Economics
for CAPE

CAPE

Economics

Colin Bamford
Narissa Mohammed

CAMBRIDGE
UNIVERSITY PRESS

CAMBRIDGE
UNIVERSITY PRESS

University Printing House, Cambridge CB2 8BS, United Kingdom

Cambridge University Press is part of the University of Cambridge.

It furthers the University's mission by disseminating knowledge in the pursuit of education, learning and research at the highest international levels of excellence.

www.cambridge.org
Information on this title: www.cambridge.org/9780521701419

First published 2007
6th printing 2013

Printed in India by Replika Press Pvt. Ltd

ISBN 978-0-521-70141-9 Paperback

Cover design: Richard Jervis Design

Acknowledgements: PA Photos, Alamy, Stillpictures and SA photos

Contents

	page
Preface	vii
Introduction: The economist's 'tool kit' and the Caribbean Advanced Proficiency Examinations (CAPE)	1
UNIT 1 MICROECONOMICS	13
Module 1 Methodology of Economics and demand and supply analysis	15
1 Central problem of Economics	16
2 Tools of economic analysis	34
3 Theory of consumer demand	39
4 Theory of supply	58
Module 2 Market structure and market failure	71
5 Market structure	72
6 Market failure	94
Module 3 Distribution theory and applications of recent theoretical developments	115
7 The theory of income distribution	116
8 Decision-making with incomplete information	135
UNIT 2 MACROECONOMICS	141
Module 1 Models of the macroeconomy	143
9 The nature of macroeconomics	144
10 National income	159
11 Classical models of the macroeconomy	168
12 The consumption function, basic Keynesian models and investment	174
Module 2 Macroeconomic policy analysis	185
13 Demand and supply of money	186
14 Monetary policy and fiscal policy	196
15 Public debt	206
Module 3 Growth and development and international economic relations	215
16 Growth and development	216
17 International trade	231
18 Economic integration	243
19 Balance of payments	250
20 Exchange rates	259
21 International institutions	266
22 Foreign direct investment and globalisation	272
Preparing for examinations	281
Glossary	289
Index	301
Multiple choice questions	309
Answers to multiple choice questions	316

Preface

This book has been specifically produced for the Caribbean Advanced Proficiency Examinations (CAPE) of the Caribbean Examinations Council.

The text is divided into two main units, Unit 1: Microeconomics and Unit 2: Macroeconomics. These units are preceded by an Introduction that contains supporting information on the 'economist's tool kit' and are followed by a short section on the CAPE examinations. The book also contains an extensive glossary of terms and concepts that are introduced in the two subject units. Overall, it provides a self-contained programme of study for the external assessment components of the examinations for school/college and private candidates.

The book has certain distinctive features:

- Whenever possible, examples from the Caribbean area have been used in the text to support and amplify the subject content. This is particularly the case with Unit 2.
- It is arranged in the same order as the CAPE Economics syllabus and is written in such a way as to match in full the learning outcomes and subject content of each topic.
- Self-assessment tasks, some of which are drawn from recent CAPE question papers, are included in all topics. These will help teachers deliver the syllabus and also provide on-going tasks for students to complete.
- Each chapter contains key economic terms and concepts, which are identified in bold print when they first arise and are later defined in the Glossary.

Although this book has been specifically produced for the CAPE syllabus, it will also be of value to students and teachers of A Level Economics particularly in developing economies.

Finally, could I record my thanks to the various people who have made the production of this text possible. First, to my fellow authors of CIE AS Level and A Level Economics (CUP 2001), small parts of which have been used in updated form in Unit 1 especially. Secondly, to Anne Rix for her useful comments on the draft text and her skill in managing this project. Thirdly, to Sarah Clarke and Diane Bramley for word processing the text. Finally, not least, to my wife Elisabeth and daughters Emily and Alice for their understanding and patience during the many hours that I have spent on the book's production.

I wish you every success in the CAPE Economics examinations.

Colin G Bamford
April 2007

Introduction
The economist's 'tool kit' and the Caribbean Advanced Proficiency Examinations (CAPE)

On completion of this introduction you should:

- have a broad idea of what is meant by Economics
- know how economists seek to explain economic phenomena
- be aware of the 'tool kit' of skills required for a study of Economics
- be aware of the requirements of the CAPE Economics syllabus

What is Economics?

There are almost as many definitions of Economics as there are economists! Although a definition of the subject is to be expected, it is probably more useful at this stage to set out a few examples of the sort of issues that concern professional economists. These topics occur in an introductory form in the CAPE Economics syllabus.

Let us take yourself first of all. Most teenagers find that they want to lead an exciting and full life but unfortunately do not always have the money necessary to do everything they would like to do. So, choices have to be made or as an economist would say, individuals have to decide:

'How to allocate scarce resources in the most effective way?'

A body of economic principles and concepts has been developed to explain how people, and also businesses, react in this situation. This is a typical example of what an economist would refer to as '**microeconomics**'.

It is not only individuals and firms who are faced with having to make choices. Governments face many such problems. For example, how does a Caribbean government decide how much to spend on health or social security and how much should go into providing new roads and infrastructure for tourism? This is the same type of problem facing all of us in our daily lives but on a different scale.

The Caribbean governments also have extensive responsibilities in looking after the well-being of their national economies. The Finance Ministers for example prepare an annual budget for their economies, in which taxation and government expenditure plans are reviewed. It is also an opportunity to 'manage the economy', by seeking to ensure that policy objectives are being met. As the economist would say, the Finance Ministers have to decide: 'how to keep the rate of change of prices (inflation) under control' or alternatively 'how to reflate the economy to increase the number of jobs that are available'.

These are typical topics which come under the broad heading of '**macroeconomics**' since they relate to the economy as a whole.

As you progress through this text you will come across many other economic problems and issues of both a micro and a macro nature. You may now find it useful to complete the self-assessment tasks below.

Self-assessment tasks

1 Make a list, in your own words, of some of the economic decisions that:
   - you are facing;
   - your family has to take;
   - your country has to take.

2 Pick up any quality newspaper. Look through it systematically and make a note of the various:
   - microeconomic,
   - macroeconomic

   problems and issues you find.

   Have you found it easy to classify problems in this way?

The last part of the task is designed to get you to appreciate that many economic problems and issues cannot be satisfactorily classified as micro or macro. In other words, such problems encompass both of the main branches of Economics. For example, an increase in taxation on alcohol may reduce the demand for alcohol; depending on the extent of this, there is an effect on the income of individuals and the government and, in turn, this affects the economy as a whole. So, there can be complex inter-relationships coming into play. In many respects this makes Economics an interesting subject to study.

As you progress through this text, you will be introduced to concepts, theories and simple models that are used by economists to explain the many economic problems and issues that come within the scope of Economics. In time, you will build up a portfolio of such techniques, from a micro- and a macroeconomic perspective. Virtually all have their origin in some sort of empirical investigation, i.e. a study of real economic phenomena. Some concepts have their origin 200 years ago, others are much more contemporary or may have been refined and revised in the light of the growing complexity of the present-day global economy. Again, this serves to enhance the interesting nature of the subject.

To conclude, therefore, it is appropriate to give a clear definition of 'What is Economics?' For a start, Economics is a social science – it adopts a scientific framework but is particularly concerned with studying the behaviour of humans, as consumers, in business or in taking decisions about the economy as a whole. More specifically:

> 'Economics is the study of how scarce resources are or should be allocated.'

All of the problems and issues you come across fit into this broad definition.

Regardless of what you may think about Economics and economists at this stage of your CAPE studies, few would deny that Economics is a logical subject and that the advice provided by economists is derived from a set of well-established principles relating to the operation of the market economy. Figure 1 shows in simple terms how economists think and how they seek to explain real problems and issues like those you will have come across in the first two self-assessment tasks.

At this stage, bear this process in mind and return to it whenever you are learning new concepts as it will help you understand how economists think and operate.

Economists cannot always be certain about what they say or the advice they might provide. Much of the content of this book though consists of **positive statements** which are descriptive and usually acceptable to all economists. For example:

- the inflation rate in 2006 was 2.5 per cent;
- the inflation rate of 2.5 per cent in 2006 produced an improvement in business confidence;
- the quantity theory of money can be used to explain why inflation occurs in an economy.

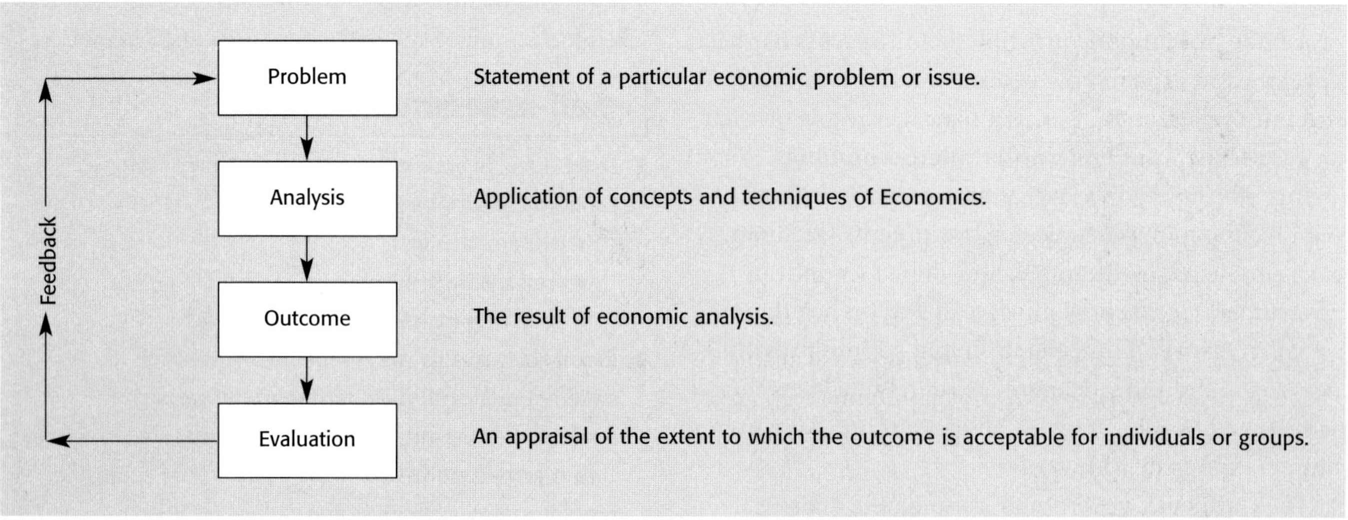

Figure 1 The road to economic explanation

On other occasions, economists make **normative statements** involving value judgements. For example:

- the government should cut fuel tax to reduce the rate of inflation,
- public sector workers should reduce their demands for higher wages.

These latter statements are expressing an opinion as to what ought to happen. Unlike positive statements, where economists can use data and empirical evidence, normative statements involve value judgements that are often drawn from the economist's personal views, political beliefs and ethics. As you study the content of the modules, keep this important distinction in mind. You will also need to think about it when answering some of the more demanding CAPE examination questions.

To conclude, therefore, it is appropriate to give a clear definition of 'What is Economics?' For a start, Economics is a social science. More specifically, it is 'the study of how society provides for itself by making the most efficient use of scarce resources so that both private and social welfare may be improved' (CAPE Economics Syllabus). Economics provides a framework whereby it is possible to study how individuals, households, firms, governments and global organisations behave and take a wide range of decisions.

Just what this involves will become much clearer as you work through the various units in this book.

Self-assessment task

Think again about what you have found out in completing the first self-assessment task. Now read the article from *The Economist* on the so-called puzzling failure of Economics. Do you agree at this early stage of your studies with what the author is saying? Why might you not yet be in a position to make a proper evaluation?

The economist's 'tool kit'

The economist has a varied 'tool kit' – the term that can be used to describe the skills and techniques available for the analysis of economic problems. Two which are of particular relevance for the CAPE examination are:

- the ability to interpret and use data,
- the ability to write in a clear and effective way.

Each of these will now be considered. *You may find it helpful to return to these parts intermittently when you are undertaking some of the self-assessment tasks in the two Units and various modules of the book. You should also refer back to this part before you take any of the CAPE examinations.*

Data skills

Five main skills are required in the CAPE examination – these skills are:

- the ability to pick out the main features in a data set,
- a knowledge of trends and the rate of change in a set of time series data,
- a working knowledge of index numbers,
- how to calculate a simple average and know what it means,
- how to interpret economic information produced in visual form.

In addition, you will find it useful to know:

- how and why economists make forecasts.

Each of the above will now be looked at. It is important that you feel confident in handling data – these simple skills will help you. You will also gain confidence as you become more familiar with economic data and complete the various self-assessment tasks in each module.

Economic data generally are of two main types. These are:

Time series data – as the name suggests, the same information is recorded over a period of time, namely for a period of years, for months in a year, days in a week and so on.

Cross-sectional data – the easiest way to imagine this type of data is in terms of a 'snapshot', i.e. a picture taken at a given time.

Another important introductory point concerns the nature of the data itself. Again two types can be recognised, namely:

Discrete data – the simplest way to imagine this is in terms of values that are shown as whole numbers, e.g. the number of people or number of cars.

The puzzling failure of economics

If the world were run by economists, would it be a better place? You might expect economists, not to mention a newspaper called *The Economist*, to think so. After all, many of the policies that people fight over have economics at their core – jobs, wages, investment, growth. Economists, professional and otherwise, are forever criticising those who do run the world for making such a mess of it, and are keen to change the way people think so that things will be run more to their liking. As one Nobel laureate put it, 'I don't care who writes a nation's laws ... if I can write its economics textbooks.'

Paul Samuelson, the author of that remark, has seen his wish fulfilled. His 'Economics', first published in 1948, has sold millions of copies and is still, with its 16th edition in preparation, doing well. Down the editions, the book's views on policy have changed, as have those of the profession at large. These shifting ideas have in turn influenced policy, and to a degree that would make other social scientists drool. Lately the results have been good. During the past decade, some of the worst economic incompetence has ended: central planning has given way to 'transition economies' in Eastern Europe and the former Soviet Union; many developing countries have opened their economies to the outside world; every week another state-run company is put up for sale. Textbook wisdom seems to prevail.

The message and the messenger

But don't praise the dismal scientists too much. Who designed those earlier policies, which failed so disastrously? Economists. Where were those theories of planning, of demand management, of industrial dirigisme and public ownership that did such harm in the third world so persuasively set out? In economics textbooks.

These days, it is true, the advice is better – but it often gets dangerously garbled in transmission. Trade is the best example. By pitting exporters against importers, successive rounds of trade negotiations have encouraged politicians in many countries to lower trade barriers. Yet this effort is based on a false premise: that freeing trade is good for you only if other countries do the same. This basic misunderstanding, left unattended, may one day lead governments to turn back the clock on liberal trade.

Other good policies have likewise been founded on bad economics. Privatisation, for instance, has more often been seen as a way to raise revenue than as a way to promote competition; and deregulation is often portrayed by governments as something that global markets have forced upon them, rather than as a way of raising living standards. As for bad policies based on bad economics, these remain too numerous to mention, despite Mr Samuelson's prodigious efforts.

Why has economics not done better? Economists tend to blame others for being too lazy or too stupid to understand their textbooks. There is doubtless something in this. Economics is hard to teach well. To the uninitiated, its basic principles often seem surprising or odd. And whereas most people will admit their ignorance of physics or biology, the armchair economist is convinced that he knows exactly what he is talking about.

But the economics profession itself also deserves much of the blame. Crucial ideas about the role of prices and markets, the basic principles of microeconomics, are uncontroversial among economists. These are the first ideas that politicians and the public need to grasp if they are to think intelligently about public policy, and the fact is that they are not widely understood. Yet because economists take these essential ideas for granted, they spend their time arguing about much more contentious notions, developed in one disputed way or another from those common underlying principles. The public and their politicians are treated to perpetual squabbles about the exact effects of raising interest rates or of cutting the capital-gains tax or whatever – and conclude that economists disagree about everything and understand nothing. As long as economists choose to talk loudest about the things they understand least well and to remain silent about the underlying ideas that unite them, this is unlikely to change.

And economists must shoulder a further portion of the blame for quite another reason. The biggest economic-policy mistake of the past 50 years, in rich and poor countries alike, has been and still is to expect too much of government. Statism has always found all the support it needs among mainstream economists. They are unfailingly quick to point out various species of market failure; they are usually much slower to ask whether the supposed remedy of government intervention might not, in practice, be worse.

This is not a failure of economics, in fact, but of modern (one might say Samuelsonian) economics. The classical economists viewed the market economy with a kind of awe. Amazing, it truly is, that all these workers, firms and households, acting without visible co-ordination and guided mainly by self-interest, manage to produce such extraordinarily beneficial results. Smith's 'Wealth of Nations' conveyed this sense that the market, for all its 'failures', is a marvel. Today precious few textbooks even try to guide their readers to any such inspiration. Implicitly, at least, their message is too often quite the opposite: that markets aren't perfect and governments (advised by economists) can be. Dismal is the word.

Source: *The Economist*, 23 August 1997.

- *Continuous data* – such values can usually be measured in a precise way and are not confined to whole numbers, e.g. income, inflation or economic growth.

So, when you are confronted with economic data for the first time, ask yourself:

- Are the data shown time series or cross-sectional data?
- Are the values of the data discrete or continuous?

There are three further matters to consider; these are also important when you come across a data set for the first time, particularly in the time-constrained examination situation. These are

Title and source of data – the title should give you a clear idea as to what the data are about. A lot of economic data are from governmental or other official sources such as CARICOM. This should mean they are accurate, although this may not necessarily be so. If the data have come from other sources, be a little wary as to what they show – they may have been produced in such a way as to make a particular viewpoint.

Estimates – some data will be estimates that have been made by the organisation responsible for collecting the data. This is often necessary as there is invariably a time lag in producing more accurate information. In other instances it may be an estimate as no data have been collected.

Forecast – as explained below, economists rely heavily on forecasts in order to take policy decisions. Therefore, key economic variables are often forecasted in order to assist this process. Such data are likely to be reasonably accurate but should never be taken to be precise.

Data skill 1 – How to pick out the main features in a data set

Consider the data in table 1. This gives the average unemployment rates in CARICOM members in 2005.

The first skill you need to develop is what is known as 'eyeballing'. All this means is looking at a data set and going down the columns (or across the rows) very quickly to pick out the main features. This is a very useful thing to do, particularly in examinations when it could give you a clue as to what questions might follow.

Country	Percentage
Antigua and Barbuda	11.0
Bahamas	7.8
Barbados	10.4
Belize	12.8
Dominica	23.1
Grenada	17.0
Guyana	9.1
Jamaica	13.0
St Kitts/Nevis	4.5
St Lucia	18.1
St Vincent & the Grenadines	15.0
Suriname	10.6
Trinidad and Tobago	14.2
Average CARICOM	11.90

Table 1 Average percentage unemployment in 2005
Source: Caribbean Community Secretariat, 2006.

Looking at table 1, you can quickly see that:

- There is a wide variation in average unemployment rates for CARICOM members in 2005.
- Dominica has the highest rate at around 23 per cent, whereas unemployment was lowest in St Kitts/Nevis at 4.5 per cent.
- The CARICOM average therefore would not seem a particularly meaningful statistic.
- For the two largest members, Jamaica and Trinidad and Tobago, their average unemployment rate was just above the CARICOM average.

The average of 11.90 per cent that is shown is often used to summarise a particular set of data. In this case, it is what is known as a 'weighted average', the weights being the actual numbers unemployed in each of the 13 countries listed in table 1. The weights are necessary since the populations of the countries are different. If they were all equal, the average would be the sum of all the percentages divided by 13. As they are not equal, the average is calculated using the formula

$$\text{Weighted mean} = \sum_{i=1}^{n} \frac{wx}{w}$$

where w is the population of each country
x is the unemployment rate
n is the number of countries

As hinted earlier, the average or mean can be affected by extreme values. To some extent, the use of weights reduces this problem compared with a situation where all values have an equal weight.

Data skill 2 – How to pick out trends and the rate of change in a data set

Now look at the data in table 2. This shows the average annual percentage change in the consumer price index for Trinidad and Tobago. (As you will learn later this is a good indicator of inflation in an economy.)

This data set is of course time series data. You can get an overview of the data by looking at how the data changed on a year-to-year basis and over the time period as a whole. When you do this, you will see that:

- The annual percentage change in the consumer price index peaks in 1998, closely followed by 2001.
- There is a slight increase in the average change at the end of the time period compared with the beginning.
- In all years, the average annual change in food prices is considerably greater than the change in the 'all items' price index, also peaking in 1998 and 2001.

For time series data such as found in table 2 you might find it useful to write a '+' or a '–' sign between each year so that you can see how the rate of change varies over time. Looking at table 2, you will see that the rate of change in the 'all items' index increased for four of the year-on-year periods, yet fell in three periods. The fall was particularly significant between 1998 and 1999.

	All items	Food	Annual charge (all items)
1996	3.3	9.3	
			+
1997	3.6	9.2	
			+
1998	5.6	12.9	
			–
1999	3.4	8.8	
			+
2000	3.6	7.6	
			+
2001	5.5	12.8	
			–
2002	4.2	10.1	
			–
2003	3.8	5.5	

Table 2 Average annual percentage change in the consumer price index for Trinidad and Tobago, 1996–2003
Source: Statistical Yearbook for Latin America and the Caribbean, 2004.

A final word of warning though. Consumer prices have increased consistently since 1996, as shown by the data in the first column. The rate of change in consumer prices however has varied, as shown in the final column – in some years, such as 1999 and 2002, it has been at a lower percentage rate than in the preceding year. Prices however have continued to increase. A common error that many students make when looking at data like these is to wrongly assume that prices have actually fallen. This is not so.

Data skill 3 – A working knowledge of index numbers

With time series data especially, it is often helpful to show the data in index form, with a base year of 100. Thereafter, data for subsequent years are shown in index form, so avoiding some of the difficulties mentioned earlier when considering the rate of change in time series data.

To construct an index number:

- Choose a base value or value for a base year. This may be the first year in a time series or a year that is taken as typical. Assign this year an index of 100.
- Divide the base year value by 100 and then divide every subsequent value by this figure to calculate the index number for each particular year.

When you do this, the data in table 2 become:

	All items Index	Food
1995	100	100
1996	103.3	109.3
1997	107.0	119.4
1998	113.0	134.8
1999	116.8	146.7
2000	121.0	157.8
2001	127.7	178.0
2002	133.1	196.0
2003	138.2	206.8

In this form, you can make additional points such as:

- Food prices have more than doubled between 1995 and 2003.
- Consumer prices have risen by almost 40 per cent over the same period.
- It can therefore be assumed that the recent inflation in Trinidad and Tobago has hit the poorer sections of the population particularly hard due to spiralling prices for food.

Data skill 4 – How to interpret economic information produced in visual form

So far, the two data sets used have been in tabular format. This might give a false impression because economists often use various visual forms of presentation, particularly in the popular media, when analysing particular issues.

Figures 2 and 3 are typical examples, namely a *bar chart* and a *pie chart*. Both represent data in an effective way.

Figure 2 is a bar chart showing the trend in hotel occupancy rates in the Caribbean between 1993 and 1999. The basic principle is that the height of each bar represents the data indicated on the vertical scale – in this case, hotel occupancy rates. At a glance it is possible to make assertions about the level (in percentage terms) and the trend (from one year to another).

The pie chart in figure 3 indicates the origin of tourists arriving in the Caribbean in 2000. Very conveniently, the percentages for market share are indicated. This is not always so – the share of each segment can be determined in relation to an overall total of 360°.

Students with access to Microsoft Excel will be able to produce a wide range of bar charts and pie charts from this software.

When confronted with any bar chart or similar representation, it is very important to look very carefully at the vertical scale. In particular, see whether it has been modified to make small changes look bigger (figure 2 has). You might also check to see if the section immediately above the origin is shown as a set of straight cross lines – this can indicate that the degree of change needs to be carefully considered.

Increasingly in newspapers and magazines economic information is being represented in highly attractive ways in the form of inter-related graphics, pictures and charts. Figure 4 is an excellent example containing a lot more economic information than might seem to be the case at first sight.

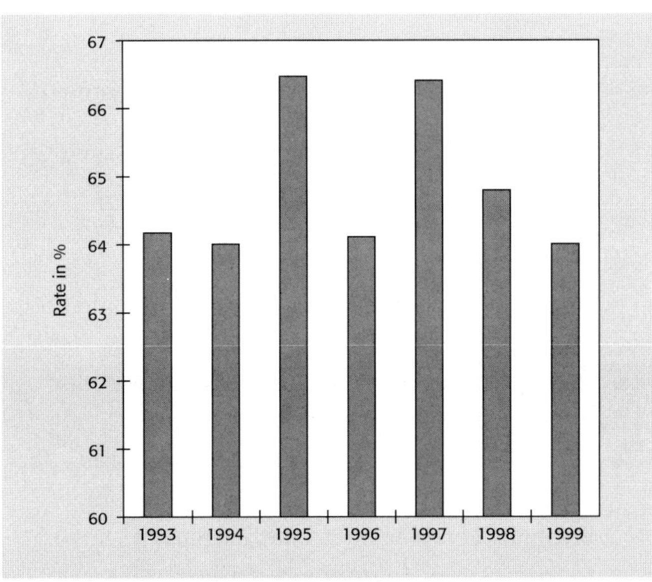

Figure 2 Occupancy rates in the Caribbean (percent)

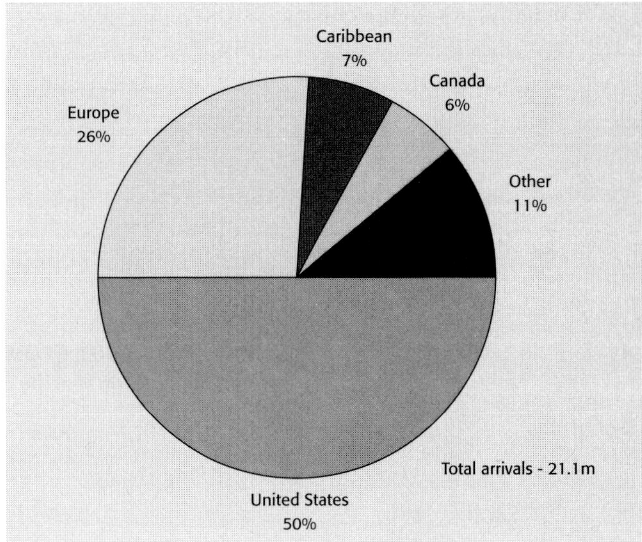

Figure 3 Tourist arrivals to the Caribbean by major markets 2000
Source: Caribbean Tourism Organisation.

Self-assessment tasks

Study the information in figure 4 and then tackle the following exercises.

1 (a) Describe the trend in:
- investment,
- GDP growth

in the Chinese economy from 2004 to early/mid 2006.

(b) What relationship can you detect between the increase in investment and GDP growth?

2 Describe the relationship between money supply growth and inflation:
- up to the middle of 2006,
- as a forecast from the middle of 2006 to the middle of 2007.

3 Comment upon why and how the boom in China's economy might be cooled.

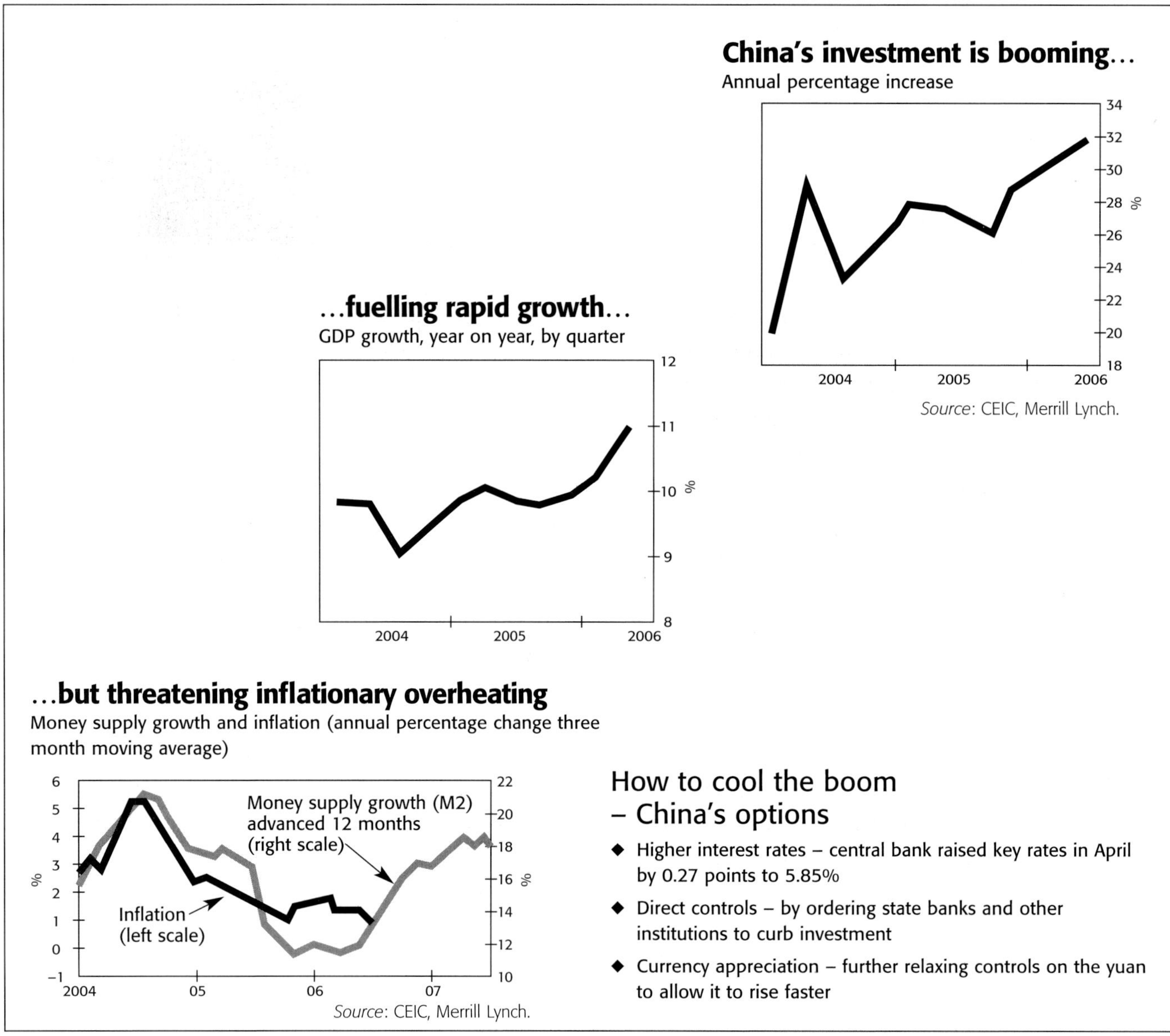

Figure 4 Can China control its economy?
Source: *The Times*, 21 July 2006.

How and why economists make forecasts

One of the most important tasks of the professional economist, whether in government or private sector employment, is to be able to forecast future economic phenomena. Many economic variables are heavily dependent upon the state of the economy. For example, forecasts of economic growth are widely used by economists for all sorts of reasons related to economic policy and business well-being.

Economists use various types of forecasting method. The three main ones are:

- statistical forecasts based on simple or complex future extrapolation techniques;
- using models to produce a range of forecasts – this is particularly true of models of the economy involving complex inter-relationships;
- forecasts based on intuition, experience or even guesswork, i.e. not involving statistical methods.

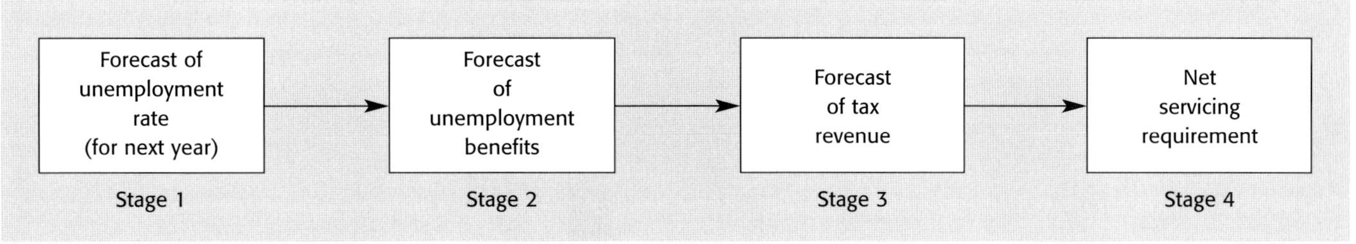

Figure 5 Use of unemployment forecasts

Macroeconomic forecasts – finance ministers and other government officials find it essential to have estimates of projected variables such as the unemployment rate, inflation rate, balance of payments position and economic growth rate. These are required on a short-term basis (one year or less) or over a longer period of time. Take the case of the unemployment rate – the importance of forecasting is shown in figure 5.

This seems quite simple. In practice though the process is much more difficult to set out and at stages 3 and 4 requires further assumptions to be made with regard to other sources of revenue and taxation.

Microeconomic forecasts – these are not quite as obvious but one example that develops out of Chapter 3 is the need to be able to make forecasts of demand. These are important for future business and economic planning.

Returning to figure 3, any business in the tourism sector has a need for a forecast of future numbers of tourists. This is by no means easy, due to the many factors involved. We can get an idea of some of these factors from the general determinants of demand that are analysed in unit 1, module 1 and include:

- the average price of tourism in the Caribbean,
- the income of tourists,
- the price of substitute destinations and the price of complements such as air travel,
- a range of non-price factors that might determine whether tourists are attracted to Caribbean destinations.

Looking at each of these it is clear that a whole set of forecasts have to be made and determinants looked at before an aggregate forecast can be made. These include:

- forecast of inflation rates in the Caribbean area,
- forecast of economic growth rates in countries generating tourists for the Caribbean area,
- forecasts of the costs of tourism in competing destinations and forecasts of the future cost of air travel,
- alternative tourism destinations and leisure options in the home market,
- safety and security issues, health issues and so on, globally as well as in the Caribbean.

As you can see, some of these are macroeconomic forecasts. So, in order to obtain what might appear to be a simple future estimate, access to a mass of other statistical information is required. It is for this reason that forecasts may not always be close to what actually occurs.

Forecasting over a longer time period is even more problematic due to all of the uncertainties involved. An example of this is the forecast that is shown in figure 6 (the underpinning theory is in unit 2, module 3). At best this should be seen as providing a very broad indication of what might be the case in 20 years time!

How to write in a clear and effective way

It is really beyond the scope of this book to include a lot of material on this part of the 'tool kit'. But having said this, much of the work of economists is communicated in a written manner, in books and newspaper articles especially. For students, examinations in Economics (CAPE included) require you to communicate your ideas in a written form. The section on examination skills later in the book gives you very specific advice on how to impress examiners.

From a more general standpoint, you must always think about what you are writing and how you might improve your writing skills. You can enhance these skills by reading a good newspaper, particularly if you read material which supports your studies.

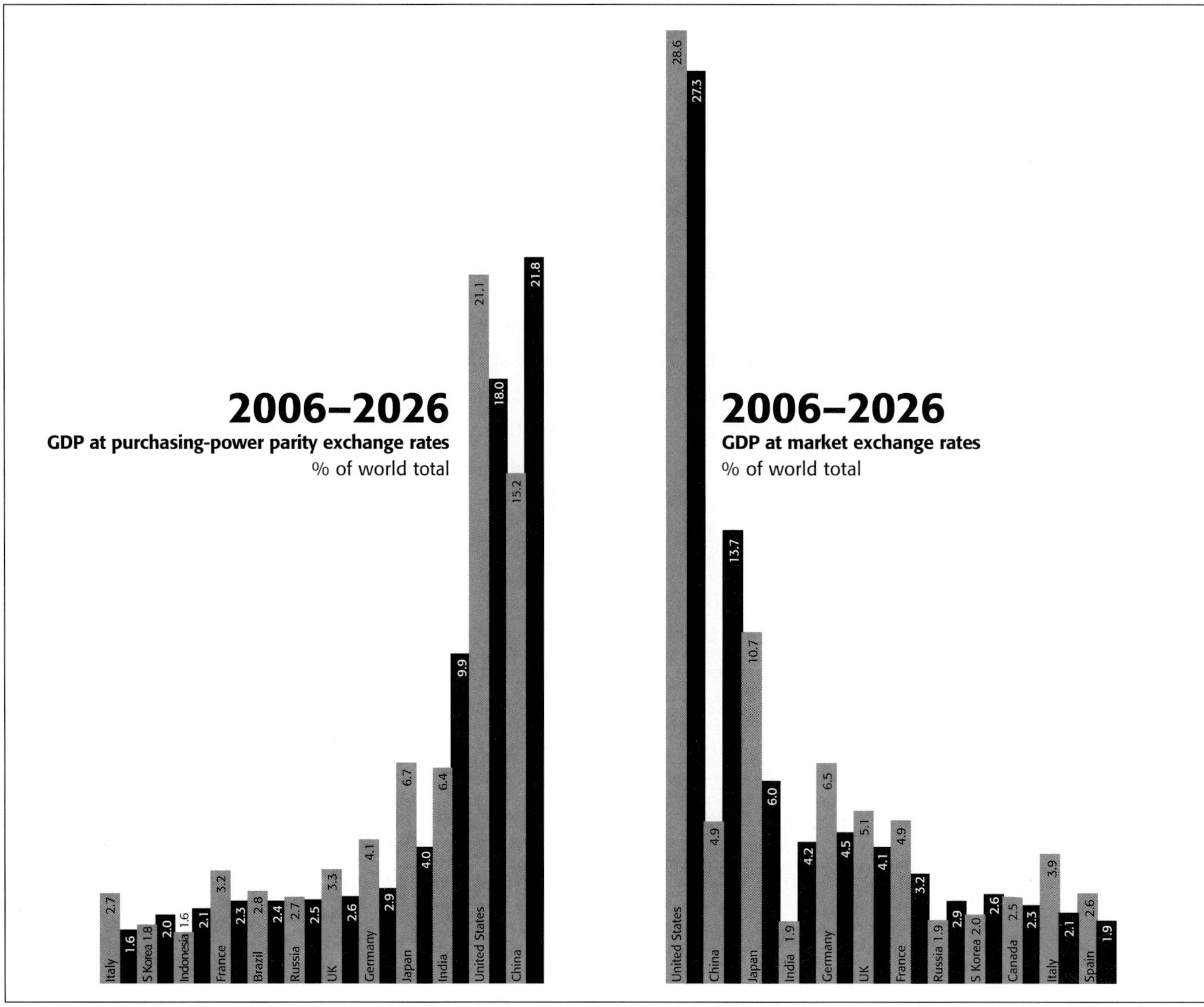

Figure 6 Forecasts of GDP in 2026
Source: Economist Intelligence Unit.

For the time being, you might like to think about the following 'Ten tips for budding writers':

1 *Be clear and precise in your writing* – use words you understand and when using technical terms be specific, not least as Economics has many terms that are very similar.
2 *Remember to match your writing to your audience* – in most cases this will be your teacher or a CAPE examiner. They are likely to be older than yourself and will be looking to read material from you which is written in a relevant way.
3 *Write impersonally* – in other words, do not use 'I' or 'we' in your written essays and examination answers. This particularly applies when you are asked to make an evaluation of an economic issue or argument.
4 *Think carefully about what tense you are writing in* – try and be consistent.
5 *Take care with sentences and punctuation* – in general, try to write short sentences, to the point and that contain words you understand and know how to use.
6 *Use one idea per paragraph and develop your ideas* – this makes it relatively easy for someone reading your work to know what your answer is about and to see how your idea has been developed.
7 *Support your arguments* – in other words, never make rash statements you cannot back up. Always try to elaborate or develop your statements and arguments.
8 *Avoid humour* – if in any doubt, leave humour and wit out of your written answers. Many economists do have a sense of humour – but examinations and essays are not the place for it to be demonstrated.

9 *Be professional* – do not insult or offend even if you do not agree with what you might have read or with the examination question. There are other ways you can make your opinions known.

10 *Keep working at your writing* – never be satisfied and keep thinking about how you can write in clear, relevant, authoritative and positive ways.

An outline of the CAPE structure

It is useful from the outset for you to know the structure of the CAPE syllabus. This is shown in table 3. There are separate requirements for school/college and private candidates.

Overall this is a unitised structure. There are two units, one in microeconomics and one in macroeconomics. These cover the main introductory areas of Economics at this level (see unit 1, module 1 for more details).

Although each unit can be taken individually, it really makes better sense to take them together. This is because Economics as a subject cannot strictly be divided up into micro- or macroeconomics. Each unit also has skills that are common to the subject as a whole as this introduction has indicated.

As you systematically work through the modules in the two units of this book, and undertake the various self-assessment tasks, you will become increasingly familiar with the subject content of Economics and the assessment methods used by CAPE.

So, good luck and welcome to CAPE Economics!

Unit 1:	**Microeconomics**	**Unit 2:**	**Macroeconomics**
Module 1:	Methodology of Economics and demand and supply analysis	Module 1:	Models of the macroeconomy
Module 2:	Market structure and market failure	Module 2:	Macroeconomic policy analysis
Module 3:	Distribution theory and applications of recent theoretical developments	Module 3:	Growth, development and international economic relations

Table 3 CAPE Economics specification

Assessment

This is the same for each unit and consists of:

External assessment (80%):

Paper 1 24 compulsory multiple choice questions.

Paper 2 1 question to be answered from 2 in each of 3 sections. Questions take a variety of forms including calculations, data response and short essays.

Internal assessment (20%):

A project report: the topic is determined by the candidate in consultation with the teacher. Private candidates take an alternative mini case study examination on a topic that is pre-circulated by the Caribbean Examinations Council.

Unit 1
Microeconomics

Module 1

Methodology of Economics and demand and supply analysis

On completion of this module you should be able to:

- appreciate the main problem of Economics, namely the allocation of scarce resources and the inevitability of choice
- view the market as the main mechanism for exchange
- understand the basic tools of economic analysis
- understand how consumers go about allocating their scarce resources to maximise their satisfaction
- understand the nature of costs and the factors surrounding the supply of goods and services

1 Central problem of Economics

This chapter covers unit 1, module 1, topic 1.
On completion of this chapter, you should be able to:

- define the concept of scarcity
- define and apply the concept of opportunity cost
- define the term production possibility frontier
- use the production possibility frontier to indicate constant returns, diminishing returns and increasing returns
- define the concept of Pareto efficiency
- define and explain private cost, external cost and social costs
- define the market and explain how it allocates scarce resources
- define the concept of market failure
- list the advantages and disadvantages of the alternative mechanisms by which resources are allocated
- define positive and normative Economics and give examples of each
- explain the difference between inductive and deductive methods of reasoning and give examples of each
- define the terms price ceilings and price floors and state their effects on resource allocation

One economic problem or many?

Economists have to deal with a whole range of **economic problems**. You may have seen TV programmes about the misery of unemployment and poverty; you may have read about the difficulties caused by inflation or heard politicians discuss exchange rate crises on the evening news. You may also be aware of debates surrounding issues such as the acute shortage of skilled labour in the Caribbean, the UK's future relationship with the European Union, the problems of global warming and the population explosion in the Third World. Despite this extensive range of issues, which economists are trained to consider, they often talk about *the* economic problem. This is the fundamental problem from which all others arise. This is the fact that we have scarce **resources** to satisfy our unlimited **wants.** As a result of this problem, which is sometimes called the problem of **scarcity**, we have to make **choices**, and it is the task of the economist to explain and analyse the nature of choice facing economic agents, such as consumers, producers and governments.

The economic problem is

SCARCE RESOURCES IN RELATION TO UNLIMITED WANTS

This is summarised in Figure 1.1.

Because the basic economic problem exists, societies need to confront three inter-related questions. These are:

1 *What to produce*

Because we cannot produce everything, we need to decide what to produce and in what quantities. We have to choose, for example, whether to produce lots of goods and services, such as food, clothing and vehicles, to improve our standard of living, or whether we need to produce lots of military hardware to improve our defences.

2 *How to produce*

This question arises from the basic economic problem that, since resources are scarce in relation to unlimited wants, we need to consider how resources are used so that the best outcome arises. We need to consider how we can get the **maximum use** out of the resources available to us. It should be noted, however, that other issues besides purely economic concerns should be considered when deciding how to produce. It may be true, for example, that through slavery or forced labour we could produce more goods and services in an economy, but there is a moral objection to such arrangements. Similarly, crop yields could well be increased through the introduction of genetically modified plants but this may lead to damage to the ecosystem. The decision to maximise output and satisfy more wants would need to consider the full impact on the environment and any potential long-term health risks.

3 *For whom to produce*
Because we cannot satisfy all the wants of all the population, decisions have to be taken concerning how many of each person's wants are to be satisfied. On a broad level we need to decide whether everyone is going to have more or less an equal share of what is produced or whether some will have more than others. In some economies there are deliberate attempts to create a more egalitarian society through policies that re-distribute wealth and income from the rich to the poor. This could be through the adoption of progressive taxation systems. In other economies there are no such policies and inequalities of wealth and income, usually based upon inheritance, remain extreme. In answering this question, moral aspects of decision making again become important.

Self-assessment tasks

Read the article below and then tackle the exercises that follow.

The economics of ageing: the luxury of longer life

In the world's rich countries, you can expect when you retire at 65 to live on average for another 15 or 20 years. A hundred years ago, you would on average have already been dead. The late twentieth century brought to many the ultimate gift: the luxury of ageing. But like any luxury, ageing is expensive. Governments are now fretting about the cost. Over the next 30 or 40 years the demographic changes of longer lives and fewer births will force most countries to rethink in fundamental ways their arrangements for paying for and looking after older people.

Thanks to state transfers, being old in developed countries mostly no longer means being poor. Old people expect decent pensions to live on; they will make heavier demands on medical services; some will need expensive nursing care since younger relatives will be concerned about making the most of their own lives. At the same time, the number of people in work – who will have to foot the bill – will stay much the same. Consequently, each worker will have to carry a much heavier burden.

Mass survival to a ripe old age will not be confined to rich countries. Most developing countries, whose populations are now much younger than the developed world's, are starting to age fast. This is particularly true of Caribbean economies such as Barbados as the population pyramids overleaf indicate. The new combination of age and relative poverty will create many problems for poorer countries – these problems are already familiar to industrialised European countries and the USA. The problem for poorer countries is that they have far fewer resources to tackle them. Ethical problems over the use of scarce resources will be magnified.

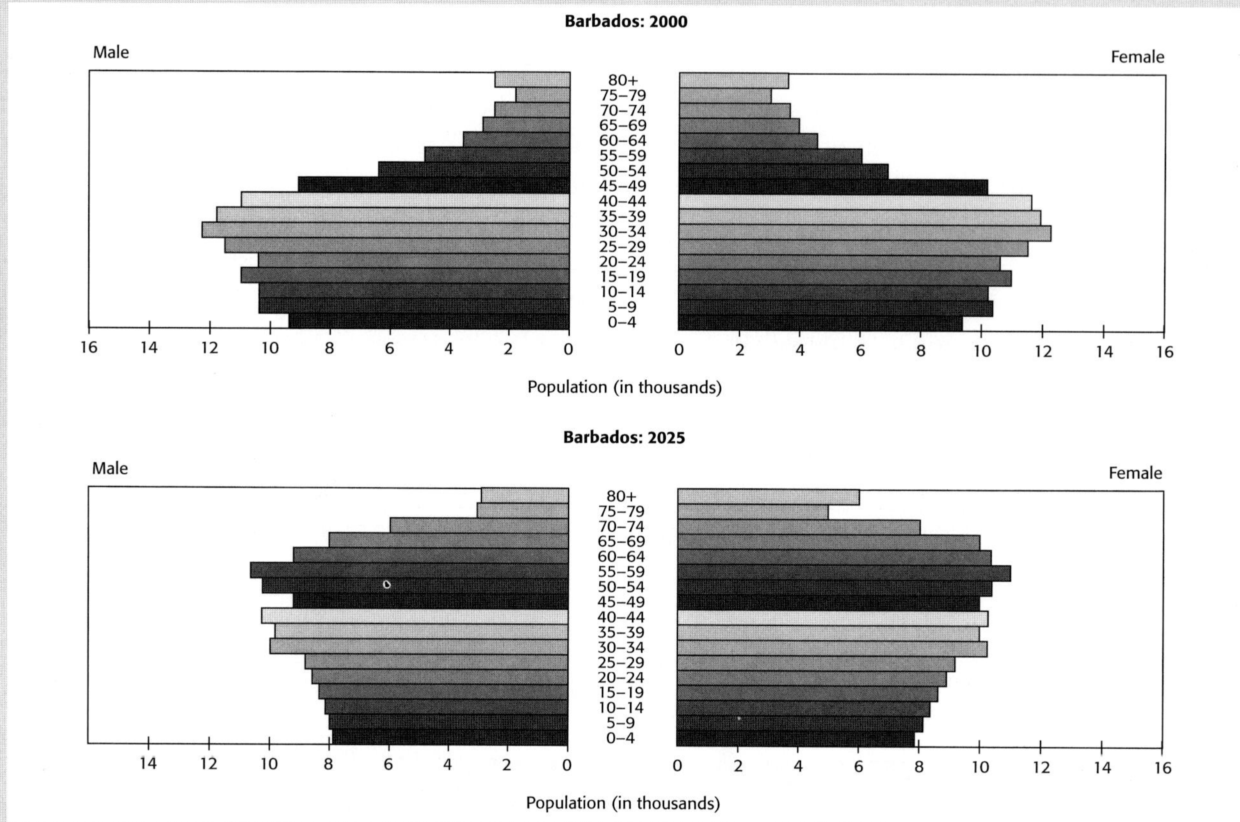

Population pyramid summary for Barbados

Source: *The Economist*, 27 January 1996 (adaptation) and the US Census Bureau International Data Base, 2006.

1 Summarise the projected changes in the population of Barbados from 2000 to 2005.

2 Discuss the effects of these changes on decisions concerning:
- ◆ what to produce;
- ◆ how to produce;
- ◆ for whom to produce.

3 Comment upon the 'ethical problems over the use of scarce resources' that are facing the government of Barbados in meeting the needs of its changing population.

Limited resources

In Economics we categorise the resources available to us into four types. These are known as **factors of production**:

1 **Land** This is the natural resource. It includes the surface of the earth, lakes, rivers and forests. It also includes mineral deposits below the earth and the climate above.

2 **Labour** This is the human resource, the basic determinant of which is the nation's population. Not all of the population are available to work however, because some are above or below the working population age and some choose not to work.

3 **Capital goods** These are any man-made aids to production. In this category we would include a simple spade and a complex car assembly plant. Capital goods help land and labour produce more units of output. They improve the output from land and labour.

These three factors are organised into units of production by firms.

4 **Enterprise** *(or entrepreneurship)* This factor carries out two functions. Firstly, the factor enterprise organises the other three factors of production. Secondly, enterprise involves taking the **risk** of production, which exists in a free enterprise economy. Some firms are small with few resources. The functions of enterprise are undertaken by a single individual. In larger, more complex firms the functions are divided, with salaried managers organising the other factors and shareholders taking the risk.

Some economies have a large quantity of high-quality

factors of production at their disposal. They can create lots of goods and services to satisfy the wants of their population. They are said to have a good **factor endowment**. Some economies lack sufficient quantities of one or more of the factors. Developing countries, for example, might have large quantities of land and labour but lack sufficient capital and enterprise. Recognising this, in Trinidad and Tobago, NEDCO is trying to develop an enterprise culture.

Production and consumption

Resources are combined in the process of **production** to create goods and services. Goods and services have the capacity to satisfy wants. The process through which individuals use up goods and services to satisfy wants is known as **consumption**. Some goods, such as a chocolate bar, are quickly used up to satisfy our wants. Others satisfy wants over a longer period of time. These are called consumer durables. Examples of consumer durables include television sets, refrigerators and vehicles.

Unlimited wants

If we were asked, we could all identify certain basic wants which must be satisfied if we are to stay alive. These include the obvious essentials of food, shelter and clothing. We might also identify those wants which are clearly less essential but which we think improve our quality of life. Some might include television sets, cars, trips to the cinema and so on. These are sometimes called luxuries but it is important to remember that what might be a luxury for one individual may be considered an essential for others. This is because we all have a **scale of preference** with our more urgent wants at the top and the less urgent ones at the bottom. Each individual's scale of preference is a product of a complex set of influences, involving our culture, upbringing and life experiences. These together influence our likes and dislikes. Unsurprisingly, since we all have different experiences, there is bound to be great variation between any two individuals' scales of preferences. You may find it interesting to conduct a class exercise in which everyone makes a list of ten wants in descending order of priority. When you compare results you may be surprised to find that, although there may be broad agreement on the first few choices, there is likely to be considerable variation as you compare people's choices over the full list. You may also consider how your list would compare to lists compiled by others with very different life experiences, such as your teacher, your grandparents or even a student of Economics in another country. A further point to consider is whether you could imagine any end to your list if you were not limited to ten choices. It is important to remember that our wants are continually expanding, developing and changing.

Some wants expand as we grow up, marry and raise a family. Imagine how our housing needs change as we go through this process or how we change from wanting a small car with two doors to wanting a large family saloon with four doors. Some of our wants develop and expand when we see others around us enjoying goods and services and we feel the need to keep up.

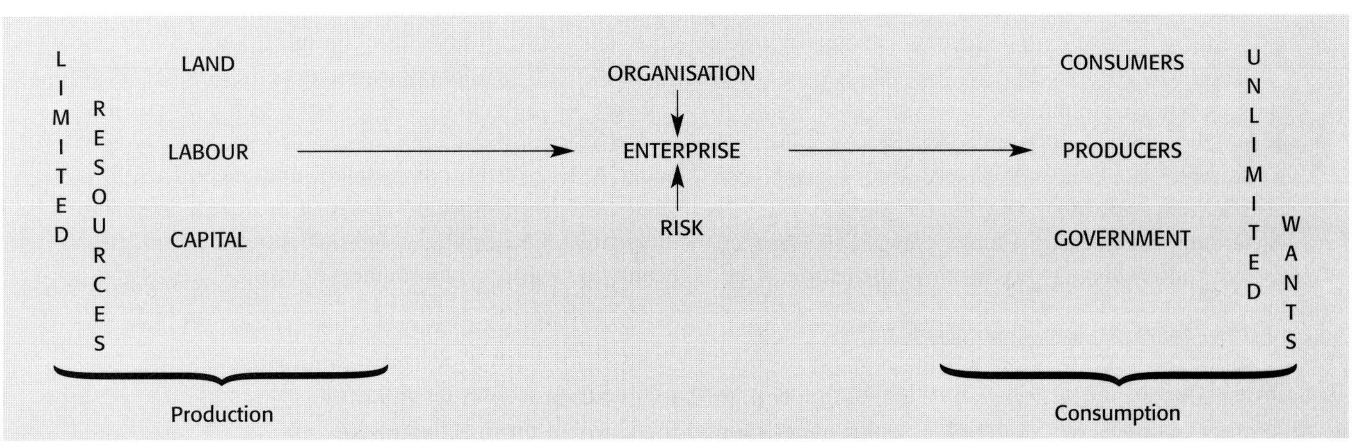

Figure 1.1 Elements of the economic problem

Sometimes our wants change as we have new experiences, for example we might become vegetarian because we have seen a TV programme on the health risks of eating meat.

All of this points to the fact that we can never imagine a time when all our wants are satisfied. Our wants are continually expanding and changing. Despite the fact that we are continually finding new, more efficient ways to produce more and more goods and services with the resources available to us, we are still faced with the basic economic problem that we have limited resources and unlimited wants. This is sometimes called the problem of **scarcity**. As a result we have to make choices.

Specialisation and exchange

One of the ways in which more goods and services can be produced in the economy is through the process of **specialisation.** This refers to a situation where individuals and firms, regions and nations concentrate upon producing some goods and services rather than others. This can be clearly illustrated at the individual level. Within the family there may be some

Self-assessment tasks

Read the case study below and answer the questions that follow.

Rich and miserable ... or poor and happy?

It's often said that those who say that money can't buy you happiness simply don't know where to shop. So when you've finished leafing through *The Guardian*, the odds are that you'll be off to the mall, armed with your plastic for a bit of conspicuous consumption.

After all, Christmas is only five weeks away and spending money makes you happy, right? Wrong. According to economists it's a myth that the more we spend, the better we feel.

The evidence – to be published in this month's edition of *The Economic Journal* – that the link between happiness and income/consumption is tenuous – is quite compelling.

The West is much richer than it was 50 years ago but:

- in the USA, reported 'happiness' has gone up only fractionally over this period;
- in Europe, 'satisfaction with life' is actually lower than it was 20 years ago.

This is evidenced in a number of ways. For example:

- in rich countries, male suicide rates have gone up;
- unemployment rates have increased – unhappiness is far more prevalent amongst the jobless.

According to Professor Andrew Oswald of Warwick University, money is to blame for this state of affairs. He argues that it buys very little well-being, yet everyone wants more of it. He says it is akin to the spectator who stands up at a football match to get a better view; by the time all of his neighbours are standing up, everybody is no better off than before.

Other economists agree:

- Yew Kwang Ng, a Chinese economist, has argued that production and consumption, 'to keep up with the Joneses', continue to impose substantial environmental costs, making economic growth happiness decreasing.
- Robert Frank, an American economist, argues that we would be better off if we all agreed to consume less. We could work less, meet other people more regularly and cut down on workplace commuting.

These arguments are unlikely to go down well in developing economies such as those in the Caribbean area. It is through growth, as in the USA and most of Europe, that people have become materially better off. It is surely wrong to deny these benefits to the populations of Barbados, Jamaica, Dominica and so on... or is it better to learn from our mistakes and encourage these economies to permit the transfer of more resources into things that make us happy such as better education, good health and a decent environment?

Source: *The Guardian*, 22 November 1997 (adapted).

This article expresses the view that, through economic growth, people may actually be worse off.

1 What other examples can you think of which might support the views of these economists?

2 Do you see any conflict between these views and your understanding of the 'economic problem'?

specialisation in the performance of household tasks, with one person doing the ironing and gardening while another does the shopping and cooking. At the workplace, of course, the fact that some people are labourers or lorry drivers while others have office jobs is also a reflection of specialisation. At this level, specialisation allows individuals to concentrate upon what they are best at and thus more goods and services will be produced. With such specialisation, however, although more is produced no-one is self-sufficient. It becomes necessary to exchange goods and services. As an individual specialises they will produce a surplus beyond their needs, which they can exchange for the surpluses of others.

With the expansion of trade and the development of markets, the benefits of regional and national specialisation became apparent. Surpluses produced by regions and countries were bought and sold, allowing world living standards to rise. Just as individuals concentrated on what they were best at, so did regions and countries.

Specialisation has clearly resulted in a massive expansion in world living standards, but there are dangers in specialisation. Given the pace of technological change in modern society, there is always the possibility that the specialist skills and accumulated experience, which any individual has acquired, may become redundant as the economy develops. Individuals need to be flexible and multi-skilled and be able to move between occupations. At regional and national levels, changes in consumers' wants can sometimes mean that the goods and services produced in a region or country are no longer required in the same quantity and unemployment can result. Policies then have to be adopted to deal with the economic and social problems that will arise. This issue will be looked at in depth in unit 2, module 2.

The division of labour

With the technical advances of the last few hundred years, production of goods and services has taken place on a much bigger scale. The concentration of large numbers of workers within very large production units allowed the process of production to be broken down into a series of tasks. This is called the **division of labour**. For example, Adam Smith, writing at the end of the eighteenth century, showed how the production of pins would benefit from the application of the division of labour in a factory. He suggested that pin-making could be divided into 18 distinct operations and that, if each employee undertook only one of the operations, production would rise to 5,000 pins per employee per day. This was compared to his estimate that each employee would be able to produce only a few dozen each day if they produced pins individually.

Although the division of labour raised output, it often created dissatisfaction in the work force, who became bored with the monotonous nature of their task. The process was taken a stage further in the 1920s when conveyor belt production was introduced in the United States car industry by Henry Ford. Ford's method of car production provided the model for much of manufacturing production in the twentieth century. In more recent times the de-humanising impact of production techniques, such as those using a conveyor belt, have been recognised and alternative methods of production have been introduced.

Choice and opportunity cost

Given limited resources and unlimited wants we have to choose which wants to satisfy. The true cost of any choice we make between alternatives is expressed by economists through the notion of **opportunity cost**. This looks at the cost of our choice in terms of the next best alternative forgone. For example, suppose you were given a $15.00 gift voucher for your birthday. You could either buy a new compact disc which costs $15.00 or two paperback books for $7.50 each. It is clear that you could not have the CD *and* the books.

Two books or one CD?

The opportunity cost of the CD, therefore, is the two paperback books. The value of the concept of opportunity cost is that it brings home to us the real cost of our choices. It can be applied in a variety of contexts in Economics and is helpful for economic decision makers, such as households, firms and governments.

Production possibility curves

How many goods and services an economy is capable of producing is determined by the quantity and quality of resources available to it, together with the state of technical knowledge. These factors determine an economy's production possibilities.

Example: An imaginary economy, given its available resources, can either produce military goods or consumer goods or a combination of each. The various possibilities are shown on the following production possibility schedule.

Military goods	*Consumer goods*
10,000	0
8,000	4,000
6,000	8,000
4,000	12,000
2,000	16,000
0	20,000

It is sometimes useful to illustrate the choices open to an economy by considering the production possibility curve. From the above schedule we can produce a production possibility curve with military goods plotted on the vertical axis and consumer goods on the horizontal axis.

Figure 1.2 shows all possible combinations of military goods and consumer goods which could be produced given the existing quantity and quality of resources in our imaginary economy and the existing state of technical knowledge. At point a, only military goods are produced, and, at point d, only consumer goods are produced, but between these two extremes lie all the other possibilities. The term production possibility curve emphasises that this shows what levels of output an economy can achieve with its existing resources. It can also be used to show what the economy is *not* able to achieve. Point *Y* on the graph represents a

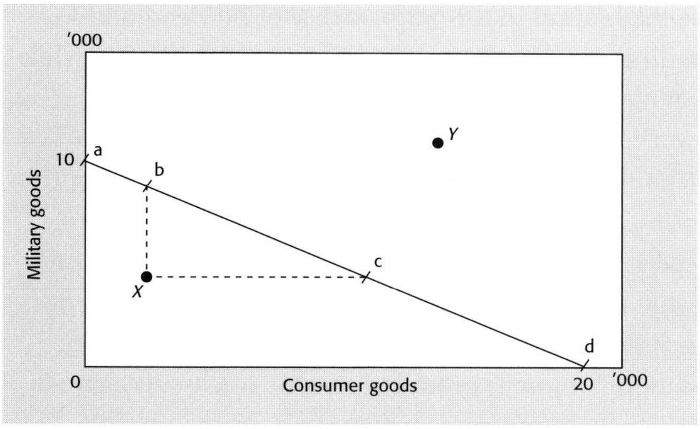

Figure 1.2 A production possibility curve

combination of military and consumer goods which it is not possible to achieve. It is beyond our production possibilities. Sometimes the curve is called a **production frontier** because it draws the boundary between what can and cannot be achieved.

This diagram is also useful in illustrating the real cost to society of unemployed resources. The point *X* on the diagram represents a production of 4,000 military goods and 2,500 consumer goods. This is possible to achieve because it is within the production frontier, but it represents a point where some resources are unemployed or not employed effectively. The economy is capable of moving to point b with more military goods and the same number of consumer goods or to point c, which would bring more consumer goods and the same quantity of military goods. Alternatively, at a point between b and c, the economy can have more of both types of goods. Looking at the diagram in this way illustrates the waste from unemployed resources. We are not satisfying as many of our wants as possible.

A further alternative name for the production possibility curve is the **product transformation curve**. This emphasises a further use for the concept in introductory Economics. As the economy moves along the curve from point a through to point d then a different combination of goods is being chosen. More consumer goods are being produced and fewer military goods. This emphasises that the cost of producing more consumer goods is the military goods which have to be sacrificed. Given the figures, we can calculate the opportunity cost of consumer goods in terms of military goods. A move from b to c on the graph leads to a gain of 4,000 consumer goods but we sacrifice 2,000 military goods. The opportunity cost of one consumer good is therefore half of a military good. This is equivalent to one military good having an opportunity cost of two consumer goods. As we move along the curve the composition of our output is being transformed. We should also note that for this to happen we need to switch our resources from one use to another. Resources have to be switched from producing military goods to producing consumer goods and vice versa. This is known as the **reallocation of resources** and in the real world, as we decide to change the composition of our output, we need to consider the costs of reallocating resources between uses. These include the costs of re-training our work force in the skills required to produce different types of goods and services. This might take a considerable period of time and might only be possible as new entrants to the labour force are trained in new skills. The extent to which resources can be reallocated from one line of production to another is known as **factor mobility** and, if we want resources to be swiftly allocated to the use we choose, we have to ensure that factors are as mobile as possible.

It should be noted that, in our example, the opportunity cost of military goods in terms of consumer goods has not changed because we have chosen different combinations of the two goods. This is in fact quite unrealistic. A more likely outcome is that the production possibility curve will illustrate increasing costs. Consider the production possibility schedule in table 1.1, which shows the quantities of agricultural goods and manufactured goods that can be produced in an economy given existing resources and state of technology.

Assume that initially the economy is producing at point p with 660 agricultural products and 100 manufactured products (figure 1.3). Then assume that it is decided to move to point q to gain an extra 100 units

Agricultural products	Manufactured products
700	0
660	100
600	200
500	300
300	400
0	500

Table 1.1 A production possibility schedule

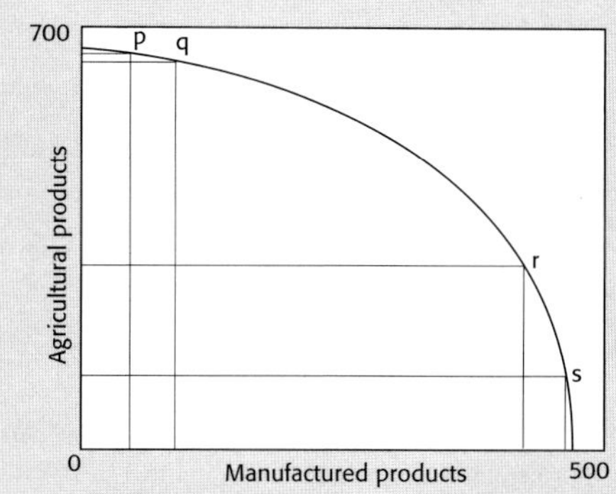

Figure 1.3 A production possibility curve with increasing costs

of manufactured products. Clearly, resources need to be reallocated from agricultural use to manufacturing. At first the least fertile land will be reallocated and only 60 units of agricultural produce will be sacrificed. This means that each extra consumer good has cost 0.6 of an agricultural good. Now compare this with a movement from r to s, to gain an extra 100 manufactured goods we have to sacrifice 200 agricultural goods. This means that one extra manufactured good has cost 2 agricultural goods. The cost has increased as we have reallocated our resources. This is because at this stage we are switching the more fertile land into manufactured good production so that agricultural output is going to be affected to a much greater extent. This diagram illustrates a production possibility curve with increasing costs.

Shifts in production possibility curve

A production possibility curve is drawn on the assumption that the quantity and quality of resources and the state of technology are fixed. Through time, of course, economies can gain or lose resources; the quality of resources and the state of technical knowledge can change. Such changes will shift the production possibility curve to a new position. Figure 1.4 illustrates the outcomes of changes in the quantity and quality of resources and changes in technology.

Figure 1.4(a) shows a situation in which the production possibilities available to an economy have expanded. This is known as **economic growth**. This could be due to an increase in the quantity and/or the quality of resources available to the economy or an improvement in the state of technology. Here the changes have improved the economy's ability to produce both agricultural and manufactured products. In figure

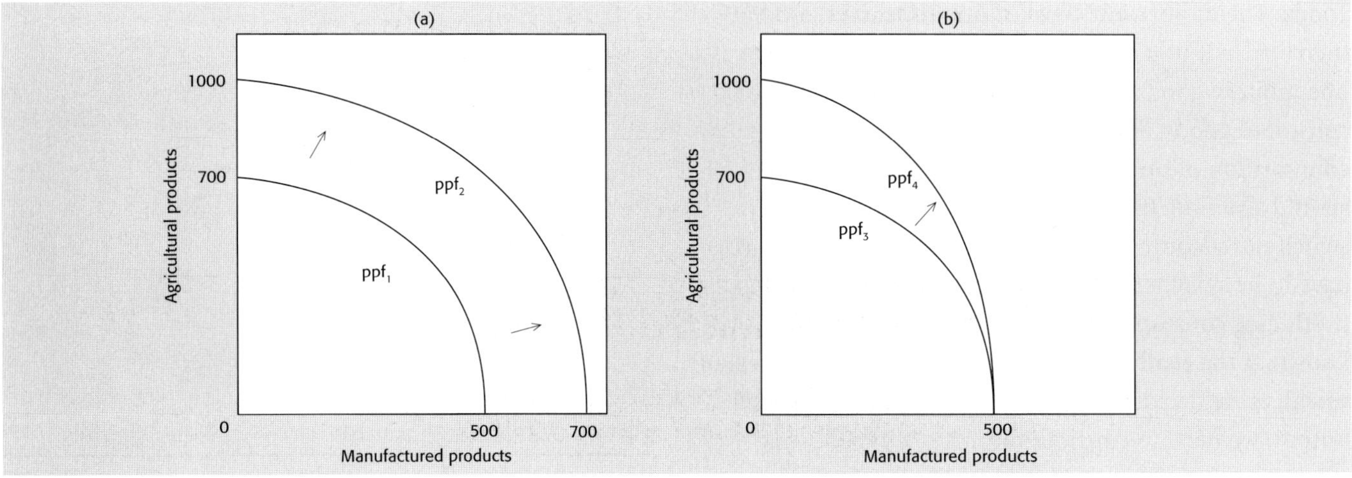

Figure 1.4 Shifts in production possibility curves

1.4 (b), however, only our ability to produce agricultural products has been improved. This could perhaps be because there has been a technological breakthrough in producing agricultural products, which does not apply to the production of manufactured products. Nevertheless, this economy's production possibilities have improved and the curve has shifted outwards from the origin.

The production possibilities could also have declined. This could be because in some way the resources available to the economy have declined. Perhaps some of the economy's natural resources have become exhausted or the working population is falling. It might also be because the technology available to us has changed. An example might be the impact of controls on global emissions, which will affect our production possibilities as controls become more rigorous.

Applications of production possibility curves

We can use production possibility curves to illustrate some of the issues facing economic decision makers in the real world.

Jam today or more jam tomorrow? As stated previously, the production possibilities open to an economy are determined by the quantity and quality of resources available. In the process of production, resources are used up and they need to be replaced if production possibilities are to be maintained. The terms **capital consumption** or **depreciation** describe the using up of capital goods during the process of production. Some resources need to be devoted to the production of capital goods if production possibilities are to be maintained. The creation of capital goods in the process of production is known as **investment**.

This can be defined as *any production not for current consumption.* A choice has to be made therefore between producing consumer goods and services or producing capital goods through the process of investment. The more consumer goods and services produced, the higher the standard of living in the current time period, but the standard of living might fall in the future if there is a failure to produce enough capital goods to replace those worn out in the process of production. In addition, the quality of an economy's capital goods will not be improved and the full benefits of new technology will not be enjoyed if there is a failure to devote sufficient resources to investment.

Figure 1.5 shows the production possibilities between capital goods and consumer goods. These possibilities are determined by the quantity and quality of resources in the economy, which include the capital goods that have

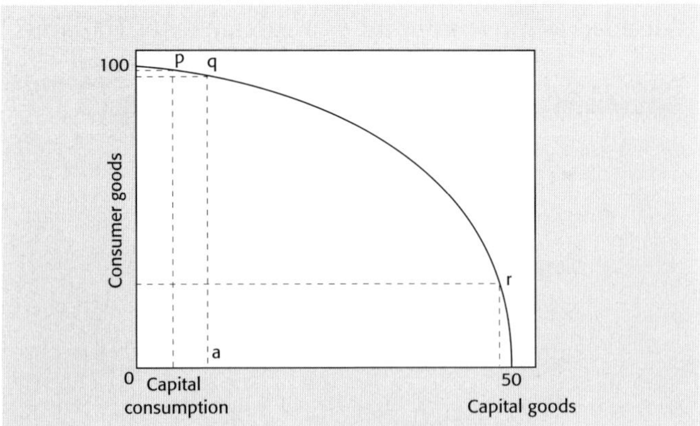

Figure 1.5 The choice between consumer goods and capital goods

been produced in the past. If we assume that the quantity of capital goods which are wearing out in each time period is shown at a, then we can see the consequences of our choices. If we fail to produce the quantity at a then our capital stock will decline. Our production possibilities will diminish and the curve will shift to the left.

We use the term 'gross investment' to describe the total quantity of capital goods produced. If we deduct from this the capital consumption allowance then we are left with net investment:

Gross investment minus capital consumption = Net investment

Self-assessment task

Use the terms gross investment, capital consumption and net investment to analyse the effect of economic decision makers choosing each of points p, q and r in figure 1.5. Explain the choices in terms of the present and future standard of living in the economy.

Hard choices for developing economies **Developing economies** are characterised by low standards of living. If they are to grow then they need to increase their capital stock. Like all economies they need to divert resources from current consumption to investment. Some resources must be devoted to consumption, however, to keep their expanding populations alive. We refer to this as the subsistence level of consumption. The difficulty they face is that in the poorest developing economies almost all their production possibilities need to be devoted to subsistence.

In figure 1.6, 0a represents the capital consumption in a developing economy and 0b represents the consumer goods required for the subsistence of the population.

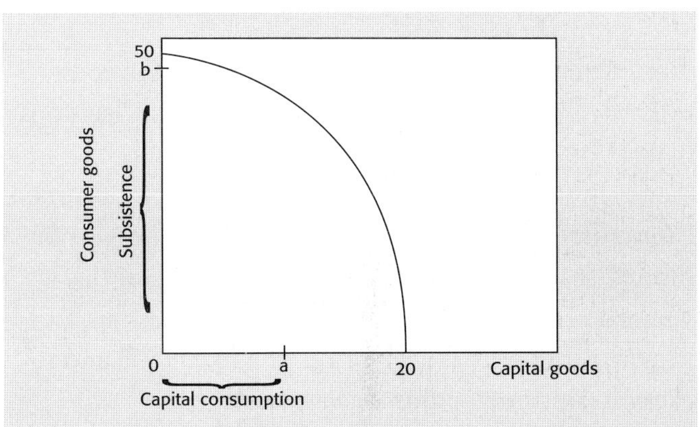

Figure 1.6 Capital consumption in a developing economy

Self-assessment task

Explain the choices facing decision makers in the developing economy shown in figure 1.6. Discuss the difficulties they face and suggest any solutions to their problems.

Different allocative mechanisms

The problem of scarcity, which in turn requires choices to be made, is one that is common to all economies, rich and poor. The choices that are made and which can realistically be made in turn are determined by the **economic system** of a particular country. This is the term used to describe the means or allocative mechanism by which its people, businesses and government make choices. Traditionally, economists have recognised three distinct types of economic system – these are the **market economy**, the **command or planned economy** and the **mixed economy**. Let us briefly consider each in turn.

The market economy

In such an economy decisions on how resources are to be allocated are usually taken by millions of households and thousands of firms – the exact number will of course depend on the size of economy. The key point is that they interact as buyers and sellers in the market for goods and services. Prices and the operation of the price system underpin this interaction; in turn prices act to indicate the likely market value of particular resources. For example, a commodity in short supply but which has a high demand attached to it will have a high price. Alternatively, one which has a high supply and low demand will have a much lower price attached to it. Prices and the self-interest of people and businesses therefore act as a guide to the decisions that have to be taken.

Economics as a subject has its origin in the notion that prices and the market mechanism are the 'best' way of handling economic problems. This notion can be particularly attributed to the Scottish economist Adam Smith, who is remembered for his reference to an 'invisible hand' (the price system) that brings together private and social interests in an harmonious way. This is the fundamental philosophy underpinning the workings of the market economy.

The government has a very restricted part to play. For example, in Smith's view, it should control national defence, act against monopolies, issue money, raise taxes and so on whilst protecting the rights of the private sector. It certainly should not try to influence the dealings of individuals in the market or to regulate the workings of that market. Figure 1.7 is a simple representation of these functions.

Before moving on, it must be made clear that the market economy is an ideal which does not exist in today's complex, globalised economy. Arguably, its most important representation is the United States of America (USA), and it should be stressed that here federal and state governments play important roles in the economy and society, as well as in providing defence, law and order and other public services.

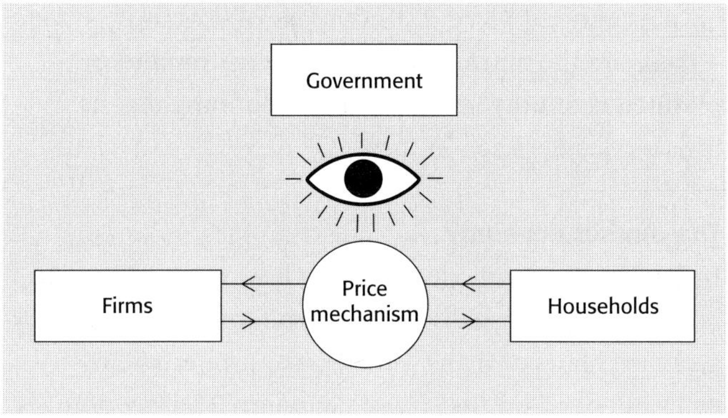

Figure 1.7 The market economy

The command economy

Like the market economy, the command or centrally planned economy in its purest form exists only in theory. In this second type of economy, the government has a central role in all decisions that are made and unlike the market economy, the emphasis is on centralisation. Decision making is taken by central planning boards and organisations to enterprises that are state-owned or under state regulation and control. Whereas in a market economy consumer sovereignty influences resource allocation, in a command economy, it is central planners who have to determine the collective preferences of consumers and manufacturing enterprises.

The planned economies of the last fifty years or so have their economic logic in the Marxian criticism of the market economy. This particular objection was essentially one of class conflict between the wealthy owners of capital and the poor working classes who provided this wealth through the production process. Marx was also critical of the built in unemployment arising out of the market system. For example, he had observed the trend to replace labour with machines (capital) and the inability of labour to secure higher wages. Under a command economy, unemployment is not an issue. Marx was also very concerned about the way in which the market economy fostered the concentration of productive resources in the hands of large monopolistic industrial and commercial organisations. As such he maintained that they corrupted the workings of demand and supply and, if powerful enough, could exert pressure on governments. Retrospectively, and in the light of empirical experience, economists have with some justification concluded that Marx's criticisms were excessive. Nevertheless, his general recognition that more centralisation should occur and that more emphasis should be placed on economic planning, have been applied by those countries which have pursued the notion of a planned economy.

So the key features of a command economy are that central government and its constituent organisations take responsibility for:

- the allocation of resources,
- the determination of production targets for all sectors of the economy,
- the distribution of income and the determination of wages,
- the ownership of most productive resources and property,
- planning the long-term growth of the economy.

From a practical standpoint, some of these decisions have to be de-centralised, either geographically or sectorally, to other government organisations. In certain cases, these bodies have control over the workings of a limited market mechanism. A good example of this is where basic foodstuffs such as bread and meat are heavily subsidised to keep prices at a fixed level and so exempt consumers from the vagaries of price fluctuation which are so commonplace in the market economy. Artificially low prices result in excess demand

Queuing for bread in the former Soviet Union
Source: Photo by Hjalte Tin, Still Pictures.

relative to supply – queuing becomes a way of life (see photograph). Also from a practical standpoint it is very difficult for all enterprise to be state-owned – there has to be a limited opportunity for the private ownership of small businesses such as shops, restaurants and personal services like hairdressing and cleaning.

The outcome of the command economy is that central planning tends to set goals for the economy that differ from those of the market economy. In particular they have a clear objective of achieving as high a rate of economic growth as possible in order to 'catch up' on the progress being made by much more advanced market economies. Popularly known as the 'guns and butter' argument, it is more correctly described as one of sacrificing current consumption and standards of living in order to achieve enhanced future well-being. This is the sacrifice that has to be made by the present generation for the benefit of future generations.

The last point can be illustrated by returning to the production possibility curve. Figure 1.8 indicates that the economy can choose between capital goods or consumer goods. The former represent an investment in machinery, equipment, infrastructure, technology and so on which will in time increase the productive capacity in the economy. Consumer goods like cars, refrigerators and televisions are for current consumption. In making this choice, command economies have chosen to produce at point *X* on their production possibility curve rather than at point *Y*, where consumer needs are satisfied in full.

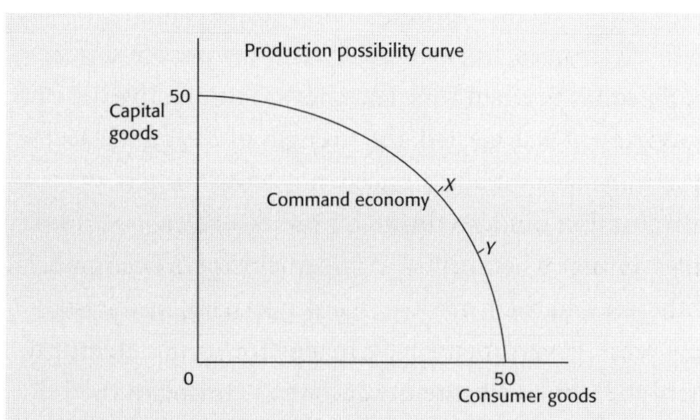

Figure 1.8 Command economies' production possibilities

This is of course a highly simplified representation of what in reality is a very complex process of centralised decision making. The extent to which economies choose *X* rather than *Y* also varies, depending on the degree to which the economy sees growth first and foremost as its only economic objective.

The mixed economy

It is clear from the brief analysis of market and command economies that, in the 'pure' sense, these types of economic systems occur in theory and not in reality. In contrast, the mixed economy is undoubtedly the characteristic form of economic organisation within the global economy. As its name indicates, it involves both private and public sectors in the process of resource allocation. Consequently, decisions on most important economic issues involve some form of planning (by private as well as public enterprises) and interaction between government, businesses and labour through the market mechanism. Private ownership of productive resources operates alongside public ownership in many mixed economies, although, increasingly, the trend is towards the privatisation of certain activities that were once in public sector hands.

The best example of this is undoubtedly the UK economy in the mid-1970s when the public and private sectors, broadly speaking, contributed equal proportions of the Gross Domestic Product (GDP). At this time the government was responsible for:

- substantial areas of public expenditure such as health, social services, education and defence;
- the direct operation of nationalised industries, such as coal, iron and steel, railways, gas, water, telephones and electricity;
- providing support for large areas of manufacturing, such as vehicle production, aerospace and electronics, in partnership with the private sector.

Since 1979, when Mrs Thatcher's Conservative government was elected, the strength of the public sector has been substantially reduced, not only through privatisation but also through a policy of non-intervention when private companies experience financial difficulties in their markets. Controversially, in the last few years, governments have made little or no attempt to stem the virtual closure of car manufacturing in the UK as, one by one, former British-owned companies have been rationalised by their non-UK owners.

The modern view of UK governments, Conservative and Labour, is that their responsibilities are for the overall management of the macroeconomy and for the funding of particular public and merit goods which overall would be underconsumed if left to the private sector alone to provide. It is also the case that new forms of regulation and control have had to be introduced in order to protect consumers from possible exploitation by the private sector providers of essential services. A very popular outcome of the UK experience is that millions more people now hold shares in such businesses.

Elsewhere, there have been similar trends. One of the most dramatic has been the restructuring of the economy of the former Soviet Union (*perestroika* as it is sometimes called). Under President Gorbachev's reforms, small private businesses could be set up in the service sector (for example, cafés, retail shops, garages and taxi hire) and workers could form their own co-operatives to market and sell surplus production from monolithic state manufacturing companies.

The US economy is also an example of a mixed economy, somewhat contrary to common perception. For example:

- the government at all levels is an important employer and provides basic services, such as education and various types of medical care;
- government agencies regulate and control the provision of some essential services, such as energy, telecommunications and transportation;
- indirect support is given to various strategically important companies.

These are over and above the expected provision of external defence and internal security services.

Trinidad and Tobago is a particularly good example of a Caribbean mixed economy. In the late 1980s, government involvement in the economy was through subsidies, transfers and joint ventures between itself and the private sector. The government has a share in many major companies in banking, agriculture, utilities and manufacturing. It is the largest single employer. Free enterprise, especially the foreign sector, is highly regulated by the government. This is also true in Barbados where tourism developments take the form of a Social Partnership between the Government, private sector investors and the labour unions.

Just how important a role the government plays in any particular mixed economy is not easy to explain.

About the only real explanation that can be given is that in most cases it is usually a consequence of differing political philosophies. Figure 1.9 provides a largely normative assessment of where particular economies fall in terms of the relative strengths of market and planned systems of resource allocation. In all cases, except arguably for Albania, the prevailing wind is to move their economic structures towards that of an ever-increasing role for the market mechanism.

In more recent times, the experience of the newly industrialising countries (NICs) is interesting. In terms of allocative mechanisms, some, such as Singapore and Hong Kong, opted for a strong focus on the market to allocate resources and through this have created an economic situation where enterprise can be encouraged and rewarded. Other South East Asian Tigers have placed more emphasis on central planning, whilst China's phenomenal growth over the last decade has been based on the controlled management of the economy within a global context.

The new **Tiger economies** of Central Europe, particularly the Czech Republic, Hungary and Poland, have re-orientated their economies to foreign investors. In this way, they hope to achieve forecasted growth rates of around 5–7 per cent per annum. These are very much in line with those experienced by their Asian counterparts, yet significantly higher than those experienced in the past by more developed economies.

Looking at the Caribbean area, it is possible to identify examples of economies that closely match each of the three main types of economic system. The majority of countries, including Barbados, Jamaica and Trinidad and Tobago, have mixed economies. The public sectors provide a wide range of goods and public services for the benefit of their populations. Education up to secondary level is perhaps the best example but there are also publicly funded health services, police and fire services as well as various forms of transport infrastructure such as roads. At the same time, the private sector often works alongside the island governments to provide rail freight and passenger services, power services, telephones and in some cases, port facilities. All are vital for the well-being of the local tourist industry which is controlled by the private sector as are the mineral and extractive industries.

The Bahamas and Cayman Islands provide something of a contrast, particularly the latter which is a tax haven in so far as residents do not pay any direct taxes. Here

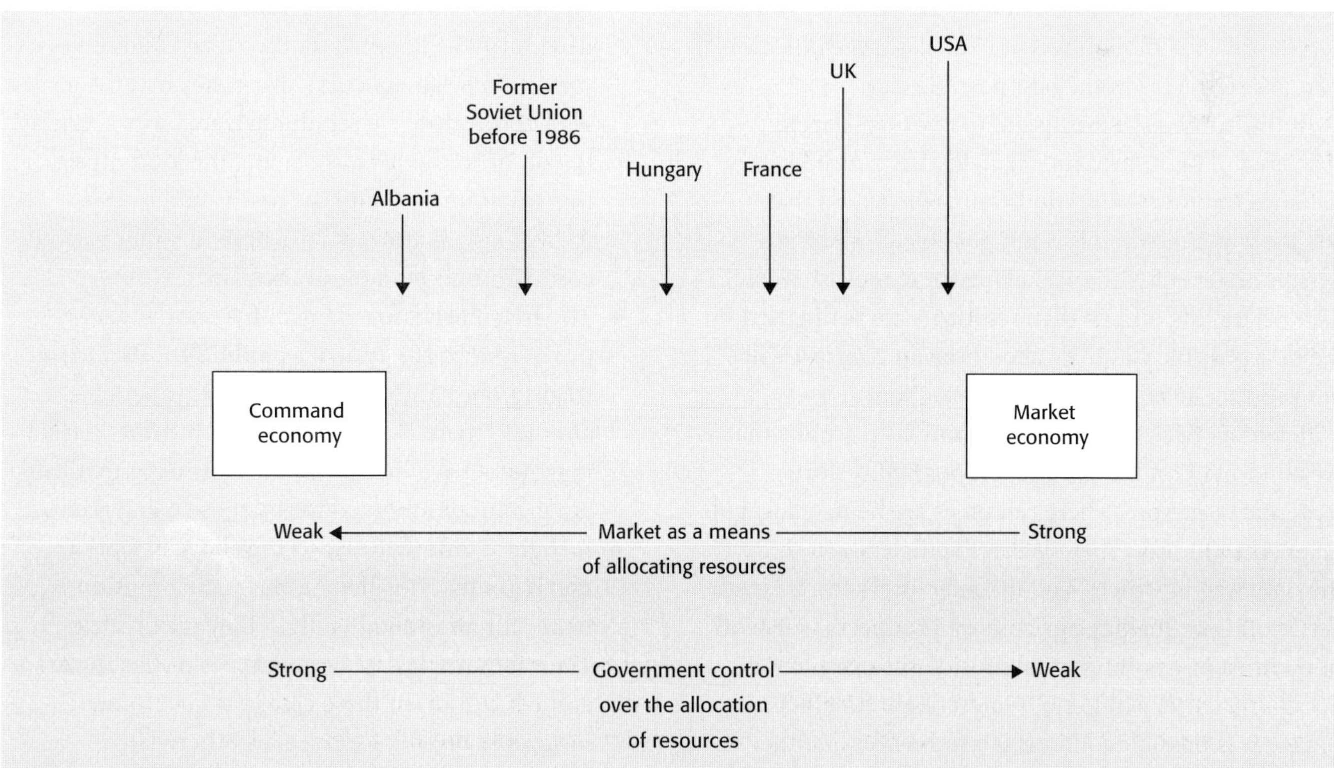

Figure 1.9 Mixed economic systems

the private sector is responsible for generating a very high percentage of GDP and the free market has a major role to play in the allocation of resources. At the other extreme is Marxist Cuba, where the private sector has only a relatively minor role in the economy and resource allocation. Housing and many areas of employment remain under state control, making Cuba a rather extreme type of economy. In recent years, the private sector has had an increasing part to play, although this has been small and underdeveloped compared with the rest of the Caribbean area.

Efficiency in Economics

The first few pages of this topic established that Economics involves a study of how 'best' to use scarce resources to meet infinite wants. Whether resources are being used in the 'best' way possible is referred to in Economics as **efficiency**. So, when all resources are being used in the most effective way to meet the greatest level of consumer wants, then this is a situation where economic efficiency is being achieved. Irrespective of the type of economy we are considering, all economies aspire to achieve economic efficiency. As you work through the various topics in units 1 and 2, this concept of efficiency will occur in many different contexts. The common factor though is that in all cases the objective is to use resources in the best possible way.

At this early stage it is useful to consider **Pareto efficiency**. This approach is named after a well known Italian economist, Wilfredo Pareto, who stated that efficiency exists 'when it is not possible to make any one person better off without making someone else worse off'. Where this occurs, then resources are being used in the best possible way. Any alterations in contrast will not produce as high a level of satisfaction.

Referring back to figure 1.3, points p, q, r and s that are all located on the production possibility curve represent situations where resources are being allocated in an efficient way. There is Pareto efficiency in so far as the only way in which (say) manufacturers can be made better off is by making agricultural producers worse off. In contrast any point that falls inside the production possibility curve would not represent Pareto efficiency as here it is possible to increase production of either or both types of products, making all concerned better off.

As mentioned earlier and as you will see later on in this unit, the free market is viewed in Economics as the best possible way to achieve an efficient allocation of resources. The natural forces of the price mechanism will work to produce such an allocation with no involvement from government (see figure 1.7). This is though a most unreal assumption to make in all cases – the free market invariably 'fails' to produce an efficient allocation of resources under certain circumstances.

Market failure

Market failure exists when free markets fail to produce an efficient allocation of resources. When this happens the self-regulating processes of the market mechanism do not lead to the best market outcome. In other words, the market fails to deliver what is expected. In turn this is a signal for possible government intervention. Chapter 6 will look at this in detail. At this stage it is useful to give three typical examples of market failure. These are:

- There are **externalities** present in a market. Here, someone not directly involved (known as a third party) is affected by the actions or decisions of others. For example, if you play loud music in a public place, others living nearby will not necessarily be happy with the noise you are making. The **social costs**, all of the costs associated with this action, exceed the **private costs** accruing to you or to the person playing the loud music. In this situation, an **external cost** is said to exist – the market fails as third parties have to suffer various costs through no fault of their own.
- The free market mechanism may not always provide what are known as **public goods** such as roads, police and fire services. This is because although there is a clear demand, the free market may not have a mechanism for ensuring that they are produced and paid for by those using them.
- A slightly different case to the above is that of **merit goods**, so-called because consumption is better for an individual than they may realise. Typical examples are certain types of health care and education. In these cases the government invariably provides services as otherwise individuals would not always consume them.

Secondary education in the Caribbean is provided free of charge by all governments since it is seen as so vital for future economic well-being. If a charge were made, many individuals would not pay.

Price ceilings and price floors

Reference was made above to the importance of the price mechanism in the allocation of resources in the market economy. Prices provide feedback on the extent to which resources are being allocated in the most effective way. In certain circumstances though, governments in mixed and particularly command economies find it necessary to intervene in the natural workings of the price system. Two instances are:

- **Price ceilings** or where the government fixes a maximum price that is below the price that would otherwise be set. A good example of this is the case of public housing where rents tend to be fixed at a low level for valid social and equity reasons. In such circumstances, those living in such housing are the main beneficiaries. The effect of the price ceiling will be to make demand greater – possibly diverting some tenants from private sector housing – than what can be supplied. Another example could be in the case of basic foodstuffs where prices are kept at a deliberately low level. Where this is so then the likely outcome is one of excess demand and suppliers who are reluctant to put their products on to the market.
- **Price floors** or where the government fixes a minimum price as the free market price is deemed too low. A good example is in the labour markets where minimum wages apply. Although the purpose is to reduce worker exploitation, a minimum wage might lead to less employment as some employers may be reluctant to pay a rate which they believe to be too high.

In both of these cases, the price system is not allocating resources in the most efficient way.

Positive and normative Economics

It is useful to conclude this first topic by making a distinction between **positive and normative economics**. Economics is a social science. As such it has developed through the use of positive analysis that is devoid of any value judgements. Typical positive statements are:

Hong Kong, the new jewel in China's crown

- A fall in the supply of petrol will lead to an increase in its price…
- An increase in tourist numbers in Jamaica will create more employment…
- An increase in taxation on cigarettes will result in less cigarettes being sold…

These are statements of what will happen. No value judgements are involved. When values come into the analysis, then this is normative economics. Here an opinion or value judgement is being made. The above statements can become normative, for example, by adding

… and this should be positive for the environment.

… and therefore the Jamaican government should do everything it can to help.

… and this should improve the nation's health.

Self-assessment tasks

1 Think carefully about the ways in which your own economy allocates resources. Make a few notes on the ways in which
- the government,
- the market mechanism,

are responsible for decision making.

2 Use the above information to insert your own economy into the scale shown in figure 1.9. How has its relative position changed in recent years?

3 What information might an economist use to quantify the relative importance of the government and the market mechanism within an economy?

Self-assessment tasks

On completion of this chapter you should be able to attempt the following short answer questions drawn from CAPE examination papers, 2003–2005.

1 (a) Define the following terms:
- scarcity, (2 marks)
- opportunity cost. (2 marks)

(b) Draw a 'production possibility frontier' diagram to illustrate increasing opportunity cost. (2 marks)

(Total 6 marks)

2

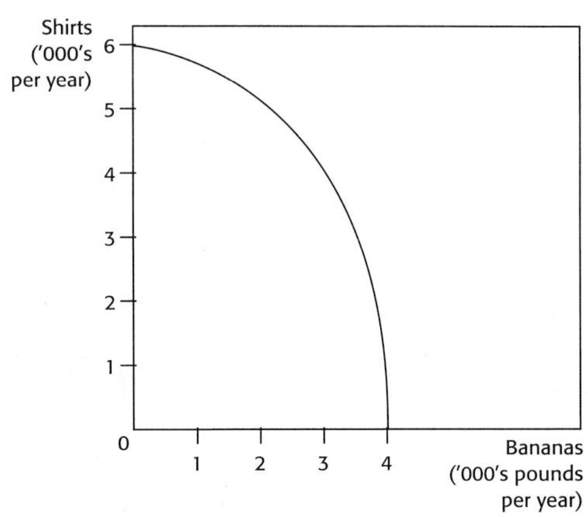

(a) Reproduce the production possibility frontier diagram shown above in your answer booklet and indicate the following:
- an inefficient production point, (2 marks)
- a production point that is unattainable. (2 marks)

(b) What is the additional cost, in shirts, of increasing the production of bananas from ONE thousand pounds per year to TWO thousand pounds per year? (2 marks)

(Total 6 marks)

3 (a) State ONE reason why it is necessary to make economic choices. (1 mark)

(b) State THREE major questions that must be asked when deciding what goods and services should be produced. (3 marks)

(c) Susan uses the two hours available to her to answer her email messages rather than study for her Economics examination. What is the cost to her of choosing to read her email messages rather than study for her Economics examination? Briefly explain your answer. (2 marks)

(Total 6 marks)

4 (a) Use the information in the following table to construct a production possibilities frontier (PPF).

Pineapples	Mangoes
0	500
200	450
350	450
425	275
475	125
500	0

(3 marks)

(b) Mark the point (300,300) on your diagram. (1 mark)

(c) State why this point does not represent an efficient use of resources. (1 mark)

(d) What does the shape of the PPF you have drawn say about the opportunity costs of producing ONE more unit of pineapples or mangoes? (1 mark)

(Total 6 marks)

Summary

In this chapter it has been shown that:

- All economies face the so-called economic problem of limited resources and unlimited wants.
- Choice is necessary in order to decide what, how and for whom to produce.
- The true cost of choices can be explained in terms of opportunity cost.
- Production possibility curves can be used to show opportunity cost, economic growth and technological change.
- Efficiency is the term used to demonstrate how well resources are being used.
- The market mechanism is a self-regulating way of allocating resources.
- Under certain circumstances the market mechanism fails to produce the best allocation of resources.
- The mixed economy is the typical form of organisation in the global economy.

Key words

Definitions of Key words can be found in the Glossary.

capital consumption
capital goods
choice
command economy
consumption
developing economy
division of labour
economic growth
economic problem
efficiency
enterprise
external cost
externalities
factor endowment
factor mobility
investment
labour
land
market economy
market failure
maximisation
merit goods
mixed economy
normative economics
opportunity cost
Pareto efficiency
planned economy
positive economics
price ceiling
price floor
production
production frontier
production possibility curve
production transformation curve
public goods
resources
reallocation of resources
risk
scale of preference
scarcity
social costs
specialisation
Tiger economies
wants

2 Tools of economic analysis

This chapter covers unit 1, module 1, topic 2.
On completion of this chapter, you should be able to:

- explain the concept of a model
- identify the maximum and minimum of a function
- distinguish between a variable and a constant
- define the following terms: 'endogenous variables', 'exogenous variables', 'coefficients' and 'parameters'
- use linear and non-linear diagrams for economic representation
- prepare a scatter diagram using basic economic data
- present economic data in tabular form

This chapter is different from all others in both units since the items that it covers are largely embedded in the subject content of Economics that will be progressively analysed as you work through the chapters. The last three items, on data representation, were briefly referred to in data handling skills 1 and 4 in the Introduction. These will be elaborated on later in this chapter.

Naomi Campbell
Source: Empics.

What is a model?

The term 'model' is used in various ways. In the fashion business, for example, it is used to describe the near perfect figures and looks of the likes of Naomi Campbell and Kate Moss; in the toy manufacturing business, it represents the scaled-down version of a real car or aeroplane. When used by economists, a model incorporates both of these characteristics – it, is 'an idealised but simplified representation of reality'.

A few examples will help elaborate on this meaning. In microeconomics:

- Chapter 3 introduces the idea of a demand curve. This is a very simple model of the relationship between the quantity demanded of a particular good and its price. It is simple in the sense that all other factors that affect the demand for a good are held constant. The demand curve model therefore is

  demand = f(price)

A more accurate model, taking all other variable factors into account, would be demand = *f* (price, price of other goods, income, taste)

- In the theory of the firm (chapter 5), the firm is modelled in terms of its cost and revenue curves. Variations in these apply in different market structures. As a consequence, the price, output and profits made by a firm can be determined. Economists can then use this information to put forward important principles as to how firms behave in particular market structures.

In macroeconomics:

- Chapter 4 introduces the basic Keynesian consumption function, $C = a + bY$. This is a simplified representation of the relationship been consumption and the level of income in an economy. Mathematically, it is no more than the equation of a straight line. In Economics this simple model has stood the test of time and continues to have some relevance more than 70 years on from when it was first developed.
- Another well-known model is that of the relationship between the money supply and inflation in an economy. This is the quantity theory of money, $MV = PT$. It assumes that if V and T are held constant, then any change in the money supply (M) will cause the same change in the price level/rate of inflation (P) in the economy. This is another model that has stood the test of time.

These are just some of the many models you will come across as you progress through the topics in this book. Economists have sought to simplify particular relationships, based on empirical evidence, and then used the resulting models to enhance awareness of an actual economic issue or problem.

Maximum and minimum of a function

The maximum value in a set of data is the highest value that it takes; the minimum value is the lowest. Both can be shown in the time series graph in figure 2.1.

The highest recorded value (maximum) was 3.5 per cent for the January–March quarter of 2003. In contrast, the lowest value (minimum) was –1.0 in the October–December quarter of 2004 when the Jamaican economy was negatively affected by Hurricane Ivan.

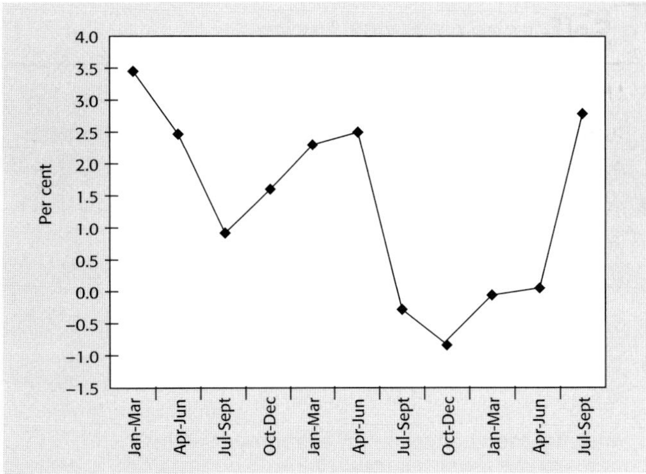

Figure 2.1 Quarterly real GDP growth in Jamaica, 2003–2005
Source: Planning Institute of Jamaica, 2006.

If we now take the consumption function,
$C = a + b\,Y$, where
C is consumption or consumer spending
a is a constant
b is the marginal propensity to consume, the proportion of any income increase that is spent on consumption
Y is disposable income

Table 2.1 shows how this function changes for various levels of income. Let us take the consumption function as

$$C = 100 + 0.8Y$$

As the table indicates, the minimum value of the function is where $Y = 0$; the maximum value is where $Y = 1{,}000$. (This is normal for a linear function like this.)

Income (*Y*)($)	*bY*	*a*	Consumption (*C*)
0	0	100	100
100	80	100	180
200	160	100	260
300	240	100	340
400	320	100	420
500	400	100	500
600	480	100	580
700	560	100	660
800	640	100	740
900	720	100	820
1,000	800	100	900

Table 2.1 Relationship between consumption and income

Self-assessment tasks

1 Using the data in Table 2.1, draw the consumption function $C = 100 + 0.8Y$ for the income range 0 to 1,000.
2 What is the value for consumption when income is $650?
3 Confirm the value of the marginal propensity to consume as income increases from $400 to $500
4 Comment upon why this simple model may not fully reflect the relationship between consumption changes and income changes in an economy.

Constants and variables

Looking back at the consumption function $C = a + bY$, a and b are constants, whilst C and Y are variables.

A **constant** therefore is something that does not change. In this case it is a coefficient that is fixed or pre-determined. Another example of a constant that is often used in economic data is the base year for a set of time series data, for instance 1995 = 100. When looking at living standards between economies (see chapter 16), it is necessary to express comparative data in a common form, usually US$, for an exchange rate at a given point in time. This is a further example of a constant.

A **variable** is defined as any statistic or measure that is liable to change. Most economic data, particularly relating to the macroeconomy, are like this and vary usually over time. This applies to data on consumer prices, interest rates, unemployment, growth rates and so on. In microeconomics, the list is equally extensive. Typical examples are the quantity of a good that is demanded and how this changes with price, the average cost of a firm and how this varies with output and how the marginal revenue product of labour is affected by the number of workers employed. These topics will be analysed later in this unit.

Other terms

The simple models that were described earlier usually consist of a set of variables. Where these arise out of the natural workings of the economic system, they are referred to as **endogenous variables**.

The demand function referred to at the start of this topic consists of this type of variable. The four variable factors that are used to explain variations in the quantity demanded of a good have been identified in empirical economic investigations as being of direct importance in this respect. The same is true of the variables M, V, P and T in the quantity theory of money model. Many years ago these were identified from real economic situations.

In contrast, **exogenous variables** influence the workings of the economic system from outside. They are often unplanned and unexpected. For example, political conflict in the Middle East can affect the world supply of oil, resulting in an escalation of world prices. Another example might be if there is an outbreak of food poisoning amongst tourists in the Dominican Republic. This would have an adverse effect on tourism there and could result in some tourists switching their holidays to other Caribbean islands. Another example is the pressure on the Thai baht which led to the Asian financial crisis of 1996 and the resulting negative effects on most other economies in the region. In all cases, these events were unexpected, yet they had a profound economic impact.

Returning to the consumption function, $C = a + bY$, the constant 'b' is sometimes referred to as a **coefficient** or, more specifically, the coefficient of Y. In this case it is the number that is part of an economic equation.

Finally, a **parameter** is sometimes referred to in Economics as a quantity that is taken as given in any piece of analysis. For example, in analysing how buyers and sellers behave in a competitive market, each is assumed to regard price as a parameter since they are unable to affect it through their own actions (see chapter 5). This is one of the principal features of this type of market structure. Looking at the market as a whole though, price is in itself a variable which is determined by the combined forces of demand and supply.

Further aspects of data representation

Data skill 4 in the Introduction looked at how economic information could be produced in visual form through bar charts, pie charts and other forms of pictorial representation. Figure 2, for example, represented the data on a **linear** basis – the vertical *x* scale was calibrated in an even way starting at 60 per cent. The same was true of the diagrams in figure 4.

An example of a **non-linear** form of representation is where the scale on a diagram is logarithmic. Here the logarithm of a variable is usually shown on the vertical scale. Such scales are particularly used in diagrams where time is usually on the horizontal axis and variables such as GDP or the price level are shown as logarithms on the vertical axis. With GDP, the slope of the resulting curve shows the proportional growth rate of this variable. If the resulting representation is a straight line, then this is indicative of a constant proportional growth trend.

A **scatter diagram** is often used to show basic economic data. As its name suggests, it consists of a diagrammatic representation of the distribution of a particular variable in a data set. Each piece of data is shown by a dot or cross. The individual pieces of data in Figure 2.1 above were like this.

Throughout the book, much of the data are presented in tabular form. Such tables or matrices provide a very effective way of summarising data that have been collected by government departments, global organisations, firms and so on. Table 1 in the Introduction is a simple example of this. Often though tables of data are presented in the form of a frequency distribution where individual pieces of data are grouped together in a series of frequency bands. This form of representation is useful since it can provide a very effective summary of a set of data.

Self-assessment tasks

The data in table 2.2 below shows visitor arrivals in Jamaica for the first nine months of 2004 and 2005.

Month	Total Stopover Visitors 2004	Total Stopover Visitors 2005	Cruise Passenger Arrivals 2004	Cruise Passenger Arrivals 2005
January	109,350	116,844	124,650	111,841
February	120,129	123,022	115,351	112,261
March	136,606	155,103	129,266	150,871
April	131,101	123,578	109,744	98,654
May	111,759	110,821	64,424	74,505
June	133,393	132,710	76,427	73,246
July	160,231	151,289	68,203	59,881
August	129,526	117,898	69,229	75,555
September	64,940	72,926	48,301	69,463

Table 2.2 Monthly Visitor arrivals in Jamaica, 2004 and 2005
Source: Jamaica Tourist Board.

1 (a) Draw a scatter diagram of total stopover visitors and cruise passenger arrivals covering the period January 2004 to September 2005.
(b) Use this diagram to describe trends in each of these sets of data.

2 For each of the two variables, simplify the data in table 2.2 into a frequency distribution. Use the following categories: less than 60,000, 60,000–79,999, 80,000–99,999, 100,000–119,999, 120,000–139,999, 140,000 and over. Your diagram should cover the two years of data.

Summary

On completion of this chapter, you should know:

- What is meant by a model.
- How to identify the maximum and minimum values of a function.
- The difference between a variable and a constant.
- What is meant by endogenous variables, exogenous variables, coefficients and parameters.
- How linear and non-linear diagrams are used to represent economic information.
- How to prepare scatter diagram.
- How to present data in tabular form.

Key words

Definitions of Key words can be found in the Glossary.

coefficient
constant
endogenous variable
exogenous variable
linear diagram
maximum
minimum
model
non-linear diagram
parameter
scatter diagram
variable

3 Theory of consumer demand

This chapter covers unit 1, module 1, topic 3.
On completion of this chapter, you should be able to:

- explain the concept of utility
- explain the law of diminishing marginal utility and the limitation of marginal theory
- explain consumer equilibrium using both utility and indifference curve approaches
- explain the meaning of indifference curves
- isolate the income and substitution effects of a price change
- differentiate normal, inferior, Giffen and ostentatious goods
- identify the factors that cause demand curves to shift
- define effective demand
- distinguish between shifts of the demand curve and movements along the curve
- identify and discuss the factors that determine and influence the shape of the demand curve
- explain the meaning of consumer surplus
- define price, income and cross elasticity of demand
- calculate and interpret numerical values of elasticity
- state the factors that determine the price elasticity of demand

Utility and marginal utility

Economists have long been interested in the way that consumers behave. The starting point is the notion of **utility**. This idea dates back to the nineteenth century and is a term used to record the level of happiness or satisfaction that someone receives from the consumption of a good. It is assumed that this satisfaction can be measured, in the same way that the actual units consumed can be calculated. Two important measures are:

- **total utility** – the overall satisfaction that is derived from the consumption of all units of a good over a given time period;
- **marginal utility** – the additional utility derived from the consumption of one more unit of a particular good (also known as cardinal utility).

The marginal utility gained from the consumption of a product tends to fall as consumption increases. For example, if you buy an ice cream you will get a lot of satisfaction from its consumption, especially in hot weather. If you consume a second one, you will still get some satisfaction but this is likely to be less than from the first ice cream. A third ice cream will yield even less satisfaction. This aspect of consumer behaviour is referred to as the principle of **diminishing marginal utility**. As consumption increases further, there may actually come a point where marginal utility is negative, indicating dissatisfaction or disutility.

In considering the consumer's equilibrium, it is necessary to remember that Economics assumes that consumers have limited incomes, behave in a rational manner and seek to maximise their total utility. A consumer is said to be in equilibrium, assuming a given level of income, when it is not possible to switch any expenditure from, say, product A to product B to increase total utility. This is referred to as the **equi-marginal principle** and can be represented thus:

$$\frac{MU_A}{P_A} = \frac{MU_B}{P_B} = \frac{MU_C}{P_C} \cdots = \frac{MU_N}{P_N}$$

where MU = marginal utility

P = the price

A, B, C and N = individual products

It is possible to use marginal utility to derive an individual demand curve. The fundamental principle of demand is that an increase in the price of a good will lead to a reduction in its demand. Using the above principle, this can now be proved. The value of the expression $\frac{MU_A}{P_A}$ will now fall as the price of A has increased. So, the marginal utility of A per $ spent will now be *less* than on any other goods. The consumer will therefore increase total utility by spending less on good A and more on all other goods. This will in turn reduce the value of their marginal utility. In other words, the consumer only maximises total utility by buying less of good A. The conclusion is that the demand curve for a good is downward sloping.

Self-assessment tasks

1 The table below shows the total utility gained from the consumption of lemonade in a week.

Quantity consumed (bottles)	Total utility
0	0
1	20
2	35
3	45
4	53
5	58
6	54
7	48

(a) Calculate the marginal utility.

(b) Sketch the total utility and marginal utility curves (put utility on the vertical axis, quantity on the horizontal axis).

2 If the price of lemonade increases from $1 to $2 per bottle, how might it affect consumption? Explain your answer using the data above.

Budget constraint

All consumers are constrained in what they are able to buy because of their income and the prices of goods they wish to buy. These two important underpinning principles of consumer behaviour are brought together in the idea of a **budget constraint** or **budget line**. This shows numerically all the possible combinations of two products that a consumer can purchase with a given income and fixed prices.

Suppose someone has $200 to spend on two products, A and B. Assume the price of A is $20 and the price of B is $10. Table 3.1 shows the possible combinations that can be purchased. Each of the combinations would cost $200 in total. Figure 3.1(a) shows the budget line for this situation. Any point along this line will produce an outcome where consumption is maximised for this level of income.

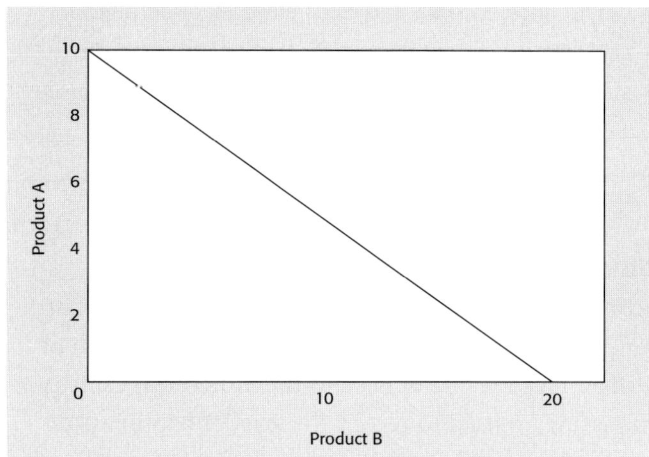

Figure 3.1(a) Budget lines for an income of $200

Quantity of A ($20 each)	Quantity of B ($10 each)
10	0
9	2
8	4
7	6
6	8
5	10
4	12
3	14
2	16
1	18
0	20

Table 3.1 Combinations of A and B with a budget of $200

If there is a change in the price of one good, with income remaining unchanged, then the budget line will pivot. For example, if the price of good B falls then more of this product can be purchased at all levels of income. The budget line will shift outwards, from its pivot at point A. This is shown in figure 3.1(b). So, if the price of B falls by a third to \$6.67, then 30 of good B can now be purchased with an income of \$200.

As the price of B has fallen relative to that of A, which is unchanged, consumers will substitute B for A. This is known as the **substitution effect** of a price change. It is always the case that the rational consumer will substitute towards the product which has become relatively cheaper. With the fall in the price of B, the consumer actually has more money to spend on other products, B included. The real income has therefore increased, which may mean that a consumer may now actually purchase more of good B. This is called the **income effect** of a price change.

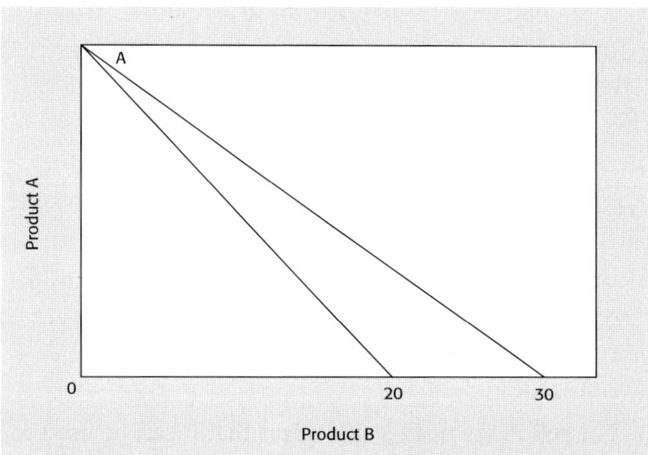

Figure 3.1(b) Budget lines – a fall in the price of B

Self-assessment tasks

1 Re-draw figure 3.1(a) to show how it would change:
   - if the price of B increased, leaving the price of A unchanged,
   - if the price of A decreased, leaving the price of B unchanged.

2 In your own words, describe the substitution and income effects of:
   - an increase in the price of a normal good,
   - a decrease in the price of an inferior good.

Indifference curves – representing what consumers want

The budget constraint referred to above showed what combination of goods a consumer could buy, given income and the prices of goods. This is only part of the reason why consumers buy particular goods – what is also relevant is consumer preference. Consumers will only buy a particular good if it is something that they actually want or prefer when having to choose between alternatives. Consumer preferences can be represented diagrammatically by what are known as **indifference curves.**

As the name suggests, an indifference curve shows the combinations of two goods with which the consumer is equally satisfied. Figure 3.2 shows two such indifference curves out of the many that can apply to a particular consumer. Considering indifference curve I_1, the consumer is indifferent with respect to combinations X, Y or Z since each are on the same indifference curve. If the consumer moves from point Z to Y, then the consumption of good B falls at the expense of an increase in consumption of good A. Point Y, though, still represents a situation where the consumer is still equally happy with the combination of goods that are being consumed.

The slope of the indifference curve is important – it represents the extent to which the consumer is willing to substitute one good for another. Looking at figure 3.2, all the curves slope more steeply from left to right showing that when consuming large amounts of good A, the consumer is willing to give up rather more of this good when consumption of good B is small. The rate at which the consumer is willing to substitute one good for

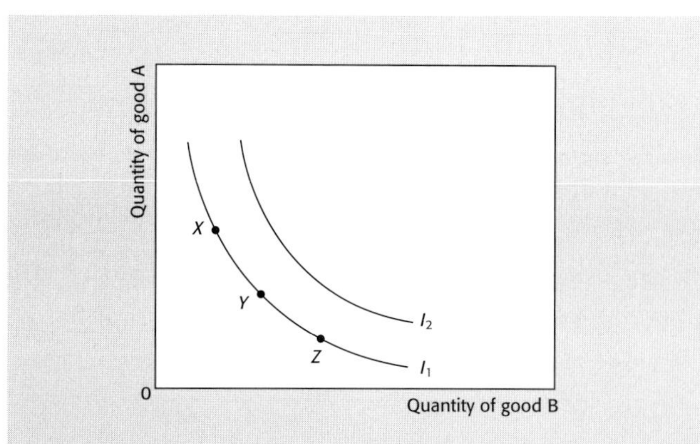

Figure 3.2 An indifference map

another in this way is known as the **marginal rate of substitution.**

Other points to note are:

- Higher indifference curves represent higher levels of consumption. Consumers therefore prefer them to lower ones.
- All indifference curves are downward sloping to indicate that a fall in the quantity consumed of one good is accompanied by an increase in the consumption of the other good.
- Indifference curves cannot cross.
- Indifference curves are concave or bowed inward to the origin.

Effect of a change in income on consumer choice

The budget constraint and the indifference curve can be used together to show the effect of a change in income on the consumption of two goods. This is indicated in figure 3.3. A consumer's choice is optimal at the point where the budget line touches or is at a tangent to the highest indifference curve. So, E_1 will give the consumer the maximum combined consumption of goods A and B given the budget constraint shown by the budget line B_1.

If income increases, then this will allow the consumer to choose a better combination of goods A and B. This will usually be more of each good. So, if the budget constraint rises to B_2, then the consumer will increase consumption of good A and also of good B, albeit to a lesser extent. E_2 is the new optimal position, where more of both goods are being consumed. The change in position from E_1 to E_2 is what occurs when both goods are **normal goods.** If the increase in income or budget constraint results in less of one good being consumed, then this is an **inferior good.**

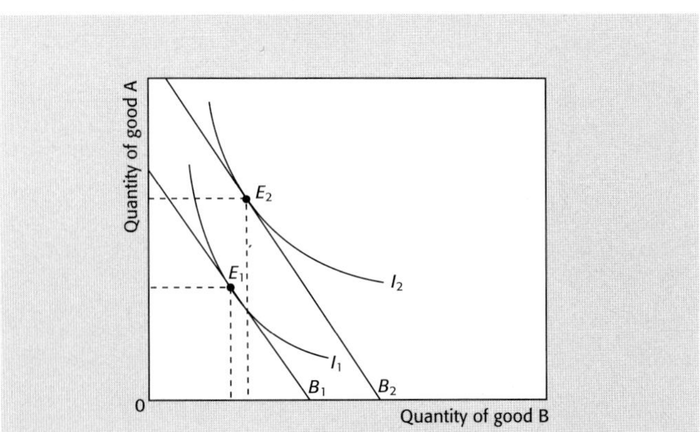

Figure 3.3 The effect of an increase in income

Income and substitution effects of a price change using indifference curves (Slutsky approach)

The income and substitution effects of a price change were outlined earlier. These effects will now be interpreted using indifference curves. This is shown in figure 3.4.

If the price of good A falls, then this means that the consumer has more spending power. This is represented by the new budget constraint B_2. The price of good B remains the same, which is why B_2 pivots upwards to a new position. The extent of change that occurs consists of two stages. These are:

- A movement along the initial indifference curve I_1 to point E_2. This is the substitution effect. It is so-called since the consumer buys less of good B as it is now relatively more expensive than good A.
- A shift upwards to a higher indifference curve, moving from point E_2 to E_3. This is the income effect. As the consumer has more spending power, it is positive in the case of both goods, resulting in an increase in consumption of good B as well as good A.

In the case of good A, the income and substitution effects are both positive, resulting in a substantial increase in consumption. For good B, the substitution effect is negative, but the fall in consumption is to some extent offset by the positive income effect. So here the income and substitution effects are pulling in opposite directions. In figure 3.4, there is a fall in consumption of good B as the substitution effect is stronger than the income effect.

The relevance of this analysis is that it can be used to derive the **demand curve** for a product. As we shall show below, the demand curve shows how the price of a

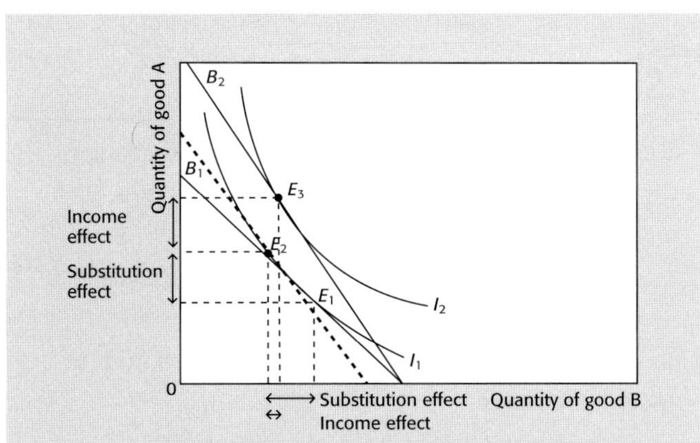

Figure 3.4 The income and substitution effects of a price change

good affects the quantity that is demanded. It is therefore a summary of the decisions arising from a consumer's budget constraint and indifference curves.

Demand

To an economist:

> **demand** refers to the *quantities* of a *product* that *purchasers* are *willing and able* to buy at *various prices* per *period of time, other things remaining the same.*

Definitions are of critical importance in Economics, so let us break this definition down to understand in some depth what this means.

- *Quantities* – economists often deal with numerical values and very often try to represent information in a quantitative way. This point is reinforced by the use of the term 'prices'.
- *Product* – this is a general term that simply refers to the item that is being traded. It can be used for goods or services. We could also stretch this to include tradable items like money or other financial assets such as shares.
- *Purchasers* – these are the buyers of the product and are often referred to as 'consumers', although they may simply be intermediaries in the production–consumption chain, for example Nestlé purchasing large amounts of cocoa to be used in the production of chocolate for sale to the final consumer. We could look at an individual purchaser's demand for a product or, more usefully, we can aggregate this to look at the demand of an overall market or sub-market.
- *Willing to buy* – clearly purchasers must want a product if they are going to enter into the market to buy it. Economists use the terms 'satisfaction' or 'utility' to describe the benefit or pleasure that the final consumer derives from the product.
- *Able to buy* – to an economist, the **notional demand** for a product, which emerges from wanting it, must be backed by purchasing power if the demand is to become **effective**. Companies are only willing to sell a product if the purchaser has monetary ability to pay for the product – the world is full of wishful thinkers who would love to own something they just cannot afford. It is, however, effective demand that is of real importance for economists.
- *Various prices* – prices are crucial to the functioning of a market. Although demand for a product is influenced by many things, it is at the moment of purchase, when we have to hand over our money and pay the price, that we really judge whether the product is value for money, that is, whether we really are willing and able to buy it. As the price goes up, and provided no other changes have occurred, more and more people will judge the product to be less worthwhile.
- *Per period of time* – demand must be time related. It is of no use to say that the local McDonalds sold 20 Big Macs to consumers unless you specify the time period over which the sales occurred. If that was per minute then demand is probably quite high, but if that was per week then clearly there is little demand for Big Macs in this sub-market.
- *Other things being equal* – we will see shortly that there are numerous potential influences on the demand for a product. Analysing the connections between the various elements is very difficult if lots of these elements are changing simultaneously. The process is similar to that of a scientist who, when conducting an experiment, will control the general conditions except for the two elements that he/she wishes to investigate. So, for simplicity, we start with the assumption that all the other factors are constant and analyse the response of purchasers on the basis that price alone changes. We will relax this assumption as we progress. Economists often use a Latin phrase, **ceteris paribus**, to indicate this assumption – this simply means '*other things being equal*'.

The demand curve

Let us now take the definition of demand and represent it diagrammatically to construct what is known as a **demand curve**. We will make up an example based on the overall market demand for PCs to illustrate the point. Let us make an assumption that we can identify a typical PC, that is one with a set of standard specifications. Remember we can break the analysis into sub-markets later if we want to become more detailed. Let us also assume that we have collected statistical data about people's preferences and that the quantity of PCs that people are willing and able to buy at various prices

Consumers sit outside their local McDonalds. But if these young people are not buying or the rest of the day is very quiet, it is not reflective of high demand

per period of time, ceteris paribus, can be represented by the data in table 3.2. This is known as a **demand schedule**. We can now plot the **market demand** schedule on a graph to see how the quantity demanded of PCs relates to variations in price. This demand curve therefore represents the aggregation of many individual demand curves. Figure 3.5 shows the market demand curve for the data in table 3.2.

Points to note:

- An inverse or negative quantitative relationship between price and quantity demanded.
  When price goes up, there is a **decrease** in *quantity demanded.*
  When price goes down, there is an **increase** in *quantity demanded.*

Price of a 'standard' PC ($)	Quantity demanded per week – demand curve D_0
2,000	1,000
1,800	2,000
1,600	3,000
1,400	4,000
1,200	5,000
1,000	6,000
800	7,000

Table 3.2 Market demand schedule

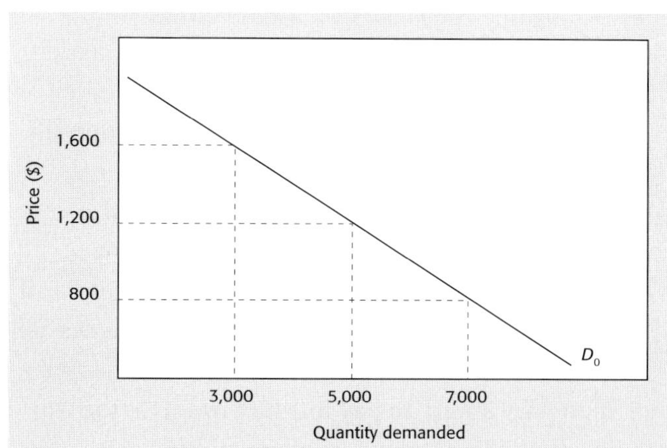

Figure 3.5 The market demand curve for PCs

Notice the language that is being used here – changes in price cause *changes in quantity demanded* and we illustrate this by movements up and down the demand curve.

- A causal relationship – we are saying that changes in price cause changes in quantity demanded.
- A linear relationship – this demand curve has been drawn, again for simplicity, as a straight line. However, it is perfectly acceptable for price and quantity demanded to be related in a non-linear manner.
- A continuous relationship – we could look at the diagram and find out at what price consumers would be willing and able to buy 1,259 PCs.
- A time-based relationship – the time period here is weekly.

Note that we are also assuming ceteris paribus – you should briefly review what this means.

Notice how important it is to label diagrams – the price axis, the quantity demanded axis, the demand curve and the P and Q_D reference points on each axis.

Figure 3.5 is a very useful diagram since it allows us to visualise a quite complex relationship – simple pictures are usually easier to understand and remember than a large number of words. It also allows us to estimate how much consumers may spend when buying PCs, or conversely how much revenue companies may receive from selling PCs. If the price of each PC is $1,800 and the above information is accurate then consumers will buy 2,000 units and their total spending will be equal to $3,600,000, which, of course, will be the revenue that companies receive from selling this quantity of the product. (Note that, since we do not know the firm's production and distribution costs, we are as yet unable to say anything about profit.)

Self-assessment tasks

1 How many PCs per week are people willing and able to buy if the price is $1,100?

2 What price will persuade people to buy 1,350 PCs per week?

3 What assumptions are you making when you answer these questions?

A typical personal computer
Source: Hewlett Packard.

Self-assessment task

Explain how the area under the demand curve could be used to illustrate total consumer expenditure/total revenue of the firms selling PCs.

Consumer surplus

The underlying principles behind the demand curve are relatively simple to understand. They are also ones which many of us follow in our daily lives. For instance, when a product is on 'special offer' in a local shop, and its price has been reduced, more will be demanded and purchased.

For any good or service, though, there are always some people who are prepared to pay above the given price to obtain it. One of the best examples where this happens is in the case of tickets to concerts or a cricket match. If all the tickets are sold out, there will always be some people who are willing to pay over the stated price to obtain a ticket. Another example might be the case of a chocoholic who is prepared to pay over the odds to get a bar of his or her favourite chocolate. To the economist, such situations introduce the concept of **consumer surplus**.

Some people will be willing to pay sky-high prices, over the ticket price, to watch a live concert by a performer such as Rihanna.

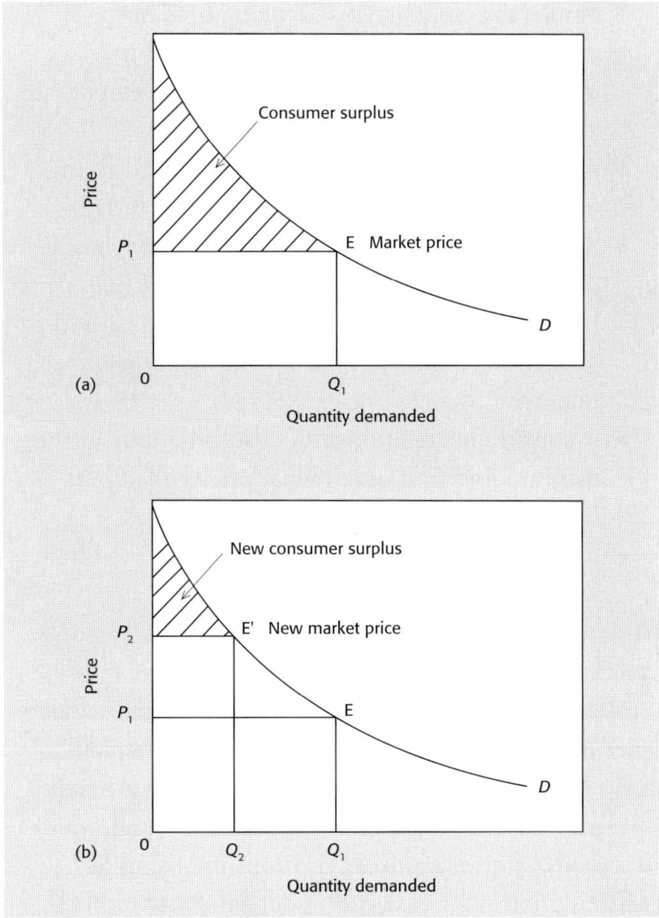

Figure 3.6 Consumer surplus

Consumer surplus arises because consumers would be willing to pay more than the given price for all but the last unit they buy. This can be illustrated in figure 3.6(a) where consumer surplus is the shaded area under the demand curve and above the price line. More specifically, it is the difference between the total value consumers place on all the units consumed and the payments they need to make in order to actually purchase that commodity.

If the market price changes then so does consumer surplus. For example, if the price increases then consumer surplus is reduced as some consumers are unwilling to pay the higher price. This reduction is shown in figure 3.6(b). The loss of consumer surplus is shown by the area P_1P_2E'E.

Shifts in the demand curve

Whilst the above analysis is useful, it is clearly limited because the price of a PC is not the only, or in many cases not the most important, factor influencing demand for it – other things play a part and are not always constant. Changes in these 'ceteris paribus' factors can be illustrated by shifts in the demand curve. A rightward shift indicates an increase in demand; a leftward shift indicates a decrease in demand. Notice how the language changes here when we are talking about a shift in the whole curve rather than simply a movement along it – a **change in demand** rather than quantity demanded (see table 3.3 and figure 3.6).

Points to note:

- *Explanation in terms of the horizontal shift* – consumers are now willing and able to buy more PCs at each and every price. So, whereas previously they had only been prepared to buy 3,000 units per week at $1,600 each, now they are prepared to buy 4,000.
- *Explanation in terms of the vertical shift* – consumers previously were prepared to pay $1,600 for 3,000 PCs, now they are prepared to pay $1,800 each for that quantity.

Price of a 'standard' PC ($)	Quantity demanded per week – demand curve D_2
2,000	2,000
1,800	3,000
1,600	4,000
1,400	5,000
1,200	6,000
1,000	7,000
800	8,000

Table 3.3 Shifts in the demand curve

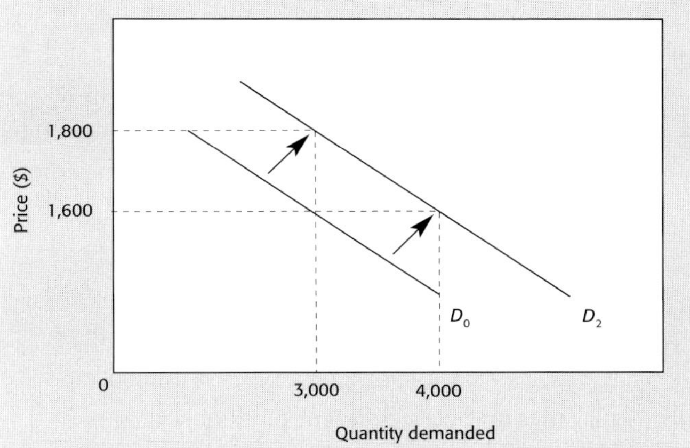

Figure 3.7 A shift to the right in the market demand curve for PCs

Self-assessment task

Use the information below to draw a demand curve and explain what has happened to that demand curve – you are showing a decrease in demand. Draw in demand curve D_0 from figure 3.7 as well so that you can use it as the basis for your comparison.

Price of a 'standard' PC ($)	Quantity demanded per week – demand curve D_1
2,000	0
1,800	1,000
1,600	2,000
1,400	3,000
1,200	4,000
1,000	5,000
800	6,000

Causes of shifts in the demand curve

Individuals may differ widely in their attitudes towards products. We could therefore spend a lot of time constructing a very long list of non-price influences. This might be useful in certain circumstances but not in all cases. Fortunately, economists have identified that there are three key non-price categories that can be used to describe and analyse the factors that influence the demand for most products. They are:

(a) the financial ability to pay for the product;
(b) our attitudes towards the product itself;
(c) the price, availability and attractiveness of related products.

Let us look at each in turn.

The financial ability to pay

We have already noted the importance of effective demand. So what influences someone's ability to pay for a product? The key factors are:

- the purchasing power of their income after taxation;
- the availability of loans/credit and the interest rate that must be paid on loans or credit card balances.

In general we would expect a positive relationship between the financial ability to pay and the demand for a product. So an increase in purchasers' financial ability to pay generally leads to an increase in demand, and this would be represented by a rightward shift in the demand curve from D_0 to D_2 in figure 3.7. A decrease in the ability to pay would lead to a decrease in demand, and this would be represented by a leftward shift in the demand curve from D_2 to D_0.

There is an important qualification to this general rule. The single most important influence on people's financial ability to pay for goods and services is generally considered to be income. In most cases there is a positive relationship between income and product demand – that is, as income rises, normally the demand for the majority of goods and services also increases; as income falls, so does the demand for most products. Products that are characterised by such a relationship are labelled normal goods.

However, there are some products that are characterised by a negative relationship between income and demand. As income rises the demand for dated types of PC, such as 386 and 486MHz speed PCs, will fall; as income rises people tend to choose better quality clothing. Products that are characterised by such a relationship are referred to as inferior goods.

Self-assessment task

Draw diagrams and briefly explain how you expect changes in the following to influence the position of the demand curve for PCs:

- an increase in interest rates;
- a large increase in unemployment;
- a sustained rise in earnings from work;
- a reduction in income tax.

Attitudes towards the products

We all buy products for a reason, that is our behaviour is purposefully motivated, at least at the time of purchase! Economists usually consider our behaviour to be a reflection of our tastes and preferences towards different types of goods and services. You may buy a particular type or brand of PC because of its reputation for reliability. You may buy a pair of brand-name trainers because you want to play sport and you genuinely believe them to be of better quality or you may buy them simply because they are fashionable and you want to look cool.

Self-assessment task

Would you classify the following products as normal goods or inferior goods? In each case draw a diagram to explain how a decrease in income will shift the demand curve. Explain your reasoning. What difficulties did you have in deciding? What information would you need to resolve these difficulties?

◆ Premium brand orange juice	Supermarket own label orange juice
◆ Holidays overseas	Holidays at home
◆ Portable TV sets	Nicam stereo, digital TVs

Detailed understanding of the psychological motives that determine our behaviour are beyond our scope here, but clearly we are influenced by our own individual likes and dislikes, by peer pressure and by advertising and the marketing images that surround us. Nowhere of course is this more evident than in markets for clothing and recorded music, where tastes and preferences can be extremely volatile.

Self-assessment tasks

1 What, at present, is the dominant brand of sports clothing? Why do you think it is dominant? Is it because it is of genuinely superior quality or is there another explanation?

2 Think of a successful advertising campaign that is running on the TV at present. Why is it successful and what impact would you expect it to have on sales over the next six months?

The price, availability and attractiveness of related products

Economists classify types of related products into two categories: **substitutes** and **complements**.

- *Substitute products* are alternatives – products that satisfy essentially the same wants or needs. The range of substitutability can be fairly narrow, for example in terms of different product brands: Hewlett Packard and Dell computers, Casio and Accurist watches and Ford and General Motors cars. Or the range of substitutability can be broad, in terms of product groups, for example different types of transport – rail, buses and cars; different types of soft drinks – lemonade, Pepsi Cola, or fruit juices. Changes in the price or attractiveness of one of these products will have an impact on the demand for all substitutes.
- *Complements* are products that enhance the satisfaction we derive from another product. Common examples are fish and rice, TVs and video recorders, airline flights and hotel accommodation, PCs and modems or software. In some cases, without the complement the main product would be useless. Examples here include: cars and fuel; video recorders and video tapes. Once again changes in price or attractiveness of one of these products will have an impact on the demand for the complementary product.

Self-assessment tasks

1 What would you expect to happen to the demand for Dell PCs if Hewlett Packard cut their prices?

2 What would you expect to happen to the demand for all PCs if the price of software and printers came down sharply?

Use a diagram to help explain your answers.

Exceptions to the downward sloping demand curve

As explained above, it is normally the case that when the price of a good rises, people buy less of it. This results in the downward-sloping demand curve that was shown in figure 3.5. Exceptions to this principle are the special cases of **Giffen goods** and **ostentatious goods**. In both cases the demand curves are thought to slope upwards, indicating that as the price of the good rises, more will be bought. The circumstances where this occurs though differ.

A Giffen good is an inferior good for which the negative income effect outweighs the positive substitution effect, resulting in an upward-sloping demand curve. This term is named after Sir Robert Giffen who first noticed this phenomenon in the case of the Irish potato famines of the 1840s. Potatoes were a staple foodstuff. When the harvests failed, their price rose but people demanded still more as they cut back on luxurious food items such as meat. Examples of Giffen goods today are very rare and restricted to similar examples of staple foodstuffs that are purchased by very poor families.

Although displaying the same tendency with respect to price, ostentatious goods (or snob goods) are ones which are relatively rare yet highly sought after. An example could be the highest quality jewellery or the very latest mobile phone, both of which consumers would obviously like to own and above all, be seen to own. Status in the community is attached to having something that most can only aspire to.

Only the very rich can afford a Rolls Royce such as this

The importance of elasticity

We now want to add more depth to our understanding by looking at the *extent* of demand changes and whether there is likely to be a large or a small impact on the equilibrium. In some cases, a small increase in income, for example, may have a really big impact on demand and this in turn may have a really significant impact on the equilibrium price. In other cases, the same increase in income may have little impact on demand and the market equilibrium. We need some tools or concepts to help us understand these changes more precisely. The concept that allows us to move forward in this way is **elasticity**.

Elasticity is simply a way of quantifying cause and effect relationships. It is defined generally as a numerical measure of *the responsiveness of one economic variable (the dependent variable) following a change in another influencing variable (the independent variable), ceteris paribus*! Where relationships are elastic (responsive), a small change in the cause or the independent variable has a big effect on the other dependent variable. Where relationships are inelastic, a large change in the cause has limited effects on the dependent variable. This might seem a bit confusing, so let us look at specific examples of elasticity – this general definition will then start to become clearer.

Price elasticity of demand (PED)

Price elasticity of demand is a numerical measure of the responsiveness of demand for one product following a change in the price of that product alone. If demand is elastic, then a small change in price will result in a relatively large change in quantity demanded. On the other hand, if price goes up by a lot and quantity demanded only falls slightly, then demand would be price inelastic. A numerical example will help clarify this. First, however, we need a way of expressing PED in a numerical form – the formula we will use at this stage is

$$\text{PED} = \frac{\text{\% change in quantity demanded of a product}}{\text{\% change in price of that product}}$$

Let us take two specific examples of price changes for two general products that we will call product A and product B (see figure 3.8). Assume that both of these unrelated products currently are priced at \$100 and demand for them is 1,000 units per month. Consider what is expected to happen to the demand for A and B if the price rises to \$105. The quantity demanded of product A only falls from 1,000 to 990, whereas the

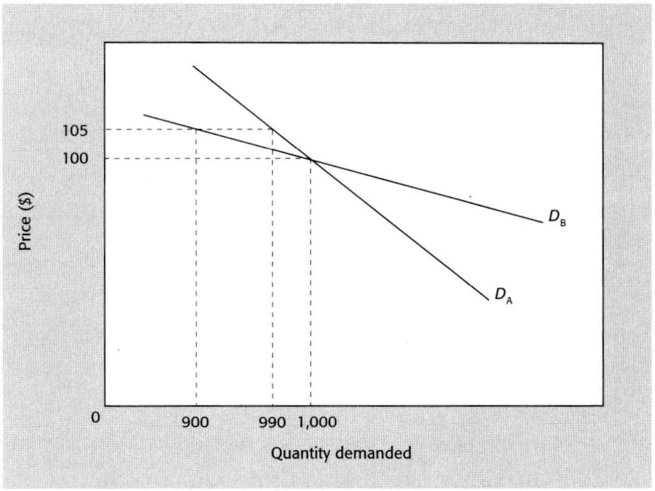

Figure 3.8 Price inelastic and price elastic demand curves

quantity demanded of product B falls from 1,000 to 900. Now let us put these values into the PED equation to calculate the elasticity.

$$\text{Product A} \quad \frac{\text{\% change in quantity demanded of A}}{\text{\% change in price of A}} = \frac{1\% \text{ fall}}{5\% \text{ increase}} = (-)0.2$$

$$\text{Product B} \quad \frac{\text{\% change in quantity demanded of B}}{\text{\% change in price of B}} = \frac{10\% \text{ fall}}{5\% \text{ increase}} = (-)2.0$$

Notice that in both cases a negative figure is given. This is because of the negative (or inverse) relationship between price and quantity demanded, that is, as the price goes up, the quantity demanded goes down. Conventionally economists refer to PED in absolute terms by ignoring the negative sign.

Product A – because the numerical value (0.2) is less than one we say that the demand for this product is relatively inelastic or unresponsive to price changes. Over this particular range of prices, the 5 per cent increase has resulted in a much smaller change in quantity demanded.

Product B – because the numerical value (2.0) is greater than one, we say that the demand for this product is relatively elastic or responsive to price changes. Over this particular range of prices, the same 5 per cent price change has caused a much bigger change in quantity demanded.

Some special PED values

It is important to realise that mathematically PED values can range from 0 to infinity. These values need explanation. Consider, for example, the demand curve shown in figure 3.9. Irrespective of the price charged, consumers are willing and able to buy the same amount – in this case demand would be said to be perfectly inelastic. Let us just look at the PED calculation for an increase in price from \$10 to \$11

$$\text{PED} = \frac{\text{\% change in quantity demanded}}{\text{\% change in price}} = \frac{0\%}{+10\%} = 0$$

Hence, when the PED = 0, demand is perfectly inelastic, perfectly unresponsive to price changes.

Consider the demand curve in figure 3.10. At below a price of \$10 per unit consumers are not prepared to buy any of this product; however, if price falls to \$9, they will buy all that is available. The relative change in

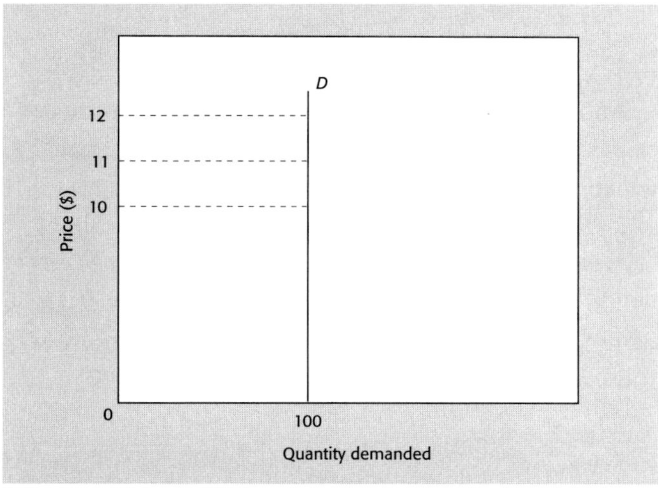

Figure 3.9 A perfectly inelastic demand curve

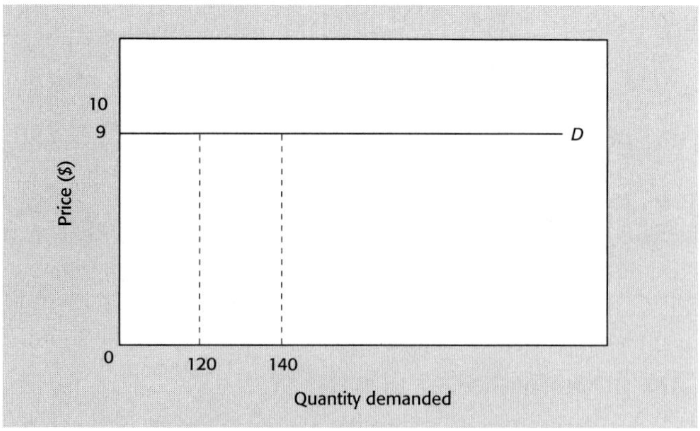

Figure 3.10 A perfectly elastic demand curve

quantity demanded here, of course, is infinite, since the original demand was zero

$$\text{PED} = \frac{\%\ \text{change in quantity demanded}}{\%\ \text{change in price}} = \frac{\infty}{-10\%} = (-)\infty$$

Unitary elasticity

If the relative increase in price is exactly matched by the relative fall in quantity demanded, then the PED value will equal (–)1 and demand will be said to have **unitary elasticity** over that particular price range. So, for example, if the price of the product goes from $1,000 to $1,050 and quantity demanded decreases from 10,000 to 9,500, then the PED will equal (–)1 over this particular range of prices.

Factors that influence price elasticity of demand

There are three key factors that influence whether, over a particular price range, demand for a product is likely to be price elastic or inelastic.

- *The range and attractiveness of substitutes* – the greater the number of substitute (alternative) products and the more closely substitutable those products are, the more we would expect consumers to switch away from a particular product when its price goes up (or towards that product if its price falls).

  It is important, however, to distinguish between the substitutability of products within the same group of products and substitutability with goods from other product groupings. For example, different types of orange juice are a group of products in their own right; they are also part of a larger group of fruit juices and part of the even bigger category of products that we could label as 'drinks'. If we are concerned with the price elasticity of demand for a particular type of orange juice produced by a specific manufacturer, then it will have a fairly high PED (probably) because of the range of substitutes. As we aggregate products into groupings, such as 'fruit juices', or 'all soft drinks', demand will start to become more price inelastic.

  Other substitutability issues to consider include:
  - the quality and accessibility of information that consumers have about products that are available to satisfy particular wants and needs;
  - the degree to which people consider the product to be a necessity;
  - the addictive properties of the product, that is, whether the product is habit forming;
  - the brand image of the product.

- *The relative expense of the product* – a rise in price will reduce the purchasing power of a person's income (real income). The larger the proportion of income that the price represents, the larger will be the impact on the consumer's real income level of a change in the product's price. For example, a 10 per cent increase in the price of a flight to Malaysia will have a bigger impact than a 10 per cent rise in the price of a bus trip into town. The greater the relative proportion of income accounted for by the product, the higher the PED, ceteris paribus!

Self-assessment tasks

1 Calculate the PEDs in each of the following cases and explain whether demand would be considered price elastic or price inelastic.

Original price	New price	Original quantity demanded	New quantity demanded
(a) $100	$102	2,000 units per week	1,950 units per week
(b) $55.50	$54.95	5,000 units per week	6,000 units per week

2 With the aid of a numerical example of your choice explain the meaning of these PED values:
(a) PED = (–)1.5, (b) PED = (–)0.6.

Self-assessment tasks

1 Classify the following products into whether, in your opinion, the PED is likely to be relatively high (elastic) or relatively low (inelastic):

- Coca Cola
- Pepsi Cola
- soft drinks in general
- Nike trainers
- Cadbury chocolates
- all sweet products
- a particular brand of petrol
- all forms of car fuel

Justify your classification.

2 A manufacturer has received a market research estimate of PED values for their shirts that are currently sold in three markets: to independent retailers, to prestige fashion stores and via mail order.

Market	Current price	Current sales	PED value
Independent retailers	$8	40,000 p.a.	−1.0
Fashion stores	$15	10,000 p.a.	−0.2
Mail order	$10	3,000 p.a.	−3.0

Explain and comment upon the PED values shown above.

- *Time* – in the short term, perhaps weeks or months, people may find it hard to change their spending patterns. However, if the price of a product goes up and stays up, then over time people will find ways of adapting and adjusting, so the PED is likely to increase over time.

PED and a downward-sloping linear demand curve

So far the impression may have been created that PED and the slope of a demand curve are the same – this, however, is incorrect. Table 3.4 and the associated self-assessment task will help you see the difference.

Price of product R ($/unit)	Quantity demanded of product R (units per week)
10	0
9	1,000
8	2,000
7	3,000
6	4,000
5	5,000
4	6,000
3	7,000
2	8,000
1	9,000
0	10,000

Table 3.4 Demand schedule for product R

Income elasticity of demand

Income elasticity of demand (YED) is defined as a numerical measure of the responsiveness of demand following a change in income alone. Once again if demand is responsive, then it is classified as elastic; if unresponsive, it is inelastic.

The formula used in this case is

$$\text{YED} = \frac{\%\text{ change in quantity demanded}}{\%\text{ change in income}}$$

It is important to recognise that the relationship between income and demand changes may not always be positive. If an increase in income leads to an increase in demand (or a decrease in income leads to a decrease in demand), then there is a positive relationship and the product is classified as normal, and the YED has a positive value. However, there are some products (inferior goods) that exhibit a negative relationship between income and demand. Here an increase in income would cause a decrease in demand (a decrease in income would cause an increase in demand) and the YED has a negative value. So the sign that precedes the

YED tells you the nature of the relationship between income and demand; the numerical value tells you the strength of that relationship.

For example, there has been a 2 per cent increase in consumer income and that has led to the following changes in demand.

	Original demand (per period of time)	New demand
Product A	100 units at the current price ($10)	103 units at the same price ($10)
Product B	100 units at the current price ($10)	99 units at the same price ($10)
Product C	100 units at the current price ($10)	101 units at the same price ($10)

Self-assessment task

Use the information in table 2.6 to calculate the PED values as price falls from $10 to $9, from $9 to $8, from $8 to $7 and so on. You should see that the PED value falls as you move down the demand curve in figure 3.11. In the top half of the demand curve, PED > 1; in the bottom half of the demand curve, PED < 1. We could show that for very small changes in price, PED $= 1$ at the mid point of the demand curve. That is why, in theory, a demand curve with unitary price elasticity throughout can be drawn – it is called a **rectangular hyperbola**. Total expenditure (the area beneath this curve) for any price quantity combination is constant.

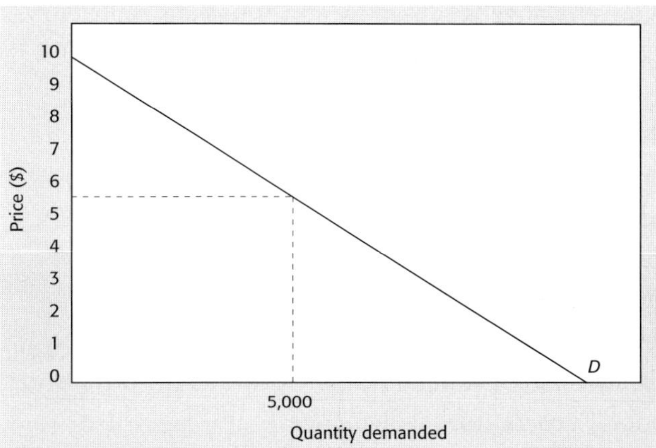

Figure 3.11 The demand curve for product R

$$\text{The YED of A} = \frac{3\%\text{ increase in demand}}{2\%\text{ increase in income}}$$
$= +1.5$ (normal good – elastic response)

$$\text{The YED of B} = \frac{1\%\text{ decrease in demand}}{2\%\text{ increase in income}}$$
$= -0.5$ (inferior good – inelastic response)

$$\text{The YED of C} = \frac{1\%\text{ increase in demand}}{2\%\text{ increase in income}}$$
$= +0.5$ (normal good – inelastic response)

Cross elasticity of demand

Cross elasticity of demand (XED) is a numerical measure of the responsiveness of demand for one product following a change in the price of a *related* product alone. Note the causal relationship that is being measured; and, since this has altered the conditions of demand, we would illustrate the impact of this change in the price of a related product by a shift in the demand curve (similar to YED above).

Self-assessment task

Use figure 3.12 to explain the YED calculations for the three products A, B and C. Note: the sign indicates the direction in which the demand curve shifts, the numerical value indicates how far the curve shifts at the original price.

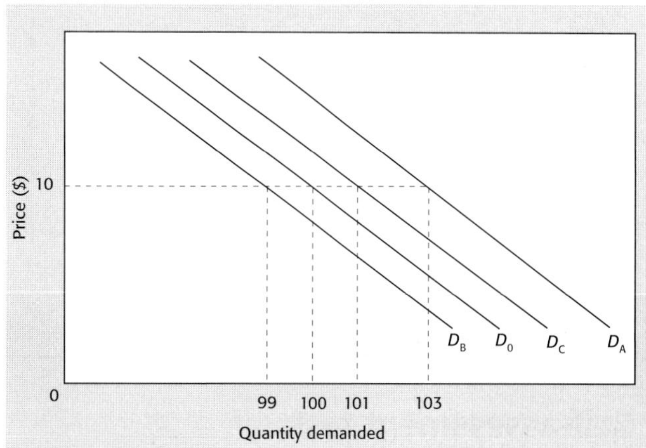

Figure 3.12 The effect of alternative income changes on the demand curve

The formula used is

$$\text{XED} = \frac{\text{\% change in quantity demanded of product A}}{\text{\% change in the price of product B}}$$

Products that are substitutes for each other (for example, different types of laptop computer) will have positive values for the XED. If the price of B goes up, then people will begin to turn to product A because of its more favourable relative price. If the price of B falls, then consumers will start to buy B instead of A. Products that are complements (for example, computers and printers or software) will have negative values of XED. If the price of B goes up, the quantity demanded of B will drop and so will the complementary demand for A.

A numerical and diagrammatic illustration Assume the current average market price of a standard type of personal computer is $1,000 and current sales are 100 units per day (figure 3.13). Consider what might happen if, following a 2 per cent decrease in the price of laptop computers (a substitute product), demand for PCs falls from 100 units to 98 units per day at the original price (D_0 to D_1). Our calculation becomes

$$\text{XED} = \frac{\text{2\% fall in demand for PCs}}{\text{2\% decrease in price of laptops}}$$
$$= +1$$

The positive sign indicates that the products are substitutes.

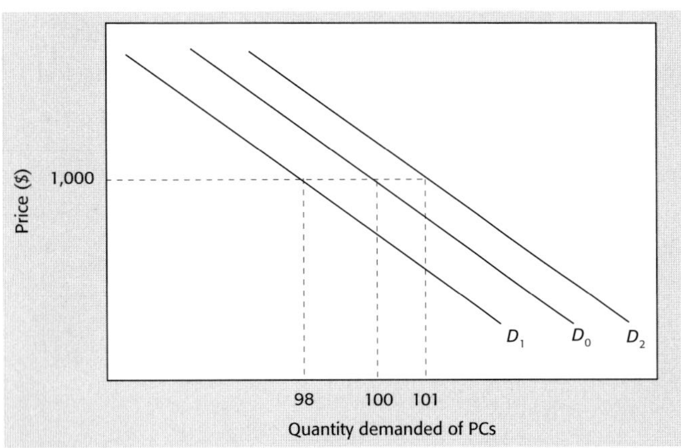

Figure 3.13 A change in the demand for PCs

Self-assessment task

What would have happened to the demand for PCs if, following the same change in the price of laptops, the XED had been +2. Redraw figure 3.13 to illustrate this.

Now consider that the average price of software (a complement) falls by 5% – this encourages extra sales of PCs so that demand for PCs rises to 101 per day at the original price and the demand curve shifts from D_0 to D_2.

The elasticity calculation is

$$\text{XED} = \frac{\text{1\% increase in sales of PCs}}{\text{5\% fall in price of software}} = -0.2$$

Note again that the sign indicates the nature of the relationship (a negative one between complements), and the numerical value indicates the strength of that relationship.

Self-assessment tasks

1. What would happen if demand for PCs had risen to 110 units per day? Calculate the XED and redraw the diagram to illustrate what has happened.
2. The owner of a local golf course loans out equipment to non-members who want to play occasional rounds. She estimates that in June and July, if she lowers the hire price of clubs by 10 per cent, the number of non-members playing will increase by 25 per cent. Calculate and comment on the XED. What other factors should the owner consider?

Business relevance of elasticity

PED and total expenditure/total revenue

PED can help us understand how total spending by consumers will change as price rises or falls assuming the price change is caused by a shift in the supply curve.

Total expenditure = $P \times Q$ = Total revenue of a firm or industry

In figure 3.14, assume there are two products each with the same equilibrium price ($10) and quantity traded (100 units per day). Total expenditure by consumers per day = $10 × 100 = $1,000 – this is of course equal to the revenue received by companies. Now, if the price rises to $11, the differences in PED indicate that consumers respond in different ways, and the total expenditure will change:

- D_e is relatively price elastic over the relevant price range, and quantity falls considerably to 80 units (PED = –2). Total expenditure is now down to $880

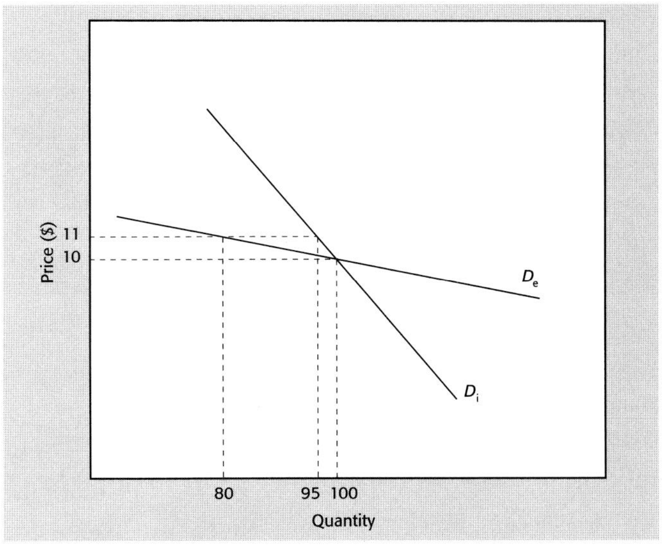

Figure 3.14 Price elastic and price inelastic demand curves

per day – the reason, of course, is that the relative fall in sales is greater than the relative increase in price.

- D_i is relatively price inelastic over the relevant price range and the quantity traded only falls slightly to 95 units (PED = –0.5). Total expenditure actually rises even though less is traded! The reason is that the increase in price exerts a more powerful influence in this case.

Income elasticity of demand

Since YED provides information about how demand varies as income changes, the concept is potentially of great importance to planners in business organisations and government.

If the YED for a normal good exceeds unity, then demand for that product will grow more rapidly than consumer incomes during normal periods of economic growth – hence considerably greater productive capacity

Self-assessment tasks

1 You used this demand schedule when we looked at PED on a linear demand curve at the beginning of this chapter. Figure 3.15 shows the resulting demand curve.

Refer back to how PED varies along a linear demand curve – note, in the top half of the demand curve PED > 1 whereas in the lower half PED < 1.

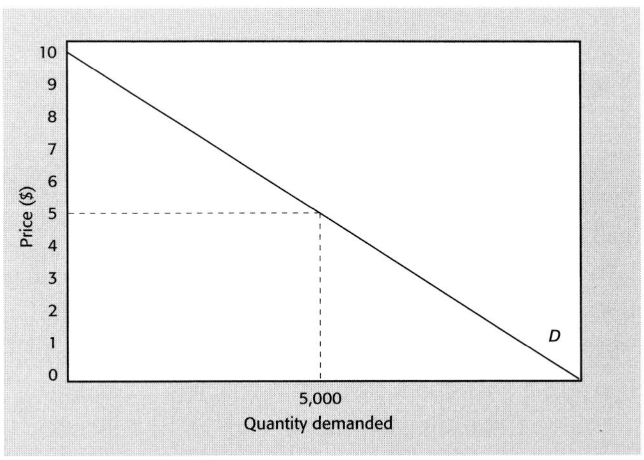

Figure 3.15 The demand curve for product R

Calculate the total expenditure (TE)/total revenue (TR) figures and graph the resulting values underneath the demand curve in figure 3.15 (put TE on the vertical axis and quantity on the horizontal axis – it will help if you use the same scale on the horizontal axis).

Price of product R ($/unit)	Quantity demanded of product R (units per week)	Total expenditure $ per week
10	0	
9	1,000	
8	2,000	
7	3,000	
6	4,000	
5	5,000	
4	6,000	
3	7,000	
2	8,000	
1	9,000	
0	10,000	

- What do you notice about TE/TR figures as price is cut from $10 towards $5 per unit?
- Why does this happen?
- What do you notice about the TE/TR figures as price is raised from $0 to $5?
- Why does this happen?
- Where is TE/TR maximised?

2 If a government is interested in raising more revenue from indirect taxes, such as VAT or excise duties, should it tax products that are price elastic or price inelastic? Explain and illustrate your answer with diagrams and examples.

Self-assessment tasks

1 What will happen to sales of a product whose YED = + 0.6?
2 How could you use YED values to advise a company on how to produce a mix of goods and services that would reduce the risk often associated with only producing a very narrow range of products?
3 Why might government planners be interested in the YED values of different products?

may be required. However, during a recession, when incomes fall, firms producing this sort of product will be extremely vulnerable, given the large reduction in demand that might be expected.

If the YED is negative then firms producing such inferior goods will see their sales decline steadily over time as the economy grows – however, they may be the sort of business to benefit from the hard times of recession.

Cross elasticity of demand

Many companies are concerned with the impact that rival pricing strategies will have, ceteris paribus, on the demand for their own product. Remember that substitutes are characterised by a positive XED: the higher the numerical value, the greater the degree of substitutability between these alternatives in the eyes of the consumer. In such cases there is a high degree of interdependence between suppliers, and the dangers of a rival cutting price are likely to be very significant indeed.

Companies are increasingly concerned with trying to get consumers to buy not just one of their products but a whole range of complementary ones, for example computer printers and print cartridges. XED will identify those products that are most complementary and help a company introduce a pricing structure that generates more revenue. For instance, market research may indicate that families spend most money at the cinema when special deals are offered on ticket prices, even though the PED for ticket prices is low. In this case, for example, the high negative cross elasticity between ticket prices and the demand for food, such as ice cream and popcorn, means that, although the revenue from ticket sales may fall, this may be compensated for by increased sales of food. This points to the need for a more sophisticated pricing structure within the cinema looking at the relationships between the demand for all products and services offered.

Self-assessment tasks

1 (a) Explain the difference between price elasticity of demand, cross elasticity of demand and income elasticity of demand.
(b) Discuss how an understanding of these concepts might be useful to a professional football club in deciding the price of tickets for its matches.

2 A market research company has recently published estimates about UK consumers' demand for holidays in certain countries. A summary of the main findings is given below:

Holiday destination	Price elasticity of demand	Income elasticity of demand
Spain	−1.8	−0.1
USA	−1.2	+1.3
Caribbean	−0.5	+2.0

Price refers to the average combined price of a direct flight (economy class) and seven days' accommodation, half board in a standard hotel.

With reference to the above data:
(a) Explain the difference between normal and inferior goods.
(b) Explain how an increase in consumers' income might affect the demand for each of the holiday destinations shown.
(c) Use the figures to discuss the possible effects that a 10 per cent increase in the 'average price' of each of the holiday destinations shown might have on demand.

Self-assessment tasks

On completion of this chapter you should be able to attempt the following short answer questions from CAPE examination papers, 2003–2005.

1 (a) Define the term 'utility'. (2 marks)

(b) What is an indifference curve? (2 marks)

(c) Why is the slope of an indifference curve negative? (2 marks)

(Total 6 marks)

2

Quantity of gasoline (litres)	Marginal utility of gasoline (utils)	Quantity of fishburgers	Marginal utility of fishburgers (utils)
1	36	1	22
2	27	2	19
3	17	3	18
4	9	4	10
5	5	5	8
6	4	6	6

Additional information:

Income	\$13.00
Price per litre of gasoline	\$ 1.00
Price of one fishburger	\$ 2.00

(a) State the optimal purchase rule. (2 marks)

(b) Given the data above, state the quantity of gasoline and the quantity of fishburgers that will maximise consumer satisfaction. (2 marks)

(c) What is the total utility, in utils, from EACH commodity at equilibrium? (2 marks)

(Total 6 marks)

Summary

In this chapter it has been shown that:

- An understanding of utility can be used to derive an individual's demand curve for a product or service.
- Consumer equilibrium can also be explained by means of the budget constraint and indifference curves.
- For most goods, there is an inverse relationship between price and the quantity demanded; exceptions are Giffen goods and ostentatious goods.
- A change in price of a good is represented by a movement along the demand curve; a change in any other factors affecting demand is shown by a shift of the demand curve.
- Consumer surplus occurs when consumers are willing to pay more than the given price for a good.
- Elasticity is a concept that measures the responsiveness of demand to a change in another variable such as price, income and the price of substitutes or complements.
- The numerical estimates of elasticity have important business implications; more specifically, the change in total spending on a good is dependent upon the price elasticity of demand.

Key words

Definitions of Key words can be found in the Glossary.

budget constraint/budget line
change in demand
complements
consumer surplus
cross elasticity of demand
demand
demand curve
demand schedule
diminishing marginal utility
effective demand
elasticity
equi-marginal principle
Giffen goods
income effect
income elasticity of demand
indifference curves
inferior good
marginal rate of substitution
marginal utility
market demand
price elasticity of demand
normal good
notional demand
ostentatious goods
rectangular hyperbole
substitutes
substitution effect
unitary elasticity
utility

4 Theory of supply

This chapter covers unit 1, module 1, topic 4.
On completion of this chapter, you should be able to:

- identify the factors of production (as outlined in chapter 1)
- define and explain the term 'production function'
- calculate total, average and marginal physical product and explain the relationships among them
- calculate total, average, marginal and other costs and explain the relationships among them
- explain why supply curves are usually positively sloped
- explain the shape of the short-run and long-run supply curves
- explain the law of diminishing returns to scale and the concept of economies of scale
- distinguish between the factors that cause supply curves to shift and those that cause supply curves to change their slopes
- explain the impact of time on elasticity of supply
- calculate and interpret elasticity of supply

Principles of production and the production function

Introduction

At the beginning of chapter 1 we identified four factors of production. These were land, labour, capital and enterprise. In all cases, the demand for these factors of production comes from a producer, who wishes to use them to make various goods or products. The producer is normally a firm or business whose demand for factors of production is derived from the needs of its operations. Let us take the case of a clothing manufacturer to elaborate this important point.

As a consequence of globalisation, many clothing items are now produced in the developing economies of South East Asia, north Africa and central Europe. Designer labels, such as Nike, Reebok, Ellesse and Kappa, are no longer produced in the home country of their corporate producer. Producers in these countries need all of the factors of production in order to make their products for sale in markets which are mainly in developed economies. Their task is to combine the factors of production in an effective way to be efficient, competitive and profitable in the world market. In particular, the most important decision they have to make concerns the relative mixture of labour and capital. The task for the firm therefore is to find the least cost or most efficient combination of labour and capital for the production of a given quantity of output.

Clothing is a typical example of a business where labour and capital are in direct competition with each other. If labour costs are relatively cheap, as is the case in developing and emerging economies, then the production process is likely to take place using much more labour than capital. In most developed economies, though, the reverse is true. High-tech machines can often be used to replace labour, largely because it is more cost effective to do so. So, in this case, the same amount of output is produced using more capital and far less labour than if it were taking place in a developing economy.

Clothing factory
Source: Alamy.

Firms therefore have to choose between alternative production methods. Returning to the case of the clothing manufacturer, figure 4.1 shows three different methods of production, each of which combines different levels of labour and capital to make items of clothing. Line A shows a method whereby labour and capital are used in equal proportions; line B shows a production method which uses twice as much capital as labour and line C shows the output resulting from twice as much labour as capital being used. On these lines, points *X*, *Y* and *Z* show the respective amounts of labour and capital that are needed to produce 100 units of clothing. If we join these points then it gives us what is known as an isoquant, a curve which joins points which give us a particular level of output. This isoquant can of course be extended for other combinations of labour and capital not shown on figure 4.1.

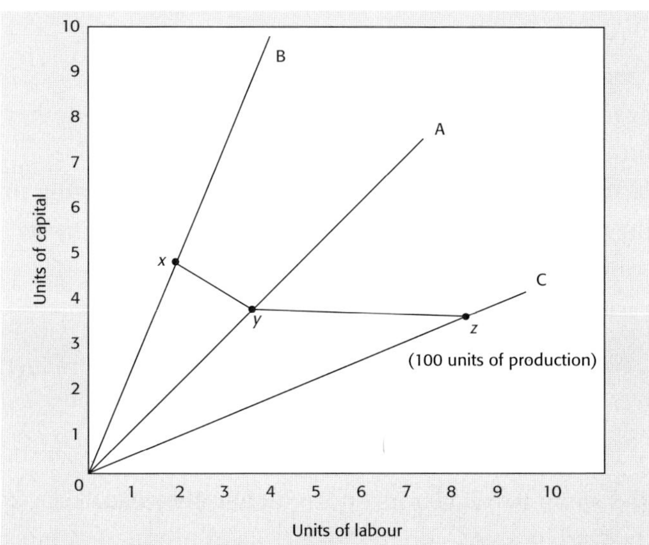

Figure 4.1 Alternative production methods

The production function

To simplify our analysis, let us assume that the size of a clothing factory is fixed and that the only way in which the units of clothing produced can be varied is through varying the input of labour. This is referred to as the **short run**. Table 4.1 shows how the quantity of clothing produced depends on the number of workers employed. For example, if there are no workers in the factory, there is no output; with one worker, output is 100 units. When there are two workers, the total output is 180 units and so on.

Number of workers	Output of clothing	Marginal product	Average product
0	0		0
		100	
1	100		100
		80	
2	180		90
		60	
3	240		80
		20	
4	280		70
		15	
5	295		59
		11	
6	306		51

Table 4.1 Production data

Figure 4.2 is a graph of the first two columns of data in table 4.1. It shows the relationship between the quantity of factor inputs (labour/workers) and the **total product** or quantity of output (clothing). It is called the **production function**. Column 3 of table 4.1 shows the **marginal product**, the increase in output that occurs from an additional unit of input (labour in this case). The data in this column show that, when the number of workers goes from one to two, output increases by 80 units; when it goes from two to three workers, the marginal product is 60 units. As the number of workers increases the marginal product declines. This property is referred to as **diminishing returns**.

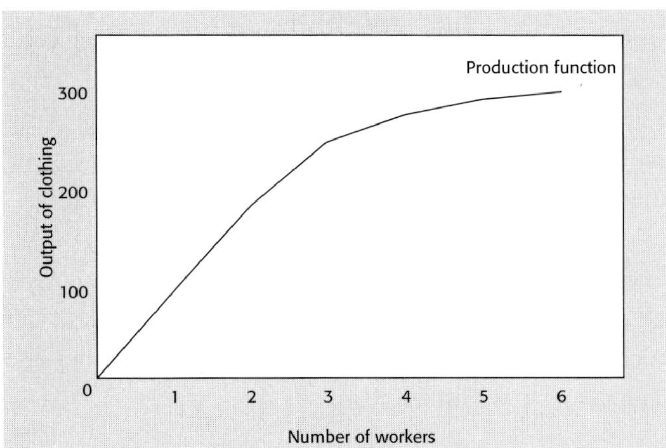

Figure 4.2 A production function

The final column of table 4.1 shows another important variable, **average product**. This is calculated by dividing the total product (output produced) by the number of workers employed. It is a simple measure of labour productivity, that is how much output is produced by each worker.

Self-assessment tasks

1 Using data from table 4.1, draw graphs which show:
   - the marginal product of labour,
   - the average product of labour.

2 What do you notice about the shape of these two graphs?

3 What implications do these graphs have for a clothing firm planning how much to produce?

From short run to long run

As stated above, the short run is a period of time in Economics when at least one of the factors of production is fixed. The factor that takes the longest to change is capital; the factor that tends to be easiest to change is labour as we have already seen. Students often ask the question, 'How long is the short run?'. This is not an easy question to answer, as it tends to differ for different industries. In the clothing industry it is likely to be no more than a few weeks, the time that is taken to install new capital equipment and to get this operational to produce clothing. In other industries, it will be much longer. A country building a new hydro-electric power station will, for example, take much longer to plan, install and make such a new facility operational. Ten years may well be a realistic estimate in this case. This time is still referred to as the short run since capital is fixed over this time.

In the long run, all factors of production are variable. This therefore gives the firm much greater scope to vary the respective mix of its factor inputs so that it is producing at the most efficient level. So, if capital becomes relatively cheaper than labour or if a new production process is invented and this increases productivity, firms can reorganise the way in which they produce. Firms must therefore know the cost of the factors of production they use and see this in relation to the marginal physical output which accrues. The right combination of factors can be arrived at as their price varies. Firms should aim to be in a position where

$$\frac{\text{Marginal product factor A}}{\text{Price of factor A}} = \frac{\text{Marginal product factor B}}{\text{Price of factor B}} = \frac{\text{Marginal product factor C}}{\text{Price of factor C}}$$

and so on for all factors of production they use. For them to be able to do this all factors of production must be variable.

If we go back to the principles introduced in figure 4.1, it is possible to derive the long-run production function for a firm by initially constructing an isoquant map. This shows the different combinations of labour and capital that can be used to produce various level of output. This is shown in figure 4.3.

Let us again assume that this is for a clothing manufacturer. Part (a) of this figure consists of a collection of isoquants for output levels 100, 200, 300, 400 and 500 units of production. From this it is possible to read off the respective combinations of labour and capital that could produce these output levels. Remember that as yet this is only looking at output from a physical standpoint.

If you look at the diagram carefully you will see that as production increases from 100 to 200, relatively less capital and labour is required per unit of output. This is referred to as **increasing returns to scale**. As production expands further, increasing amounts of capital and labour are needed to produce 100 more units and so move up to the next isoquant. In contrast, this indicates **decreasing returns to scale.**

In the long run, both labour and capital can be varied and, as stated above, the actual mix will depend upon their prices. Figure 4.3(b) shows what are known as isocosts, lines of constant relative costs for the factors of production. On this figure, therefore, each of the isocosts shown has an identical slope. In deciding how to produce, the firm will be looking for the most economically efficient or least cost process. This can be obtained by bringing together the isoquants and isocosts, so linking the physical and economic sides of the production process. The point where the isocost is tangential to an isoquant represents the best combination of factors for the firm to employ. Hence, on figure 4.3(b), the expansion path or long-run production function of the firm can be shown by joining together all of the various tangential points.

It is important to recognise that the above analysis is highly theoretical. In practice:

- It is often very difficult for firms to determine their isoquants – they often do not have the data or the experience to be able to derive them.
- It is also assumed that in the long run it is quite possible to switch factors of production. This may not always be as easy as the theory might indicate.
- Some employers may be reluctant to switch labour and capital – they may feel that they have a social obligation to their workforce and will therefore not alter their production plans with a change in relative factor prices.

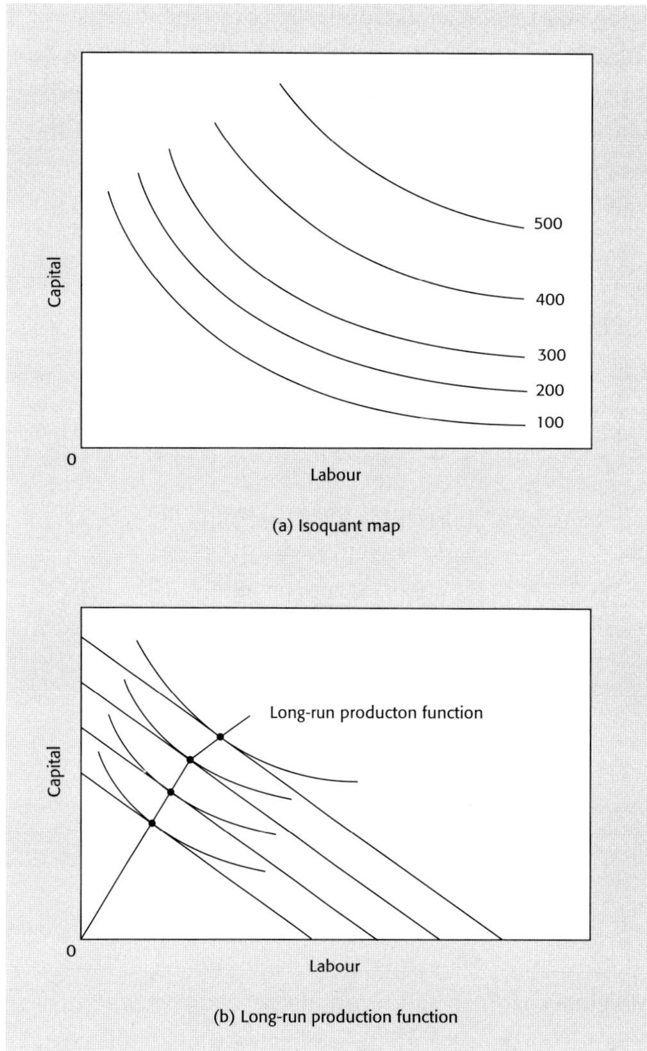

Figure 4.3 Isoquants and isocosts

Short-run costs

Fixed costs These are the costs that are completely independent of output. Total fixed cost data when drawn on a graph would appear as a horizontal straight line. At zero output, any costs that a firm has must be fixed. Some firms operate in a situation where the fixed cost represents a large proportion of the total. In this case it would be wise to produce a large output in order to reduce unit costs.

Variable costs These include all the costs that are directly related to the level of output, the usual ones being labour and raw material or component costs. Sometimes a cost has elements of both, for example, a firm's electricity bill may consist of the heating and lighting cost of the premises and the power to operate production machinery. Electricity could therefore be considered to be a semi-fixed and semi-variable cost:

TOTAL COST (TC) EQUALS FIXED COST (FC) PLUS VARIABLE COST (VC).

From this information all the relevant cost concepts can be derived.

AVERAGE FIXED COST (AFC)

$$\text{equals} \quad \frac{\text{TOTAL FIXED COST}}{\text{OUTPUT}}$$

AVERAGE VARIABLE COST (AVC)

$$\text{equals} \quad \frac{\text{TOTAL VARIABLE COST}}{\text{OUTPUT}}$$

AVERAGE TOTAL COST (ATC)

$$\text{equals} \quad \frac{\text{TOTAL COST}}{\text{OUTPUT}}$$

Marginal cost is the addition to the total cost when making one extra unit and is therefore a variable cost.

The most important cost curve for the firm will be the ATC, showing the cost per unit of any chosen output. For most firms the decision to increase output will raise the total cost, that is the marginal cost will be positive as extra inputs are used. Firms will only be keen to do this when the expected sales revenue will outweigh the extra cost. Rising marginal cost is also a reflection of the principle of diminishing returns (see above). As more of the variable factors are added to the fixed ones, the contribution of each extra worker to the total output will begin to fall. These diminishing marginal returns cause the marginal and average variable cost to rise, as shown on figure 4.4.

The shape of the short-run ATC is the result of the interaction between the average fixed cost and the average variable cost. AFC + AVC = ATC. As the firm's output rises the average fixed cost will fall because the total fixed cost is being spread over an increasing number of units. However, at the same time, average

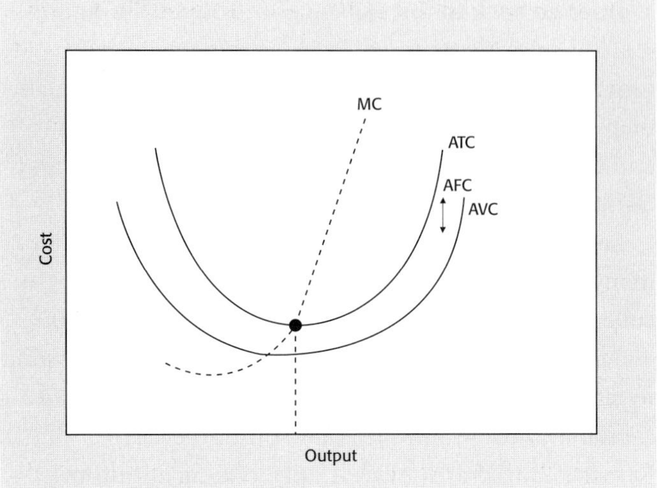

Figure 4.4 Short-run cost relationships

variable cost will be rising because of diminishing returns to the variable factor. Eventually this will outweigh the effect of falling AFC, causing ATC to rise. This gives the classic 'U' shape to the ATC. On a graph of cost data, the MC will always cross AVC and ATC at their lowest point. In this situation, the most efficient output for the firm will be where the unit cost is lowest. This is known as the optimum output. It is where the firm is productively efficient in the short run, but the most efficient output is not necessarily the most profitable (see next topic for details). For a firm wishing to maximise its profits, its chosen output will depend on the relationship between its revenue and its costs.

Costs in the short and the long run As we have already stated, the short run for the firm is a period of time when it cannot alter its fixed inputs. The level of production can only be changed by altering the variable inputs, such as labour. The time taken to alter fixed factors differs, depending on how easy it is to get new capital installed.

In the **long run**, the firm can alter *all* of its inputs, using greater quantities of land, capital and labour, operating on a bigger scale. All the factors are now variable.

In the very long run, technological change can alter the way the entire production process is organised, even the nature of the products themselves. In the case of airlines, the introduction of the jumbo jet suddenly raised the passenger miles per unit of inputs by 50 per cent. In a society with rapid technological progress this will be shrinking the time period between the short run and the long run and suddenly shifting the firm's product curves up and its cost curves down. There are now examples in consumer electronics where whole processes and products have become obsolete in a matter of months as a result of more powerful microchips increasing the volume and speed of the flow of information.

Costs in the long run It is possible that a firm can find a way of lowering its cost structure over time. One way might be by increasing the amount of capital used relative to labour in the production process, with a consequent increase in factor productivity.

The long-run average cost curve shows the least cost combination of producing any particular quantity. Moving from its short-run equilibrium shown in figure 4.5(a), part (b) of this figure shows a firm experiencing falling ATC over time. This would enable it to lower the price without sacrificing profit. Products, such as electronic watches, personal computers and CD players, are examples where prices have fallen through competition and changing technology.

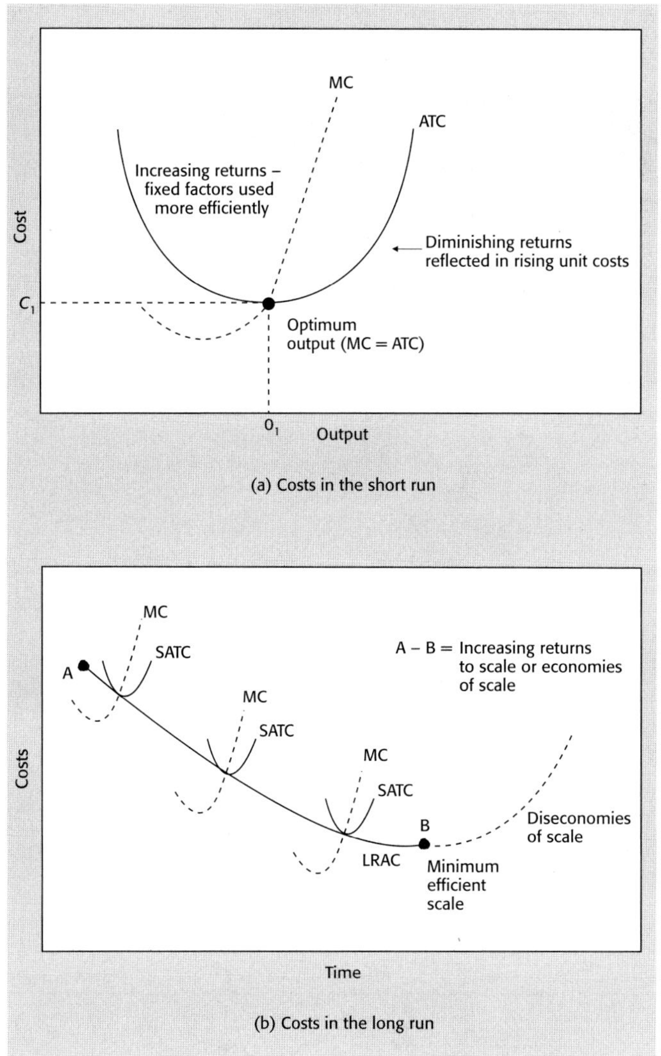

Figure 4.5 A firm's costs in the short run and in the long run

Economies of scale Where an expansion of output leads to a reduction in the unit costs, the benefits are referred to as **economies of scale. Internal economies of scale** are the benefits that accrue to a firm as a result of its own decision to produce a larger output. They occur because the firm's output is rising proportionally faster than the inputs, hence the firm is getting increasing returns to scale. If the increase in output is proportional to the increase in inputs, the firm will get constant returns to scale and the LRAC will be horizontal. If the output is less than proportional, the firm will see diminishing returns to scale or **diseconomies of scale**.

The key advantage a firm obtaining economies of scale gains is a reduction in the cost per unit produced, i.e. a fall in the ATC. The nature of the possible economies depends on the nature of the economic activity. Some of the following may apply in a particular industry.

- **Technical economies** These can take various forms such as:
  - the benefits that large-scale firms can gain through investing in expensive specialist machinery in order to reduce average costs;
  - splitting the production process into a series of separate tasks so that the workforce in a firm can specialise;
  - through the law of increased dimensions whereby a doubling of the height and width of a cube leads to a more than proportionate increase in capacity.

  Such economies of scale can apply to Caribbean agriculture, both from a production and processing standpoint. In the highly competitive export market, large multinational producers of sugar cane, bananas, coffee, pineapples and other crops are constantly seeking ways to reduce average costs as the scale of their operations increases. Concentrating processing in a central plant for example will achieve this relative to the firm operating a larger number of smaller plants.
- **Marketing economies** This is where large firms can achieve savings in unit costs from advertising

Large multinational companies can obtain the benefits of economies of scale in the processing of coffee beans ... the harvesting remains labour intensive
Source: Alamy.

or packaging. The usual one is the benefit of lower prices by buying in bulk from suppliers. Large supermarket chains are very good examples of firms that gain in this way.

- **Financial economies** Large firms will find both the access to borrowed funds easier, and the costs lower, than smaller firms will. This is because the perceived risk of lending to large-scale operators is lower.
- **Managerial economies** Firms producing on a large scale may be able to reorganise their structure in order to get a more efficient management of resources. They may also attract the best management talent through higher salaries. Overall this will lead to falling long-run costs of managing the business.
- **Risk-bearing economies** These might explain why, as firms get larger, they become more diversified. It is a way of spreading business risks. A diversified conglomerate can cover any losses in one activity with the profits from another, an option not open to smaller firms. Risks can be further reduced, by co-operating with rivals on large capital projects.

The last example above may be an illustration of an **external economy of scale** since firms can benefit from savings in research and development costs. This particular economy of scale is a benefit received by all the firms in the industry as a direct consequence of the growth of the industry and may be one reason for the trend towards the concentration of rival firms in the same geographical area. The advantages may include the availability of a pool of skilled labour or a convenient supply of components from specialist producers who have grown up to make the items for all the firms. They may all benefit from greater access to knowledge and research and the better transport infrastructure that will result from general expansion in the economic activities.

Firms where the fixed costs are a very high proportion of total cost have an incentive to increase their output as much as possible, because the marginal cost will be very low. ATC will continue to fall and profits will rise. These low costs may act as a barrier to the entry of competitors and this would be an example of a **natural monopoly** where competing firms are less efficient than the huge firm with a dominant market share.

It must be recognised that there are limits to economies of scale. A firm can expand its output too much with the result that unit costs start to rise. This may be the beginning of what are known as diseconomies of scale. The most likely source of these lies in the problems of co-ordinating large organisations and the effect size has on morale and motivation. In the same way as internal diseconomies of scale are possible, the excessive concentration of economic activities in a narrow geographical location can also have disadvantages. External diseconomies may exhibit themselves in the form of:

- traffic congestion which increases distribution costs,
- land shortages and therefore rising fixed costs,
- shortages of skilled labour and therefore rising variable costs.

A firm that is producing at its optimum output in the short run and the lowest unit cost in the long run (sometimes called the **minimum efficient scale**), has maximised its efficiency. Industries where the minimum efficient scale is low will have a big population of firms. Where it is high, competition will tend to be between a few large players.

The advantages of size in the form of economies of scale suggest that there will be a tendency for firms to get bigger over time.

Self-assessment tasks

1 The following items are a selection of business costs. Indicate whether each one is likely to be fixed, variable or a mixture of both in the short run:
- the rent of a factory,
- taxes paid on business premises,
- workers' pay,
- electricity bill,
- raw materials,
- advertising expenditure,
- interest on loans,
- management salaries,
- transport costs,
- depreciation on fixed capital.

2 Study the diagram below and then answer the question that follows.

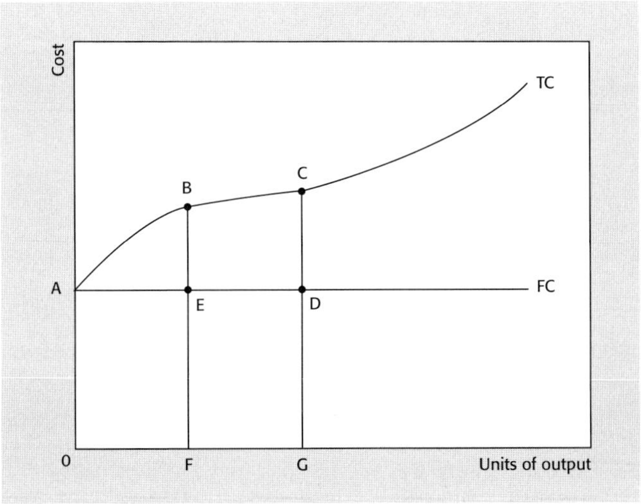

(a) What is the ATC at output G?
AVC at output F?
AFC at output G?
TC at output F?

The supply curve

Supply is the term used in Economics to describe the production that firms are able and willing to produce for the market. We need to take this definition and represent it diagrammatically to construct what is known as a **supply curve**. We could do this for an individual firm selling PCs or, by aggregating each separate company's supply curve, we could get the industry or market supply curve for PCs. Assume again that we have collected statistical data about companies' selling intentions and that these plans can be represented by table 4.2 (this is known as a market **supply schedule**). We can now plot this supply schedule to see how the quantity of PCs supplied relates to variations in price. Figure 4.6 shows the supply curve (S_0) for the data in the table.

Price of a 'standard' PC ($)	Quantity supplied per week – supply curve S_0
800	1,000
1,000	2,000
1,200	3,000
1,400	4,000
1,600	5,000
1,800	6,000
2,000	7,000

Table 4.2 Market supply schedule

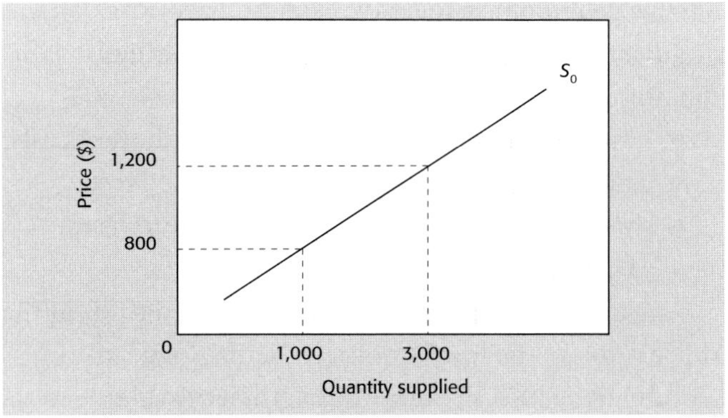

Figure 4.6 The market supply curve for PCs

Points to note:

- A positive or direct relationship between price and quantity supplied.
  When price goes up there is an *increase* in *quantity supplied.*
  When price goes down there is a *decrease* in *quantity supplied.*
- Again notice the language that is being used – changes in price cause changes in quantity supplied and we illustrate this by movements up and down the supply curve (again some economists prefer to use the terms 'extension of supply' for a movement up the supply curve and a 'contraction of supply' for a movement down the curve).
- A causal relationship – we are saying that price changes cause the change in quantity supplied.
- A linear relationship – the supply curve has been drawn for simplicity as a straight line, but of course there is no reason why the supply curve should not be represented in a non-linear way.
- A continuous relationship – we could look at the curve to find out how many PCs companies would plan to supply at a price of $1,150.

Self-assessment tasks

1. How many PCs per week are companies planning to supply if the price is $1,100?
2. What price would persuade companies to supply 1,350 PCs?
3. What assumptions are you making when you answer these questions?
4. What might be the advantages and disadvantages of using a diagrammatic form such as in figure 4.6 to represent supply?

- A time-based relationship – the time period again is weekly.

Note we are also assuming ceteris paribus – any other factor influencing supply is assumed to be unchanged.

Shifts in the market supply curve

Whilst the above is useful, one of the limitations is that companies' supply intentions are influenced by factors other than the price of the product (which, if you think about it, is the most tangible expression of consumers' buying intentions). Other things are most certainly not always equal. Changes in these 'ceteris paribus' factors can be illustrated by shifts in the supply curve.
A rightward shift indicates an increase in supply; a leftward shift indicates a decrease in supply. Notice again how the language changes when we are talking about a shift in the whole curve rather than simply a movement along it – a change in supply rather than quantity supplied (see table 4.3 and figure 4.7).

Price of a 'standard' PC ($)	Quantity supplied per week – supply curve S_2
800	2,000
1,000	3,000
1,200	4,000
1,400	5,000
1,600	6,000
1,800	7,000
2,000	8,000

Table 4.3 An increase in supply

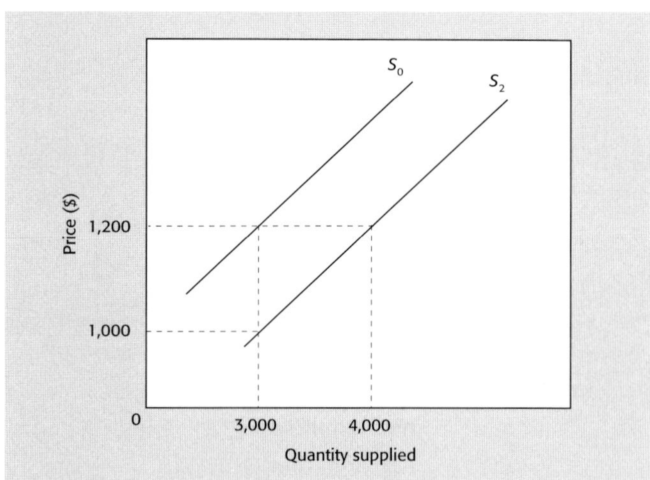

Figure 4.7 A shift to the right in the market supply curve for PCs

Points to note:

- *Explanation of horizontal shift* – companies are now more willing and/or more able to supply PCs at each and every price. Previously they had only been prepared to supply 3,000 units per week at $1,200; now they are prepared to supply 4,000.
- *Explanation of vertical shift* – companies previously wanted $1,200 per unit to persuade them to supply 3,000 units per week; now they are prepared to accept $1,000.

Causes of shifts in the supply curve

Companies clearly differ in their willingness and ability to supply products and, as with demand, we could spend a long time building a list of possible factors other than price that will affect supply. If we were required (and paid!) to conduct a detailed analysis of supply conditions in a particular industry, that might be justified. For our purposes we need to simplify and generalise about the factors that can influence supply in most industries. As with demand, we can focus on three main influences:

- the costs associated with supplying the product;
- the size, structure and nature of the industry;
- government policy.

Let us discuss each in turn.

Self-assessment task

Use the information below to draw a new supply curve (S_1) and explain what has happened to that supply curve – remember you are showing a decrease in supply. Draw in supply curve S_0 as well so that you can use it as the basis for your comparison.

Price of a 'standard' PC ($)	Quantity supplied per week – supply curve S_1
1,000	1,000
1,200	2,000
1,400	3,000
1,600	4,000
1,800	5,000
2,000	6,000

Costs

In a market-based economy, no firm (in the absence of government support) can exist indefinitely if it makes losses, so companies will make supply decisions on the basis of the price they can get for selling the product in relation to the cost of supplying it. You will see later how costs may rise as a firm increases production with a given capacity – this will influence the shape of the supply curve. What we are interested in here, however, is what factors can influence the position of the supply curve – in other words, what factors can cause an increase or a decrease in the costs of supplying each and every unit, since it is likely that this will impact on the price that companies charge per unit. Below are listed some potentially influential factors – if the factor pushes up costs, there is likely to be a leftward shift in the supply curve or decrease in supply; if the factor lowers costs, there is likely to be an increase in supply:

- wage rates;
- worker productivity (output per worker);
- raw material and component prices;
- energy costs;
- equipment maintenance costs;
- transport costs;
- the state of technology.

Self-assessment task

Go through each of the above factors in turn and work out what sort of change in that factor will cause:

- an increase in supply,
- a decrease in supply.

The size and nature of the industry

If it is clear that there is substantial profit to be made by selling a product, firms inside and outside the industry are likely to react. Firms currently in the industry may invest in capital equipment in an attempt to grow bigger and take advantage of the situation. Firms outside the industry may try to enter this market and of course new firms may set up in business. The ease with which they can do so will depend on whether there are any **barriers to entry** into the industry and, if there are, how easy it is to overcome them (see next chapter). Nonetheless if the size of the industry increases, because there are more firms or bigger firms, then it is likely that the supply of the industry will increase. Equally, if firms in the industry start to compete more intensively on price, it is likely that the supply curve will shift to the right as the effects of this price competition start to affect the price that all companies are willing to accept for their products. Of course if a fierce price war does break out, then consumers, at least temporarily, may enjoy very much lower prices for any given level of supply.

Self-assessment tasks

1 Why might firms choose to leave an industry?
2 What is likely to happen to the industry supply if the size of the industry shrinks?
3 What might happen to supply if all firms decide to try and increase the amount of profit they make on each unit they sell?

Government policy

Governments influence company decisions in many ways. Legislation designed to protect consumers or workers may impose additional costs on companies and this may affect the supply curve. Governments may also impose indirect taxes (excise duties or value added tax) on companies. These taxes can act like a cost increase because companies may seek to pass the tax on to the consumer in the form of higher prices. As such, indirect taxes often result in a decrease in supply. On the other hand, a relaxation of certain types of legislation or government subsidies can increase supply by encouraging firms to reduce prices for any given level of output.

Self-assessment task

Refer to the supply curve S_0 in figure 4.6. What would happen to this curve if the government introduced a tax of:

- $100 per computer?
- 10% on the pre-tax selling price?
- legislation that raised companies' costs by about 20 per cent on average?

Other supply-influencing factors

As with our treatment of demand, this is not intended to be a complete list of the factors that influence supply. Each industry will have some features that are relevant to it. For example, the supply of agricultural produce is particularly influenced by weather conditions. Some industries may be able to switch production from one product to another fairly easily and so the relative profitability of alternative product areas may be important. In financial markets, like the stock market or the foreign exchange market, supply may be significantly influenced by expectations of future prices. Once again the skill of the economist is to use theory, insight and observation to identify the key influences on supply in any situation to explain the past or to try to predict the future.

Price elasticity of supply or elasticity of supply

Price elasticity of supply (PES) is a numerical measure of the responsiveness of supply to a change in the price of the product alone. The supply could be that of an individual firm or group of firms; it could of course refer to the supply of the overall industry. It is expressed as

$$\text{PES} = \frac{\text{\% change in quantity supplied}}{\text{\% change in price}}$$

Since the relationship between the price and quantity supplied is normally a direct one, the PES will tend to take on a positive value. If the numerical value of PES is greater than 1, then we say that supply is relatively price elastic, that is supply is responsive. If the numerical value of PES is less than 1, then supply is relatively price inelastic, that is supply is unresponsive.

Figure 4.8 shows five supply curves each with different PES values.

Factors influencing PES

The key words in understanding PES are supply flexibility – if firms and industries are more flexible in the way they behave, then supply tends to be more elastic. The main influences on PES are:

- *The ease with which firms can accumulate or reduce stocks of goods.* Stocks allow companies to meet variations in demand through output changes rather than price changes – so the more easily manufacturing firms can do this, the higher the PES. Companies that provide services are, of course, unable to build up stocks.
- *The ease with which they can increase production.* In the short run firms and industries with spare

productive capacity will tend to have a higher PES. However, shortages of critical factor inputs (skilled workers, components, fuel) will often lead to inelastic PES. This is particularly the case with agricultural products.

- Over time, of course, companies can increase their productive capacity by investing in more capital equipment, often taking advantage of technological advances. Equally, over time, more firms can enter or leave an industry and this will increase the flexibility of supply.

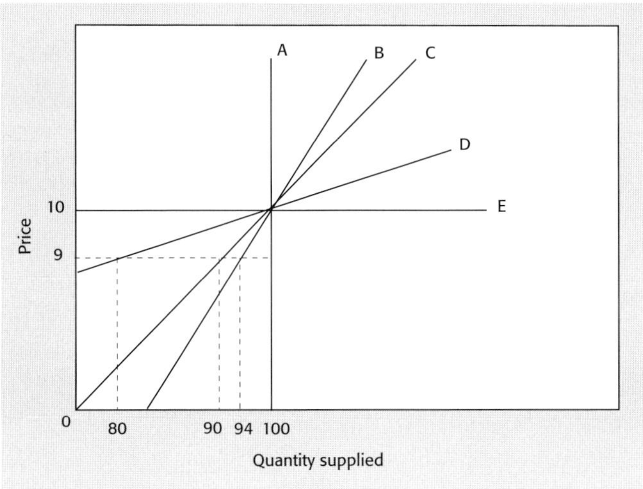

Figure 4.8 Five different supply curves

Supply curve	% change in quantity supplied	/ % change in price	= PES	Description
A	0%	/ 10% decrease	= 0	Perfectly inelastic
B	6% decrease	/ 10% decrease	= +0.6	Relatively inelastic
C	10% decrease	/ 10% decrease	= +1.0	Unitary elasticity
D	20% increase	/ 10% increase	= +2.0	Relatively elastic
E	Firms are not prepared to supply any at a price below $10 but will supply as much as they can at $10 (or above!)		= + ∞	Perfectly elastic

Self-assessment tasks

The following short answer questions have been set in recent CAPE examinations, 2003–2005.

1

No. of workers	Total product	Marginal product	Average product
0	0	0	0
1		3	
2			4.50
3	14		
4		3	
5	19		
6		1	

Draw the table above in your answer booklet and complete it. Where applicable, calculate your answer significant to two decimal places. (6 marks)

(Total 6 marks)

2 (a) State the law of 'diminishing marginal returns'. (2 marks)

(b) Define the term 'returns to scale'. Give an example. (2 marks)

(c) Distinguish between the 'long run' and 'short run' as they relate to production (2 marks)

(Total 6 marks)

3 The table below shows the production costs of bananas at various output levels.

1 Total output of bananas	2 Total fixed costs	3 Total variable costs	4 Total cost	5 Average total cost	6 Marginal cost
0	10	0			
1	10	10			
2	10	18			
3	10	25			
4	10	30			

In your answer booklet, complete columns 4, 5 and 6. (6 marks)

(Total 6 marks)

4 (a) Define the term 'price elasticity of supply'. (1 mark)

(b) What is meant by the statement 'the supply of bread is inelastic'? (2 marks)

(c) The information in the table below shows the supply of bread per week.

	Price of bread	Loaves of bread supplied per week
A	$100	6,500
B	$125	7,000
C	$150	8,000

Calculate the elasticity of the supply of bread when the price increases from $100 to $125. (3 marks)

(Total 6 marks)

Summary

In this chapter, you have learned that:

- In the theory of supply, factors of production are combined in the production process and that the production function shows the relationship between factor inputs and the total output.
- In physical terms, various product measures can be derived to show the relationships between factor inputs and outputs; a range of cost measures can also be derived to explain why firms produce a particular level of output.
- There is an important distinction between the short-run and long-run periods – diminishing returns occur in the short run, whilst in the long run, firms may benefit from falling average costs arising from economies of scale.
- The supply curve of a firm is upward sloping due to a positive relationship between price and the quantity supplied.
- The elasticity of supply measures the slope of the supply curve; it is affected by various factors, depending upon the business situation.

Key words

Definitions of Key words can be found in the Glossary.

average total cost
average product
barriers to entry
decreasing returns to scale
diminishing returns
diseconomies of scale
economies of scale
external economies of scale
financial economies
increasing returns to scale
internal economies of scale
long run
managerial economies
marginal cost
marginal product
marketing economies
minimum efficient scale
natural monopoly
price elasticity of supply
production function
risk-bearing economies
short run
supply curve
supply schedule
technical economies
total cost
total product

Module 2

Market structure and market failure

On completion of this module you should be able to:

- appreciate the distinction between the different types of market structures
- develop awareness of the causes of market failure and the measures that can be adopted to reduce or eliminate such failure

5 Market structure

This chapter covers unit 1, module 2, topic 1.
On completion of this chapter, you should be able to:

- list the characteristics of the different market structures
- compare market structures and provide examples of such structures
- identify the strengths and weaknesses of the marginalist approach
- calculate and interpret measures of industrial concentration
- explain the factors that influence the pricing and output decisions of the firm

The firm

In the last topic we referred to the firm when explaining the various types of cost that apply in the theory of supply. Before studying market structures, it is necessary to define what is meant by a firm, what is the usual objective of a firm and how the firm's revenue can be derived. These are essential preliminaries for a study of market structures.

Essentially a firm is used by economists as a unit of decision making that has particular objectives such as **profit maximisation**, the avoidance of risk-taking and achieving its own long-term growth. At its lowest level, the firm may be a sole trader with a small factory or a corner shop. The term is also used for the national or multinational corporation with many plants and business establishments. In economic theory all firms are headed by an entrepreneur (see chapter 1).

An entrepreneur must consider all the costs of the factors of production involved in the final output. These are the private costs directly incurred by the owners. Production may create costs for other people but these are not necessarily taken into account by the firm (see next chapter). The firm is simply the economic organisation that transforms factor inputs into goods and services for the market.

An accountant's view of a firm's costs is that they are incurred when the firm makes a recognised expenditure. They are production expenses paid out at a particular time and price. **Profits** are what are left when the expenses are deducted from the firm's income or sales revenue.

The economist's view of costs is wider than this. The accounting view does not fully recognise the private cost of economic activity. As well as money paid out to factors, there must be an allowance for anything owned by the entrepreneur and used in the production process. This factor cost must be imputed or estimated and included with the other costs. In addition, the concept of opportunity cost is relevant. As seen in chapter 1, opportunity cost involves the sacrifice of the closest alternative and is the value of what has been given up. The entrepreneur may have capital that could have been used at no risk elsewhere and would have earned an income. There will be a minimum level of profit that the entrepreneur will expect, reflecting what his capital and labour would have earned elsewhere. This is the concept of **normal profit**. Economists regard this element of the entrepreneur's reward as a cost of production, because without it there would be nothing produced by the firm. Profit, to an economist, is:

Total revenue (unit price multiplied by number of units sold)
minus total cost (including normal profit).

If this is positive, then it is **abnormal profit**. It is the prospect of making abnormal profit that motivates the entrepreneur to take the business risks in supplying goods and services to the market.

Measures of industrial concentration

Reference was made at the start of the chapter as to how a concentration index could help establish the market structure of a particular activity. Let us consider this in more detail.

The retail grocery market in the UK is now dominated by a small number of large supermarket companies. Table 5.1 below shows their estimated market shares in 2004. These data, which are in percentage form, can be easily used to calculate an industrial concentration ratio.

Tesco Stores	28%
Sainsbury's	19%
Asda	18%
Morrisons	15%
Waitrose	6%
Co-op	5%
Others	9%

Table 5.1 Estimated market shares of UK grocery retailers in 2004
Source: Institute of Grocery Distribution, 2005.

A four firm concentration ratio would seem most useful since there are clearly four very large companies that dominate the market. This ratio is 80%, indicating a very high degree of concentration in the hands of the four largest companies. If the data were tracked back over time, then this would clearly indicate that the grocery market was increasingly in the hands of large retailers. The market structure is a very clear example of **oligopoly** (see below). One consequence of increasing concentration is that many small grocery retailers, particularly local corner shops, have gone out of business as they are unable to compete with the huge buying power of the major supermarkets. (Note that in this example the calculation is straightforward – the percentage market shares have been derived from the total market sales.)

Within the Caribbean and Latin America, the banana industry is an example of an oligopoly. It is dominated by five main multinational growers. Although data is not easy to obtain, it is estimated that:

- Chiquita and Dole have about half the total market;
- Del Monte, Noboa (Ecuador) and Fyffes have the remainder of the market.

The power of these oligopolies is demonstrated through the way in which they control the whole supply chain of bananas from the grower through to their retail distribution to major retailers and wholesalers in the USA and Europe. Because of their size they can gain benefits from various types of economies of scale (see previous topic) as well as use their market power to exploit growers who have little or no power in the industry. Although we do not have data, the five firm concentration ratio would seem to be almost 100%.

An alternative, more sophisticated measure of concentration in an industry is the **Herfindahl index** (sometimes known as the Herfindahl–Hirschman index). The index calculates the sum over *all* firms of the squares of their market shares, expressed as proportions. It can be represented algebraically as

$$H = \sum_{i=1}^{n} S_i^2$$

where S_i is the market share of the *i*th firm.

If all firms in an industry had an equal market share, then H would be equal to $1/n$. The highest value it can take is 1 – this is an industry where there is a monopoly with full control over the market. Apart from this extreme case, the value of H rises as the degree of concentration in an industry increases. In practice this measure is not easy to calculate since it requires market share data for each firm in an industry (see self-assessment task).

The bulk distribution of Chiquita fruit by rail

Self-assessment tasks

Read the case study below and then tackle the exercises that follow.

Rough times in the Caribbean cruise market

The cruise market for visits to the Caribbean is an interesting yet very unusual example of an oligopolistic market. The table below shows the market shares of the principal US-based cruise lines for the second quarter of 2003.

Cruise Line	Passengers (thousands)	% of Total passengers
Carnival Cruise Line	723	36.2
Royal Caribbean International	510	25.5
Norwegian Cruise Line	186	9.3
Princess Cruises	156	7.8
Celebrity Cruises	153	7.6
Holland America Line	141	7.0
Disney Cruise Line	101	5.1
Cunard Cruise Line	13	0.6
Costa Cruise Line	8	0.4
Crystal Cruises	7	0.1

Source: US Dept of Transportation.

Like most tourism markets, that for cruises to the islands of the Caribbean is a mixed blessing. The main operators are very powerful businesses. This can be very clearly shown by their rejection of the proposal made in 2003 for a $20 per passenger tax on all cruise passengers, the purpose of which was to help the various Caribbean islands handle the negative effects of cruise traffic on their communities.

At the time, the head of Carnival Cruise Lines called the tax proposal 'outrageous'. Through the Florida Caribbean Cruise Association, Carnival and other leading operators imposed intensive pressures on the Caribbean governments to back down on the $20 per passenger tax. This has now happened, leading to claims that the cruise ship operators were using tactics that 'put the fear of God' into Caribbean governments.

Source: Oligopoly Watch, November 2003.

1 (a) Using the information in the table calculate
- ◆ the five firm concentration index,
- ◆ the Herfindahl index.

(b) Explain what each calculation means.

2 Later in 2003, Carnival Cruise Line bought P and O Princesses Cruises (including Princess Cruises). How does this acquisition change the above indices?

3 Use a diagram to explain the likely impact on the Caribbean cruise market of the $20 tax that had been proposed.

4 Why might the management of Carnival Cruise Line find it appropriate to meet senior managers from arch rivals, Royal Caribbean International?

Self-assessment tasks

Read the case study below and then tackle the exercises that follow.

The telecommunications market in the Caribbean

For over 100 years, Cable and Wireless had a monopoly over the provision of telecommunications services in the Caribbean area. Through its various subsidiaries, this UK-based company has successfully operated 'native incumbent' services in Jamaica, Trinidad and Tobago, Cayman Islands, Barbados and elsewhere. In 2005 it had a turnover of £550m from its Caribbean businesses; this was about one-third of Cable and Wireless's group turnover. Moreover the Caribbean subsidiaries have consistently contributed to the profitability of the parent company.

The present position is that Cable and Wireless's monopoly is gradually being challenged by other providers as a result of governments liberalising the telecommunications market in their countries.

Governments throughout the Caribbean have become increasingly concerned about the problem of telephone penetration, the rate at which households subscribe to the telephone service. In 1999, with Cable and Wireless as the monopoly provider, telephone density was 19 lines per 100 people in Jamaica and 9 lines per 100 people in the Dominican Republic. This compared with 66 lines per 100 people in the USA and 33 lines per 100 people in neighbouring Puerto Rico. In a shrinking world, policy makers were becoming increasingly concerned that Caribbean economies would fall even further behind due to inadequate internet access for their businesses and people.

Two factors have led to change in recent years. The first has been the development of wireless technology and with it, the opportunity for those who can afford, to own mobile telephones. The second has been the way in which island governments have recognised the importance of competitive communications markets in promoting vibrant economies.

In February 2000, the Jamaican Parliament led the way by passing legislation to end Cable and Wireless's telephone monopoly. The legislation provided for a three-year transition to a fully competitive market. In addition, a regional regulatory body, the Eastern Caribbean Telecommunications Authority, has been established to oversee revisions to telecommunications laws across the Caribbean area.

More recently, Digital has begun to offer what it claims to be 'highly competitive' mobile telephone services in Trinidad and Tobago, Antigua and Barbuda and in the Turks and Caicos Islands. Their claim is that they can provide a better service at a lower cost to users than the Cable and Wireless owned Telecommunications Services of Trinidad and Tobago.

1 What evidence might an economist need to investigate whether a firm such as Cable and Wireless was abusing its monopoly position in the market?

2 How might other companies compete with Cable and Wireless in the
- ◆ provision of telephone land line services,
- ◆ provision of mobile telephone services?

3 How might Cable and Wireless react to the new competition in its former monopolistic markets?

The firm's revenue

In the theory of the firm, there are only two possible revenue relationships. In a competitive market, each firm has to accept the ruling market price. Its demand curve is horizontal at this level. Any firm in any other market will face a downward-sloping demand curve for its product. If the firm chooses to increase its output, the extra sales will depress the price. To look at it another way, the sales will only increase if the price is reduced from its present level. An increase in price would lead to a fall in the volume of sales. The following definitions are used by economists when looking at a firm's revenue:

> **Total revenue** (TR) is price multiplied by quantity
> **Average revenue** (AR) is total revenue divided by output

The firm's demand curve therefore is the average revenue line or the price line.

The **marginal revenue** (MR) is the addition to the total revenue resulting from the sales of one extra unit. Because the firm can only sell more by reducing the price, it follows that the value for MR will always be lower than AR. Figure 5.1, derived from the accompanying data, shows that when the price moves from 9 to 8, the MR is 7. The addition to TR is gradually falling as the price falls until when five units are sold MR = 0. At this point total revenue is maximised.

The relationship between price elasticity of demand and revenue In the above example the firm would be facing a straight line demand curve. Even so, the consumers' reaction to a price change varies at different prices due to the way in which the price elasticity of demand (PED) varies along the demand curve.

As the price falls in steps from \$10, sales increase more than proportionally, giving PED a value greater than 1, until the output of 5 when total revenue is unchanged. This gives a PED value of 1. Beyond this output PED has a value less than 1 and the result is that further price cuts will reduce total revenue.

A relationship between elasticity and marginal revenue can also be seen. In the elastic part of the demand curve where PED > 1, the marginal revenue is positive and total revenue will be increasing. When the

Revenue data

Price (*P*)	Units sold (*Q*)	*TR* (*P* x *Q*)	*MR*
10	0	0	
9	1	9	9
8	2	16	7
7	3	21	5
6	4	24	3
5	5	25	1
4	6	24	–1
3	7	21	–3
2	8	16	–5
1	9	9	–7

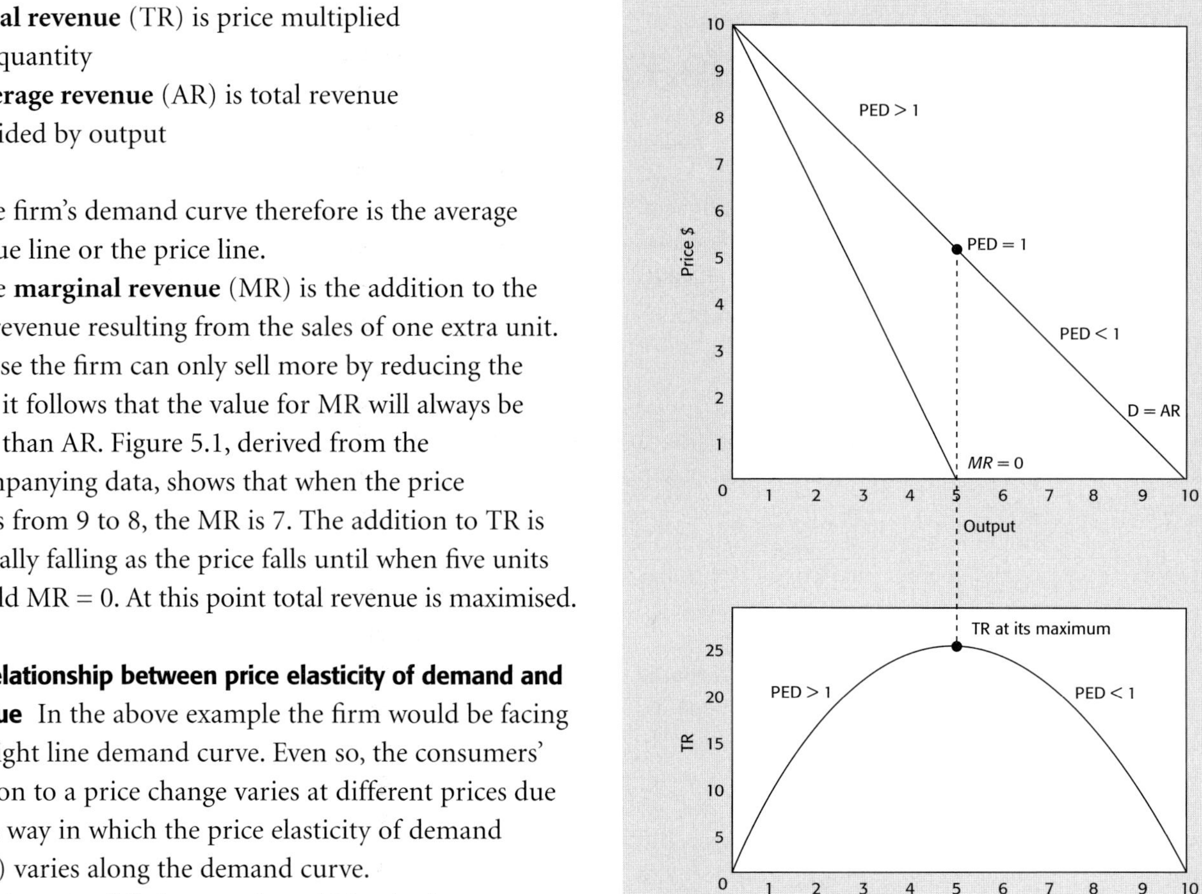

Figure 5.1 The relationship between average revenue, marginal revenue and total revenue

PED = 1, MR will be zero and total revenue will be maximised. When PED < 1, MR will be negative, reducing the total revenue.

The most important thing about the concept of price elasticity from the firm's point of view is that it

Self-assessment tasks

Wok, Stock and Barrel is a small family-run engineering company with a production capacity of 9,000 units per year. Market research suggests that the market will take up all of this output at a price of $8. The firms cost structure is as follows:

direct labour $1.50 per unit,
raw materials $0.50 per unit,
other variable costs $1.00 per unit,
the total fixed costs are $27,000 a year.

1 Calculate:
- AFC,
- AVC,
- ATC,
- AR.

2 If the factory produced its capacity output, what would the firm's abnormal profit be?

3 Suppose that consumer tastes change away from the product and the firm has to reduce the price to $6 in order to get rid of unsold stock. What situation is the firm now in?

determines what happens to total revenue when the price is altered. It would make sense for any firm operating in the elastic part of the demand curve to reduce price and boost total revenue. Conversely, in the inelastic part, the firm should raise its price if it wants to see higher revenue. In this example revenue is maximised at five units of output with a price of 5.

With knowledge of the firm's cost structure and revenue situation, and the firm's objectives, we are now in a position to make some predictions about the output the firm will choose to put on the market.

The firm and the industry

A firm As referred to earlier, a firm is a business organisation that buys or hires factors of production in order to produce goods and services that can be sold at a profit. The types might include:

- sole traders or one person businesses,
- partnerships,
- co-operatives,
- private companies,
- public limited companies,
- state-owned firms,
- multinational or transnational firms.

They can range from small simple organisations to ones that are almost too complex to control, and where there is some conflict of interests between the members. The characteristics and behaviour of the firm depend on the type of economic activity and the nature of competition. The factor mix in firms varies enormously, with some firms in the service sector being highly labour intensive. This contrasts with some manufacturing that is capital intensive. The decisions that firms take will vary according to the cost and availability of factors of production in different economic systems. There has been a trend in the rich western economies to make large parts of manufacturing more capital intensive, to the point where some major activities, such as car manufacturing, can largely be done by robots and computer-controlled machinery. Another trend has been increased concentration of ownership in the hands of large multinational conglomerates.

An industry In a competitive market structure, the industry is simply the sum of all the firms making the same product. This is the total market supply.

In other markets, the industry is taken to be the total number of firms producing within the same product group, i.e. things which are close substitutes for each other. It is sometimes difficult to draw the line between different industries; for example are motor cars and motor cycles in the same product group? In reality many multi-product firms operate in more than one industry at the same time. A multinational conglomerate can be in several industries right across the global economy.

The industry is therefore a collection of business organisations which supply similar products to the market. When a firm's market share is discussed it tends to be in terms of the sales of the firm divided by the total sales of the entire industry. The terms 'industry' and 'market' are interchangeable in this context.

The firm's objectives

Profit maximisation The standard assumption made by economists is that firms will seek to maximise their profits, that is maximise the gap between the firm's total revenue and total cost (including normal profit). A firm making the minimum level of normal profit is said to be producing the break-even output. Firms will want to make abnormal profit as a reward for managing the resources and taking business risks.

If the firm produces up to the point where the cost of making the last unit is just covered by the revenue from selling it, then the profit margin will have fallen to 0 and total profits will be at their greatest. In figure 5.2, a firm producing an output to the left of *Q* is sacrificing potential profit. It can raise total profit by increasing its output, because each marginal unit sold adds more to revenue than it does to costs. A firm producing to the right of *Q* is making a loss on each successive unit, which will lower the total profit. It would be better off cutting the output back to *Q* where MC = MR and the area of abnormal profit will be at its highest.

There may be several reasons why firms do not operate at the profit-maximisation output:

1 In practice it may be difficult to identify this output. The firm may simply work out the average total cost and add on a profit margin in order to determine the selling price. This cost-plus pricing technique may not result in maximum profit.
2 Short-term profit maximising may not be in the long-term interest of the company since:
   - firms with large market shares may wish to avoid the attention of government watchdog bodies, such as the Competition Commission in Britain;
   - large abnormal profit may attract new entrants into the industry;
   - high profits may damage the relationship between the firm and its stakeholders, such as the consumers and the company workforce;
   - profit maximisation may not appeal to the management, who may have different objectives;
   - high profits might trigger action by the firm's rivals and it could become a target for a take-over bid.

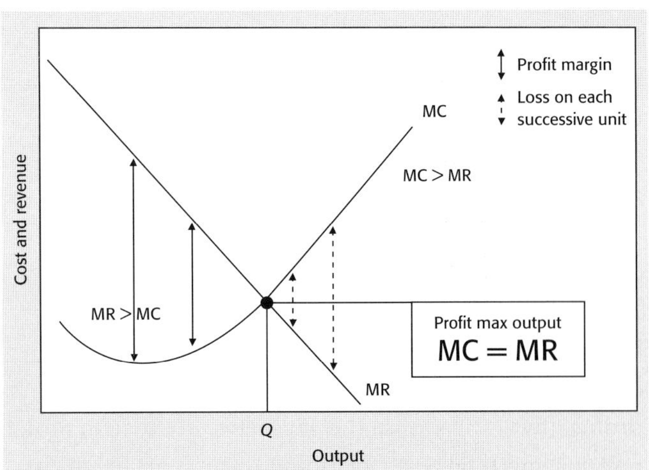

Figure 5.2 The profit maximisation rule

Alternative objectives to profit maximisation

Dissatisfaction with the simple assumption of profit maximisation has led to a number of alternative assumptions that have been labelled as managerial or behavioural theories.

Sales revenue maximisation A firm may be prepared to accept a lower price and produce above the profit-maximising output in order to increase its market share in a growing market. This is a penetration pricing policy. A firm choosing to maximise its sales revenue would raise output beyond MC = MR until MR had fallen to zero. Extra sales after this would contribute nothing to total revenue, therefore it is at its maximum. There may still be abnormal profit if total revenue is higher than total cost. The reason why sales revenue maximisation might be chosen in a large firm is that management salaries might be linked to the value of sales. Shareholders might be more interested in profit. The solution to this conflict of interests is to offer management some shares as a bonus or link their salaries to profits.

Sales maximisation This option maximises the volume of sales rather than the sales revenue. In this option the firm would increase output up to the break-even output where the total revenue just covered the total cost. A higher output implies loss-making behaviour. The only situation where this would be possible is where the firm could use the profit from some other activities to cover these losses using the principle of cross subsidisation. It could be that in a state-owned firm, there are social objectives lying behind price and output decisions. The company might be instructed to keep prices down, to cover their ATC, or to make sufficient profit to be self-financing when it comes to new investment.

A firm in the private sector would not go beyond the break-even output in order to expand sales unless it is part of a diversified grouping where cross subsidisation is being practised. Deliberately cutting the price to reduce profit might be a strategy to deter new entrants into the market. If they still appear, a price war may be a tactic to squeeze them out.

Satisficing profits This behaviour would occur when a firm is determined to make a reasonable level of profits, sufficient to satisfy the shareholders but also to keep the other stakeholding groups happy, for example the workforce and of course the consumers. The firm is seen as a coalition of interest groups, each with its own objectives which may change over time. Workers will expect pay rises and improvements in working conditions which may raise costs. Consumers may expect to see prices falling, particularly if there are rival producers. This is a long way from the simple profit-maximising theory as firms may choose to sacrifice some potential short-term profits to satisfy these expectations.

Where the firm's shareholders are divorced from control of the firm, there may be a conflict of interests. The management's motives may be concerned with growth rather than profit. They may place a lot of importance on comfortable working conditions, job security, status and fringe benefits, such as company cars, private health care and pension rights. Time and money spent on these issues can raise costs. If the firm has close rivals, it may make management more cautious because the risk of failure will threaten their job security and career advancement prospects. Firms may have charitable or environmental objectives which must be financed at the cost of profit. Satisficing can also be a feature of firms that have enjoyed a high market share over a long period of time. Complacency can lead to firms losing their focus on the cost structure or failing to devote resources to either product or process innovation. Either situation can lead to a loss of profits.

One must be careful of sweeping statements concerning firms' short-run behaviour and recognise the difference in objectives that can exist in different countries. Extra long-run profits may follow from short-term sacrifices. As a working assumption, it is still valid to see profit maximisation as the major long-term objective of privately owned firms operating in a free market system. The search for abnormal profit will be a major factor in explaining firms' behaviour throughout the world.

Self-assessment tasks

Read the following short case study which looks at some of the objectives of the firm, and then tackle the exercises that follow.

Chefaid plc

A row has broken out in the boardroom of Chefaid plc, the kitchenware company, over the firm's prospects and future direction. The marketing director announced a record level of sales for the last quarter and suggested that there should be a 10 per cent target for the growth of sales revenue over the coming year. It was suggested to him that this was unwise. The firm's latest product, an exclusive set of kitchen tools, has yet to break even. The sales record owes a lot to the current popularity of cookery programmes on TV; there is a danger that the sales boom is a flash in the pan.

The managing director was more interested in the firm's profitability. He was under pressure to declare higher future dividends and to get the funds to finance the planned new factory. He believed that a profit-maximisation strategy was the best way forward. The production director warned the meeting that cost pressures were building up and that industrial relations with the workforce were fragile because of the beginning of talks about wages and new working conditions. Management in general had been delighted with the new share option scheme and the bonus linked to sales performance.

It was suggested that the prospects for growth in general were good, because of the increase in consumer confidence, and the firm's market share had benefited from the closure of two large rivals during the recession. It was argued that the market structure was becoming less competitive and this might give an opportunity for price rises. The company must not lose sight of its long-term drive to raise profitability by reducing unit costs. This sparked further disagreement over the firm's sponsorship commitments, its promotions budget and its charitable contributions.

1 What do economists understand by the phrase 'the market structure is becoming less competitive'?
2 What will be the best output for the firm if the profit-maximising strategy wins the day?
3 What are the risks associated with this strategy?
4 What output would maximise turnover?
5 What does the phrase 'fail to break even' mean? What advice would you give to improve the performance of the new product?
6 Explain why the management may not favour profit maximisation.
7 To what extent does the case study show that businesses have a range of objectives?
8 Discuss the idea that each business decision to reach an objective has risks attached to it.

Market structures

The term 'market structure' describes the way in which goods and services are supplied by firms in a particular market. In economic theory, a range of models has been developed within what is called the spectrum of competition. These models are shown in figure 5.3. The extreme or limiting models may only exist in theory but give a framework for understanding real world competition. The following stages can help to identify a market structure within this spectrum of competition:

- By counting the number of firms. The bigger the total, the closer to perfect competition the market stucture will be.
- A better guide will be to use sales **concentration ratios** to see the combined market share of the biggest 3, 5 or 7 firms in the industry as a percentage of total industry sales. The bigger the percentage, the closer the industry will be to the oligopoly and monopoly models.
- By considering how easy or difficult it is for new firms to set up and how easy it is for firms to exit the industry. These barriers are indicative of market structures on the right-hand side of the spectrum.
- By considering the importance of economies of scale to the firms. The more important they are the closer the industry will be to an oligopoly structure.

Figure 5.4 provides an elaboration of the above – understanding this figure is very important for the rest of this section.

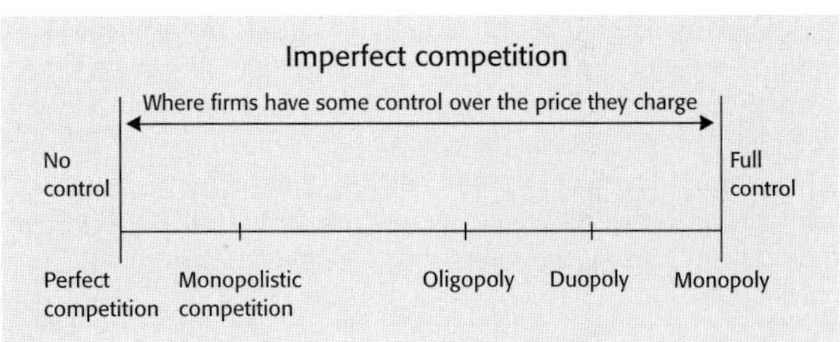

Figure 5.3 The spectrum of competition

Perfect competition

Perfect competition is a theoretical extreme in the spectrum of competition. The main point of studying this model is that it can act as a benchmark for real-world competition. The performance of actual firms can be judged against the most efficient model possible. Some of the characteristics are shared by the next most competitive model, which somewhat confusingly to students is known as monopolistic competition.

Perfect competition has the following characteristics:

1 There is a large number of buyers and sellers who have perfect knowledge of market conditions and the price.
2 No individual firm has any influence on the market price. Firms are described as being price takers. The ruling price is determined by the forces of market demand and the aggregate output of all the firms.
3 The products are homogeneous. They are all of the same quality and are identical in the eyes of the consumer.
4 There is complete freedom of entry into and exit from the market.
5 Each firm will be seeking to maximise its profits.

The only industry which comes anywhere near this theoretical model is agriculture. The problem in searching for an example is in finding products that are homogeneous. Perfect competition has a lot of appeal as a yardstick because if it were to operate, there would be consumer sovereignty and efficient production with no possibility of exploitation.

In perfect competition, the firm cannot do anything that will influence the market price. Each individual firm makes such a small contribution to the industry output that no alteration in its own output can significantly affect the total supply. The firm can choose to produce any quantity it likes and will be able to sell all of it at the ruling price. The demand curve facing the firm is therefore perfectly elastic at this price. In this situation if the firm sells an extra unit of output it will get the same price as the one before. The marginal revenue is therefore equal to the price or the average revenue. In figure 5.5, all the firm's revenue information is in the line

$$D = \text{AR} = \text{MR}$$

Choosing the output would be the only decision that the firm has to make. This will be done by considering the relevant costs of production. Given the assumption that the firm wants to maximise profits, the chosen output will be where MC = MR.

The firm's total revenue would be the price multiplied by the output sold. If the total cost of producing this output is lower than the total revenue,

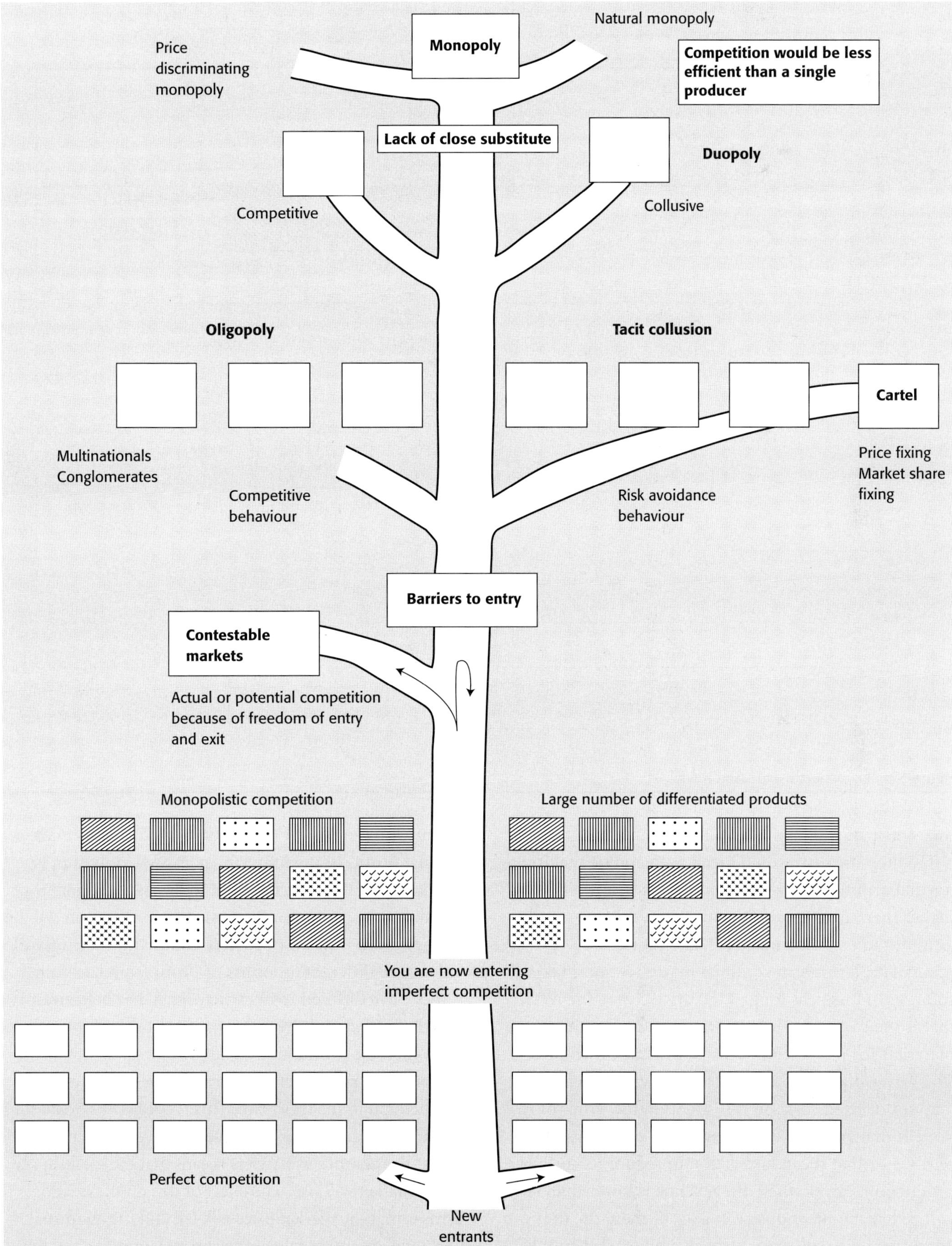

Figure 5.4 A competition road map

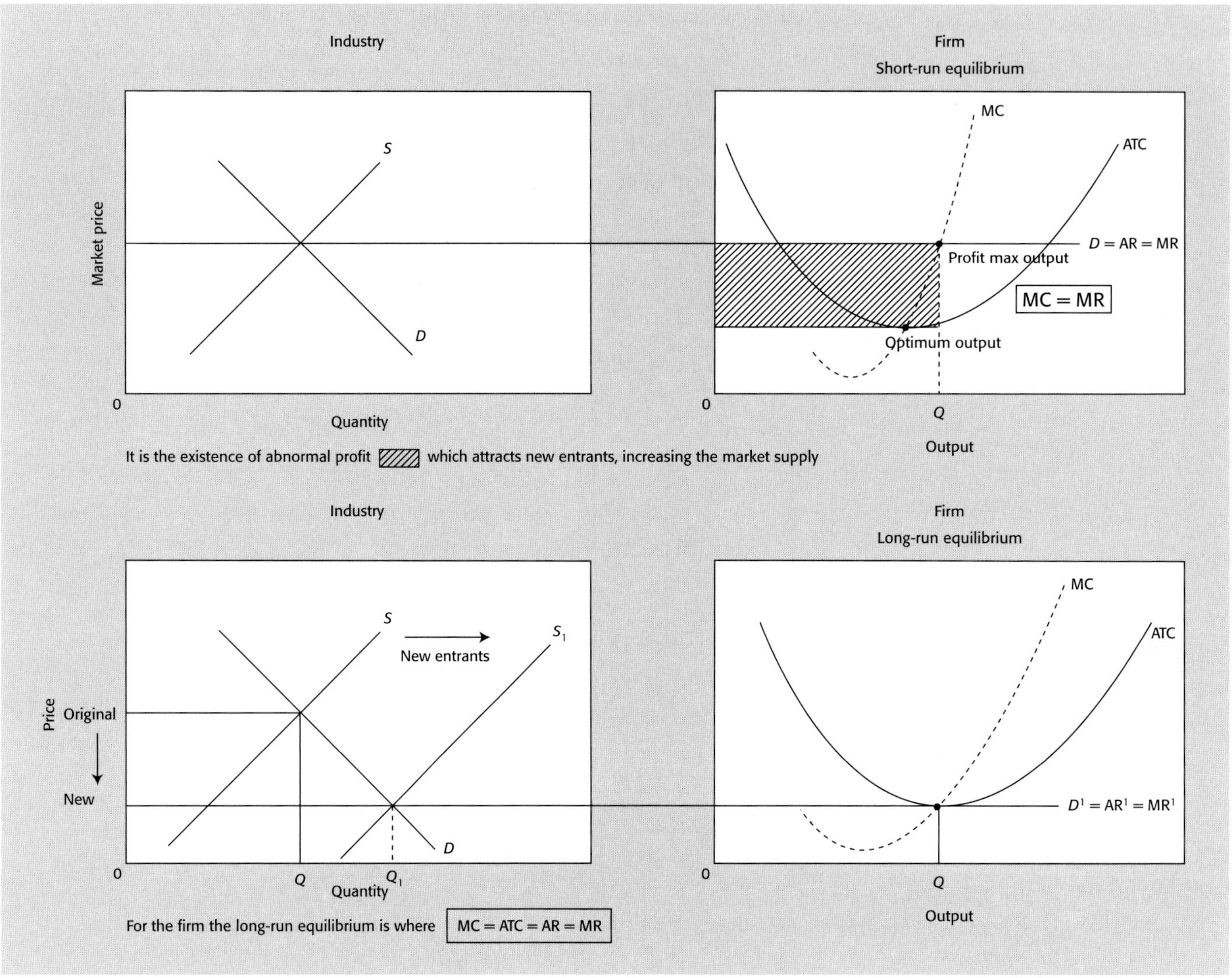

Figure 5.5 The perfect competition model

then the firm will be making an abnormal profit. If TC = TR, then the firm would break even and be making a normal profit. It is possible that the costs could be higher than the revenue, in which case the firm would be about to exit the industry. This may not be immediate, a firm can continue in production making short-term losses, as long as the price covers the AVC, that is the cost of paying the wage bill and buying the materials for production. This is the shut-down price. The firm would be making a loss equivalent to the amount of fixed costs. In this situation the firm's only hope is that the market price will rise to increase its revenue or that it can take action to reduce its costs of production. Firms where the revenue is lower than costs will be leaving the industry. If a lot of them do, the effect will be a reduction in the overall market supply which will raise the market price giving the rest an opportunity to continue producing and at least make a normal profit. In the long run, firms will only supply the market if they can cover all their costs and make a normal profit. The minimum supply for the firm will be the optimum output. In perfect competition, firms will only make different amounts of profit from each other if they have different cost structures. Their behaviour is strictly limited and the only way to boost profit would be to increase productivity and lower average total cost.

Abnormal profit will only be a feature of perfect competition in the short run. This is because its existence will act as an economic incentive for the entry of new firms. The absence of barriers means that the total supply in the market will rise. The effect of this on the existing firms is that the market price will fall and the abnormal profit will diminish. When the abnormal profit goes, the entry of new firms dries up, and the existing ones will simply be covering costs. It is the competitive force of large numbers of new entrants that destroys abnormal profit.

The long-run equilibrium is therefore where the only firms left are the most efficient ones, making a normal profit.

In this model, there is no action that the firm can take to prosper at the expense of rivals. It has no market power. Firms' behaviour in this market structure is easy to understand. The appeal of this model is that abnormal profit is competed away and the only firms that participate in the market in the long run are completely productively and allocatively efficient. It is the efficient economic performance which would occur in perfect competition that can be used to criticise real-world competition.

Self-assessment tasks

1 Study the diagrams below and tackle the exercises that follow.

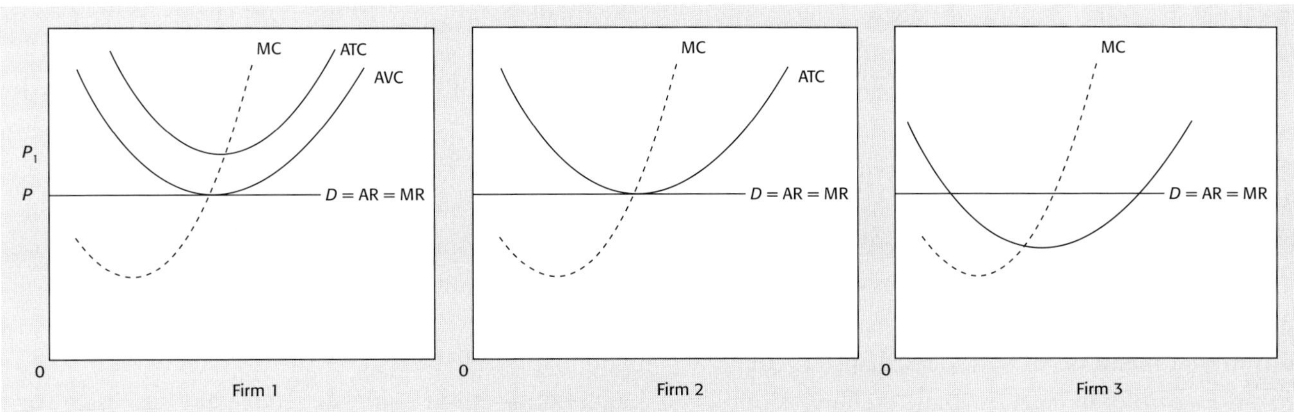

(a) Describe the situation of each firm regarding profit.
(b) If market demand increased and the price rose to P_1, how would it affect each of them?
(c) According to the theory what will happen next?
(d) What output does a firm in perfect competition choose?
(e) How can an individual firm increase its profits?

2 Read the article below and then tackle the exercises that follow.

Shedding light on competition

In Guangdong, people do not hide their light under a bushel. 'Guizhen: Lighting Capital of China', proclaims the sign beside the highway into the village (more of a town), which two decades ago was an unpaved track. Factory after factory, every one of them advertising light fittings, lines the road. In town, hundreds of shopfronts display their variations on a theme: street lights, chandeliers, bedside lights, halogen lights, lights of any sort, from the modern to the eternally tasteless. Guizhen has 60,000 registered inhabitants, says the party secretary, Mr Wu, frantically talking on his cellphone, and though there are officially 1,000 lighting factories, 'there are also 600 or so underground ones . . . they all count.'

One resident in every 40 men, women and children, then, is a factory owner, and that does not take into account the wholesalers and shop owners. On top of that there are some 40,000 migrant workers. It is an intensely competitive industry. The Guizhen factories on average change their designs every fortnight. The specialist designers of light fittings have to come up with three new ideas a day. In return, they are paid 600,000 yuan ($72,000) a year, many times the salary of China's prime minister.

Since the first factory opened in 1986, little-known Guizhen has captured 46% of China's total domestic lighting market. One in every two light fittings you see in China has been trucked out past that bragging highway sign.

Source: *Economist* survey of China, 8 April 2000 (adapted).

(a) Is this an example of perfect competition or monopolistic competition? Justify your choice.
(b) Give examples of Caribbean market structures that are (i) perfectly competitive and (ii) monopolistically competitive. Justify your choice.

Monopolistic competition

This is the market structure closest to the model of perfect competition because of the large number of competing suppliers.

Monopolistic competition has the following characteristics:

1 There is a large number of buyers and sellers.
2 There are few barriers to entry into the market and it is easy for firms to recoup their capital expenditure on exit from the market.
3 Consumers face a wide choice of differentiated products. Each firm has a slight degree of monopoly power in that it controls its own brand.
4 Firms have some influence on the market price and are therefore price makers.
5 Each firm will seek to maximise profits.

Each firm is competing with a large number of similar producers. In this situation the demand curve facing the individual firm will be downward sloping but relatively price elastic because of the presence of substitutes. It might be an option for firms to reduce their price in order to increase total revenue. As in perfect competition, the firms can make abnormal profit in the short run but the key restraint on their power is the free entry of rivals. In the long run, the prediction is that the profit-maximising firms will only be able to achieve a normal profit covering all the production costs and the opportunity cost of capital.

It is easy to open a local store but not so easy to stay in business

The clue to the behaviour of firms in this market structure lies in the concept of product differentiation. The development of a strong brand image must be seen as an act of investment on the part of the individual firm. This highlights the important role that advertising and promotions play in this market structure. Successful advertising will not only shift the firm's demand curve to the right at the expense of the rivals but will also reduce the price elasticity if the consumers feel there are no close substitutes. This is what is meant by brand loyalty – people will not easily shift back to rival products. There are problems associated with advertising because it will be a competitive tool taken up by all the firms. In this case one could argue that the advantage will be temporary and that advertising will simply add to the firm's costs and bring little benefit to its demand curve. If advertising is not equally effective, the successful firms might take advantage of their greater market share and brand loyalty to charge a higher price. It would increase its sales revenue by doing this in the portion of the demand curve where price elasticity of demand has a value less than 1.

It is easy to see how each firm can try and strengthen its market power in the short run. The constraint on firms is that there is freedom of entry into the market, which will threaten the existence of abnormal profit in the long run. By a combination of marketing and product innovation, the individual firms may be able to postpone the long-run equilibrium, if the total market is growing.

At the heart of this model of competition is the fact that there are a large number of competitors using a combination of price and non-price competition to try and increase their market power. If there are few barriers to entry then their success will only be temporary. There are many typical examples of this market structure in operation. For example, local hairdresser's shops, take-away food stores and travel agents exhibit the characteristics of this market structure.

Figure 5.6 shows the equilibrium price and output in monopolistic competition. In the short run, the profit-maximising firm will be seen to make abnormal profits.

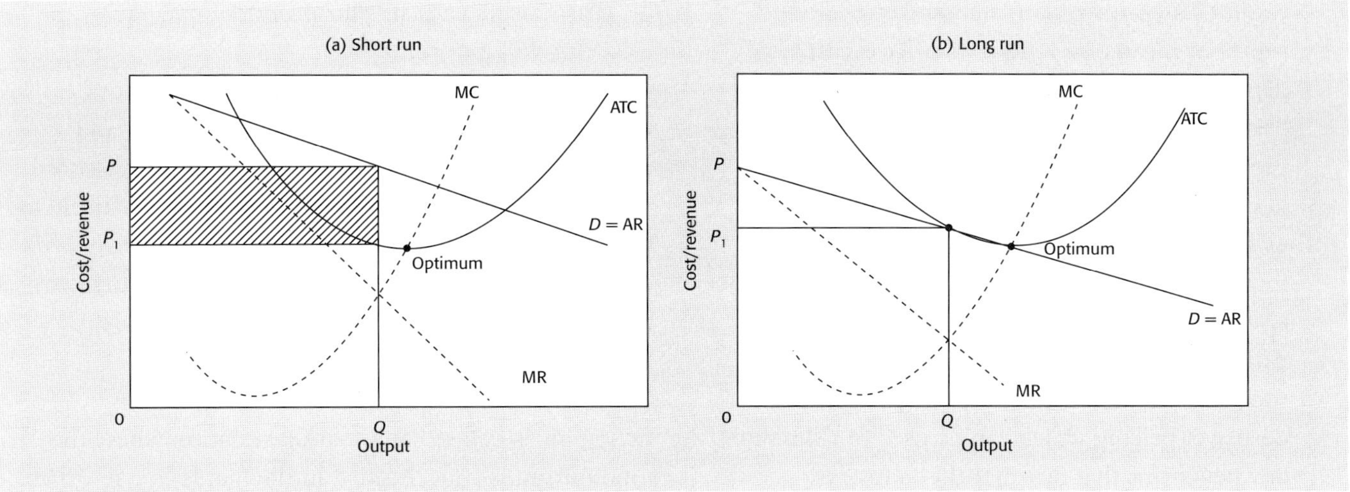

Figure 5.6 Monopolistic competition in the short and long run

In time these will be competed away by the entry of new firms which will shift the original firm's demand curve to the left. The process will continue until the only firms in the industry are making normal profit. A key point though is that in both the short and the long run the firm is inefficient. It is below the optimum point, giving a situation of excess capacity.

Barriers to entry

In the spectrum of competition, it is the existence of **barriers to entry** of new firms into an industry that differentiates oligopoly and monopoly from the others.

Barriers are a mixture of obstacles that deter or prevent new firms from entering a market to compete with the existing firms. They give firms a degree of market power in that decisions can be made by existing firms without the risk of their market share or the price being challenged from outside. The construction and maintenance of these barriers can become part of the firm's behaviour. Below are some of the main barriers that can be identified:

- In some countries, it may be impossible for new firms to enter an industry because the economic activity is state owned or the good is produced under licence from the government. This is a legal monopoly created to achieve social and political objectives. The economic justification might lie in the concept of a natural monopoly, where it is more efficient to have a single producer than to have competing firms. In countries where the state-owned resources have been privatised and the market has been deregulated, the economic justification has been that the injection of competition will bring economic and social benefits. Some economists though believe that there is no such thing as a natural monopoly.
- The high fixed cost or setup cost in activities such as electricity generation, aircraft and car production and pharmaceuticals may deter potential entrants. The barrier here is access to capital. Only very large firms will be able to fund the necessary investment. Research and development costs will represent a high proportion of total costs and it will require high sales over a long period of time before the activity becomes profitable.
- If these costs cannot be recovered in the case of the firm shutting down, because the resources are specialised and are not easily transferable to other uses, they are regarded as sunk costs and act as a *barrier to exit* from the industry because the capital investment will be lost. It is therefore the risk of entering and the high cost of failure that deters potential entrants.
- Advertising and brand names with a high degree of consumer loyalty may prove a difficult obstacle to overcome. This explains why firms regard their expenditure on advertising and promotions as an act of investment. Existing firms can make entry more difficult through brand proliferation, giving the customers an apparent abundance of choice and closing market niches. Successful advertising

cannot only shift a firm's demand curve to the right but it can also reduce its price elasticity of demand. This gives the firm greater market power because consumers do not see the rival firm's product as a close substitute.

- Economies of scale can be a barrier because the existing large producers are able to produce at a lower average cost than those just starting up. They also give the large firm an opportunity to cut its price in order to eliminate any high-cost producers. This is the concept of predatory or destroyer pricing which can be used to eliminate any new firms that do enter the industry.
- The production process or the products of a firm may be protected by a legal monopoly in the form of a patent, whereby competitors cannot copy without the permission of the owner. The idea is to guarantee a reward to entrepreneurs with original ideas for a reasonable period of time. The barrier here is really access to either technology or information.
- Some existing firms may have a monopoly access to raw materials, components or retail outlets, which will make it difficult for new entrants. Vertically integrated manufacturing businesses will be protected by the fact that their rivals' costs will be higher.
- In activities such as computer manufacturing and consumer electronics, the pace of product innovation is so rapid that the existing firms will be working on the next generation of products whilst launching the current range. Unless the new entrants have original ideas or can exploit a new market segment, they are destined to fail.
- It may be possible for existing firms to hide the existence of abnormal profit by what is called entry limit pricing. This involves deliberately setting a low price and temporarily abandoning profit maximisation. It may be in the interest of all the players to do this and it therefore becomes a form of collusion.
- Collaboration between existing producers to develop new products may act as a barrier in that the resources necessary to compete are beyond the means of single producers.
- Market conditions, such as a fall in demand resulting from economic recession, can leave producers with surplus production capacity and this will deter entry.

The concept of barriers to entry is central to understanding where the models of oligopoly and monopoly begin within the spectrum of competition.

Where the barriers are strong, the market is likely to be dominated by a few large producers. New firms will only enter if they think that the economic returns will be greater than the cost of breaking the barriers.

Oligopoly

Oligopoly is defined as a market situation where the total output is concentrated in the hands of a few firms. It is possibly the most realistic economic model but ironically the theory does not provide the definite predictions regarding the price and output of the firm that exist in every other model. An effective oligopoly can exist in an apparently competitive industry if a handful of firms dominate the market. Duopoly, where the market is shared between two big players, can be seen as an extreme form of oligopoly.

An oligopoly has the following characteristics:

1. The market is dominated by between two and up to about ten firms.
2. Their decisions are interdependent. Firms must decide their market strategy to compete with close rivals, but they must also try and anticipate their rivals' reactions and think what the next step should be in the light of this response.
3. There are significant barriers to entry.
4. The products may be homogeneous or differentiated.
5. The uncertainty and risks associated with price competition may lead to price rigidity.
6. Firms may or may not choose to maximise profits.

The difficulty in studying oligopoly is that the behaviour can follow two very different routes. There are examples of aggressive competition in some industries whilst in others there is a suggestion of co-operation and even collusion.

Oligopolists are price makers but one of the dangers of using this weapon is that the firm can get drawn into a price war. An oligopolist would only start a price war if its costs of production were significantly lower than its rivals. A price war may be the natural outcome of economic events, such as overcapacity in the industry or the appearance of new firms. Where the firms are highly diversified, a firm may be prepared to sacrifice profits by cutting the price, in an attempt to increase market share. Profits from some of its activities may be used to cover short-term losses on others.

Although they each have market power in the form of influence over the price they charge, the uncertainty surrounding the outcome of competitive tactics means that firms may prefer **non-price competition**. The observation that prices tend to be similar between oligopolists and are stable with time might be explained by the kinked demand curve theory (see figure 5.7).

The diagram illustrates a situation where one firm suspects that it faces a relatively elastic demand curve below the existing price. The temptation would be to cut the price in an attempt to increase total revenue. The outcome depends on the rivals' response. If they also cut their price, then the firm will sell relatively little extra output. It could be worse off than it was before the price cut. It can also be shown that the firm could lose out if it chose to raise the price. Whatever the elasticity was, if the price increase is not copied by the rivals, then the firm will lose a disproportionate amount of sales because the product will look overpriced against rivals. The firm would be better off concentrating on non-price competition to increase revenue. This may include the following:

- Advertising and promotions.
- Product innovation. This is the attempt to further differentiate the products in the eyes of the consumers.
- Brand proliferation. This is where the firm produces lots of brands to saturate the market and to leave no gaps for rivals.
- Market segmentation. Producers may decide that there are sub-markets where the consumers have different characteristics and needs. These market niches will be catered for through product innovation.
- Process innovation. This is usually seen as a way of reducing average costs, allowing the firm to cut the price without sacrificing profits.

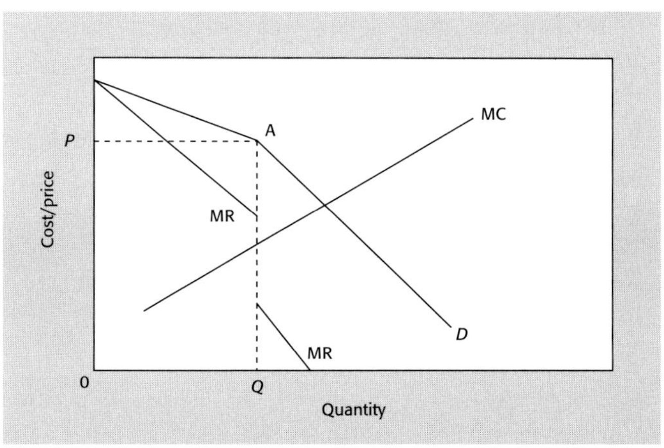

Figure 5.7 The kinked demand curve

One way for a firm to grow rapidly would be to take over one of its rivals. As seen earlier, this so-called horizontal integration may in fact be the cheapest way of getting growth in sales if the competing oligopolists are a similar size. If a takeover or merger is likely to be resisted, a firm wanting to get rapid growth may prefer to look elsewhere. This leads to a prediction that diversification becomes a feature of businesses in an oligopolistic market. This could explain the growth of conglomerate enterprises which start to look for profits by producing in different countries and eventually become multinational enterprises.

The difficulty of choosing competitive strategies and of predicting the response of rivals may change the objectives of the firm. Profit-maximising strategies may be replaced by satisficing (see above). The firm's management becomes more cautious, preferring to make just enough profit to keep the shareholders happy. The focus shifts towards maintaining market share.

Co-operation and collusion between oligopolists There are situations where big firms find that it is in their interest to co-operate with rivals. One of the best examples is where the research and development costs are high as a proportion of total costs and where the pace of technical change is very rapid. It is in the interests of all the firms to pool their knowledge and agree on technical standards, perhaps taking part in joint ventures.

Collusion is altogether different. It is an anti-competitive action by producers. Informal or tacit collusion usually takes the form of **price leadership**, where firms automatically follow the lead of one of the group. The objective is to maximise the profits of the whole group by acting as a single monopolist. This illegal activity is difficult to prove since there is no written evidence. A formal **price agreement** or output agreement is known as a **cartel** arrangement. The big problem that the participants have is that there is an incentive for individual members to cheat on the agreement.

Collusion of any kind will work best when:

- there is a small number of participants;
- a strong element of trust exists between them;
- they have similar cost structures;
- there is a clear leader;
- the agreement can be policed;
- there is no danger from new entrants;
- the market conditions are stable;
- the government will not intervene.

Collusion is more likely to be tacit where the behaviour of each firm is the result of an unwritten rather than formal agreement. One of the simplest forms is a follow-the-leader agreement, where each firm will only adjust its price following a move by the dominant firm. There are other price leadership models, such as using a typical firm as the yardstick for price. This will only change if a rise in costs affects the profit margin. The principle is the same: each firm will act in the same way in the interests of the group as a whole.

In practice it is difficult to identify either tacit or formal agreements. This is because price similarities can be the result of either aggressive pricing in a competitive oligopoly or the outcome of a collusive agreement.

Monopoly

In theory, a **monopoly** or pure monopoly is where a single firm controls the entire output of the industry. In practice, many governments define a monopoly as where one firm has a large market share, say 25 per cent. Another type is a **natural monopoly**, where, due to the benefits of economies of scale, there seems little sense in duplicating provision, for example in the case of railways or water supplies.

A monopoly will be protected from competition by the barriers to entry explained earlier. The word 'monopoly' conjures up an image of giant powerful firms. However, local monopoly can exist where a relatively small firm dominates a local market either because it is too costly for others to enter or the prospect of profit is not high enough. Even when monopolists are large, the extent of power must not be exaggerated. Sometimes a domestic monopoly can be suddenly broken by new competition from imported goods and services.

A single firm monopolist in theory would face the downward-sloping market demand curve. In this situation it can decide on the price to charge or the quantity to supply, but not both. There may be situations where the monopolist is unable to make abnormal profit in spite of having market power. One such example would be where the fixed costs are so high that the necessary price would be outside the range that the consumers could afford. It may be that all the monopolist can hope for is that the revenue covers the production costs.

Figure 5.8 shows the equilibrium output of a monopolist. A profit-maximising monopolist would choose the output where MC = MR. This output will be somewhere over the price range where demand is price elastic and will be sold at the price consumers will pay. If the total revenue is higher than the production costs, it will make abnormal profit. This will be a permanent feature. In monopoly, there is no distinction between the short run and the long run because of the barriers that prevent the entry of competitors. There is no economic incentive for the monopolist to move away from the profit-maximising output *Q*.

The monopolist's profits could be increased in certain circumstances by a practice known as **price discrimination**. Price discrimination occurs where the monopolist chooses to split the output up and sell it at different prices to different customers. It is only true price discrimination if the quality of the product is identical in all market segments. The monopolist is making use of the fact that some consumers would have been prepared to pay more than the single price (see figure 5.9). At this price they would be enjoying some consumer surplus. The monopolist's aim is to charge what the consumers will pay and turn the consumer surplus into producer surplus in the form of abnormal profit.

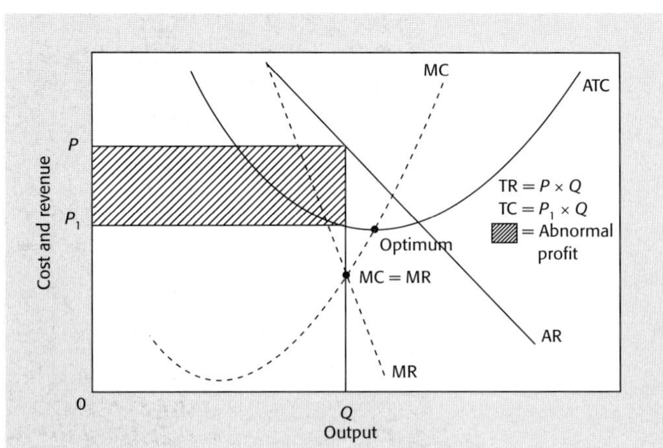

Figure 5.8 The equilibrium of a monopoly

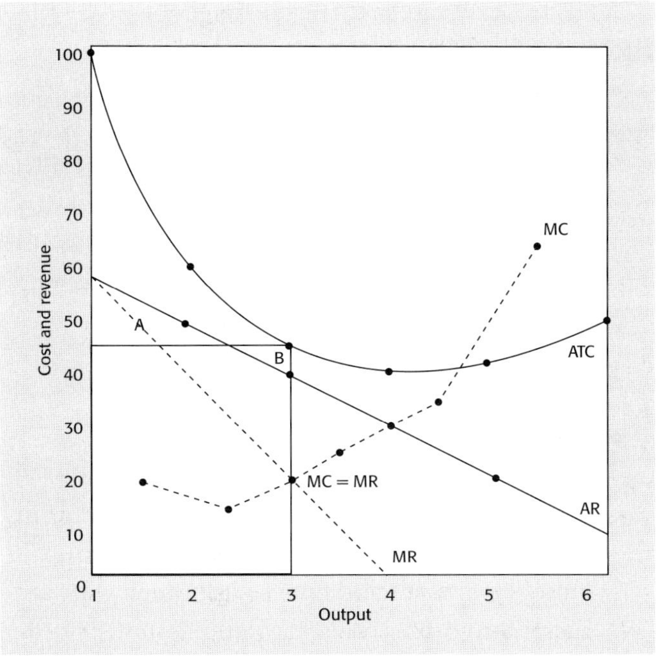

Figure 5.9 A price discriminating monopolist

It may be possible for a monopolist to use price discrimination to produce at a profit when competitive firms or a monopoly charging a single price could not cover costs. Figure 5.9 shows that at the single price profit maximisation output, the total revenue would be 3 × 40 = 120 and the total cost would be 3 × 45 = 135, giving a loss of 15. If the output was sold separately for what consumers would pay for each individual unit, the revenue would be 60 + 50 + 40 = 150, giving an abnormal profit of 15. The monopolist has effectively tapped into the consumer surplus and turned it into producer surplus or profit. If triangle A in the diagram is the same size as triangle B, which is the shortfall in cost, the firm will break even, but if it is larger then it makes abnormal profit. As long as the consumers are prepared to pay the higher price, there is no consumer exploitation. The competitive market price would generate losses and therefore there would be zero output in the long run. Price discrimination can only exist in particular circumstances and there are situations where it can be justified on economic grounds. If different groups of customers are being charged different prices because the cost of providing the service differs then it is quite acceptable. For example, at peak times of demand a firm might have to employ more staff. Price discrimination might in fact be used as a way of spreading out demand. This would account for out-of-season holiday tariffs and the lower price for off-peak telephone calls. Spreading out demand may improve efficiency, giving a further benefit to consumers. Price discrimination could be used to generate revenue on parts of a service, such as a rail network, so that the operator can cover losses on the least popular routes. Transport provides several examples of travellers being split into definite categories and charged different prices. There may be social motives for charging older people and children less than others. Consumer loyalty may be rewarded by discounts. The price of a journey may vary with the time of day or the day of the week.

If a firm wishes to split the market up into different segments and charge different prices, it must have a mechanism for keeping the markets separate. It must avoid the possibility of consumers buying in the cheaper part and the product being resold at a higher price. Price discrimination will only make economic sense if the market segments have different price elasticities of demand. The simple rule would be to charge higher prices where the demand is more price inelastic and lower prices where demand is price elastic.

Comparing monopoly with perfect competition

Figure 5.10 shows the equilibrium price and output of a monopoly charging a single price in a market free of government intervention and the situation that would occur in a perfectly competitive industry.

The classic case against monopoly is that its conduct and performance is undesirable when compared with that of firms in more competitive markets. The following observations can be made from the diagram comparing the equilibrium in both perfect competition and monopoly:

- the price in monopoly will be higher than it would be in perfect competition;
- the monopoly output is lower;
- the monopolist is making short- and long-run abnormal profits;
- the firm in perfect competition is productively efficient, producing the optimum output;
- it is also allocatively efficient, producing where price = MC;
- the monopolist captures consumer surplus and turns it into abnormal profit;

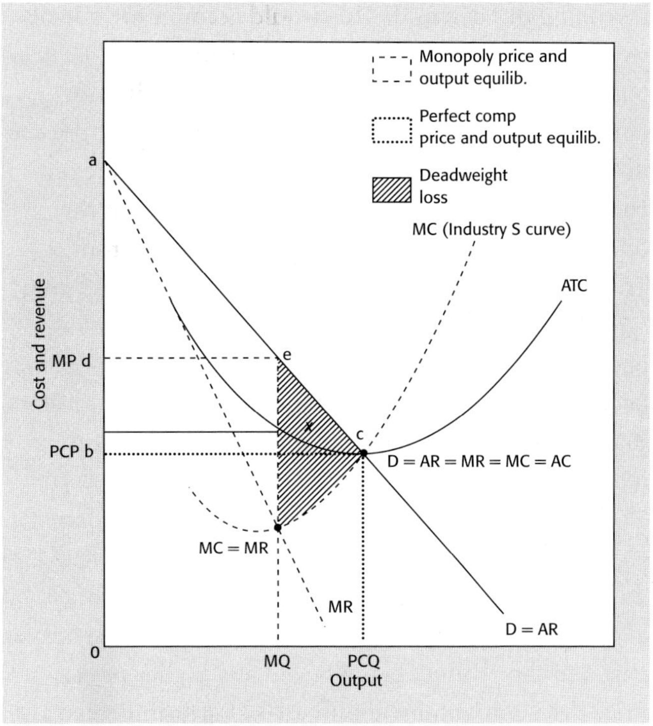

Figure 5.10 A comparison of a perfectly competitive industry with a profit-maximising monopolist

- the monopolist is productively inefficient, producing less than the optimum output in the search for extra profit;
- the price charged is well above marginal cost;
- if a perfectly competitive industry was turned into a monopoly there would be a welfare loss of area *x* in addition to greater allocative inefficiency.

The criticisms of real-world monopolies based on a comparison with perfect competition may not be valid because:

1 Perfect competition is a theoretical ideal. Monopoly must be compared with the real world models of monopolistic competition and oligopoly. These are also characterised by productive and allocative inefficiency. In addition they may involve a waste of resources in competitive advertising.
2 Figure 5.10 is drawn under the assumption that the costs in monopoly will be the same as in perfect competition. This ignores the possibility that the monopolist can achieve internal economies of scale which would reduce unit costs. It is possible that a monopolist could charge a lower price than would occur in perfect competition, making consumers better off, even though the monopolist is making abnormal profits.

A positive case can be made for monopoly in certain circumstances. These include:

- A monopolist cannot always make abnormal profit – it depends how high its costs are. There may be situations where the fixed costs are so high relative to the total cost that the market price can just cover the average costs. In this case the monopolist would only make normal profit. This is a case of natural monopoly, where it would make no economic sense to have the product supplied by competing firms.
- The concept of abnormal profit must be considered carefully. One of the criticisms of a competitive market is the uncertainty of profits in the long run. A monopolist however can plan future investment and finance it through what are guaranteed profits. This may offer customers better products and the workforce greater security.
- The investment may take the form of process innovation, implementing new techniques of production with the objective of lowering unit costs.
- Alternatively, the profit could be used to finance product innovation which will add to consumer welfare in the future, either through an improvement in the product's performance or through widening consumer choice.
- If the benefits of economies of scale and greater investment are passed on to consumers, it could be argued that they have gained from the existence of abnormal profit.

One of the criticisms raised against state-owned monopolies is that the absence of competition makes them become less efficient. The essence of the argument is that firms with a guaranteed market can be complacent. Monopolists are said to suffer from *x*-inefficiency, which means that their cost levels are higher than they would be in competitive firms because they do not have the incentive for process innovation. They become less dynamic, doing things in a particular way simply through tradition. In addition, some of their investment may take the form of erecting barriers to maintain the level of abnormal profit by excluding potential rivals. This will add to costs in the short run. This may be true but there is the possibility that these inefficiencies are outweighed by economies of scale which lower the unit costs.

It is clear that monopolies can operate in ways that lead to inefficiency or consumer exploitation. However,

Self-assessment tasks

Read the case study below and then tackle the exercises that follow.

Does OPEC have a monopoly in the supply of oil?

The Organisation of Petroleum Exporting Countries is a cartel set up in 1960 by five countries. The membership has now risen to 11. OPEC is responsible for 40% of the world production of crude oil and 14% of the world's natural gas. However, its exports of oil represent 60% of the oil that is traded internationally, and it has 77% of the world's proven oil reserves. Its declared objective was to secure fair and stable prices for producers, an efficient, economic and regular supply of oil to consuming nations and a fair return on capital for those investing in the oil industry. The cartel was in a very strong position. It had a geographic monopoly because the distribution of world oil deposits is uneven. The demand for oil has been rising on trend and has been an essential raw material with a low price elasticity of demand because of the lack of a close substitute. In this situation, any reduction in supply will increase the market price without much reduction in the volume traded. The revenue of the OPEC members will certainly increase. OPEC cut production in 1973/4 and 1979 in what have been described as oil crises. In the 1980s, oil prices fell because supply was greater than demand. The only thing that will weaken OPEC's economic power is if new suppliers outside of the cartel appear or consumers take action that will reduce consumption. Technology may provide alternatives to oil in the future. The monopoly will weaken further if there is disagreement over the target price or the production quotas allocated to each member country.

OPEC denies that it is acting as a single monopoly, cutting output in order to charge high prices to consumers and points out that western governments make more money from the tax on oil than the producing countries receive in revenues from selling the oil. At the retailing end of the industry, the supply is in the hands of an oligopoly of oil companies who deny that they are charging too much, insisting that the profit margin is low because of fierce competition. Profits are only high because of the large turnover. Some analysts predict that there will be further horizontal integration between oil companies that are already vertically integrated. The oil industry will continue to be dominated by a few big players mainly because of the high fixed cost and risks associated with exploration and drilling.

1. Is OPEC a monopoly or an example of collusive oligopoly? Justify your answer.
2. Explain the economic logic behind OPEC's decision to reduce output.
3. What factors may reduce the demand for OPEC oil over time?
4. How can the oil companies boost their profits if they have little control over the market price?

one can make a positive case for monopoly. This explains why the investigation of monopoly practices is difficult and each case must be judged on its own merits. It is dangerous to assume that monopoly is always harmful; the performance of a monopolist may be little different from that of firms in oligopoly.

Contestable markets

So far, in dealing with market structures, the models shown in figure 5.3 have been analysed. A **contestable market** is not listed here although it features prominently on the competition road map (figure 5.4). Why is this? The reason is that the concept of a contestable market does not fit neatly into the structure which has been developed by economists to study the conduct and performance of firms and the industry. By definition, a *perfectly* contestable market is one in which there are no costs of entry and exit. So, only perfect competition matches this ideal; monopolistic competition, with few relatively costless barriers to entry and exit, can match it to some extent, as can oligopoly in certain situations.

A contestable market is not so much a market structure as a means by which governments have sought to regulate industry and the provision of services. It has had particular significance in the UK since 1979, when the principle of contestability became central to the tremendous structural changes that have been made especially to the service sector of the economy.

The important features of a contestable market are:

- *Free entry.* This implies that new and existing market providers will have the same cost structure as in a perfectly competitive market.
- *The number and size of firms are irrelevant.* If a contestable market has only a few large firms, any cost differences should be a reflection of a decision by a particular firm to charge a given price.
- *Normal profits only can be earned in the long run.* If firms are making supernormal profits then this is the signal for others to enter the market. This could be on a 'hit and run' basis – a firm sees an opportunity, enters the market, collects the gains and leaves at no cost.
- *The threat of potential entrants into the market is over-riding.* Oligopolists and even a monopolist are obliged to offer consumers the benefits that they would receive in a more competitive market structure. Otherwise, new firms will enter from the pool of potential entrants.
- All firms are subject to the same regulations and government control irrespective of size.
- Mechanisms must be in place to prevent the use of unfair pricing by established firms to stop new entrants from entering the market.
- Cross-subsidisation is eliminated since firms cannot make normal profits if they sell any of their services below cost.

The application of contestability to the airline market is particularly interesting, since prior to deregulation routes were strictly regulated by governments and there was little competition. The 'open skies' policy of a deregulated market has led to lower fares and a greater choice of airline for passengers. This has particularly been the case in the US domestic market and in Europe, where new low-cost airlines such as easyJet and Ryanair have entered the market and challenged the established national carriers. A further outcome has been the response of these carriers to form alliances (see the case study).

There are other examples of contestable markets in the UK including:

- local bus services and rail services,
- the provision of public services such as electricity, gas and water supplies,
- telecommunications, particularly through the choice of network suppliers.

Self-assessment tasks

The following short answer questions have been set in recent CAPE examinations, 2003–2005.

1 (a) Define the term 'market structure'. (1 mark)

(b) List any TWO market structures and state ONE way in which they are different. (3 marks)

(c) In which market structure will you place gasoline stations in your country? (2 marks)

(Total 6 marks)

2 (a) Define the following terms:

- marginal cost, (2 marks)
- marginal revenue. (2 marks)

(b) 'Profit maximisation requires that the marginal cost of the firm MUST be equal to its marginal revenue.' Explain this statement. (2 marks)

(Total 6 marks)

3 (a) List TWO multinational corporations (MNCs) operating in any CARICOM member state. (2 marks)

(b) List TWO benefits which can be derived from the presence of multinational corporations in any CARICOM state. (2 marks)

(c) State ONE way in which the pricing practices of a multinational corporation can be disadvantageous to the country in which it is operating. (2 marks)

(Total 6 marks)

4 (a) Define the term 'normal profit'. (2 marks)

(b) How is EACH of the following calculated?

- ◆ The four-firm concentration ratio, (2 marks)
- ◆ The Herfindahl–Hirschman index. (2 marks)

(Total 6 marks)

5 (a) State TWO ways in which a firm in monopolistic competition differs from a monopolist. (4 marks)

(b) 'Monopolistic competition produces inefficiently even in the long run because it has excess capacity.' Explain this statement. (2 marks)

(Total 6 marks)

6 (a) What is the difference between price leadership in an oligopoly and a cartel arrangement? (4 marks)

(b) Give an example of a successful cartel arrangement and state why you think the example chosen is successful. (2 marks)

(Total 6 marks)

7 (a) How do oligopolists believe their competitors will respond to price rises and price reductions that result in a kinked demand curve? (4 marks)

(b) What do the beliefs explained in (a) above suggest about the elasticity of demand for the product? (2 marks)

(Total 6 marks)

Summary

In this chapter it has been shown that:

- Profit maximisation is the usual objective of firms in all market structures.
- Firms may earn normal profit or abnormal profit; the extent to which this is earned depends upon the particular market structure.
- Economists recognise different types of market structure, namely perfect competition, monopolistic competition, oligopoly and monopoly.
- The number of firms and the strength of barriers to entry are important considerations when assessing the extent to which real world market structures match the models used in Economics.
- Through government intervention, many markets are becoming increasingly contestable.
- Firms compete in various ways depending upon the market structure.
- Market structures can be compared in terms of their relative efficiency, output, profits and prices.

Key words

Definitions of Key words can be found in the Glossary.

abnormal profit
average revenue
cartel
concentration ratio
contestable market
firm
Herfindahl index
industry
marginal revenue
monopolistic competition
monopoly
natural monopoly
non-price competition
normal profit
oligopoly
perfect competition
price agreement
price discrimination
price leadership
profit maximisation
profits
sales maximisation
sales revenue maximisation
satisficing profits
total revenue

6 Market failure

This chapter covers unit 1, module 2, topic 2.
On completion of this chapter, you should be able to:

- explain the concept of economic efficiency with special emphasis on the Pareto efficiency criteria
- explain the concept of market failure with special emphasis on the efficiency criterion
- define and give examples of private goods, public goods and merit goods
- distinguish between social and private costs and social and private benefits
- explain the issues surrounding privatisation and deregulation
- explain the causes of market failure
- identify the pros and cons of government measures used to correct market failure

Efficiency in Economics

How might we judge whether any type of economic system (be it a market system or any other type of system) is 'doing a good job'? This is clearly a very important question. The answer to it might affect the whole way we would want to try to organise the running of an economy. The answer that economists give to the question is to say that an economic system is doing well to the extent that it is delivering **economic efficiency**.

Efficiency is a word often used in our society. It is usually seen as 'a good thing'. However, it is important to think what it actually means. It probably has a range of different meanings when it is used by different people in different contexts.

The best way of understanding the term 'efficiency' is to return to the key issues of Economics, as discussed in chapter 1. If Economics is a study of the use of scarce resources in order to meet our infinite wants, then efficiency is to do with using those scarce resources in the most effective way possible to meet the highest possible level of wants.

If resources are being used in this 'best' possible way, then economists are clear that this must imply that two different types of efficiency are being achieved, namely **productive efficiency** and **allocative efficiency**.

Productive efficiency

This type of efficiency is all to do with using the least possible amount of scarce resources to produce any particular product. To put it another way, it involves producing things at the lowest possible average cost.

Productive efficiency can be understood through figure 6.1, which shows a firm's or an industry's average cost schedules.

In this diagram, the point marked '*x*' indicates the point of productive efficiency. It is worth noting that productive efficiency can thus be seen as implying two things about the point of production by a firm or an industry. First, it implies that production takes place on the lowest possible cost curve. This means that the lowest possible cost techniques of production are being used. Secondly, it implies that production occurs at the lowest point on the lowest cost curve. Production at this point on an average cost curve is referred to as a point of 'technical efficiency'.

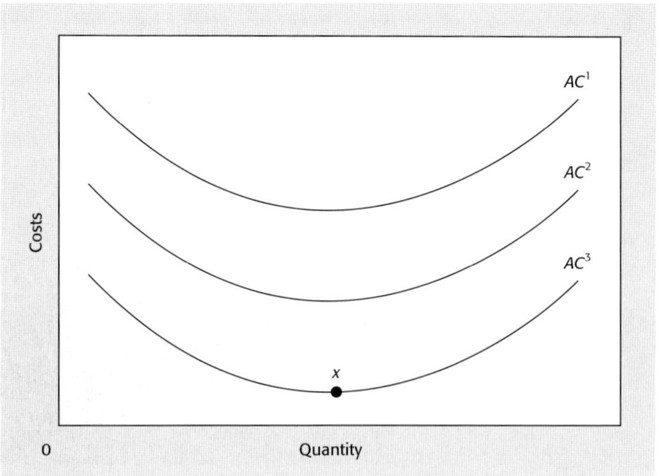

Figure 6.1 Productive efficiency

Allocative efficiency

To achieve full economic efficiency, it is not enough simply to produce goods and services at the lowest possible average cost. Even if it had been possible for the former command economies of Eastern Europe or for Cuba today to produce everything with full productive efficiency (which seems unlikely), it would be hard to argue that this represented efficiency in its full sense. Economies must not only produce things using the least possible resources, they must also make products that consumers most want. There would be little of merit in an economy that produced many products at very low cost that nobody particularly wanted and yielded little satisfaction.

Allocative efficiency is all to do with producing those products that are most wanted by consumers, given their cost of production. This can be seen from the following:

1 Two products, *x* and *y*, cost exactly the same amount to produce. However, product *x* gives consumers twice as much satisfaction as product *y*. If allocative efficiency is to exist, product *x* should be produced in preference to product *y*.
2 Two products, *a* and *b*, yield the same amount of consumer satisfaction. However, product *a* costs half as much to produce as product *b*. It would be allocatively efficient to produce product *a* in preference to product *b* in this situation.

Allocative efficiency can be thought of more precisely than this. It will exist when the selling price of a product is the same as the marginal cost of producing that product. In this situation, the price paid by the consumer will represent the true economic cost of producing the last unit of the product. This should ensure that precisely the right amount of the product is produced.

The idea that when price is equal to marginal cost there will be allocative efficiency (the right amount of the product made) is best understood through a simple example:

Quantity	1	2	3	4	5	6	7
Price ($)	5	5	5	5	5	5	5
Marginal cost ($)	2	3	4	5	6	7	8

Rotting flats in Havana – hardly the result of an efficient economic system

Self-assessment tasks

Read the article below and then tackle the exercises that follow.

Breaking the Logjam

Increasing demand for timber is a major threat to forests worldwide. Only one-fifth of the world's original forest cover is intact today. Yet United Nations data show that global wood consumption increased by 40 per cent between 1970 and 1996, and continues to grow.

Inhabitants of the US, Japan, and Western Europe consume on average about ten times as much per person as the average citizen of a developing country, even accounting for the fact that many more of the latter use wood for fuel.

There are now suggestions for consideration at the World Trade Organisation (WTO) that global trade in wood products should be further promoted. A new report by the World Resources Institute and the Centre for International Environmental Law concludes that these proposals could put yet more pressure on forests in Amazonia, the Congo Basin, South-East Asia, and the northern Boreal region. These forests are the home to most of the world's terrestrial biological diversity, and to hundreds of unique, traditional cultures.

The wealthy nations leading the charge for the timber trade – including the US, Canada, New Zealand and Indonesia – have paid scant attention to the potential negative environmental and social side effects of their actions. Perhaps this is because large, powerful forest products companies in these countries stand to benefit directly from the plan.

Source: Nigel Sizer, *The Guardian*, 1 December 1999 (adapted).

1 Explain why economic efficiency is a fundamental economic concept.

2 Consider the ways in which, according to the article, there would not be economic efficiency if the world timber trade were to be allowed to expand.

For this product, an output of one unit would not be allocatively efficient. Here, the cost of producing the product is less than the value put on it by the consumer (as represented by the price that the consumer is prepared to pay for that product). The product should clearly be produced, but there is scope for further worthwhile production from this point. This is also true when two or three units of the product are made. On the other hand, an output of seven units should not be produced. Here, the 7th unit costs $8 to produce, but is only valued at $5 by the consumer. The same problem exists with output levels of 5 and 6. Thus, there is only one ideal output level (that is, one output level that will yield allocative efficiency) and that is an output of 4 units where price is equal to marginal cost.

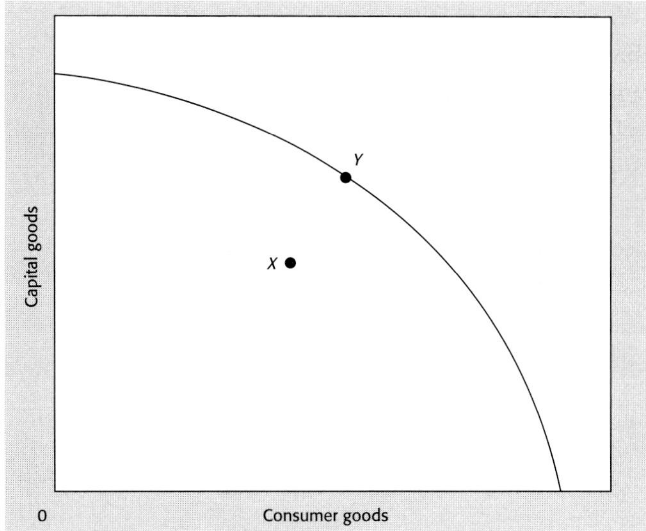

Figure 6.2 Productive efficiency in an economy

Pareto efficiency

A related way of defining economic efficiency is in terms of what economists call **Pareto efficiency** (named after an Italian economist, Wilfredo Pareto, who suggested the idea at the beginning of the twentieth century). This is said to exist when it is not possible to make any one person in society better off without making someone else worse off. If this situation exists, then there will be productive efficiency as nothing more could be produced with the resources available (and thus there is no possibility of any overall extra production). It also implies that allocative efficiency exists, because, if it does not, then it may be possible to swap production in such a way that consumers can be made better off (without necessarily having to make any others worse off).

Efficiency and the production possibility frontier

One way to illustrate the concept of economic efficiency is to think in terms of the production possibility frontier. This is illustrated in figure 6.2.

Point *y* on the diagram can be considered to be productively efficient. At this point, nothing more can be produced in total than is currently being produced. This is not true about point *x* where it is possible to increase production as some resources remain unused. Equally, point *y* can be considered to be a possible point of Pareto efficiency as it is only possible to increase the production of one product by reducing the production of another (and hence potentially making someone worse off). This is not true about point *x* from where it is possible to increase the production of either or both products without sacrificing any other production. It is only possible to establish whether point *y* (or any other point on the frontier itself) is allocatively efficient by knowing consumer preferences. This information about consumer demand is not given by the production possibility frontier alone, and thus we cannot say for sure whether this point represents the point at which the combination of products that are being produced is that which satisfies the maximum amount of wants (or gives the highest possible level of consumer satisfaction).

Competition and efficiency

It is often suggested by economists that efficiency, as defined above, will exist in a fully competitive market (specifically, a perfectly competitive market). This is seen as the crucial argument in favour of competition. It is why competition is seen as 'a good thing'.

A competitive market could lead to productive efficiency as it provides firms with the incentive to produce things at the lowest possible cost. If a firm can produce at a lower average cost than its competitors, then it will be able to gain increased profits as a product sold at the same price now yields a higher profit. A failure to keep costs as low as possible will lead to the firm going out of business if other firms do keep costs low and thus charge lower prices.

Referring specifically to perfect competition, the perfectly competitive firm will always produce at a point of technical efficiency in long-run equilibrium as it will produce at the lowest point on its average cost curve (see previous topic).

Competitive markets could also force allocative efficiency upon an economy. If firms wish to make maximum profit, then they will only succeed in doing so by producing those products that are most demanded by consumers. Equally, the threat of bankruptcy will force firms to produce only those products that are clearly in demand as a failure to do so will result in losses being made.

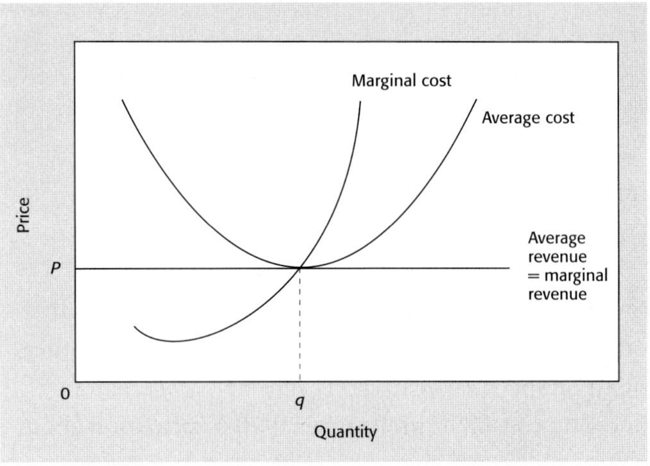

Figure 6.3 Productive efficiency and perfect competition

In perfect competition, it can be noted that the specific requirement for allocative efficiency, that the selling price is equal to the marginal cost of production, is always true. This can be seen in figure 6.3. As profit is maximised where marginal cost is equal to marginal revenue and marginal revenue is equal to average revenue (or price) in perfect competition, then it follows that price will be equal to marginal cost.

A free and competitive market can also be seen as leading to Pareto efficiency. The key to understanding this is to recognise that people will only trade with each other if they believe that trading is mutually beneficial. No one will trade with someone else unless they believe that they will benefit from that trade. If this is true, then it can be concluded that in a totally free market all trades that are advantageous to both people involved will occur, but no trades in excess of this will take place. In other words, Pareto efficiency will exist. It will not be possible to improve on the situation described by making someone better off without making someone else worse off. The free market automatically leads to Pareto efficiency.

Self-assessment tasks

Read the case study below and then tackle the exercises that follow.

Understanding the Caribbean hot pepper market

The hot pepper is a Caribbean crop that has universal appeal in the region and is exported in various forms to other markets worldwide. The Caribbean hot peppers are well known and highly regarded for their pungency and delicate flavours. The crop is sold to consumers in many forms, for example fresh hot peppers, hot pepper mash, hot pepper sauces and in ground or extract form. Within CARICOM, total production in 2001 was almost 16,000 tonnes and this was worth almost US$18m. Every CARICOM country had some production - Jamaica and Trinidad though produced around 80% of the total crop.

The average yield in Jamaica was 15 tonnes per hectare as against 20 tonnes per hectare in Trinidad. These yields are considerably lower than those in other hot pepper-growing countries. Production in the Caribbean is not very cost competitive and this is a further problem. CARICOM's main competition is from Costa Rica, where the industry is well organised and receives government support. Nicaragua is another competitor, mainly because of its cheaper labour costs. The industry in the Caribbean supports many farmers and their families - it is vital that it survives.

Source : V. Stewart, Caribbean Agribusiness Marketing Intelligence and Development Network.

1 What is productive efficiency and what are the conditions that are necessary for it to exist?
2 Draw a production possibility diagram that shows how hot pepper production in Jamaica is inefficient compared to that in Trinidad.
3 Draw a diagram to show how in theory the average cost of production in CARICOM compares with that in Costa Rica and Nicaragua.
4 Suggest ways in which CARICOM hot pepper production might become more productively efficient.

Meaning of market failure

It is stating the obvious to say that market failure exists when markets fail. However, the question needs to be asked: 'Fail at what?' The answer is: 'Fail at delivering economic efficiency.' Market failure exists any and every time that a free market, left to its own devices and totally free from any form of government intervention, fails to lead to the best, or optimum, use of scarce resources. Using earlier terminology, it is when the interaction of supply and demand in a market does not lead to productive and/or allocative efficiency. There are though reasons why this may not be the case.

Specifically, look at the following different reasons why markets fail:

- the existence of externalities;
- merit and de-merit goods;
- public and quasi-public goods;
- the concentration of power in markets, particularly a monopoly;
- concerns about distribution and equity;
- information failure;
- adverse selection or moral hazard.

Externalities (negative and positive)

Defining an externality

If the market system is to work well and lead to economic efficiency, it is important that those people who make economic decisions are those who are affected by those decisions. A transaction between a supplier and a consumer for a product needs only to affect the supplier and consumer involved. As long as this is the case, then both sides will act only so long as both feel that they will benefit from any action – all is well in the market. However, a problem could clearly arise if someone else not party to the economic decision is affected by that decision. This is the economic concept known as an **externality**.

An externality is said to arise if a third party (someone not directly involved) is affected by the decisions and actions of others. If you decide to play your radio in public, then others (third parties) not involved in making that decision are affected by the assault on their ear drums.

Private and social costs

Another way of understanding the same concept is to define an externality as any divergence between private and social costs or benefits. The **social costs** of any action are all of the related costs associated with that action. The **private costs** are those costs involved in an action that accrue to the decision maker.

Negative externalities

It is quite possible that these private and social costs are the same: all of the costs of an action accrue to the decision maker and there are no further costs. If this is the case, then there are no externalities. However, it is possible that there will be a difference; private and social costs may not be equal to each other. For example, if you make a decision to take a journey by car, you consider the costs of the petrol and the time taken. However, you do not consider the further costs that you may be imposing on others in terms of your contribution to road congestion, to atmospheric pollution and to possible car accidents. In this situation, a negative externality exists, the cost of which is called an **external cost**. The situation is illustrated in figure 6.4. Here, private costs are part of the total social costs involved in a decision. However, they do not represent all of the social costs. The difference between the two is the **negative externality**.

Private and social benefits

A similar situation can also exist with benefits rather than costs. The **social benefits** of a decision are all of

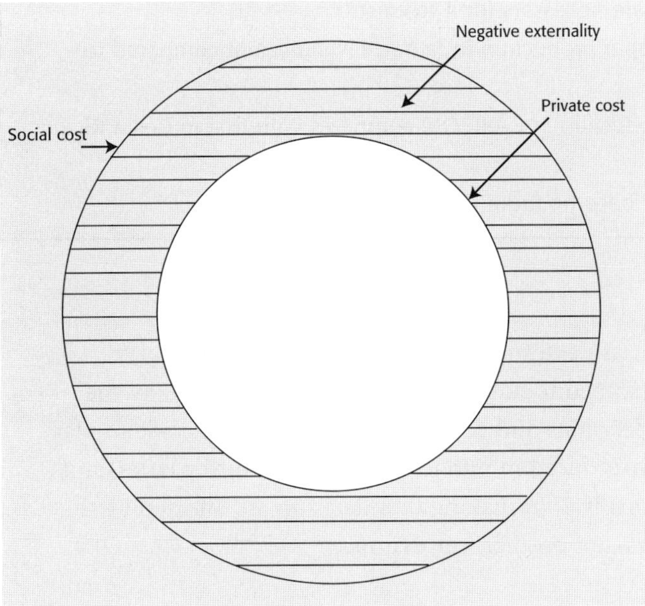

Figure 6.4 A difference between private and social costs: negative externalities

the benefits that accrue from that decision. The private benefits are those that accrue solely to the decision maker. Again, these may or may not be the same.

Positive externalities

It is possible that the social benefits of a decision may exceed the private benefits. If this is the case, then a positive externality, or **external benefit**, is said to exist. For example, if you make a decision to go to the doctor to be inoculated against a particular disease, then clearly you receive the private benefit of not catching the particular disease against which you have been inoculated. However, you may not be the only one to benefit. The fact that you do not get the disease has some possible benefit to all others with whom you come into contact, who will not now catch the disease from you.

The problem created by externalities

The essence of the problem created by externalities is that they will lead to an inappropriate amount of the product involved being produced: the free market will lead either to too much or too little production.

Consider a firm that produces a chemical. There are costs that the firm will have to meet in producing a certain quantity of this chemical. These would include such things as:

Thousands of dead fish in a polluted river – a classic case of negative externality

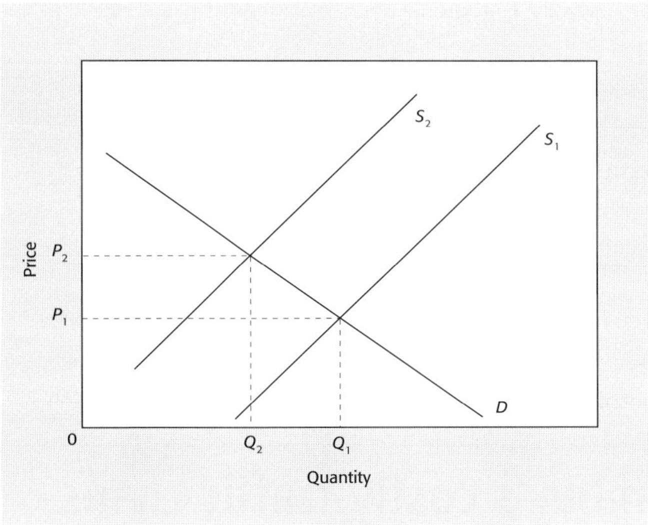

Figure 6.5 Over-production caused by a negative externality

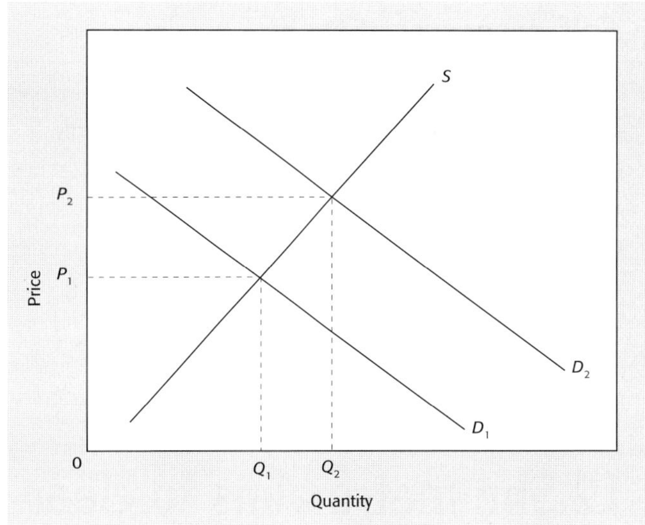

Figure 6.6 Under-production caused by a positive externality

- raw material costs,
- labour costs,
- energy costs.

All such costs would be termed private costs: they have to be paid for by the decision maker (the firm). These costs form part of social costs. However, there are further costs likely to be involved as well. These might include any dumping of chemical waste, perhaps in a local river, which creates clean-up costs, any atmospheric pollution that creates clean-up costs and ill health, and possible road congestion that results from the transportation of the chemicals. These are negative externalities. The problem is that only the private costs of producing the chemical will be taken into account by the firm when making the pricing decision about its chemical. The further external costs, which are real costs to society, will not be taken into account. This will mean that the price will be lower than if all social costs were taken into account. This means that demand and production will be higher than if full social costs had been considered. Thus, a negative externality will lead to too much of a product being produced. The situation can be seen in figure 6.5.

The price that will occur in the market will be P_1 where the supply schedule that takes account of the private costs, S_1, is equal to demand. This price is associated with production of Q_1. However, if the supply schedule took into account all of the social costs, S_2, which are greater than just the private costs, then this would result in a price of P_2. This price is associated with a lower production of Q_2. Thus, the negative externality has led to Q_1–Q_2 too much production. Too many scarce resources are being devoted to the production of this product. The market has failed.

The opposite problem is true of a positive externality. Here, the problem is that too little of the product will be produced. If only the private benefits, and not the full social benefits, are considered, then there will be under-production. This is illustrated in figure 6.6.

This time, the problem is with demand. If only the private benefits are registered, then demand is represented by the demand schedule D_1. This leads to a price of P_1 and an associated production of Q_1. However, if the further extra benefits to society were registered (which they will not be by the private decision maker involved), then demand would be greater at D_2. This would lead to a price of P_2 and a production of Q_2. Thus there is an under-production of Q_1–Q_2 associated with the positive externality. Insufficient scarce resources are being devoted to the production of this good or service. The market has failed.

We must, therefore, suggest that externalities are likely to be a source of market failure as they will mean that resources are not allocated in the ideal way: too few or too many resources are likely to be directed to the production of certain products.

Self-assessment tasks

1 Identify and explain whether each of the following involves a positive or a negative externality:

- a next-door neighbour playing his/her music loudly,
- a person being educated beyond the compulsory school leaving age,
- the dropping of litter,
- smoking in a public place,
- a new, well-designed and pleasant public building,
- the use of pesticides in agricultural production.

2 Read the following short case study and then tackle the exercises that follow.

£2.5bn metro aims to clear Bombay's costly traffic chaos

India announced a £2.5 billion metro scheme yesterday to tackle the congestion crisis in its chaotic commercial capital, Bombay.

The city has a rapidly expanding population of more than 20 million inhabitants, half of whom live in slums, and the United Nations rates it as among the world's most seriously failing metropolises.

International businessmen arriving in Bombay to take advantage of the Indian economic boom find a decrepit airport and roads so congested that it can take up to two hours to reach the city centre.

Laying the foundation stone of the project yesterday, Dr Manmohan Singh, the prime minister, said the metro was part of a £6.5 billion five-year plan to improve the infrastructure of major cities. "We have to invest in public transport", he said. "Our cities have to become more liveable and more people-friendly."

In its present state, Bombay, which like Manhattan is crammed on to an island, is one of the least people-friendly places on Earth, with sky-high property prices driving people to live in stinking, unregulated slums.

Its failings were cruelly exposed last year when monsoon floods effectively closed the city for a week, overwhelming sewers and storm drains, causing buildings to collapse and shutting the airport for 48 hours.

The three-phase metro project – a public-private venture whose partners include the French rail company Connex – promises 90 miles of railway built on elevated tracks that will criss-cross the city, cutting journey times by as much as two thirds. Construction work on the first seven-mile stretch, costing £300 million, is due to begin in October and be completed by 2011. The second and third phases are due for completion by 2016 and 2021.

Travelling in the metro will be cheap even by Indian standards. Planned fares range from six to 10 rupees (seven to 12 pence) to tempt people out of their cars and rickshaws.

At present, residents commute to work on a network of elderly trains that become so overcrowded that many people ride hanging dangerously from doors and windows. On average, seven people a day die in railway accidents.

Commuters will be hoping that the builders of the mass-transit system can match those of New Delhi's metro that has remained on schedule and within budget.

But doubts have already been raised about whether the building consortium will be able to buy enough land to push the project through such an extraordinary congested and over-built city.

Much-vaunted plans to turn Bombay into India's Shanghai had to be put on hold last year after slum-dwellers resisted the demolition of their homes to make way for new roads, shopping centres and residential complexes.

India's democratic politicians, unlike their autocratic Chinese communist counterparts, are not free to ignore the voices of the many millions of poor and dispossessed, as they rely on their votes for re-election.

Source: Peter Foster, *Daily Telegraph*, 23 June 2006.

(a) Using evidence from the case study, identify:

- the private costs and external costs of traffic congestion in Bombay (Mumbai),
- the private benefits and external benefits that might apply following the opening of Bombay's proposed metro system.

(b) Discuss the problems faced by the government in implementing the metro proposals.

Merit goods, de-merit goods and information failures

Another way in which markets may fail is due to the existence of what are termed **merit goods** and **de-merit goods**.

Sometimes, merit and de-merit goods are simply seen as an extension of the idea of externalities as discussed above. A merit good may be described as a good that has positive externalities associated with it. Thus, an inoculation might be seen as a merit good as others who will not catch the disease from the inoculated person also benefit. A de-merit good is seen as any product that has negative externalities associated with it. Thus, cigarettes can be seen as a de-merit good, insofar as secondary smoking can be viewed as a possible cause of ill health (a clear negative externality). If this is all there is to merit and de-merit goods, then they cannot be seen as a separate category of market failure from externalities.

However, merit and de-merit goods can (and indeed should) be defined in a different way, which makes them different from externalities. The essence of merit and de-merit goods in this definition is to do with an **information failure** to the consumer. Consumers do not perceive, it is suggested, quite how good or bad a particular product is for them: either they do not have the right information or they simply lack some relevant information.

The smoke from an expensive Havana cigar may not be to everyone's liking – a case of negative externality

Merit goods

With this idea of a failure of information, a merit good is defined as a good that is better for a person than the person who may consume the good realises. Under this definition, education is often defined as a merit good. The individuals who make decisions about how much education to receive (or how much to allow their children to receive) do not fully appreciate quite how much benefit will be received through being well educated. We do not appreciate how good education is for us. We do not perceive its full benefits at the time of making the decision about how much education to receive.

De-merit goods

De-merit goods, on the other hand, are those products that are worse for the individual consumer than the individual realises. Cigarettes are taken to be a good example here. It is suggested that when a person makes a decision to smoke a cigarette, he or she is not fully in possession of the information concerning the harmful effects of smoking. If he or she were in possession of such information, then there would be a greater reluctance to smoke.

It is interesting to note that the example of a de-merit good given here, namely smoking, is the same as the example of a product that can be seen as having negative externalities associated with it. However, the reason for identifying the product is different. Here, it is not due to the damage done to others that the issue arises, but rather due to the unperceived damage done to the person through consuming the product.

Merit goods, de-merit goods and value judgements

It may have been noticed in the above definitions that a significant question poses itself with regard to merit and de-merit goods. Who is to say what is 'good' or 'bad' for a person? If an individual consumer makes a presumably rational, decision to consume a product, what right has the rest of society to say that he or she is making a 'wrong' decision. It seems clear that if this is what is going on, we have entered the area of **value judgements** and thus normative economics. If society is able to say to consumers that they do not fully realise what is good or bad for them, then we are accepting that 'society knows best' and has some right to make such a judgement. In effect we are allowing **paternalism** to be a legitimate part of Economics. It is acceptable for us to say that society can judge what is, or is not, good for a person, regardless of what that person believes. In this area, then, we may have gone beyond our allegedly 'value-free' positive Economics that was introduced in the first module of this unit.

The problems caused by merit and de-merit goods

Why, then, might merit and de-merit goods be identified as a failure of the market? The problem is that their existence will cause an inappropriate amount of the products concerned to be produced.

Merit goods will be under-produced in a free market situation. Insufficient scarce resources will be devoted to their production. The problem is that the lack of information about how good the product is for individuals will result in insufficient demand being registered for the product in the market. This is illustrated in figure 6.7. Here, the 'correct' level of demand, if consumers appreciated the true value of the product to themselves, would be D_1. This would lead to a market price of P_1 where D_1 is equal to the supply of product, S. This price would be associated with a level of production and consumption of Q_1, the ideal quantity of the good. However, because consumers undervalue the product, demand is only registered as D_2. This leads to a market price of P_2 (where D_2 is equal to supply, S), which is associated with production and consumption of Q_2. This is below the optimum level. The market has failed.

Figure 6.8 illustrates the problem of a de-merit good. Here, the 'correct' demand should be at D_1, which will lead to a price of P_1 and a production and consumption of Q_1. As consumers overvalue the product, demand is registered at the higher level of D_2. This leads to a market price of P_2 and production and consumption of Q_2. The market has failed: too many scarce resources are devoted to the production of this de-merit good.

Adverse selection or moral hazard

There are numerous other examples of market failure arising from information failure. In welfare Economics two types of situation can be recognised. These are what are known as **adverse selection** and **moral hazard**.

Adverse selection can best be explained in the context of the health care market. Why does anyone go to a doctor? The most usual reason is because we are not sure how to deal with a health problem, whether this be something trivial like a sore throat or something more serious. We visit the doctor to get information – in doing this we recognise that the doctor is better informed than we are and that the whole point about making this visit is to accept the advice that is given. Adverse selection therefore is when some person in the market (in this case the doctor) is better informed than those seeking advice. If though the advice is wrong, we shall have made an undesirable choice of treatment.

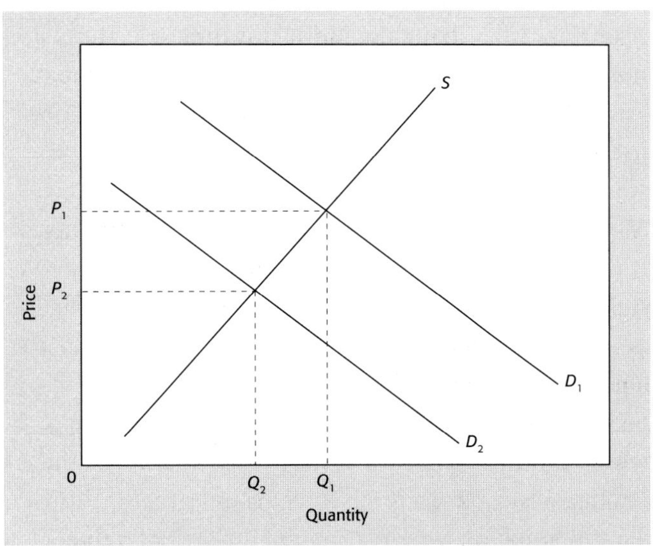

Figure 6.7 The under-provision of a merit good by the market

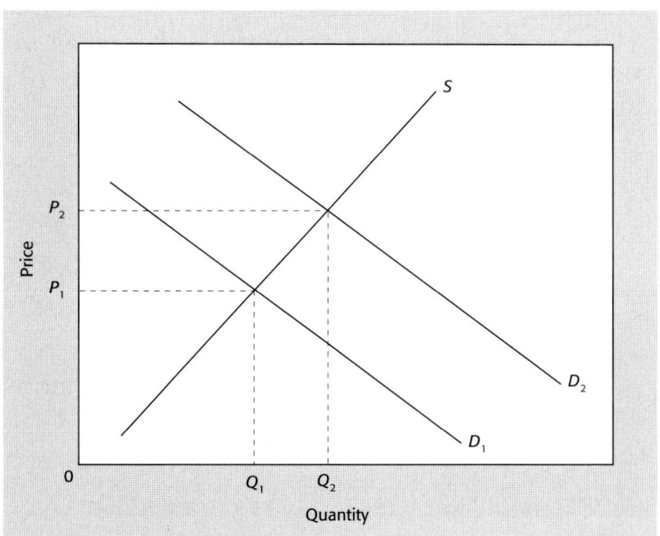

Figure 6.8 The over-provision of a de-merit good by the market

This will be a misallocation of resources and, hence, market failure.

Moral hazard is rather different. In this case, the information failure is reversed in so far as information may well be withheld or be inaccurate when it comes from say someone requiring health insurance. This puts the insurer in a position where not all the necessary information has been provided for risk to be established. If this happens, then the cost of the health premium will be too low. If this person then requires treatment for an undisclosed problem, the premiums for healthy people will have to rise. In the worst case, if premiums become too expensive, healthy people may no longer seek health insurance as it has become too expensive. This is not good news for the insurer who could be left only with 'bad risk' customers. It might even lead to the collapse of the market through the enforced withdrawal of insurers. Again, there is a misallocation of resources and hence, market failure.

Self-assessment task

Discuss whether each of the following is a merit or a de-merit good:

- compulsory secondary education,
- wearing a seat belt,
- consuming excessive amounts of alcohol,
- visiting a museum,
- playing loud music and shouting at a cricket match.

Public goods

A different type of good from a merit or de-merit that may cause the market to fail is referred to as a **public good**. Here, it is not a matter of too much or little provision of the good in question, but rather whether the product will be provided at all.

There are two specific characteristics that a good must possess if it is to be classified as a public good:

1. It must be **non-excludable**. This means that once the good has been provided for one consumer, it is impossible to stop other consumers from benefiting from the good.
2. It must be **non-rival**. As more and more people consume the product, the benefit to those already consuming the product is not diminished.

Once one begins to think about these characteristics, there are a number of goods that can be seen as public goods. Take the example of a lighthouse. Once a lighthouse is built to warn one ship at sea away from a dangerous area of rocks, then, by its very nature, this service will automatically be provided to all ships that sail within a certain distance of the lighthouse. It is non-excludable. Equally, the fact that other ships see the light given by the lighthouse and are warned away from the dangerous rocks does not reduce the benefit that any one particular ship receives from that warning. It is non-rival.

Quasi-public goods

While there may be some goods that can clearly be defined as 'public' in nature, there are others that have some of the nature of such goods without possessing fully the two required attributes mentioned above. Such goods are referred to as **quasi-public goods**. They are like public goods without truly being public goods.

In practice, it is not possible to classify all products as being either 'public' or 'private' (private goods being goods that are excludable and rival: others can be excluded from their consumption and as more people start to consume the good, those already consuming it have their satisfaction reduced). Many products lie somewhere in between these two extremes. A good that is closer to a public good than to a private good, but is not fully a public good, is called a quasi-public good.

A good example might be a sandy seaside beach. Such a beach is available to all those who wish to use it. It appears non-excludable. However, it is possible to conceive of ways of excluding consumers. Privately owned beaches have techniques of doing this. Equally, the beach is non-rival up to a point. If you are the first person on this pleasant beach on a warm sunny day, it does very little to diminish your enjoyment of that beach as a few more people arrive to enjoy the benefits themselves. However, there may well come a point at which that is no longer the case. As the beach becomes crowded, space limited and other people's conversations and music become ever more audible, enjoyment may perceptibly reduce. Thus the beach has something of the characteristic of non-rivalry, but not the full characteristic. It is a quasi-public good.

A beach is available to all those who wish to use it. Cubans enjoying a weekend swim in Santiago Bay

The problem caused by public goods

The problem that may be caused in a free market by the existence of public goods is a serious one: the market may fail to produce them at all. There may be a consumer demand for such products (consumers are willing and able, in principle, to pay for the product's services), but the free market may not have a mechanism for guaranteeing their production.

This problem is referred to as the **free rider** issue. Consumers attempt to gain a 'free ride' on the back of other consumers' purchases of the public good. It is entirely reasonable that they may attempt to do this. One of the key characteristics of public goods is that they are non-excludable. This implies that once one consumer has purchased the product, all other consumers cannot be prevented from benefiting from that product. Take the example of the lighthouse. Once one particular fisherman has provided a lighthouse close to some dangerous rocks for his benefit, then all other fishermen in the area will benefit equally from the lighthouse. Their advantage, however, is that they do not have to pay for this lighthouse: they have received a free ride on the back of someone else's purchase. The logical thing to do, then, would seem to be for all fishermen to sit back and to wait for one fisherman to be foolish enough to provide a lighthouse so that those not purchasing can benefit without paying. Unfortunately, the implication of this is that the lighthouse is never provided: everyone waits for everyone else to provide it, and nothing happens.

It could be argued that a more likely scenario to the one described above is that all fishermen in an area might agree to club together in order to make the purchase and thus the lighthouse would be provided. However, there is still a problem here as it is in the interest of any one fisherman to conceal his desire for the lighthouse, refuse to pay but still to gain the final benefit once it is provided. Again, if all fishermen behave thus, the lighthouse is not provided.

The existence of public goods may thus mean that scarce resources are not used in a way that would be desirable. People may wish for the provision of such goods (they yield utility), but the demand may never be registered in the market.

Self-assessment task

Explain whether each of the following may be described as a private, a public or a quasi-public good:

- the local police service,
- a chocolate bar,
- a public park,
- a firework display,
- a stretch of road,
- street lighting,
- a birth for a cruise ship.

Monopoly and the concentration of power in markets

Competition and markets

For markets to work well, it is generally accepted in Economics that there must be a high level of competition. To work as well as is possible, the competition needs to be as great as is possible. Economists refer to this very high level of competition as 'perfect competition' (see previous chapter).

There are good reasons for believing that a high level of competition will mean that markets work well. Some of the following are important:

- If there is a high level of competition between firms, then it is likely that these firms will produce exactly what consumers most want. There will be consumer sovereignty. Any firm that does not produce what consumers want will find itself out of business very quickly as there will always be plenty of other firms managing to produce what is most wanted.
- A high level of competition will mean that firms will produce products efficiently at the lowest possible cost. The least possible scarce resources will be used to produce the products that consumers most want. Any firm that fails to do this will be in great difficulty as other competitors will have lower costs and be able to charge lower prices for the same product.
- A competitive market will mean that firms have to charge a price to the consumer that is not much, if at all, above the cost of production. Any firm charging too high a price will soon lose out to others charging a price closer to the true production cost. Thus, when consumers buy a product, they pay a price that represents how much that product truly cost to produce in terms of scarce resources.

The problem is that in very many markets, nothing close to a high level of competition exists. This causes markets to fail.

Lack of competition and markets

There are two very valid reasons to expect many markets in developed economies not to be highly competitive:

1. The existence of economies of scale. Economies of scale imply that the larger a firm becomes, the lower the average cost of producing any particular product is likely to become. In many industries, there are considerable economies of scale available and thus firms have to become very large to benefit fully from them. In some cases, this could mean that there is room for very few or even just one firm (a monopoly) to exist in any particular industry.
2. The profit motive. As previously stated, the dominant motivation of firms is seen as being to make maximum profits. Perhaps the most effective way that profit can be made by a firm is either to get rid of all competitors or to enter into agreements with those competitors. In either case, competition ceases to exist.

The implication of these two important forces in markets is that there is often a concentration of power in many markets that means that the benefits of competition mentioned earlier are reversed:

1. Firms may not produce what consumers most want. Given the control that firms have in a market, firms may not have to produce those things that are most desired by consumers. Consumers cannot easily turn to an alternative. Thus, infinite wants may not be as fully satisfied as in a competitive situation. The market has failed.
2. Firms do not have to produce goods and services at the lowest possible cost. There is no constraint from competitors forcing firms to minimise their costs of production. Thus, firms may 'take it easy' and use more scarce resources for production than is necessary (economists refer to this as '***x***'-**inefficiency**). The market fails.

3 Firms are able to charge a price that is higher than the cost of production. With no competitors, a firm does not have to worry that consumers will turn elsewhere if price rises above costs. In this case, the price paid by the consumer is higher than the cost of production in terms of scarce resources and the demand for the product will be lower than it should be. There will be an under-production of the product. The market has failed.

Self-assessment task

Explain why each of the following situations may well arise in a market that is dominated by one or by just a few firms:

- a poor quality product,
- unnecessarily large expenditure on management perks,
- consumer dissatisfaction,
- a selling price well in excess of the cost of producing a product.

Government intervention

You have only to glance at a newspaper or listen to the news or a political debate for a few minutes to realise that one of the more controversial areas of Economics is concerned with the extent and reasons for government intervention in markets. All governments in the world intervene to a greater or lesser extent and the reasons for intervention vary enormously between them. However, the justification for intervention is usually given under two broad headings:

market failure and the desire to achieve a *fair or equitable distribution of resources* in economy.

The first intervention occurs when markets do not allocate resources efficiently and the second is concerned with ensuring that all members of society have fair access to goods and services. The role of the government is to intervene in markets that are not seen to be allocating resources in the most efficient or the most equitable manner. When governments attempt to achieve this aim it must be recognised that there is also the possibility that they will fail and create rather than remove distortions.

Methods of government intervention

Government policy and methods of intervention can be summarised under four broad headings: regulation, financial intervention, production and transfer payments. The method chosen will depend to a large extent on whether the reason for intervention is concerned with market failure or with the desire to achieve equity.

Regulation

The government uses a large number of methods of **regulation** as a means of controlling a market. Legal and other methods are used to control the quality and quantity of goods and services that are produced and consumed. For example, the government may regulate the sale of certain drugs by making them only available on prescription from a qualified doctor. Hygiene laws set standards for the production of foods. There may be *controls* on shop opening hours or the setting of a minimum age at which a person can buy certain products, such as alcohol, cigarettes and lottery tickets. Other forms of regulation may include the requirement for an individual to purchase an insurance policy before being legally permitted to drive a car, the age at which people are required to attend school and the payment of social insurance contributions.

Regulation may not only apply to the quantity and quality of goods and services sold but may also refer to prices. Examples of price controls include minimum wage legislation, maximum price and rent controls.

Financial intervention

Financial tools, such as **taxes** and **subsidies**, are also frequently used by governments to influence production, prices of commodities, incomes or the distribution of wealth in an economy. Price subsidies may vary. They might be in the form of a partial subsidy, as in the case of public transport, or total, as in the case of free eye tests for children in full-time education.

Tax instruments may also vary. In Jamaica, for example, the main indirect tax is the General Consumption Tax (GCT) which has a standard rate of 15 per cent. A higher rate of 20 per cent applies to telephone calls whilst essential items like foodstuffs and school uniforms are zero-rated or exempt. Additionally, there is a 25 per cent income tax rate for higher income earners, after direct taxes on bauxite producers and additional duties on tobacco products and alcohol and motor vehicles.

Governments also provide the finance that is needed to produce a good or service. It is very important to note at this early stage that just because the government provides the finance for a product, it does not necessarily mean it has to produce the product too. For example, the government could finance education but all schools, colleges and universities could be privately owned and run. Health care may be provided free (financial intervention) but the drugs used in prevention and cure of illness could be privately produced.

State production

In addition to providing the finance it is also possible for a government to take over the production of a good or service, either in whole or in part. State-owned industries are often referred to as **nationalised industries.** In the case of Guyana's bauxite industry, Demerara Baux, a subsidiary of the Canadian Alean Aluminium Ltd, was forcibly nationalised in 1971. Shortly afterwards, the government of Jamaica signed an agreement giving it a 51 per cent interest in the Kaiser Bauxite Company. These nationalisations were for strategic reasons, given the fundamental economic significance of these industries. Public utilities such as gas and electricity and public transport services are often state owned. This is not the case in the UK, where there has been a major shift towards privatisation (see below). It is also very common to find some goods and services being produced by both the state and the private sectors. Education and health care are particularly good examples of these types of service industries. NHS hospitals function alongside private hospitals and independent schools operate alongside state schools.

Privatisation and deregulation

Over the past 20 years or so, in seeking to enhance economic efficiency and promote competition, governments worldwide have embarked upon policies of **privatisation** and **deregulation**. Whilst the UK has led the way with the extensive privatisation and deregulation of transport, fuel and power, telecommunications and broadcasting, other governments including those in the Caribbean area have sought to gain from the UK's experience.

In a simple sense, privatisation refers to a change in ownership of an activity from the public sector to the private sector. In many instances, as in the UK, privatisation has returned activities that had been nationalised to new private owners. In a modern sense, privatisation means more than this and is now recognised to include:

Guyana's bauxite industry – a joint public sector–private sector operation

- The direct sale of government-owned and operated activities to the private sector.
- Deregulation through the removal of barriers to entry, which had protected the public sector from outside competition. Through this action, a contestable market can be created.
- Franchising. This can give a new private sector owner the right to operate a particular service or activity for a given length of time.
- Contracting out of services previously provided in-house by public sector organisations.

Why privatise?

Taking the UK economy as a particular example it is possible to recognise various reasons for privatisation. Some are economic, others much more concerned with political motivation. For example:

- In the early phase of privatisation, there is little argument that there was a deliberate commitment to reduce government involvement in the economy. A return to market forces was seen as necessary for many nationalised industries to achieve an efficient allocation of resources. Public ownership was believed to be a serious obstacle to these industries meeting their particular objectives.
- There was also a deliberate policy to widen share ownership amongst the population and amongst the employees of the privatised companies. In this way, people who previously had no opportunity to own shares could purchase small quantities of shares in businesses where they were consumers.
- Privatisation can generate benefits for consumers in the form of lower prices, wider choice and a better-quality product or service. *x*-inefficiency would be likely to be reduced as firms become more aware of the need to control costs to stay in business (see above).
- The sale of nationalised industries has generated substantial income for the UK government over a long period of time. This income generation has been very important in helping the economy to cope with deficits on the trading account of the balance of payments.
- It is further believed that privatised companies can be successful in raising capital, lowering prices and cutting out waste. In other words they are more efficient, with managers able to operate in a market-led way, without the restriction of trying to satisfy government objectives for their companies. Managerial freedom and a highly motivated workforce become the means by which economic efficiency is realised (see above).

Self-assessment task

For your own country, take each of these activities:

- water supply,
- rail transport,
- telephone services.

(a) Establish whether these activities are operated by the government or private sector businesses.

(b) If government owned, how might the private sector help to improve the economic efficiency of these activities?

(c) Why in your country might the government not wish to pursue a policy of privatisation?

Income and other transfers

Income transfers are used by governments as a means of redistributing income or transferring income from one group in society to another group, for example from people in work to those who are retired or from relatively rich people to those who are in poverty. The justification for these transfers is to achieve fairness or equity in an economy. These transfers of income may be in the form of a cash benefit paid by the government to someone with a low income. Income transfers may also be used to cover the unexpected loss of income when a person is not working due to illness or unemployment. These cash transfers include social security benefits, such as income support, a job seeker's allowance or a state pension.These will be discussed in chapter 14.

The impact of government intervention on markets

The impact of these different methods of government intervention will vary according to both the reasons for market failure and the conditions facing the markets.

Public goods

Public goods, such as defence, need to be financed by the government but they do not necessarily need to be produced by the government. The government will decide upon the optimal amount of defence expenditure and raise revenue through taxation to fund it. The problem facing the government is deciding on the best or fairest method of raising the tax revenue required. One approach is to tax individuals according their ability to pay tax. Thus those who have the highest incomes (or wealth) will pay most in taxation. Many governments use the 'ability to pay' principle as a basis for the tax system and it has a wide acceptance amongst the electorate as being the fairest means of raising tax revenue. In most countries the government takes a larger percentage of income in tax from the rich than the poor. This is called a **progressive tax** system.

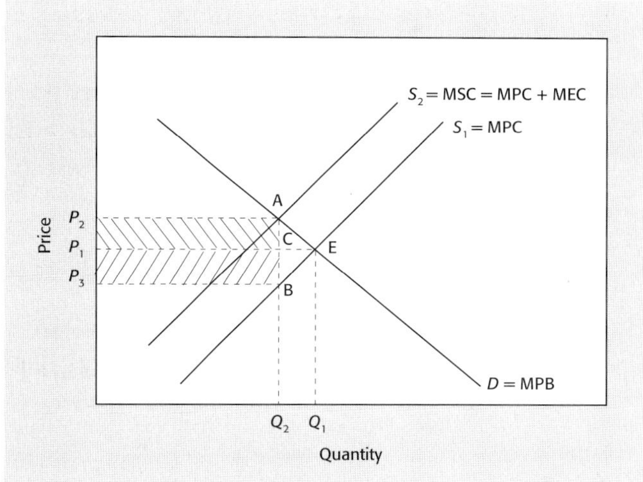

Figure 6.9 External cost and use of taxation

Externalities

Setting standards and regulation Governments frequently use regulation to overcome market failures caused by externalities. Let us consider the case of an electricity company that pollutes the surrounding countryside. The government might intervene by setting standards which restrict the amount of pollution that can be legally dumped. The government would then need to regulate and inspect the company to make sure that these restrictions are enforced. It can do this in several ways, for example by imposing large fines on any company that contravenes the law.

Exhaust fumes from cars pollute the atmosphere and to reduce this problem the government can set legal limits on the amount of carbon particles that are emitted from a car's exhaust pipe. This can be tested in the annual MOT test, although it also possible to conduct random on-the-spot tests. Regulations of this type are particularly effective when there are a large number of potential sources of the external cost. There are 17 million vehicles using Britain's roads and it is not possible to individually test every vehicle every day.

Financial intervention – taxes Financial intervention will take the form of taxes or subsidies; these can also be used in the case of externalities. A tax would normally be imposed on the individual or firm that causes the externality. If this happens then economists say that external costs are internalised.

In figure 6.9, in the case where there is no government intervention, the equilibrium occurs at point E, where supply, S_1, which is given by MPC or marginal private cost, equals demand, D, which is given by MPB or marginal private benefit. However, if external costs are included in this diagram, then the supply curve becomes S_2 or MSC, marginal social cost. The vertical distance between these two supply curves is marginal external cost, MEC. The socially optimal level of output is therefore equal to Q_2, where S_2 cuts the demand curve. At this socially optimal level of output, the marginal external cost is equal to the vertical distance AB.

The government intervenes in this market and imposes a tax which is equal to the marginal external cost. This tax is added to the cost of producing the product and thus the supply curve S_2 is also equal to the MPC plus tax. Looking at the diagram, you can see that the price at which the product is sold has increased from P_1 to P_2. This is less than the tax applied by the government. At first sight this may appear a little strange, but the producer has accepted a cut in the price received from P_1 to P_3. The producer has borne the burden of part of the tax. The total tax paid is equal to the area P_2ABP_3, of which the consumer's share of the burden is P_2ACP_1 and the producer's share is P_1CBP_3.

Financial intervention – subsidies Financial intervention to overcome market failure caused by external benefits or positive externalities will take the form of a subsidy (see figure 6.10). The equilibrium without government intervention is at point F where MPC = MPB or $D = S_1$. In this case, marginal external benefit is added to the MPB curve to give the MSB or marginal social benefit curve. The MSB represents society's demand curve for the product.

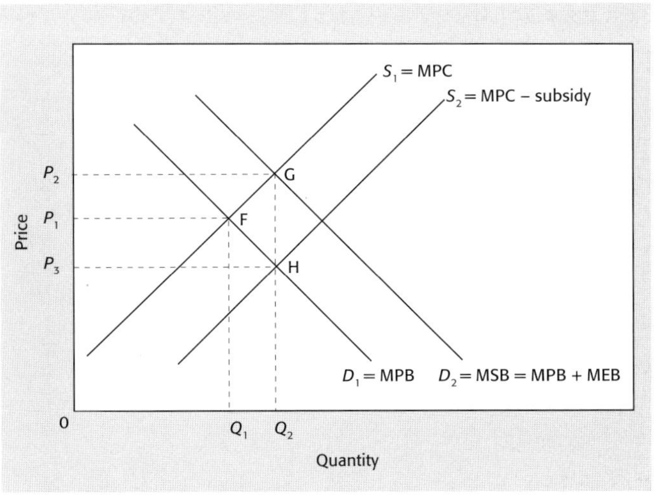

Figure 6.10 External benefits and use of a subsidy

If the government subsidises production of this product then the supply curve moves to the right from S_1, which equals MPC, to S_2, which equals MPC minus the subsidy. The marginal cost of supplying the good is reduced by the amount of subsidy and the vertical distance GH is equal to the value of the subsidy. Thus the equilibrium after the subsidy is given by point H, which is where D_1 crosses S_2 and the optimal amount of goods Q_2 is sold by the market.

As you might expect, there is considerable debate over which is the best method of government intervention when externalities are present in a market. If we accept the argument that education provides external benefits, then one solution would be to provide a subsidy to education. This can be seen in the UK where the government subsidises university education. Students still have to pay towards their education in the form of a fee, which can be represented by P_3 in figure 6.10. The government provides the difference between P_2 and P_3 by providing a subsidy.

Maximum price controls and price stabilisation

We will conclude this section by considering how governments impose maximum price controls in markets and how in agricultural markets price stabilisation policies can be applied.

Maximum price controls are only valid in markets where the maximum price that is imposed is *below* the normal equilibrium price as determined in a free market. Governments use legislation to enforce maximum prices for:

- staple foodstuffs, such as bread, rice and cooking oil;
- rents in certain types of housing;
- services provided by utilities, such as water, gas and electricity companies;
- transport fares where a subsidy is being paid.

Figure 6.11 indicates that at the price ceiling of P_1, production is not sufficient to satisfy everyone who wishes to buy the product. Consequently, as price cannot rise, the available supply has to be allocated on some other basis. The most likely way is by means of queuing, a much evidenced form of control in the former planned economies of Central and Eastern Europe. Rationing is another means of restricting demand – it inevitably leads to a black market for the products involved, with consumers then having to pay inflated prices well above the ceiling price.

Price stabilisation policies, especially in agricultural markets, are designed to lessen the effects of unplanned fluctuations in supply. A producers' association or a government-backed marketing board regulates supply by releasing stocks on to the market in order to stabilise farm incomes. By releasing buffer stocks at times of shortage or by purchasing excess stocks at times of surplus production, price can be stabilised at a predetermined level. Although theoretically simple in terms of their economic logic, such policies are often criticised as they do not promote efficiency and tend to protect farmers from the full force of competition in world markets.

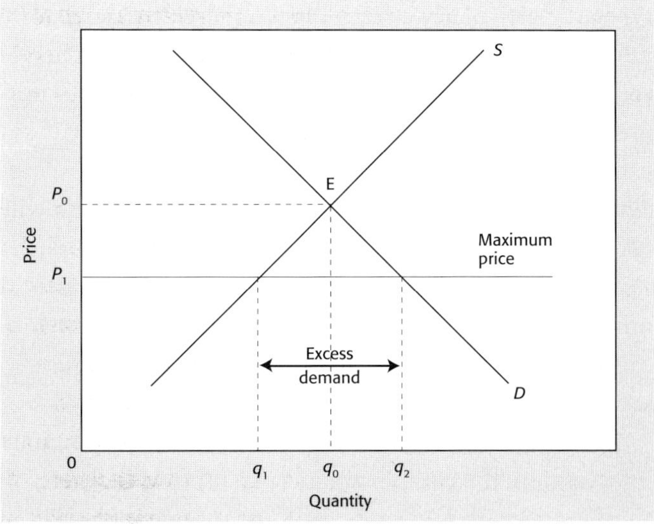

Figure 6.11 The effects of maximum price control

Self-assessment tasks

The following short answer questions have been set in recent CAPE examinations, 2003–2005.

1 (a) Define the term 'market failure'. (2 marks)
   (b) Define the term 'monopoly' and give an example of a monopoly in your country. (2 marks)
   (c) How does output and price of a firm under a monopoly differ from output and price of a firm under perfect competition? (2 marks)
   (Total 6 marks)

2 (a) Define the term 'externality'. (2 marks)
   (b) List an example of EACH of the following:
   - an external benefit,
   - an external cost. (2 marks)

   (c) Name TWO sectors in a named Caribbean country where government has intervened to correct market failure. (2 marks)
   (Total 6 marks)

3 (a) List TWO examples of 'public goods'. (2 marks)
   (b) Name TWO characteristics of public goods. (2 marks)
   (c) Briefly describe ONE of the characteristics named in (b) above. (2 marks)
   (Total 6 marks)

4 (a) Define the term 'externalities'. (2 marks)
   (b) List ONE example of an external good or benefit and ONE example of an external bad or cost that occur in your country. (2 marks)
   (c) Explain how the external good or benefit and the external bad or cost you listed in (b) above, affect efficient resource allocation. (2 marks)
   (Total 6 marks)

Summary

In this chapter it has been shown that:

- Markets do not always operate as suggested by economic theory; this results in market failure.
- Economic efficiency is used to explain how well scarce resources are allocated.
- Productive, allocative and Pareto efficiency are aspects of economic efficiency.
- The existence of negative and positive externalities in a market leads to an inappropriate level of production.
- Left to the free market, merit goods will be under-provided and de-merit goods are likely to be over-provided.
- It is necessary for governments to provide public goods as these would not be provided at all in a free market situation.
- Governments respond to market failure in a variety of ways including regulation, privatisation and various financial interventions.

Key words

Definitions of Key words can be found in the Glossary.

adverse selection
allocative efficiency
de-merit goods
deregulation
economic efficiency
external benefit
external cost
externality
free rider
information failure
market failure
merit goods
moral hazard
nationalised industries
negative externality
non-excludable
non-rival
Pareto efficiency
paternalism
private costs
privatisation
productive efficiency
public goods
regulation
social cost
subsidies
taxes
value judgements
'x' inefficiency

Module 3

Distribution theory and applications of recent theoretical developments

On completion of this module you should be able to:

understand what accounts for the returns which accrue to the owners of the factors of production

develop skills in applying recent developments of microeconomic analysis to critical social issues

7 The theory of income distribution

This chapter covers unit 1, module 3, topic 1.
On completion of this chapter, you should be able to:

- identify the rewards accruing to the owners of the factors of production – land, labour, capital and entrepreneurship
- differentiate between the size and functional distribution of income
- explain the determination of the prices of factors of production
- explain the concept of derived demand
- explain the relationship between factor rewards and costs of production
- outline the main assumptions and limitations of marginal productivity theory
- differentiate between rent and transfer earnings and apply these concepts to labour and other markets
- identify the similarities and differences of factor markets
- define the term 'labour supply'
- define the term 'potential labour force'
- define the term ' labour force'
- define and calculate labour force participation rate
- apply indifference curve analysis to labour supply
- describe the impact of labour mobility on the labour market
- explain the role of government, trade unions and employers' associations in the pricing of factors and in income distribution
- distinguish between relative and absolute poverty
- list the causes of poverty and outline the pros and cons of programmes aimed at poverty reduction

Introduction – rewards to factors of production

The four factors of production, land, labour, capital and enterprise were introduced at the beginning of this chapter. In turn these generate various rewards to their owners. These rewards are known as **factor payments** and consist of:

- **Rent** which is the payment for the use of land or buildings. Where land is productive due say to its fertility or to the natural resources that can be exploited, this payment is a form of surplus since the owner has not had to make inputs into creating what is there. The rent on buildings though is a form of quasi-rent since it includes some integral payment for the use of such buildings.
- **Wages** are the reward for the work that is carried out by labour. This is a general term irrespective of whether workers are paid on a casual, weekly or monthly basis. The factor payments made to labour vary enormously depending upon the nature of the work, the skills of the workers and where labour is employed.
- **Interest** is the price that is paid for the use of capital. Essentially, capital is everything that is man-made. It is also used to mean the additional amount of money that is paid by those borrowing money or the additional payment received by those who have invested.
- **Profits** are the difference between business receipts and expenditure over a set period of time. In most business situations, they are the reward that is paid out to those entrepreneurs who are enterprising and who are prepared to take risks.

The functional distribution of income

The income accruing to any of the four factors of production can be determined by the price (or **rental rate**) of using the factor multiplied by the quantity of factor employed. For an economy, the **functional distribution of income** shows how the national income is divided between the various factor inputs. Table 7.1 below shows these income shares for the UK economy and a typical Caribbean developing economy.

Input	UK (2003)	Developing economy[1]
Employment	62	75
Self-employment	7	10
Profits	23	10
Property rentals	8	5

Note: 1 – typical estimate.
Table 7.1 Functional distribution of income (% national income)

As the table shows, there are clear differences, due largely to variations in the economic structures of the two types of economy. Interestingly for the UK, the relative split between the factor inputs has changed little over the past generation. In developing economies there is far greater percentage income generated from the two types of employment; for profits and rent, the respective percentages tend to be lower. Over time though convergence to the UK shares can be expected.

Brian Lara
Source: Popperfoto Reuters.

The labour market

Introduction

When you leave school or college (hopefully with a CAPE Advanced Level in Economics), the wage or salary you get paid will be determined largely by what type of job you take. If you get a post as a clerk, you are likely to get more pay than if you are a street cleaner. Equally, if you go on to become a teacher, you will get paid more than a clerk. In turn, the manager of a multinational company will get paid more than a teacher. So, why is it that some workers get paid more than others? And why is it that some people with exceptional talent, for example Brian Lara, Tiger Woods or Michael Jackson, are highly paid? The answer to these questions, like many such questions in Economics, is that it all depends on supply and demand. To understand why some people get paid more than others, economists have looked at the labour market and sought to put forward various principles based on the characteristics of this market.

Demand for labour

Many of the principles introduced in chapter 3 can be applied to the labour market. There is though one fundamentally different point, namely the demand for labour is a **derived demand**. By this, we mean that the firm's demand for labour is due to its decision to produce certain goods or services. Labour is therefore demanded not for its own sake but because it is essential for the production of goods or services. Returning to our earlier examples, clerks are employed by a firm because they are necessary for a firm to carry out its business. The streets need cleaning, therefore street cleaners are needed. Children need education so teachers are required. This may seem obvious – it does though underpin the whole basis of labour economics. Brian Lara and Michael Jackson have exceptional talents

– the demand for their services is very high indeed and commands a high return.

The analysis that follows is based upon two important assumptions:

- The firm which wishes to hire labour is operating in a competitive market; there are in particular many buyers and sellers of labour, and no single firm or worker can affect the wage which is paid.
- The firm is a profit-maximiser; its demand and supply of labour are based on it maximising the difference between total revenue and total costs.

Do not worry too much about these assumptions at this stage as their importance will become much clearer during the rest of this chapter.

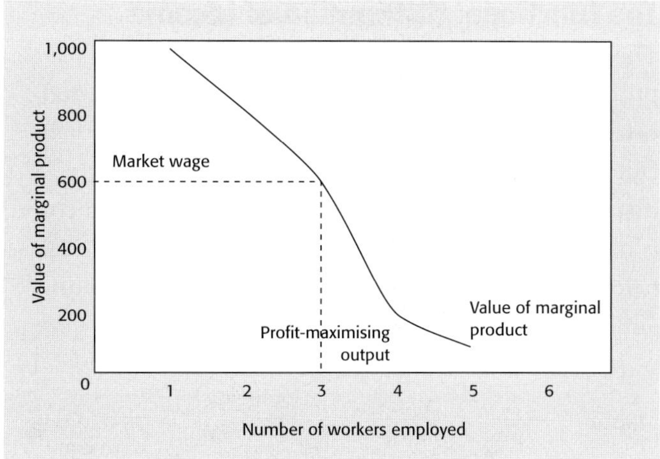

Figure 7.1 The value of the marginal product of labour

The marginal revenue product of labour

So far in our analysis of the demand for labour we have only been concerned with physical inputs and outputs. This is somewhat unrealistic because, in reality, the profit-maximising firm is concerned with how much this output is worth to the firm. We must therefore take into account the cost of employing labour – the wage rate. Let us assume that this is $600 per month and, using data from table 4.1, let us assume that a unit of clothing sells for $10.

When the firm hires the first worker, this worker generates $1,000 of revenue for the firm; this in turn represents $400 of profit. The amount of revenue generated by an additional worker is referred to as the marginal revenue product of labour. Adding a further worker generates another $800 and $200 profit. There comes a point when, after the third worker has been employed, a further worker adds more to costs than to revenue (it still costs $600 to employ the worker but only $400 worth of clothing is produced). So, above this level of employment, the value of the marginal product that is being produced is less than the wage. This clearly makes no sense to the firm. It can therefore be deduced that the firm should hire workers up to the point where the value of the marginal product of labour equals the wage that is being paid. *The demand curve for labour can therefore be represented by the value of the marginal product curve.* This is shown in figure 7.1.

So, in general terms:

- a firm should continue to hire labour as long as the additional worker adds more to revenue than he or she adds to the firm's costs;
- the market wage is determined by the **marginal revenue product** of labour;
- the marginal revenue product curve for labour is the firm's demand curve for labour;
- if the wage rate rises or falls then fewer or more workers will be employed.

It follows from this analysis that the wages paid to workers are a direct reflection of their marginal revenue product. So, a street cleaner has a lower marginal revenue product than a clerk, who in turn has a lower marginal revenue product than a teacher and so on. It also follows that it is actually possible to measure marginal revenue productivity. This is a very big assumption to make. In a manufacturing firm it may be possible to do this, but in many occupations this is not possible. How, for example, can we measure the marginal revenue of a teacher? The answer is 'with great difficulty'. We therefore need to look at the other side of the labour market, that involving the supply of labour, to give a proper explanation of how wages are actually determined. This will now be considered.

Supply of labour

The labour supply or supply of labour refers to the total number of hours that labour is able and willing to supply at a particular wage rate. In general terms the principles of supply introduced in chapter 4 apply here. With the supply of labour though it is important to remember that we are dealing with people and their willingness to participate (or otherwise) in the labour market depending upon the rate or price that they are

A Caribbean junior school teacher – how can her marginal revenue product be estimated?

offered for their services. It is useful therefore to consider labour supply at three levels: that of the individual worker, that of a firm or industry and that of the economy as a whole. Different factors affect supply depending upon which of these levels we are dealing with. Let us look briefly at each in turn.

The individual's labour supply

As with any supply, price (or wage in this case) has an important bearing on the decision of any individual worker to enter the labour market. If the wage is too low for example, someone may determine that it is not worth the effort of going to work and decide to stay at home. Not many people are in this position – most of us need to work to live. Economic theory assumes that there is a positive relationship between labour supply and the wage rate. So, as the wage rate increases, more people are willing to offer their services to employers. This is shown diagramatically by the labour supply curve, which is upward sloping in the main (see figure 7.2). Beyond a certain point, though, individuals will take the view that they prefer leisure to work. This point is indicated on figure 7.2 by the backward-sloping curve from point *X*. Before this point, an individual worker is more willing to supply his labour as the wage rate increases. It must be stressed that this point depends on the individual's attitude to work and leisure – just where point *X* is on any individual's supply curve will vary.

A further factor that can affect an individual's supply of labour is the income tax rate. In all countries this tends to be progressive. Low-wage workers pay little or

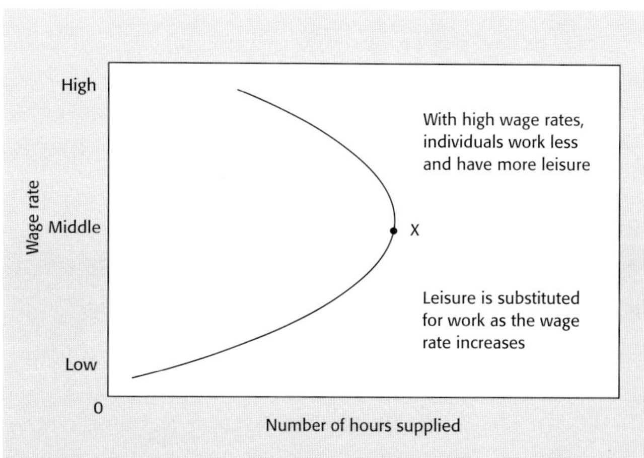

Figure 7.2 An individual's labour supply curve

no tax. As wages rise, more of the increase is paid in tax to the government. In the UK, for example, the standard rate of income tax in 2001 was 22 per cent, with a maximum rate of 40 per cent for high-income earners. In many other countries this higher rate is above 40 per cent. The downside could be that a high tax rate stifles the incentive to work. Governments must therefore be very careful to not do this as it will adversely affect economic prospects if key workers are not encouraged to work because of the high tax rates.

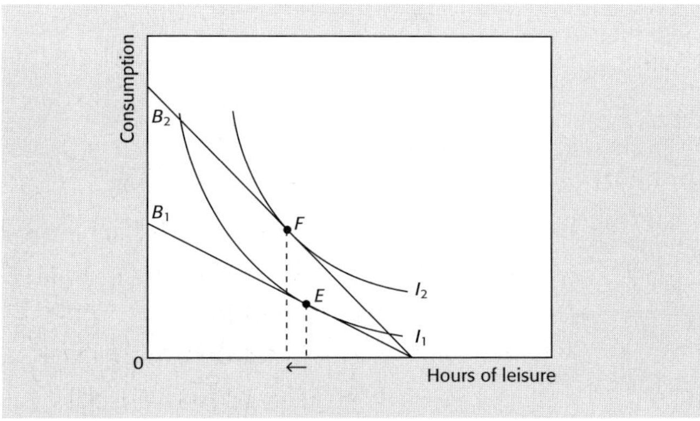

Figure 7.4 An increase in wage leading to a decrease in leisure

Indifference curve analysis applied to labour supply

Figure 7.2 indicated that as an individual's wage rate increased, then a point was reached beyond which that individual would prefer to have more leisure time than time spent at work. Indifference curve analysis can be used to show how this unusual supply curve is derived.

Let us take an individual who has a professional job such as a lawyer or an accountant. Figure 7.3 shows that if this individual spends all the time at work, then a weekly consumption income of \$200 will be earnt but the person has no time for leisure. If the individual works 40 hours, then weekly consumption is \$80 but 60 hours can be spent as leisure. The three indifference curves show the respective preferences for work and leisure. In working 40 hours, this is below the optimum point *E* – if the wage rate were to rise, then the individual would be prepared to sacrifice some leisure time in order to increase consumption income. This situation is shown in figure 7.4.

The increase in wage is shown by a pivotal change in the budget line from B_1 to B_2. The new budget line has a steeper slope, indicating that this individual gets more consumption for every additional hour of leisure time that is given up. This is represented earlier on figure 7.2 by the upward-sloping part of the labour supply curve.

In figure 7.5, the individual's response is different – here, the increase in wages prompts the person to enjoy more leisure hours at the expense of less hours worked. Referring back to figure 7.2, this can be represented by the backward-sloping part of the labour supply curve beyond point *X*.

So, why is this? The answer lies with the income and substitution effects of a higher wage. With respect to figure 7.4, this is explained by the substitution effect – as wages rise, leisure becomes more costly relative to consumption, encouraging the individual to give up some leisure time for the benefits that arise from increased consumption. As for the income effect, the increase in wages has resulted in this person moving to a higher indifference curve, I_2.

As the individual is better off, this increase in income is being used to enjoy both higher consumption and greater leisure hours.

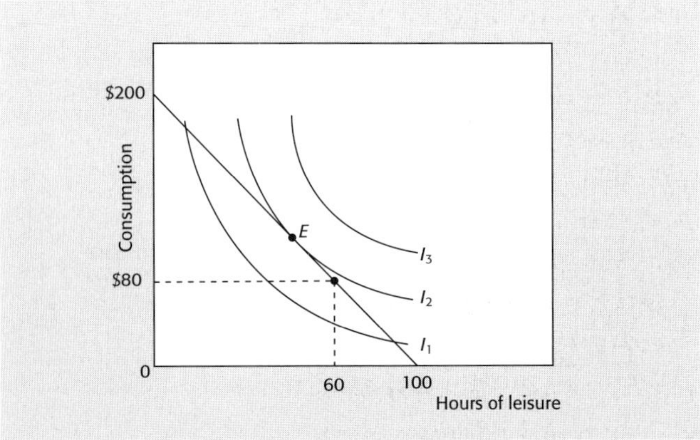

Figure 7.3 The work–leisure decision

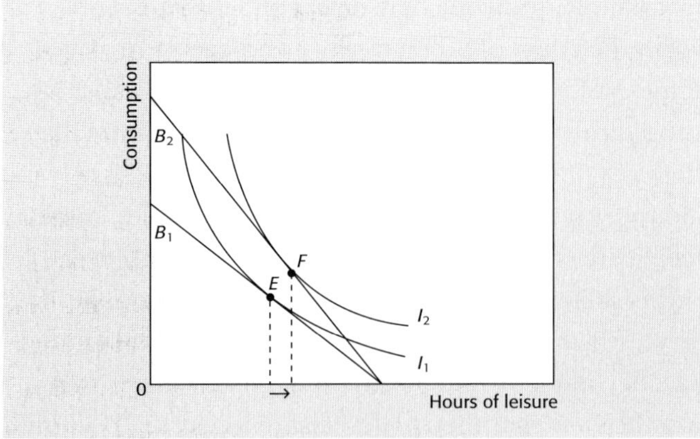

Figure 7.5 An increase in wage leading to an increase in leisure

For any one individual, the response to an increase in wages depends upon personal preferences. At low levels of wages, individuals are more likely to want to work more hours. Top wage earners may use an increase in wages as an opportunity to work less and spend more time away from work. To the economist:

- If the substitution effect is greater than the income effect, the individual will work more hours.
- If the income effect is greater than the substitution effect, the individual will work less hours.

So, for any individual the labour supply curve may be either upward or backward sloping.

Labour supply to a firm or industry

This supply curve consists of the sum of the individual supply curves of all workers employed in a firm or industry. It is usually upward sloping throughout (see figure 7.6). As with the individual, the number of workers wanting to supply their labour increases with the wage rate that is offered. The slope of this supply curve is measured by the elasticity of supply of labour – the extent to which labour supply responds to a change in the wage rate. Figure 7.6 shows two different supply curves, one inelastic (L_1) and the other elastic with respect to the wages being paid.

There are various reasons for this difference. An obvious one is the skills required to carry out a particular occupation. In general, the more skills required, the more inelastic will be the supply of labour. This also applies to the amount of education and training that are required to carry out a particular job. Anyone who teaches has to spend at least four years acquiring the necessary qualifications. Supply to such an occupation will be more inelastic than to, say, road sweeping, where no skills and little or no education and training are needed.

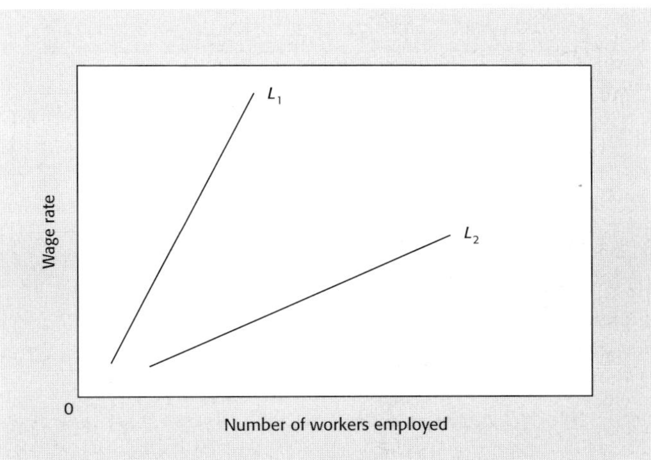

Figure 7.6 The supply curve of labour to a firm or industry

The supply curve L_2 in figure 7.6 is therefore likely to be that for an industry where wages are low and where there is a plentiful supply of labour with no particular skills or training.

In a competitive labour market, the wage rates offered in all other industries or occupations will be important in determining the supply of labour to a particular industry. In developing economies, an obvious example could be the difference in wages in agriculture compared with wages in emerging manufacturing industries or food-processing industries which usually pay more to their workers.

The long-run supply of labour

This is of particular significance to the economy as a whole. There are important contrasts here between developed and developing economies, involving wider economic factors including:

- *The age structure of the population.* In many developed economies, the total population is relatively stable. This is more or less true of the UK and France; in the case of Italy, the population is actually declining quite markedly. With life expectancy increasing, there are relatively fewer people of working age and this affects the long-run supply of labour. In such cases, therefore, the long-run supply curve of labour is shifting to the left. In contrast, in most developing economies, there is an increase in the overall supply of labour as there are an increasing number of people joining the labour market. Here, the long-run supply curve for labour shifts to the right, indicating that more workers are willing to supply their labour at a given wage rate. These contrasting situations are shown in figure 7.7.
- *The labour force participation rate.* This is the term used to determine the proportion of the population of working age actually in employment. In many developed economies, workers often choose to leave the labour market, by taking 'early retirement', before the normal age for retirement, so reducing the labour participation rate. At the lower end of the age range, with more students electing for higher

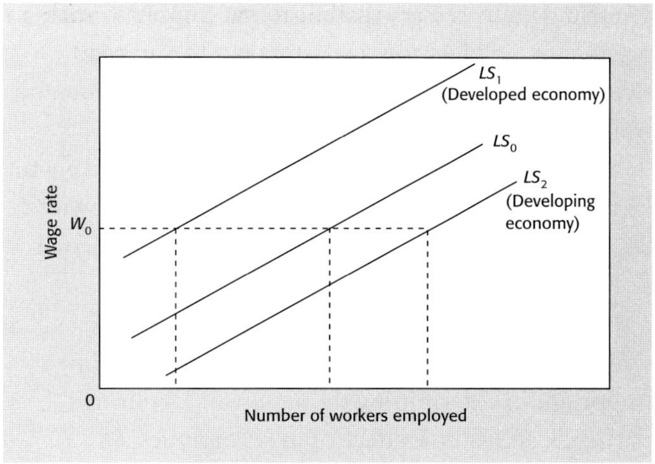

Figure 7.7 Shifts in the long-run supply of labour

education, the labour participation rate is also falling slightly. The combined effect of these has been for a slight reduction in the labour participation rate, so shifting the long-run labour supply curve to the left.

- *The tax and benefits levels.* As was shown in figure 7.7 for the individual, there comes a point where the work–leisure trade-off affects labour supply. This also affects the supply of labour for the economy as a whole, particularly in developed economies. Governments therefore have to be very careful in their taxation and social security policies to ensure that the long-run supply of labour is not adversely affected through a reduction in the willingness of people to work. In the UK, as previously stated, the top rate of income tax is now 40 per cent – 15 years ago it was much more progressive, with marginal tax rates as high as 80 per cent of the increase in income for the highest paid. In such circumstances, there is clearly a huge disincentive for someone to stay in the labour market. The level of unemployment and social security payments can also affect the long-run supply of labour in a similar way. Through their supply-side policies therefore governments seek to provide incentives for certain types of labour to remain active in the labour market.
- *Immigration and emigration.* These too affect the long-run supply of labour in an economy. Where there are labour shortages, as was the case in the UK during the late 1950s and early 1960s, immigration from Commonwealth countries, often to relatively low pay industries and the public services, increased the supply of labour. Emigration from these countries in turn relieved pressures in their labour markets. At the present time, the UK faces labour shortages in nursing, teaching and 'high-tech' industries. Selective immigration from many developing economies is being used to reduce such shortages (see case study opposite).

Wage determination under free market forces

So far, we have established two important features of the workings of the labour market. These are:

- the wage paid to labour equals the value of the marginal product of labour;
- the willingness of labour to supply their services to the labour market is dependent upon the wage rate that is being offered.

In some respects, it might seem surprising that the wage can do both of these things at the same time. There is no surprise – it is all tied up with how wages are actually determined in a competitive labour market.

The price of labour, the wage, is no different to any other price in so far as it depends on demand and supply. So, the wage and quantity of labour adjust to balance demand and supply. This is shown in figure 7.8. As the demand curve reflects the value of the marginal product of labour, in equilibrium, workers receive the value of their contribution to the production of goods and services. Each firm therefore purchases labour until the value of the marginal product equals the wage. So, the wage paid in the market must equal the value of the

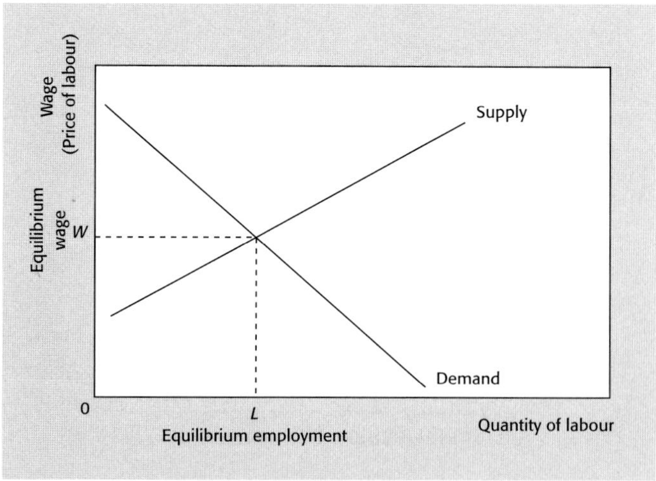

Figure 7.8 Equilibrium in the labour market

marginal product of labour once it has brought demand and supply into equilibrium. The market therefore *clears* at the equilibrium wage.

Like any market though, the labour market is dynamic – any change in the demand or the supply of labour will change the equilibrium wage. The value of the marginal product of labour will also change by the same amount, as, by definition, it must always equal the wage rate.

Let us now analyse how a change in the demand for labour and a change in the supply of labour affect the market equilibrium.

Returning to the earlier example of clothing, an increase in the income of consumers in developed economies will shift the demand curve for clothing to the right, indicating that more will be demanded at any price. In turn, this affects the demand for labour producing the clothing – this is shown in figure 7.9 by a

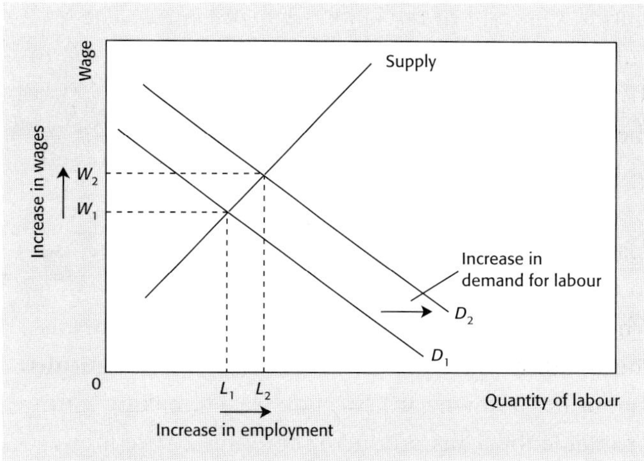

Figure 7.9 Effects of an increase in labour demand

Caribbean nurses and teachers being exploited

Bridgetown, Barbados: An official with the Commonwealth Secretariat says some of the Caribbean's qualified nurses and teachers who migrate to the United Kingdom are being manipulated and grossly exploited after being lured by recruiters.

Education Adviser, Dr Roli Degazon-Johnson, made the comments as she presented a paper on '*Brain Drain, Gain and Circulation – The Recruitment, Migration and Retention of the Highly Skilled in the Caribbean*' at the 7th annual conference of the Sir Arthur Lewis Institute for Social and Economic Studies which recently concluded in Barbados.

She said the exploitation of highly skilled migrant labour is a feature of migration that is either unknown or not readily acknowledged.

Dr Degazon-Johnson contended in her paper that 'the highly skilled can be manipulated at best and grossly exploited at worst by those who are recruiting them, be they recruitment businesses and agencies, education or health bodies, even schools and hospitals which often recruit directly'.

She says many of these Caribbean people have been treated disrespectfully and placed at a disadvantage following their migration.

'There is wide-spread evidence of qualified and competent teachers and nurses being prevented or restricted in benefiting fully from the compensation and benefits which they could be earning', she said.

The Commonwealth official noted that while there is a directive within the European Union which stipulates that once a graduate obtains a degree from a European tertiary institution, they have a right to be employed and treated equally anywhere in Europe, the same is not true of Commonwealth teachers.

'They are told because they do not hold United Kingdom qualifications that they do not have 'Qualified Teacher Status' and they cannot be paid on the same basis as a qualified teacher from the UK', she says in her report.

'Overseas nurses are also obliged to pursue a three-to-six month programme before they are permitted to carry out their professional duties in the UK. A long waiting list for this programme exists and in the interim the nurse would be employed as a nursing assistant at less than the salary and benefits that should be accrued to a qualified nurse.'

To deal with the problem, Dr Degazon-Johnson has suggested that Caribbean governments – through their Ministries of Education, Health and Labour – lend support to the International Labour Organisation, Education International, the World Health Organisation and the Commonwealth Secretariat which are seeking to ensure that when Caribbean people migrate, they're properly treated, their rights are respected, their qualifications are not discounted and they have the benefit of ethical recruitment procedures.

Source: Dawn Bennett, 5 April 2006.

shift to the right of the labour demand curve. The outcome is that the equilibrium wage rises from W_1 to W_2, and employment increases from L_1 to L_2. As before, the change in the wage rate reflects a change in the value of the marginal product of labour.

A change in the labour supply will also affect the market equilibrium. Suppose that there is an increase in immigration which increases the number of workers who are able to produce clothing. When this happens, the labour supply curve shifts to the right. This surplus labour has a downward effect on wages, making it more profitable for firms producing clothing to hire more labour. As the number of workers increases, then so their marginal product falls, as does the value of their marginal product. The outcome in this case is that wages are reduced for all workers, although the level of employment rises. This is shown in figure 7.10.

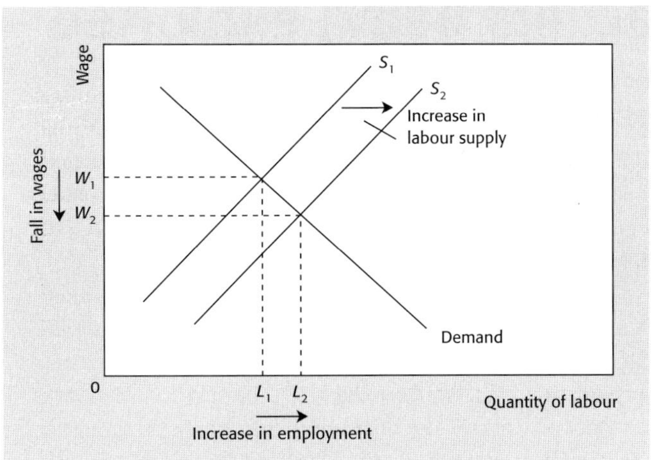

Figure 7.10 Effects of an increase in labour supply

Self-assessment tasks

1 Why might the demand for labour in an industry fall? Use a diagram to show the effects of this on the equilibrium wage in that industry.

2 Why might the supply of labour available for an industry fall? Use a diagram to show the effects of this on the equilibrium wage in that industry.

3 Combine figures 7.9 and 7.10 to show the overall effects of an increase in labour demand and an increase in labour supply on the market equilibrium. Write a few sentences to explain what your diagram shows.

The role of trade unions and government in wage determination

So far in our analysis of how wages are determined we have assumed that the respective forces of demand and supply operate freely with no intervention. In many respects this is an unreal assumption as in many labour markets, the demand and supply of labour are affected by the actions of trade unions and the government. Such interventions produce what are sometimes referred to as **imperfections in the labour market**.

Trade unions are organisations that seek to represent labour in their place of work. They were set up and continue to exist because individually, labour has very little power to influence conditions of employment, including wages. Through **collective bargaining** with employers, they act on behalf of their members to:

- increase the wages of their members,
- improve working conditions,
- maintain pay differentials between skilled and unskilled workers,
- fight job losses,
- provide a safe working environment,
- secure additional working benefits,
- prevent unfair dismissals.

Traditionally, trade unions have been strong in manufacturing and less important in the service sector. This is particularly true in the Caribbean area where trade unions in extractive industries have been very strong and in some cases militant in their quest to see an increased share of national income going to labour. The process of collective bargaining referred to above though does apply.

Economic analysis suggests that, in a competitive labour market, a powerful trade union is able to secure wages for its members above the equilibrium wage rate explained in figure 7.8. The basis for this claim is shown in figure 7.11. At the equilibrium wage, the quantity of labour employed is L. If a strong trade union can force up wages to say W_u, which is above the equilibrium, the number of workers who are offered jobs by employers falls to L_u. At this wage though the number of people who would *like* to work is higher. This is shown by L_c. Consequently there is a shortfall between those who actually want to work and those who can actually work, due to the influence of the trade union. This is shown on figure 7.11 as the difference between L_c and L_u.

Empirically, it is really quite difficult to prove whether or not this theory actually applies in labour

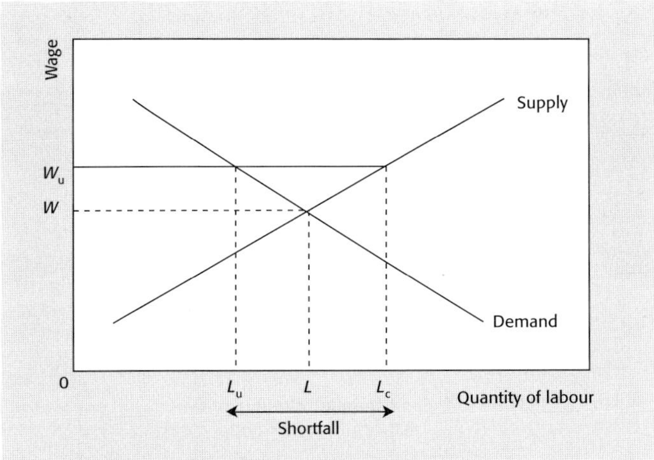

Figure 7.11 The effect of a strong trade union in a competitive labour market

markets. A much quoted example is that of actors and actresses in the UK and USA where there are very strong unions which restrict the numbers able to work in films, television and theatres. The wages of their members are supposedly supported in this way. Other examples are likely to be in labour markets where a trade union has a monopoly over workers with a particular type of skill. Increasingly though, the closed-shop policies of trade unions such as the above have been made illegal, so restricting their powers to act in this way. The case of the print unions in the UK was another typical example. However, new technology has removed their power to secure exceptionally high wages for their workers.

With ever-increasing globalisation, trade unions who try to behave in this way are playing a dangerous game with employers. The fear is that because of high labour costs and restrictive practices employers will go out of business or transfer production to countries which have lower wage levels. This threat has been particularly severe for UK car manufacturers – production has been switched to other EU countries, such as Spain, Poland, Hungary and the Czech Republic, where labour costs can be as little as one-fifth of those in the UK. Consequently, trade unions have very little real influence over the wages paid to their members.

The labour market has seen explicit government intervention through the introduction of national minimum wages. In the UK, after considerable deliberation, the government's Low Pay Commission recommended a national minimum wage of £3.60 per hour from early 1999 (£5.35 in 2007) for all workers above the age of 21. The main aim of a minimum wage such as this is to reduce poverty and the exploitation of workers who have little or no bargaining power with their employers. In the UK, many women employed in shops, small businesses and low-skill jobs, such as home working and cleaning, were being paid very low wages and, in the eyes of the government, were being exploited. The introduction of the minimum wage was of particular significance for them.

Whether there should be a minimum wage is controversial. Some of the aims have been given above. Additionally, it was argued that the amount of state benefits being paid to low-income families would be reduced with the introduction of a minimum wage. There might also be a small increase in tax revenue. Opponents were not convinced by these arguments, believing that jobs would be lost and that other low-pay workers would seek an increase to maintain their differential with the lowest paid. Cost-push inflation could well result, so affecting the economy as a whole.

The economics of a minimum wage are shown in figure 7.12. The effect on an industry is particularly dependent upon the elasticities of demand and supply for labour in that industry. Part (a) of this figure shows the effects where there is an inelastic demand for labour. The loss of jobs here is much less than shown in part (b) where the demand for labour is more wage elastic. In both cases there is an excess supply of labour at the higher minimum wage. This excess is more pronounced in part (b) where both the demand for and supply of labour are relatively elastic. It can also be seen that the higher the minimum wage is set above the competitive equilibrium (£2.50 in the case of figure 7.12), the greater will be the excess supply of labour willing to work at the national minimum wage.

Monopsony in the labour market

A **monopsony** occurs in the labour market when there is a single or dominant buyer of labour. In such a situation this monopoly buyer is able to determine the price which is paid for the services of the workers that are employed. Unlike other examples we have looked at, in this situation we are now dealing with an imperfect rather than competitive market.

Figure 7.13 shows how the monopsonist can affect the market equilibrium. The monopsonist will hire workers by equating the marginal cost paid to employ a worker

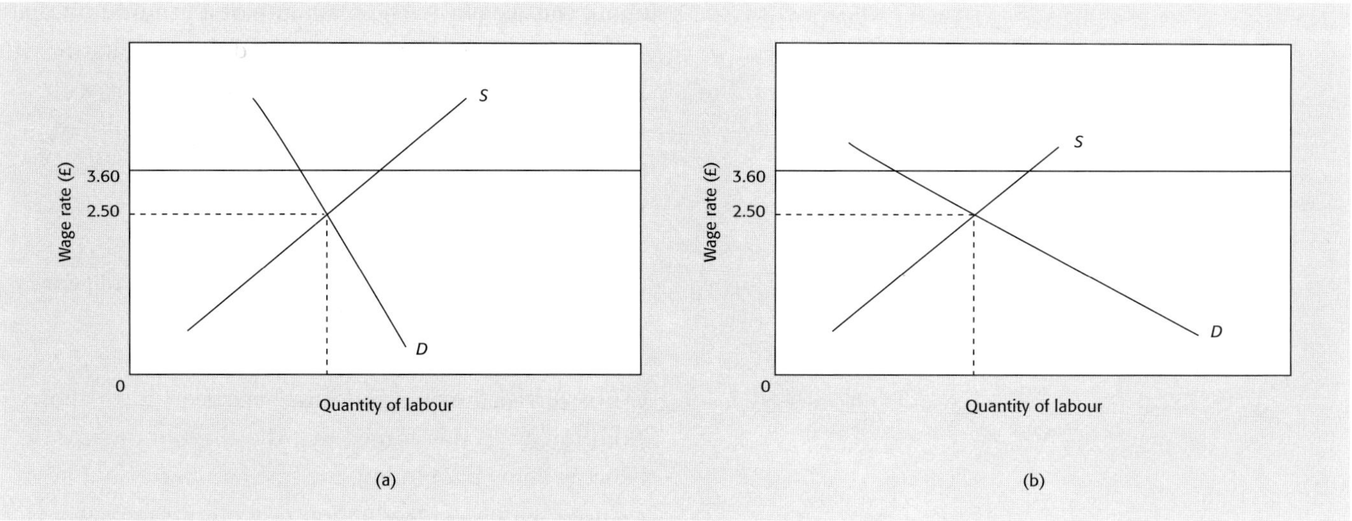

Figure 7.12 The effects of the introduction of a minimum wage

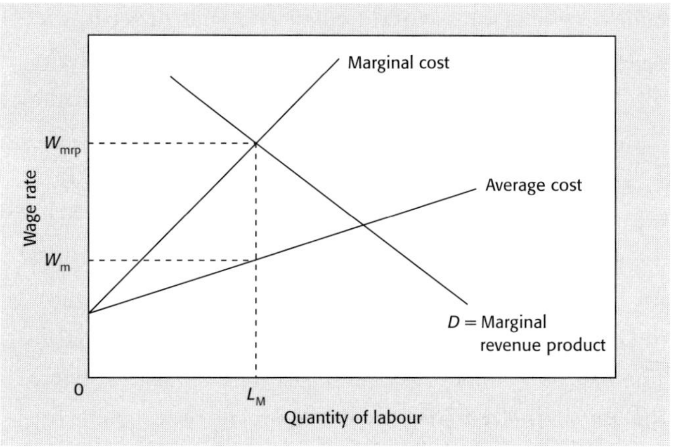

Figure 7.13 A monopsony buyer of labour

with the marginal revenue product gained from this employment. This is the profit-maximising position. The wage that the monopsonist pays to hire labour is W_m. This is actually below the wage that should be paid if he was paying the full value of their marginal revenue product, that is W_{mrp}. The level of employment is L_m.

In this situation the power of the employer in the labour market is of overriding importance and the employer can set a low wage because of this buying power. Monopsonists often exist in local labour market situations, for example where there is just one major employer in a town or where workers may be employed in an extractive industry located well away from where they may normally live. In this way the employer dominates the labour market, setting down wages and all other conditions of employment.

Transfer earnings and economic rent in the labour market

In our introduction to the labour market we posed the question:

> Why is it that some people with exceptional talent, for example Brian Lara, Tiger Woods or Michael Jackson, are highly paid?

The answer to this question can in part be given in the same way as to that as to why a teacher is paid more than a street cleaner – supply and demand. To fully answer why these earnings differences occur, economists find it useful to split earnings down into two elements. These are:

- **transfer earnings** – this is the minimum payment necessary to keep labour in its present use;
- **economic rent** – any payment to labour which is over and above transfer earnings.

Both are shown on figure 7.14(a). Transfer earnings are indicated by the area under the labour supply curve. As we have seen this is upward sloping. Although the equilibrium wage is *W*, at wage rates below this, there are workers who are willing to offer their services to employers. In fact, at any wage rate from zero upwards, workers will join the labour market, until at wage *W*, *L* labour supply is available. In all cases up to *W*, the wage that a worker receives is their best alternative. For those workers willing to work for less than *W*, then any wages they get over and above what they will accept is their economic rent. This is shown by the triangular area on figure 7.14(a).

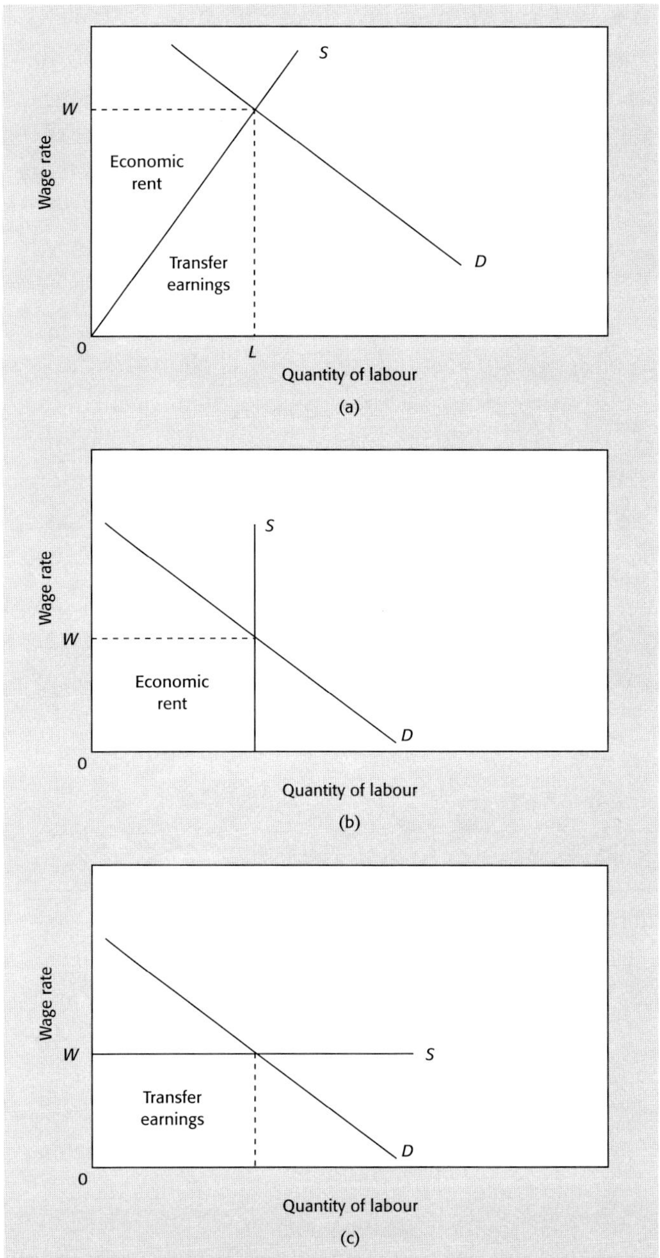

Figure 7.14 Transfer earnings and economic rent in the labour market

It follows, therefore, that different workers receive different amounts of transfer earnings and economic rent even in the same job. Take a bus driver as an example. Some people are very willing to drive buses for a low wage. These have low transfer earnings and large economic rent. Others though will be just induced by the equilibrium wage paid to bus drivers. In such cases they have little or no economic rent, the wage almost entirely consisting of transfer payments.

The case of superstars such as Brian Lara, Tiger Woods and Michael Jackson can be explained using figure 7.14(b). Such people have a scarce and, in some respects, unique talent. Their labour supply curve is completely inelastic and their earnings consist entirely of economic rent. In contrast, workers who have a completely elastic supply, such as many unskilled workers and others in menial jobs, have no economic rent at all; their earnings consist entirely of transfer earnings. Employers can hire an infinite supply of labour at the market wage, *W*. This situation is shown in part (c) of figure 7.14.

Other labour market imperfections

The basis of a competitive labour market is that workers are free to move in relation to demand. So, if there are vacancies in one geographical area or in one occupation, unemployed labour will be mobile and fill these vacancies. The mobility of labour is shown in figure 7.15, where in theory, labour will migrate to the South from the North in order to meet the former's demand for labour.

The reality of the labour market is that this seemingly simple operation does not occur as economic theory might expect. In reality, much labour is immobile and not able to flow geographically or occupationally for the following reasons:

Passengers disembarking from public transport, Holguin Province, Cuba
Source: Alamy.

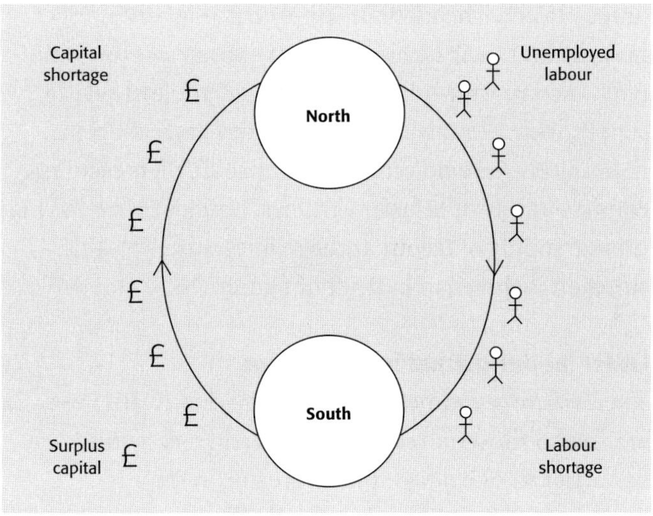

Figure 7.15 Factor mobility in a competitive market

- *Geographical* **immobility of labour**. Many people are reluctant to move away from friends and relatives and their local area even when unemployed. The cost of moving, in financial and personal terms, may also be prohibitive. In the UK for example, the cost of housing in areas with job vacancies usually prohibits workers from moving from the lower-cost areas where they live. A lack of information also tends to restrict geographical mobility.
- *Occupational immobility of labour*. This refers to a situation where labour is restricted in the type of job that can be taken up. For example, a street cleaner cannot fill a vacancy for a teacher; a teacher though is likely to be able to clean streets. This issue becomes much more difficult in specialist occupations where extensive training is needed to complete a particular job. A good example is that of dentists, who have to study for a minimum of five years in order to be able to practise. An unemployed worker could clearly not take on such a position.

Another particular issue in labour markets is that of **wage differentials**, namely the differences in wage rates for different groups of workers. The following differentials can be recognised:

- *Between different occupations*. Non-manual jobs tend to pay more than manual posts, due to the high levels of skill that are required. The greater the skill the higher the marginal revenue productivity of labour.
- *Between different industries*. Industries with a strong trade union, as shown earlier, are likely to pay more than those with a weak trade union. Capital-intensive industries usually pay more than labour-intensive industries as worker productivity is likely to be higher. Industries where there are risks, such as the chemical industry, are likely to pay higher wages than many other types of manufacturing.
- *Between males and females*. In all countries the average pay for women is below that for men. In part this is due to many women working part time and not full time, but it is also due to many more women being employed in occupations, such as nursing and secretarial work, where pay levels are often very low.
- *Between regions in the same country*. This is certainly true in the UK where the average pay of workers in peripheral regions, such as Scotland and the north of England, is less than in one of the main cities, such as London or Bristol.

Self-assessment task

Think about the labour market in your country:

(a) What information might you obtain to determine whether labour is mobile, both geographically and occupationally?

(b) What policies does your government use to improve labour mobility?

(c) Explain the main wage differentials that apply. What information might you obtain in order to provide evidence for these differentials?

Inequality and measures to reduce income inequality

It should be clear from our analysis of the labour market that within any economy there are high income earners at one extreme and very many times more people earning low wages. This aspect of income distribution is referred to as **inequality**.

A **Lorenz curve** is a simple diagrammatical way of representing such inequality in an economy. Figure 7.16 shows a typical example. If there was a completely egalitarian distribution of income, then this would be represented by the 45° line on this diagram. The extent of inequality is shown by area A – as inequality rises, this area will increase, moving towards the bottom right of the diagram. Area A shrinks as the distribution of income amongst the population becomes more equal.

The **Gini coefficient** is a numerical measure of the extent of inequality. On figure 7.16, this is calculated as area A/area A + area B. If the income distribution is equal, this coefficient will have a value of 0. At the other extreme, if all income accrues to just one person or household, then the Gini coefficient is 1. Both extremes of course never occur in reality. What is the norm is for coefficients to be somewhere between these two extremes. Typical examples are shown in table 7.2.

There are measures that governments can take to reduce income inequality. These include:

- A progressive direct tax system. Income tax is usually the main source of government revenue in developed economies such as the UK and USA. A progressive system, whereby the tax rate is higher for top earners, is a very positive way of reducing income inequality. In the UK, for example, the top tax rate is 40% as against a basic rate of 22%. In developing economies though the collection of income tax is often more problematic, resulting in more emphasis on indirect taxation. This tends to make it more difficult for governments to reduce inequality.
- Subsidies. The impact of a subsidy is to reduce prices of goods and services to consumers. By subsidising public transport, basic types of food and certain essential services, the poorer groups in the economy benefit much more than better-off groups.
- Government spending. Certain types of spending on services such as state education, health and social services will benefit lower income earners, particularly where private sector alternatives are available. By providing a good education, free at the point of use, the government hopes to provide children from poorer families with the opportunity to obtain good educational qualifications. Over time, this should enhance their earnings potential and reduce income inequality.

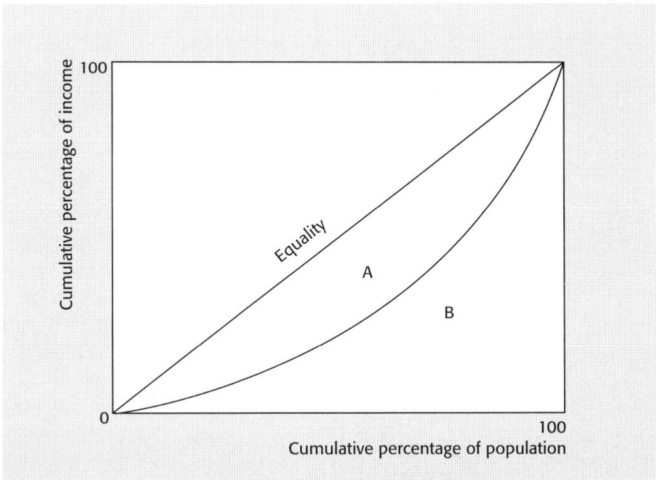

Figure 7.16 The Lorenz curve

Bermuda	0.33
Jamaica	0.38
Trinidad and Tobago	0.40
Barbados	0.49
Bahamas	0.49
UK	0.34
USA	0.41

Table 7.2 Selected Gini coefficients for Caribbean and other economies in 2003
Source: United Nation's Food and Agricultural Organisation.

Self-assessment tasks

Study the information in table 7.2 and then tackle the exercises that follow:

1 Briefly describe the differences in the Gini coefficients between:
- the five Caribbean economies
- the Caribbean economies and the USA.

2 For your own country, analyse the ways in which your government is trying to reduce income inequality. How might you know if it has been successful?

Poverty and measures to reduce poverty inequality

Poverty is not easy to define. In a simple sense, it means to be poor, or, in other words, where it is not possible for a person or family to be able to afford an adequate standard of consumption. What this standard is varies between countries and also over time.

Economists recognise two aspects of poverty. The first is **absolute poverty**, which is used to describe a situation where a person or family is living below some minimum consumption level. Where this occurs, basic human needs in terms of food, clothing and shelter are not being met. This is clearly far more of a problem in the world's poorest economies, although there is substantial poverty in the richest economies.

Relative poverty refers to a situation where people are unable to afford what is the typical average consumption level. It is a function of all economies that the distribution of income is unequal. This in itself creates relative poverty, particularly in economies where the income distribution is becoming more unequal such as in some of the world's most developed economies.

The measurement of poverty is not easy. The **poverty line** is often used for this purpose – it is the level of income that is just sufficient to avoid inadequate consumption. Just what this level is depends on a wide range of factors, not least because needs differ between countries. For example, a telephone of some sort may be essential in some economies but not in others. It also depends on consumption patterns for food – a necessity in one economy may well be a luxury item in a poorer country. The same is also true of housing and the relative housing needs of people in different economies.

The UN's **Human Development Index** (HDI) measures overall progress from an economic development standpoint. It uses four statistical measures: life expectancy at birth, GDP per capita, adult literacy rates and combined gross enrolment rates in schools. This is a reasonably comprehensive measure, although it clearly does not include all aspects of human development, particularly those aspects that are difficult to quantify such as respect and the ability to participate in the decision-making process. Table 7.3 shows the HDI rankings for a range of countries, including those in the Caribbean for 2004.

Governments can use various means to reduce poverty. These measures include:

- Progressive taxation (see above also). For those on low incomes, increasing the income threshold before tax is paid can lead to a greater incentive to work and so reduce poverty. For high income earners, as the earlier analysis of the backward-sloping labour supply curve indicated, increasing income taxes may actually increase their incentive to work. These increased taxes in turn generate

Absolute poverty

High development	Middle development	Low development
1 Norway	67 Suriname	142 Pakistan
8 United States	71 St Lucia	153 Haiti
12 United Kingdom	79 Jamaica	162 Tanzania
29 Barbados	87 St Vincent & the Grenadines	177 Sierra Leone
51 Bahamas	93 Grenada	
52 Cuba	95 Dominica	
54 Trinidad & Tobago	99 Belize	
55 Antigua & Barbuda		

Table 7.3 Human Development Index rankings for selected countries, 2004
Source: Human Development Report, United Nations, 2005.

more revenue for the government; some of this can be spent on reducing poverty.

- Minimum wage (see above also). A minimum wage raises the level of pay of people in the lowest-paid jobs. Its introduction may well lift some people out of poverty. It is also a means of enhancing the bargaining power of many workers who have little or no influence on wages paid in the labour market.
- Benefits. Where these are means-tested, namely only provided for those in most need, they can be an effective way of reducing poverty. Some of the benefits may be tied to getting more people into the workforce. In countries such as Jamaica, this is done through various income tax allowances.

Other factor markets

So far, our analysis of distribution theory has concentrated on the labour market. Other inputs are used with labour in the production process and, like labour, have their own prices. Of these inputs, capital and land are assets and their owners rightly expect payment for them when they are used.

Capital as a factor of production takes two forms. These are **fixed capital**, for example industrial machinery, buildings or vehicles, and **stocks** or inventories of goods that have been produced for sale or inputs that are being stored for production. The cost of using fixed capital is known as the rental rate (see above); for stocks, the **asset price** is the amount of money for which stock can be bought, so providing its owner with a stream of income in the future.

In considering capital as a factor of production, it is necessary to recognise two types of cost. These are:

- The opportunity cost of funds that are used to purchase capital. These funds have an alternative use and, if invested, can generate interest to their owner.
- The cost of depreciation. Over time the value of certain types of capital falls.

For any type of capital, the **required rental** is the minimum income that allows the buyer of a capital asset to break even over a given time period. The firm's demand for capital, as for labour, is a derived demand. The marginal revenue product of capital is the additional revenue that the firm obtains when using an extra unit of capital. This falls as more capital is used. A firm will rent capital up to the point where the rental rate equals its marginal revenue product. This is shown in figure 7.17. The assumption here is that all other inputs and influences on the demand curve for capital are constant.

The demand curve for capital can shift for a variety of reasons. These include:

- an advance in technology that makes capital used by firms more productive,
- a higher market price for the outputs of capital, making output more valuable.

In the short run, the total supply of capital is fixed. This is shown by the vertical supply curve in figure 7.18. In the long run the supply of capital can be increased as

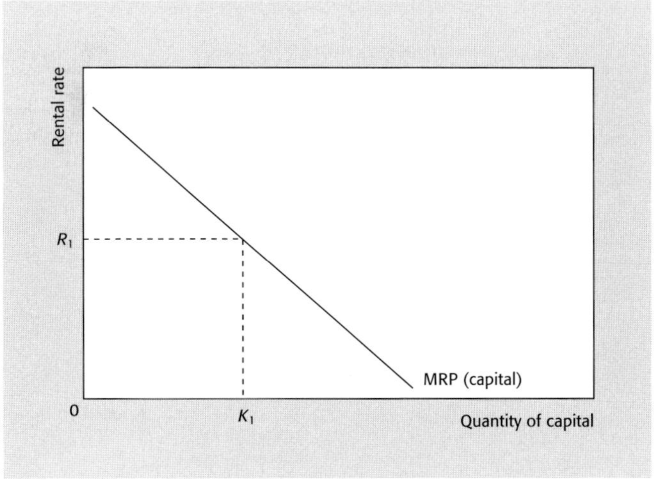

Figure 7.17 The demand curve for capital

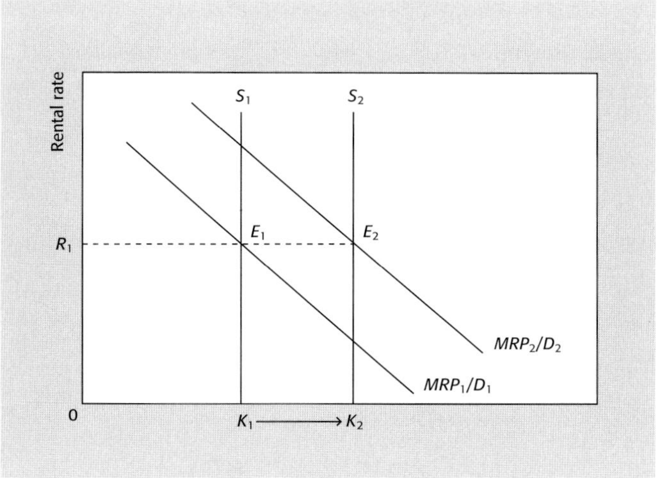

Figure 7.18 An increase in demand and supply of capital

new factories are built, new machines ordered and new vehicles purchased. An increase in the supply of capital can be shown by a shift to the right of *S*. Conversely, a reduction in the supply of capital is shown by a shift to the left.

Figure 7.18 shows how this affects the equilibrium position. The demand curve for capital and the supply of capital both shift to the right. Consequently, for the given rental rate R_1, an increased quantity of capital will be demanded.

Land is best seen as fixed in supply. The demand for land services, like that for labour and capital, is a derived demand since users of land can generate a rental rate from growing crops or using the land for buildings such as houses, offices and factories. Figure 7.19 shows how this rental rate is determined and how it changes if

New houses being built on land in Trinidad

the derived demand for the use of land falls – this could be due to a fall in agricultural prices or an oversupply of new factories and offices. As supply is fixed at S_1, a fall in demand for the use of land reduces the rental rate from R_1 to R_2.

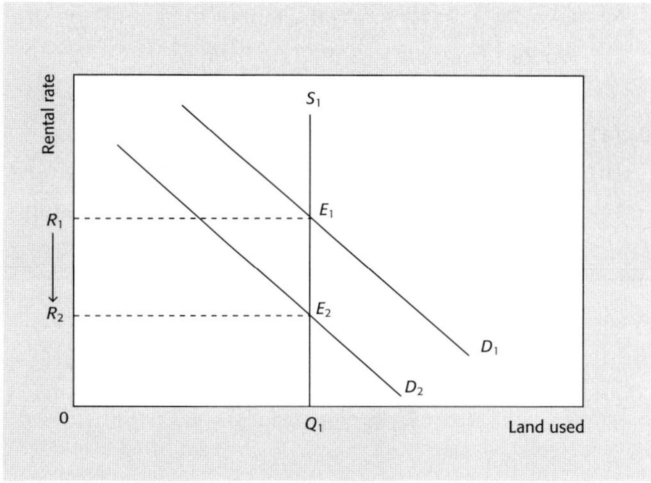

Figure 7.19 A decrease in the derived demand for land services

Self-assessment tasks

The following short answer questions have been set in recent CAPE examinations, 2003–2005.

1 (a) Why is the demand for capital a 'derived demand'? (2 marks)
(b) Explain the term 'Marginal Revenue Product (MRP) of capital'. (2 marks)
(c) How is the demand curve for capital related to the Marginal Revenue Product curve for capital under perfect competition? (2 marks)
(Total 6 marks)

2 (a) Define the following:
- potential labour force, (2 marks)
- labour force. (2 marks)

(b) Use the information in the table below to calculate the labour force participation rate. (2 marks)

Potential Labour Force	Employed	Unemployed
500,000	250,000	50,000

(Total 6 marks)

3 (a) Draw and label the Lorenz curves to represent the following Gini coefficients:
- 0.43
- 0.46 (5 marks)

(b) Which of the curves drawn in (a) above represents greater equality? (1mark)
(Total 6 marks)

4 (a) Define the term 'labour supply'. (2 marks)
(b) What is the difference between the 'actual labour force' and the 'potential labour force'? (2 marks)
(c) If the potential female labour force is 400,000, the number of females actually employed is 200,000, and the number of females seeking employment is 50,000, what is the participation rate of the female labour force? (2 marks)
(Total 6 marks)

5 (a) Define the term 'labour mobility'. (2 marks)
(b) State TWO reasons why the labour market of one CARICOM country may be attractive to workers from other CARICOM countries. (2 marks)

(c) Give TWO reasons why the labour market of one CARICOM country may NOT be attractive to workers from other CARICOM countries. (2 marks)

(Total 6 marks)

6 (a) Define the term 'poverty line'. (2 marks)

(b) State why someone whose income is above the poverty line may be regarded as poor. (2 marks)

(c) List TWO causes of poverty in any CARICOM country. (2 marks)

(Total 6 marks)

Summary

In this chapter it has been shown that:

- Factor payments in the form of rent, wages, interest and profits accrue to the owners of factors of production; the income from any of the factors of production is sometimes called the rental rate.
- The functional distribution of income shows how the national income in an economy is divided between the various factor contributions.
- The demand for all factors of production is a derived demand.
- The concepts of economic rent and transfer earnings can be used to show how the earnings of a particular factor of production have been determined.
- Common principles of demand and supply can be applied to the operations of all types of factor market.
- Indifference curve analysis can be used to derive an individual's supply of labour.
- Poverty and inequality are consequences of an unequal distribution of income; governments seek to tackle both through policies that include the use of progressive taxation, subsidies and regulation.
- Poverty and inequality can be described in a variety of numerical and more subjective ways.

Key words

Definitions of Key words can be found in the Glossary.

absolute poverty
asset price
collective bargaining
derived demand
economic rent
factor payments
fixed capital
functional distribution of income
Gini coefficient
Human Development Index
immobility of labour
imperfections in the labour market
inequality
interest
Lorenz curve
marginal revenue product
poverty line
profits
relative poverty
required rental
rent
rental rate
stocks
trade unions
transfer earnings
wages

8 Decision-making with incomplete information

This chapter covers unit 1, module 3, topic 2.
On completion of this chapter, you should be able to:

- explain the concept of social welfare
- explain and apply the concepts of moral hazard, adverse selection and asymmetric information
- identify the costs and benefits of government involvement in the provision of health care, the housing market, education, transport and environmental pollution, national security, social security and income redistribution

Social welfare

As referred to in chapter 6, allocative efficiency is achieved when firms produce a level of output at the point where the marginal cost of production equals price or average revenue. At this point, the value consumers place upon a particular product is reflected in the price they are prepared to pay. These are the products consumers want and they are made in the right quantities. In this respect **social welfare** is maximised.

For an economy, allocative efficiency is achieved where it is producing on its production possibility curve. This is known as the **socially optimum output** – it is so-called as this is best for society in so far as social welfare is maximised. Figure 8.1 shows this position. It assumes that education is a good that society values highly in so far as a well-educated population is likely to be more able to succeed and be content from a social well-being standpoint than one where education is not highly valued. If this is the case, then point A is more likely to be the point of allocative efficiency than point B, even though both points are on the PPC.

An alternative way of representing this position is shown in figure 8.2. The output that most benefits society is where marginal social cost equals marginal social benefit. At this level of output the value that consumers place on the last unit of output is equal to the full (social) cost of its production. In this case, the market is providing the best allocation of resources. Market failure is not occurring. In the real world, it is really very difficult to know if this is the case. In theory, it assumes that the costs and benefits of a particular activity can be accurately identified and measured.

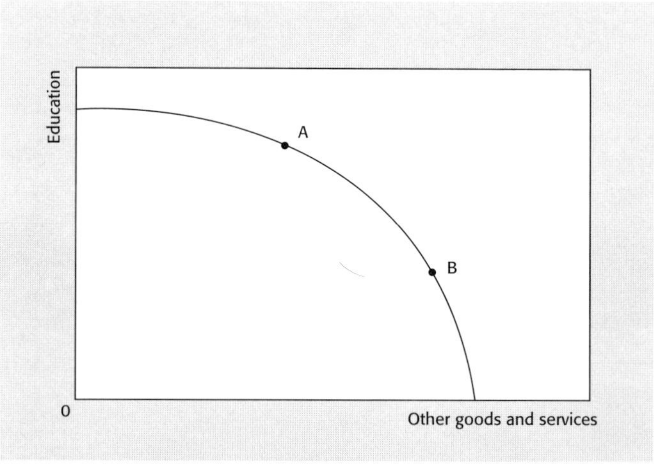

Figure 8.1 Socially optimum output

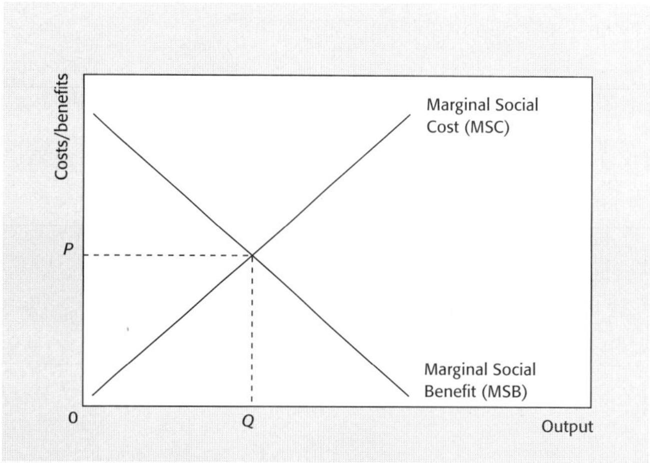

Figure 8.2 Allocatively efficient output

Information failure

Increasingly, particularly through the internet but also through better labelling on consumer products such as food, drink and medicines, we are provided with endless information about the products we might wish to buy. In principle this should enable us to take the rational decisions that are needed to maximise our own welfare and that of society. If this is the case, then one of the conditions of perfect competition is being met and hence there is no market failure.

The problem of information failure though is that the decisions being taken by consumers, firms and even governments, are being taken based on inaccurate information and, in some cases, ignorance of proper information. For instance:

- in the case of merit goods (see chapter 6);
- where there is a lack of information, for example in the case of someone who is unemployed not being aware of the potential job opportunities that are available;
- where advertising and product packaging lead to inaccurate information being provided to increase sales of a product.

Examples of the last two cases of information failure are shown in the self-assessment task below.

Self-assessment tasks

Read the case studies below and then tackle the questions that follow:

Claims 'misleading'

An advert for a Clinique anti-wrinkle cream made misleading claims about its effect on the skin, the industry watchdog said today.

The cosmetics giant's advert for Repairwear said the cream enabled the skin to steer 'hearty cells' to the base of wrinkles.

It then triggered the skin's own natural collagen production, the magazine advert said.

The Advertising Standards Authority (ASA) said Clinique could not stand up claims about their cream's physiological effect on users' skin.

It found the advert in breach of the advertising code in relation to truthfulness, health and beauty products, cosmetics and substantiation.

The ASA told the cosmetics company not to repeat the claim and to consult an advice team for guidance on future adverts.

An expert working for the watchdog said a scientific study provided by Clinique was based on laboratory test results which had not been proven on consumers' skin.

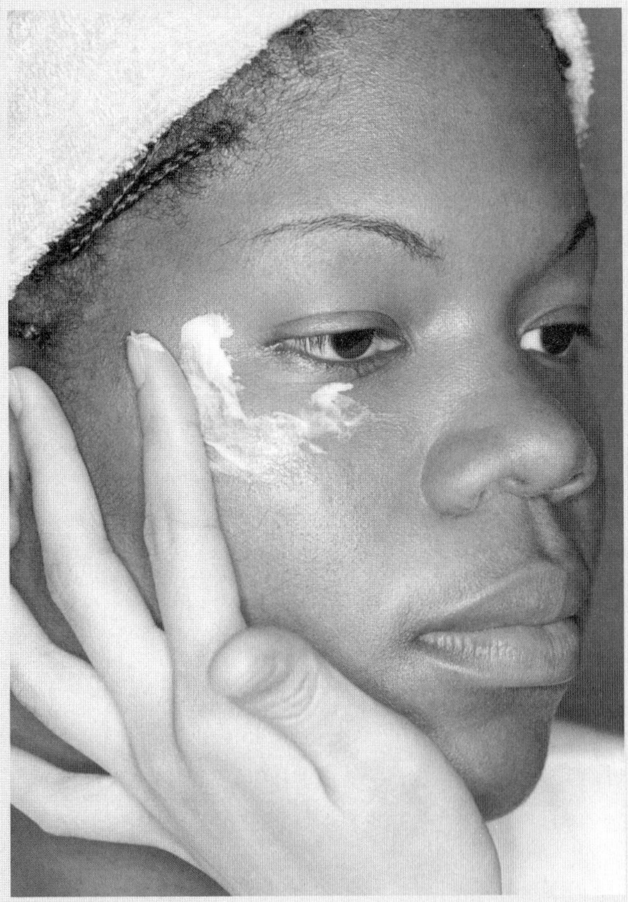

Charity's epilepsy warning to thousands of women

Tens of thousands of women with epilepsy are being put at risk because of a lack of access to information about significant times in their lives, says a national charity.

Having the condition and taking anti-epileptic drugs can affect a woman's choice of contraception, her ability to have children and, later in life, her choices about hormone replacement therapy, says Epilepsy Action.

Equally, events such as adolescence, childbirth and the menopause can all have an impact on seizure control.

With about 40,000 women having seizures that could be prevented, Epilepsy Action is urging women to seek medical advice to guide them through these stages.

The charity says all healthcare professionals should be aware of the complex issues faced by the 230,000 women with epilepsy in the UK.

1 For each case study:
   - explain why there is information failure,
   - explain how information failure has affected consumption of the two products.

2 Discuss what interventions might reduce these information failures.

In some situations, the problem of information failure is known as one of **asymmetric information**. This is the term used to describe circumstances where information is not shared equally between two agents or parties carrying out a transaction. Typical examples include:

- Health care. When you visit your doctor with an illness or problem you do not have the same medical knowledge as the doctor. You are therefore relying on their experience and competence to give you the treatment you need.
- Insurance. When applying say for health or car insurance, as the purchaser you know far more about your circumstances than the company who is selling you a policy. The company relies upon your integrity and honesty in making the decision on whether to issue a policy to you.
- Financial services. The information (small print) provided by banks and credit card companies is often very difficult to understand. What might seem a good deal could turn out not to be the case. This is also true when purchasing a mobile phone contract. In both cases, the seller has far more knowledge of the information provided than the purchaser.
- Housing. Buying or renting somewhere to live can be fraught with difficulties. Real estate agents and others try to paint a glowing picture of what they are trying to sell. Purchasers usually have to accept this and yet may find that what they have been told is not entirely the truth.
- Environment. As individuals we invariably know very little about the environmental consequences of driving cars or throwing waste into the drains or the sea. Environmental authorities though are much more aware of our actions as they will have studied the effects of our actions.

The insurance market

Two particular problems due to imperfect information are those of adverse selection and moral hazard. They can be best explained with reference to the insurance market (see also chapter 6 above).

The insurance market is a huge complex business. It is possible to purchase policies that cover buildings, personal contents, health, cars, life cover, business fidelity, travel and, in some countries, your pets. In virtually all cases, the procedure is that the client completes a proposal form which they have to sign or, if purchased over the internet, declare is correct. In some cases, it may not be to the client's advantage to divulge all of the information that is asked for, as it might lead to an increased premium. Examples would be a driver who has a string of convictions for speeding not making these known or someone who has a family history of heart problems not making these known when seeking health insurance.

Where this occurs, then there is adverse selection. The insurance company will take on clients it would otherwise reject and, in so doing, charge them the same premiums as clients with far less risk. As a consequence, the insurance company has to bear the burden of the increased probability of a claim being made. When this occurs, premiums for all clients have to rise forcing some clients with low risk characteristics to move to another insurer or withdraw from the market. Over time, a company could well be left with high risk clients forcing premiums to rise even higher. If insurers cannot make a profit, they may eventually be forced to withdraw from the market.

The problems faced by insurance companies are compounded by the additional difficulty of moral hazard. This is a term used to describe the effects that being insured has upon an individual's behaviour. With most forms of insurance, this may be seen as an incentive to behave in a less capable way as the person insured knows that there is this 'cushion of comfort' there. A car owner, for example, may be careless and leave a vehicle unlocked, knowing full well that, if it is stolen, the insurance company will provide compensation. In the health field, where someone has insurance, they may end up making more visits to the doctor than if they had to pay for each visit. As with adverse selection, the outcome could be that insurance firms suffer losses and may withdraw from a particular market. The market has therefore failed to give an efficient allocation of resources.

So what can insurance companies do to overcome these problems?

- In the case of adverse selection, they can use so-called proxies to establish risk. This may be based upon age, in the case of life and car insurance, or location, in the case of house insurance. Premiums are varied accordingly in relation to risk.
- With moral hazard, insurance companies can offer 'no claims' bonuses to customers or raise the excess payment required in cases where clients make regular claims. Both of these ought to encourage more responsive behaviour than where there are no penalties.

Self-assessment tasks

The following short answer questions have been set in recent CAPE examinations, 2003–2005.

1 A large number of workers are leaving country A for jobs in country B.

(a) How will this movement of labour affect wage rates in country A and country B? (2 marks)

(b) Sick persons are persons more likely to buy health insurance than persons who are healthy, and persons with fire insurance are less likely to take proper precautions against fire. To which of the following do the behaviours described above refer?

- asymmetric information,
- moral hazard,
- adverse selection.

(4 marks)

(Total 6 marks)

2 (a) What do you understand by a 'social welfare programme'? (2 marks)

(b) Define the term 'asymmetric information'. (2 marks)

(c) State TWO measures taken by the government of your country to improve social welfare. (2 marks)

(Total 6 marks)

Summary

In this chapter it has been shown that:

- Social welfare is maximised where the products that consumers want are being made efficiently and in the right quantities.
- A lack of information or misleading information leads to a situation whereby the market fails to provide the best allocation of resources.
- In some market situations, buyers and sellers have to make decisions in circumstances where the volume and quality of information available is unequal.

Key words

Definitions of Key words can be found in the Glossary.

asymmetric information
socially optimum output
social welfare

Unit 2
Macroeconomics

Module 1

Models of the macroeconomy

On completion of this module you should be able to:

understand the subject of macroeconomics and the difference between microeconomics and macroeconomics

appreciate the notion of national income accounting and the importance of these accounts for macroeconomic theory and policy

develop awareness of the reasons underlying the stability of an economy

appreciate the arguments suggesting that government intervention may not necessarily improve economic performance

understand the reasons why an economy may be characterised by unemployment and how intervention may be used to improve economic performance

understand the different explanations of the consumption function

appreciate the role of saving as a vehicle for economic growth

understand the reasons why investment spending is an important component of aggregate demand

understand the accelerator theory

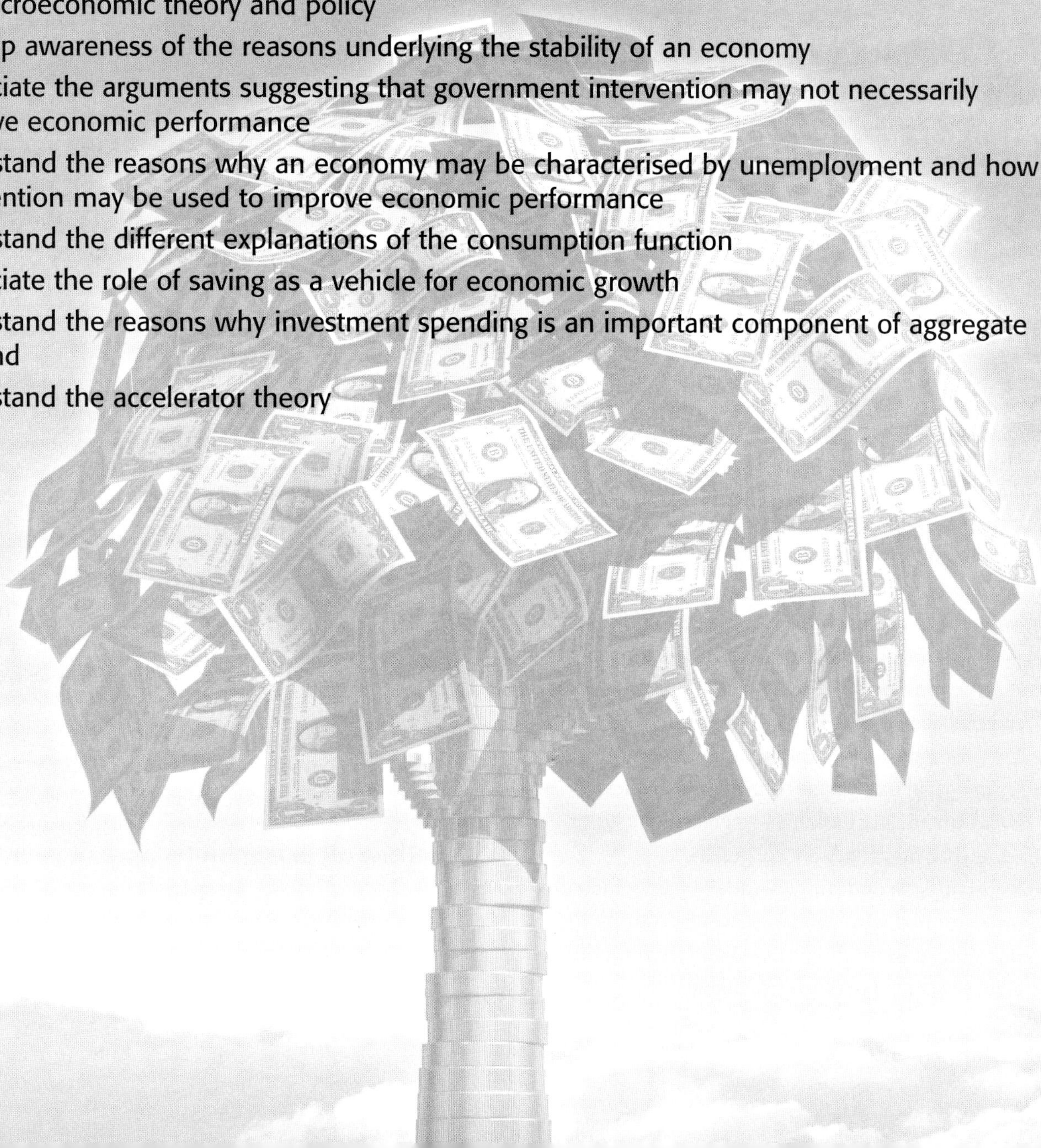

9 The nature of macroeconomics

This chapter covers unit 2, module 1, topic 1.
On completion of this chapter, you should be able to:

- outline the major differences between microeconomic and macroeconomic theory
- define the major macroeconomic variables
- explain the importance of, and the relationship, among macroeconomic variables
- explain how the major macroeconomic variables are measured
- calculate and interpret data related to macroeconomic variables
- explain the views of Keynesian and Monetarist Schools

From microeconomics to macroeconomics

The Introduction to this book defined what is meant by Economics and how from a general standpoint, it is possible to distinguish in principle at least between microeconomics and macroeconomics. Now that you have completed unit 1, you should have a good knowledge and understanding of microeconomics.

To some extent, macroeconomics differs from microeconomics in its scale and scope. In looking at problems, issues, theories and concepts that affect the economy as a whole, macroeconomics covers a much wider range of subject matter. In the twenty-first century, no study of macroeconomics would be complete without some understanding of the global context, since globalisation has had a profound effect on the well-being and operation of all of the world's economies, from the poorest African state to the mega-rich United States of America (see chapter 22).

At the same time, though, macroeconomics draws upon some of the concepts of microeconomics but uses and applies them in a wider context. For example:

- Production possibility curves and opportunity cost can be used to explain economic growth.
- The price elasticity of demand for a good or service is an important consideration when governments are looking at increasing taxes or reviewing how taxes are collected.
- Demand-side and supply-side policies, which are underpinned with similar concepts to those introduced in module 1 of unit 1, are fundamental ways in which governments manage their economies.
- Combating market failure can have a direct bearing on how governments collect taxes and allocate resources to various forms of government spending.

These are just a few examples of how in some respects the difference between microeconomics and macroeconomics is not at all clear cut.

Returning to macroeconomics, it is the case that every day in a good newspaper or on the television news, there are features that come under the scope of macroeconomics. Typical headlines could include:

'Inflation falls to its lowest level since 2001'

'Interest rate increase is bad news for mortgages'

'US dollar continues to slide on world market'

'Jobless total rises as tourism is hit by hurricanes'

'The economy continues to grow at a steady rate'

'Falling oil prices hit balance of payments surplus'

'Government spending is out of control'

These stories appear in the media since in all cases they affect the lives of people and over time or in turn, economic well-being and prosperity. Each has a particular significance for all economies, whether these be developing Caribbean ones or developed economies such as the UK and the USA.

Self-assessment task

A good newspaper usually contains useful information on the macroeconomy. In some cases, this information makes comparisons with the economies of other neighbouring countries. For your own country:

- see what articles you can find on some of the macroeconomic variables in this topic,
- make a few notes on why these variables have attracted the newspaper's attention.

Inflation

Inflation is a situation in an economy where there is a general and sustained increase in the price level. In all economies the control of inflation has become the main objective of government economic policy–price stability is crucial for governments to achieve their macroeconomic objectives. (This is why inflation is the first variable to be considered in this chapter and why it will be considered in more detail than some other variables.)

Some initial points of perspective should be noted:

- An increase in a small number of prices does not constitute inflation. The key thing is that the increase in prices should be evidenced across a wide range of goods and services purchased by consumers (see below). The one possible exception is the price of oil – when increasing, this can have a substantial effect across the economy as a whole.
- The increase in prices should be sustained over time for it to be seen as inflationary. The rate of increase on a year-by-year basis is likely to be variable. Although there are some exceptions, particularly in South American economies and Zimbabwe (see Self-assessment on next page), inflation in the twenty-first century has been more controlled than at any stage since the mid-1970s.
- A low and steady rate of inflation may not be a bad thing for an economy. This puts pressure on businesses to be competitive and at the same time, produces a situation where there is broad confidence in the macroeconomy.

Virtually all of the developed economies have managed to contain inflation to less than 5 per cent per annum over the past decade. Emerging and developing economies have not found this to be the case, although globally inflation rates are now more under control than has been the case in the past. Table 9.1 shows the average annual rates of inflation for selected economies in the region from 2002 to 2004, with a comparison from 1985 to 1990.

	2004	2003	2002	1990	1985–90
Bahamas	0.9	3.0	2.1	4.5	5.1
Barbados	1.4	1.6	0.2	3.1	3.7
Jamaica	13.6	10.3	7.1	22.0	13.2
Trinidad and Tobago	3.7	3.8	4.2	11.0	9.7
Argentina	4.4	13.4	25.9	2314.0	583.8
Brazil	6.6	14.7	8.5	2862.4	653.8
Mexico	4.7	4.5	5.1	26.7	69.7
Nicaragua	8.4	5.1	4.0	7485.2	3246.9
Venezuela	21.7	31.1	14.0	40.7	78.2

Table 9.1 Average annual rates of inflation for selected Caribbean and South American economies (% change on previous year)
Source: ECLAC Statistical Yearbook, 2005.

Self-assessment tasks

Read the newspaper article below and then tackle the questions that follow.

The millionaires who cannot afford to buy anything

The 100,000 Zimbabwean dollar note that went into circulation this week was officially worth just over 50p. On Harare's burgeoning undercover markets it was worth just 16p. Hours after printing, the price of a loaf of bread shot up by about 40 per cent to Z$130,000. These new notes are strictly speaking not currency – they are 'bearer cheques' signed by the governor of the central bank and have an expiry date of 31 December 2006.

At present, the highest denomination banknote is Z$50,000. A typical restaurant meal for four is about Z$15m – it is likely to take almost as long to count out the notes to pay the bill as it does to eat the meal! Other prices in May 2006 include

1 litre fresh milk	Z$80,000
1 litre Coca-cola	Z$120,000
1 chicken	Z$1.2m
Small portable TV	Z$23m
Mercedes-Benz C180	Z$15bn

For Zimbabwe's people, everyday life is a misery. They stand in shops with two bags, one full of money the other for the food they are purchasing. Many cannot afford public transport and many of those in employment get up in the middle of the night to walk to work. The currency is worth less each day. A barter system is rapidly emerging and farm workers invariably prefer to be paid in produce rather than a stack of banknotes that lose value as soon as they are received. Only condoms, which cost Z$300 because they are heavily subsidised by the international community, seem to be inflation-proof.

Source: *The Times*, 8 May 2006 (adaptation).

Children gather eggs at a rubbish dump. In the worst economic crisis since Independence in 1980, Zimbabweans cope with acute shortages of food, gasoline and imports
Source: PA Potos.

1 Zimbabwe is clearly experiencing severe hyperinflation. What effects is this having on the internal and external operation of the macroeconomy?

2 See what you can find out about how countries such as Argentina, Brazil and Nicaragua have dealt with similar hyperinflation problems.

It is clear from this table that all of these economies have experienced some form of inflation over the past 20 years or so. Their experience has been variable – the following conclusions can be made:

- Inflation is now far less of a problem for all of these economies than it was 15 to 20 years ago.
- Caribbean economies have not experienced the hyperinflation that affected South American economies in the late 1980s and that peaked in 1990.
- With the exception of Jamaica, recent rates of inflation for the other Caribbean economies give little cause for concern.

Table 9.2 may be useful in determining the relative extent to which inflation is a macroeconomic problem for an economy.

% change per annum over a period of time	Outcome
<5	Very mild inflation, which can actually aid competitiveness.
5–10	Mild inflation, which must be kept under control to avoid future difficulties.
10–19	Build up of inflationary pressures with increased wage demands and high interest rates; savings begin to be affected. Strict policies essential if problem is to be resolved.
20–50	Serious inflation. Economic relationships in real danger of breaking down. Confidence in money is seriously eroded.
50 and above	Signs of hyperinflation. Depending on severity, domestic economic structures collapse and currency becomes worthless on foreign exchange markets and also internally.

Table 9.2 Degrees of inflation

The general price level and price indices

The general price level is a recognised measure of the cost of living in an economy at any one point in time. Changes in the general price level on a year-by-year basis in turn are a measure of the rate of inflation in an economy (see above).

In its simplest form, the general price level in an economy is calculated periodically using some form of **price index**. In the UK, the Retail Prices Index (RPI) is a measure of changes in the prices of consumer goods bought by people in the UK. Much attention is paid to this index by the media, politicians, business people and consumers (see Introduction also).

The RPI is a weighted price index. Its calculation is a major statistical task, involving three main stages. These are:

- a survey to find out what families buy and how much they spend on particular items – this provides the **weights**;
- recording how much the prices of some 600 selected items have changed – this information is collected from all main types of retail outlet, as well as from gas, water, electricity and transport suppliers;
- the percentage change in price for each item is then multiplied by its weight – from this the average change in the RPI is determined.

Although not all countries have such a comprehensive price index, the basic principles of construction remain the same irrespective of the level of sophistication.

$$\text{Cost of living index, year 1} = \sum_{i=1}^{n} \frac{W_{i1} P_{i1}}{W_{i0} P_{i0}} \times 100$$

where W = weight of item in family expenditure
P = price of item
n = total number of items in index

If the index is calculated to be over 100 in year 1, then the cost of living has increased compared with the base date, year 0. For example, if the index is 105, then the cost of living has increased by 5 per cent since the base year. An index of below 100 in year 1 would indicate a fall in the cost of living.

The change in the cost of living index is usually measured in **nominal** terms, that is in terms of the prices operating in the year in which the goods are produced.

What's in and what's out – UK RPI basket

Food and drink:
In: salmon fillets; organic fruit and veg; mayonnaise; french stick/baguette; chilled desserts; herbal/fruit tea bags; cereal snacks; soft drinks; large multipacks
Out: rainbow trout; leeks; salad cream; streaky bacon; delivered milk, sterilised milk

Household goods:
In: home office computer desks; cutlery sets; crockery sets; laminate flooring; greeting cards
Out: nest of tables; table knife; bread bin

Household services:
In: bank overdraft charges; home removals; catering for a function; foreign exchange commission
Out: bank custody of a sealed envelope

Clothing and footwear:
In: women's vest/strappy tops; women's evening dress; baseball caps
Out: women's ski pants

Price comparisons

	1947[1]	**1997**
Frock[2]	£15.10	£69
Women's suit[2]	£23.15	£203.99
Women's cardigan/jumper[2]	£4.16	£35
Cold cream	11p	£2.65
Bar of chocolate (1/2lb bar)	7p	79p
Road tax	£1.00	£145
Family saloon car[2]	£416.03 (Austin A40)	£12,280 (Ford Escort 1.4cl)
'Over to you' by Roald Dahl	38p	£5.99
Six bedroom house, Wimbledon	£7,250	£775,000
2 weeks in Lucerne	£57.75	£815
Headache tablets	7p	£1.85
Man's wristwatch	£6.40	£29.50
Copy of *The Observer*	1p	£1.00
Copy of *Daily Hansard*	3p	£5.00
Music recording	24p (12" classical)	£15.99 (Spice Girls' album)

Notes: [1] – equivalent decimal price [2] – subject to rationing

Source: *Daily Telegraph*, 20 March 2001.

Self-assessment tasks

1 Thinking of your own country, briefly describe how you might construct an appropriate cost of living index.
2 If such an index exists, how does it compare with your own ideas on how it might be constructed?

Interest rates

As noted in chapter 7, interest is the price that is paid for the use of capital. This is looking at interest from a microeconomic standpoint with respect to factors of production. Interest rates though have wider macroeconomic significance as will become clearer throughout the course of this Unit. It is also the case that in practice there is more than one interest rate that is being applied in the economy by the central bank or monetary authority (see table 9.3).

Despite all of these rates, the main purpose of an interest rate is to make the borrower aware of what will have to be repaid on top of the principal taken out on a loan, or, for a saver, to indicate the return for depositing a sum of money with a bank. As far as an economy is concerned, the base rate of interest is a clear statement as to the state of the economy. More specifically:

East Caribbean Central Bank	
ECCB discount rate	6.5%
Minimum savings rate	3.0%
Weighted inter-bank rate	6.0%
Treasury bill rate:	
◆ 91 days	5.82%
◆ 5 years	5.50%
Other rates	
Bank of England base rate	3.75%
European Central Bank base rate	3.0%
US Federal Reserve Bank (3 month rate)	5.2%

Table 9.3 Caribbean and other interest rates (as at 20 October 2006)

- when interest rates are low or are falling, the message is that the government or its central bank is seeking to encourage expansion in the macroeconomy, particularly through increased private sector investment;
- a period of relatively high interest rates indicates that the government or its central bank is concerned about inflation and that it expects such rates of interest to lead to less inflationary pressures as borrowing money is expensive.

The interest rate paid to savers by a bank is called the **nominal interest rate.** When corrected for inflation, it is called the **real interest rate.** Their relationship with inflation is:

Grenada to benefit from lowered interest rates from IMF

St George's, Grenada: The International Monetary Fund (IMF) has lived up to its promises to ease the financial constraints on low income countries when the IMF Board took a decision on 21 January 2005 to lower interest rates on its natural disaster assistance loans.

Now the Government of Grenada will benefit from lower interest rates it has received from the IMF. The Ministry of Finance has announced that the IMF has taken the decision to reduce the interest rate on the IMF loan to Grenada from 3 per cent to 0.5 per cent, effective immediately.

As part of its assistance to Grenada, following Hurricane Ivan, Grenada received a loan of US$4.4 million at a rate of 3 per cent. Grenada also received a similar loan in 2003 after Tropical Storm Lily. The interest rates on both loans are now 0.5 per cent.

The Government of Grenada is currently engaged in a debt restructuring programme in an effort to reduce the country's debt obligation. In this regard, financial and legal advisors have been contracted and are working closely with the Ministry of Finance, according to a release from the Government of Grenada.

Source: Caribbean Net News, 2 February 2005.

Hurricane damage in Grenada
Source: Alamy.

Real interest rate = Nominal interest rate – Inflation rate

The real interest rate therefore shows how much actual purchasing power has increased over the length of the savings deposits.

In most economies, it is obvious that if savings are to be encouraged the real rate of interest must be positive. In recent years there have been extreme cases of economies where interest rates have been at zero (Japan in 2001) or near zero (Hong Kong had a 0.01 per cent rate in early 2004). In these examples, the respective governments were trying to reflate their economies after a period of severe recession, falling consumer prices and low business confidence.

For developing economies, interest rates are charged by commercial banks and the International Monetary Fund for loans that are provided to aid economic growth and reconstruction. The boxed item on Granada is clearly good news for this small Caribbean economy that has seen dramatic reconstruction following the devastation caused by Hurricane Ivan. (The People's Republic of China has also helped to finance reconstruction including Grenada's National Stadium.)

Exchange rates

An exchange rate is simply defined as the price of one currency in terms of another. For example, in mid October 2006, £1 sterling was worth US$1.87 and 1.49 euros. Taken the other way round, US$1 was worth £0.54 and 1 euro was worth £0.67. Table 9.4 shows some exchange rates for the East Caribbean dollar against other currencies at the same period.

US dollar	2.6882 (buying rate)
Pound sterling	5.0838
Euro	3.4043
Canadian dollar	2.3984
Swiss franc	2.1447
Barbados dollar	1.3500
Guyana dollar	0.0135

Table 9.4 East Caribbean dollar exchange rates in mid October 2006
Source: East Caribbean Central Bank.

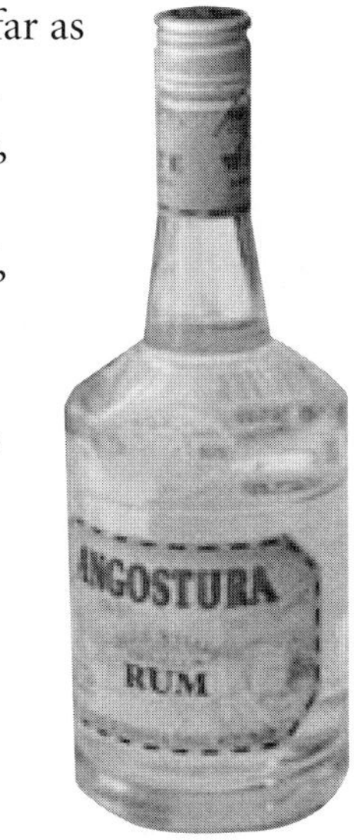

The exchange rate is a price in so far as it is determined by the demand for a currency and its supply. For example, when a UK resident buys a bottle of Jamaican rum imported into the UK, currency exchange must take place. This is because the UK resident will use sterling to buy the rum in a shop but the Caribbean producer will require payment to be made in local currency. This exchange of one currency for another takes place in the foreign exchange market.

In looking at exchange rates, it is possible to recognise three different types. These are:

- **nominal exchange rates**. This is the price of one currency in terms of another. The above examples can be described in this way. Changes in the nominal exchange rate are likely to occur on a regular, usually daily, basis depending on demand and supply. These changes can affect the transaction price of goods and services traded between any two countries. For example, if the Jamaican dollar depreciates in value relative to the UK pound, a bottle of rum bought in the UK will cost less. Significantly, the cost of a holiday in Jamaica will also fall for UK tourists resulting in Jamaica being a more attractive than other competing destinations. Nominal exchange rates are bilateral since just two country's exchange rates are being compared.
- **trade-weighted exchange rates**. This is a more useful measure of the overall relative strength of a currency. It takes into account that in today's global economy countries trade with lots of other countries and that in so doing nominal exchange rates may not always move in the same direction. The UK pound for example could be stronger against the $US over a period of time yet be weaker against the euro. The weights used for a trade-weighted exchange rate vary according to the relative importance in trading terms of the currencies used in trading transactions. So, if the UK undertakes three times as much trade with the rest of the EU than with the USA (which is the case), the euro is given three times the weight of

the $US in calculating the trade-weighted index. Table 9.5 shows some examples of this form of exchange rate for selected economies, again in October 2006.

Country	Trade-weighted exchange rate, 2000 = 100	
	Mid October 2006	Mid October 2005
UK	102.2	99.0
Canada	127.2	123.4
France	108.5	107.5
Germany	110.2	108.9
Japan	79.3	83.2
USA	85.0	86.6

Table 9.5 Trade-weighted exchange rate for selected developed economies
Source: *The Economist*, 21–27 October 2006.

This table shows that:

- The external value of the UK's currency has been relatively stable since 2000 compared with the various currencies of its trading partners.
- The $US and Japanese yen have both declined relatively to the currencies of countries with whom they trade. In principle this should make imports from these countries relatively cheaper and exports, more expensive. Their current balance positions could not be more different – the US had a huge deficit of over $860bn last year, whilst Japan had a surplus of $160bn. The conclusion that can be made is that the yen is still overvalued on world markets, making it very difficult for many exporters to sell their goods in the Japanese market.
- Where the index exceeds 100, then this country's currency has appreciated relative to others. This makes imports from such countries relatively more expensive than goods that are being exported to it.
- The **real effective exchange rate**, as its name suggests, takes into account differences in inflation rates as well as changes in exchange rates between trading countries. A simple example will show why this can be a useful measure. If a country's exchange rate is depreciating against another, it means that goods exported from this country are now cheaper in foreign markets. At the same time, the exporting country might have been experiencing a higher rate of inflation than its trading partner. As a result, in real terms, its export prices could have increased. Whether the effective prices of exports have increased will depend on the relative strength of the depreciation and the increase in prices of domestic goods for export. This measure of the exchange rate is therefore very relevant and is increasingly used to evaluate the competitiveness of an economy's goods and services in global markets.

In macroeconomics, the exchange rate of a currency is the most important, but not necessarily the only, factor in determining the health of the balance of payments in an economy (see below). This particularly applies to the current account balance. Changes in the exchange rate can also influence the rate of inflation, unemployment and growth in an economy.

Unemployment

Unemployment is the total number of people who are not in employment but who are actively seeking work. This is not the same as the **rate of unemployment**, which is the number of employed people as a percentage of the labour force. The labour force consists of those in employment and those who are officially classed as unemployed.

Measuring unemployment and the rate of unemployment, particularly in developing economies, is not easy. This is because the benefit systems in such countries are invariably less favourable than in developed economies such as the UK where the 'claimant count' method is used to measure unemployment.

The International Labour Office (ILO) has an internationally recognised definition of unemployment that includes all people who are actively seeking and available to start work irrespective of whether they are receiving welfare benefits. This definition therefore includes housewives who might be seeking to return to work or secondary school leavers looking for their first job. Table 9.6 shows the rates of unemployment in CARICOM countries in 2004.

The rates of unemployment in most Caribbean economies are high when compared with many developed economies where unemployment rates of

Antigua & Barbuda	11.0	Jamaica	13.0
Bahamas	7.8	St Kitts/Nevis	4.5
Barbados	10.4	St Lucia	18.1
Belize	12.8	St Vincent & the Grenadines	15.0
Dominica	23.1	Suriname	10.6
Grenada	17.0	Trinidad & Tobago	14.2
Guyana	9.1		

Table 9.6 Unemployment rates in CARICOM countries in 2004 (average %)
Source: CARICOM.

10% give rise to serious economic and political concerns. Notwithstanding, interpreting unemployment data is not easy for various reasons such as:

- the data are likely to be inaccurate due to problems of data collection;
- some people who are unemployed may be working illegally in the informal economy;
- the data give no indication as to how long a person has been unemployed;
- someone who was previously unemployed may be prepared to accept a low paid job that has no impact on a country's output.
- seasonal unemployment is a particular problem in the economies of the Caribbean area; agriculture and tourism are both activities where labour demand varies enormously at different periods of the year.

The measurement of unemployment is important from a macroeconomic standpoint. If there is unemployment:

- Output will be below its potential level. The economy will be operating within its production possibility curve (see chapter 1). Resources are not being fully used. As employment increases, the economy will reach its production possibility frontier when there is full employment.
- Tax revenue for the government will be lower at times of high unemployment. If welfare benefits are paid to those who are unemployed, the cost of these will be higher.
- A high level of unemployment may result in civil unrest, increased crime and substantial stress for the unemployed and their families. The gap between those in work and those who are unemployed can be a wide one, particularly in developing economies where state support for the unemployed is invariably limited.

Self-assessment tasks

1. For your own country, see what information you can obtain on:
   - the number of people in employment,
   - the number of people who are unemployed,
   - unemployment rates,
   - activity rates for males and females.
2. What trends can you identify in these statistics over the past few years?
3. What comments might you make about the quality and accuracy of this data.

Economic growth

Economic growth is defined as the increase in output in an economy. It is usually expressed as a percentage change over a period of a year. When measured in real terms, it gives a true indication as to how output has grown. Over the longer term, it can be represented by an outward shift of the production possibility curve of an economy.

Growth rates can be negative as well as positive. Table 9.7 shows recent growth rates for CARICOM economies in monetary terms from 2003 to 2005.

Country	2005	2004	2003
Antigua & Barbuda	5.6	5.2	4.7
Barbados	3.9	4.8	2.0
Belize	3.1	4,6	9,2
Dominica	3.6	3.1	0.1
Grenada	5.2	−3.0	7.5
Guyana	−3.0	1.6	−0.7
Jamaica	1.4	0.9	2.3
St Kitts/Nevis	7.0	6.5	2.2
St Vincent & the Grenadines	2.8	5.4	4.1
St Lucia	7.3	3.6	4.3
Suriname	5.7	7.7	6.1
Trinidad & Tobago	7.0	6.5	13.4

Table 9.7 Average annual rate of growth of GDP (% change on previous year)
Source: ECLAC Statistical Yearbook, 2005.

A positive annual rate of growth indicates that output is higher than in the previous year. So, in 2005, the output of Barbados was 3.9 per cent higher than in 2004. (This figure is likely to be less when expressed in real terms.) This figure is slightly less than in 2004 when there was an increase in output of 4.8 per cent from 2003. It is important to bear in mind that output has actually increased since 2003 – a fall in the growth rate means that output has increased at a slower rate than in an earlier year.

A negative growth rate, particularly over a a few years, is bad news for an economy. Looking at table 9.7, Guyana has suffered from negative growth in two of the years that are shown. As a consequence, output in 2005 has fallen in the period since 2002, despite the 1.6 per cent growth from 2003 to 2004.

In comparing economic growth rates over time and between countries, care has to be taken over a number of issues. These include:

- The official GDP figures may understate the true change in output due to the hidden or informal economy. This is the term used to describe undeclared economic activities such as people working and not declaring their income to the tax authorities or the selling of goods for cash and for which no records are declared.
- There are no problems of valuing the output of goods and services provided by the government and for which no direct charge is made.
- There are also the problems of valuing the output of goods produced by people for their own use, for example in the case of subsistence agriculture.

The balance of payments

It is important that governments have an accurate record of all the transactions that take place between residents of their country and all other countries in the rest of the world. These transactions are recorded in the balance of payments. In practice this record is a very complex financial statement – though there is an internationally agreed method for its presentation. This has been recommended by the International Monetary Fund (IMF) and permits economists to make international comparisons. The basics of this method are outlined below.

The balance of payments consists of the **current account**, the **capital account**, the **financial account** and the **international investment position**. We can use the UK accounts to explain the various components of the accounts.

It should be noted that the balance of payments accounts are simply a record of flows of money between residents of the UK and non-residents. Following basic accounting principles this means that every credit (+) entry is matched by a debit (–) entry. For example, if a UK resident exports goods abroad, this is recorded as a credit entry (+) in the accounts. We also have to record how foreign residents paid for these exports. Perhaps the foreign resident had a bank account in the UK which was used to pay the exporter. This would be shown in the accounts as a debit entry as a decrease in UK liabilities abroad (–). This means that the foreign resident has less of a claim on a UK bank account. The important point is that we have accounted for the spending and recorded both sides of the transaction. Since every credit item is matched by a debit item in the accounts, it follows that in an accounting sense, the balance of payments must always balance. In practice however, we cannot have fully accurate information. As a result, a section of the accounts is entitled 'net errors and omissions' to allow for discrepancies in the calculations.

The current account

The current account consists of four main headings:

- trade in goods,
- trade in services,
- income,
- current transfers.

Trade in goods

The goods account covers items that can be touched, weighed or counted as they are traded. For this reason, they are sometimes known as visibles. For example, the import of cars from Germany is a debit item in the current account of the UK, whereas the export of cashmere sweaters to Japan is a credit item. The difference between visible exports and imports is sometimes referred to as the **balance of trade**.

Trade in services

The services account covers exports and imports of services. For example, if a UK resident purchases an airline ticket from a foreign airline, this has the same impact as the import of a good and is recorded as a debit item. However, if a merchant bank in the City of London raises a loan for a foreign firm, the fee charged by the bank is equivalent to an export and will be recorded as a credit item. The difference in trade in such items is known as the invisible balance.

Income

The income account is made up of payments made to employees, for example, those who work abroad and send money home, and income from investments abroad. The former is not very significant for the UK but investment income is very large. This covers any earnings from foreign investment and financial assets and liabilities. For example, any dividends paid on foreign shares held by UK residents are recorded as credits, whereas interest paid to foreign holders of deposits in UK financial institutions is recorded as a debit item.

Current transfers

Current transfers are made up of central government transfers (for example, payments and receipts from the EU) and other transfers by private individuals (such as gifts of cash).

Capital account

The capital account records transactions which involve the transfer of ownership of fixed assets and the acquisition or disposal of non-financial assets. An example of the former might be a government investment grant to undertake a large construction project, such as a water purification plant abroad. An example of the latter might be land purchased or sold by a foreign embassy.

Financial account

The financial account was formerly known as the capital account. This section of the accounts records the forms of investment overseas by UK residents and the inward flow of investment funds from foreign residents. It is this flow which gives rise to flows of investment income in the current account.

Balance of payments examples

Table 9.8 shows a summary of the balance of payments current accounts for selected countries in 2004. (For ease of comparison all of the data are shown in $US.) It shows some interesting contrasts such as:

	Exports of goods	Imports of goods	Current account balance	Foreign direct investment
Developed economies				
Canada	321,967	275,799	25,870	6,273
Germany	914,839	717,491	104,301	25,568
Japan	565,490	454,530	172,059	6,238
UK	345,610	461,983	−46,879	20,696
USA	819,026	1,526,380	−665,939	39,889
Emerging economies				
China	593,369	561,423	45,875	53,505
Hungary	54,175	59,216	−8,819	2,506
Malaysia	126,497	105,176	13,381	2,473
Poland	74,094	87,849	−3,585	4,123
Singapore	179,547	163,820	28,183	11,431

Table 9.8 Extracts from the balance of payments for selected economies in 2004 ($USm)
Note: Foreign direct investment is the net inflow of investment into an enterprise operating in an economy other than that of the investor.
Source: World Development Report, 2006.

Proton Gen 2 car at the manufacturing plant in Proton City, Malaysia
Source: Andy Wong/AP/PA Photos.

- The UK has traditionally experienced a deficit in its annual trade in goods and services. This is particularly the case for trade in goods.
- The USA has a massive deficit on trade in goods and services; in contrast, both Germany and Japan have substantial surpluses.
- Emerging European economies invariably have a deficit in their trade in goods and services; Malaysia and Singapore have substantial export earnings from manufactured goods and financial services.
- Net income from investments abroad is very high for Japan; its multinationals have widespread interests across the world.
- A persistent deficit on the current account is a cause for concern.

Compiling information on the balance of payments of an economy is a major and in some respects difficult statistical task. Information has to be drawn from various sources. This is not always accurate and consistent and is why a net errors and omissions item is included in a country's balance of payments record. This compensates for the fact that in theory the balance of payments should by definition always balance, with the net of the current, capital and financial accounts equalling zero.

The data shown in table 9.8 is for one year only. In looking at the balance of payments issues in an economy, one year taken in isolation is of little relevance – what is far more useful is to see a trend over time, taking size into account. Data over a period of time could for instance indicate that:

- a country with a persistent deficit on the trade in goods may not be price competitive or its goods may be of inferior quality compared to those from elsewhere;
- persistent deficits in the current balance not compensated for in the capital account can result in serious indebtedness for an economy;
- a surplus on the financial account is likely to have a positive effect on the economy in the longer term.

Self-assessment tasks

Study the information below on the Balance of Payments of Barbados and Trinidad and Tobago for 2004 and then tackle the questions that follow.

Current account	**Barbados $USm**	**Trinidad & Tobago $USm**
Exports of goods	278.2	6,402.9
Imports of goods	−1,260.0	−4,894.2
Credit on services	1,181.4	932.0
Debit on services	−519.8	−420.4
Balance on income	−122.0	−450.4
Balance on transfers	88.2	52.6
Balance on current account	−354.0	1,622.5
Other		
Balance on capital account	n.a.	n.a.
Balance on financial account	120.7	−1,361.6
Errors & omissions	63.1	473.1
Global balance	−170.2	734.0

Source: Annual Statistical Yearbook of Latin America and the Caribbean, 2005.

1 Using the above information, compare the balance of payments for Barbados and Trinidad and Tobago. How might you explain any differences?

2 Comment upon the extent to which the current accounts of these Caribbean countries matches the current accounts of the emerging economies shown in table 9.8.

Fiscal deficit The fiscal deficit is defined as the difference between a government's total expenditure (on education, social services, defence etc) and its total receipts (largely from taxation). Borrowing is excluded. There are two components of a fiscal deficit. These are:

- the revenue deficit, the difference between current government expenditure and current receipts;
- capital expenditure such as interest repayments on loans and government bonds.

When a government is in a situation where there is a fiscal deficit, this can be financed from its central bank or by borrowing from banks on the international money market. Debt of this form raises the interest burden for governments and in turn, issues that impact upon the management of the macroeconomy.

One of these issues relates to how the interest burden can be reduced. One way is to print more money – this is likely to be inflationary if the economy is operating at full capacity. If there is spare capacity, printing money could be a realistic possibility. Alternatively, the interest burden could be reduced through the government increasing its receipts from taxation. This would not be popular, yet it would be more beneficial than if the government reduced its own expenditure.

A further issue is the possible drain on governmental finances due to the interest burden required to service fiscal debt. Whilst printing money could be an option, a safer means is to raise more revenue through taxation. For developing economies this could also mean securing a sound tax basis to fund future revenue and tightening up on areas where there is tax evasion.

Keynesian and Monetarists' views on major macroeconomic issues

As you progress through this unit, you will appreciate that economists do not always agree on how macroeconomic issues such as those described above should be tackled in terms of macroeconomic policies. Various schools of economic thought persist as to what is the best way to deal with say, unemployment, rising inflation, a current account deficit, sluggish economic growth and so on. Figure 9.1 summarises the two main approaches.

The **Keynesian** view stems from the idea and work of the British economist John Maynard Keynes (1883–1946). Keynesian economists believe that market failure in the macroeconomy is a serious problem. In particular, if left to market forces, there is no guarantee that the economy will achieve a full employment level of GDP. Indeed, in times of severe recession, they maintain that the level of GDP can fall below the full employment level by a large amount and for long periods of time.

Keynesians maintain that government intervention is needed to improve the workings of the market. So, if there is high unemployment, they argue that the government should engage in deficit financing to raise the level of spending in the economy. The role of government is to assess the appropriate amount of spending to inject into the economy and to act accordingly. For most Keynesians the avoidance of high unemployment is seen as a key priority.

Keynesian principles for managing the macroeconomy were very much to the fore in many economies, the UK especially, up to around the mid-1970s. Today, many Keynesian principles persist. The **new classical economists** take the view that markets usually work efficiently. In their view, government intervention is not required apart from ensuring that laws, regulations and institutions are in place to allow market forces to operate in an appropriate way. Deregulation and reducing government involvement in the provision of goods and services are central to their strategy for returning the economy to a situation where market forces determine how the macro- as well as the microeconomy operates.

Monetarists take a different view to Keynesian economists. They see the control of inflation as the top priority for a government. This group, the most well-known being the American economist Milton Friedman, argue that the prime macroeconomic function of government is to control the money supply. By controlling the money supply, inflation can be controlled. They also maintain that the attempts to reduce unemployment by increasing government spending will have the negative long-term effect of raising inflation. They believe that economies are in the main stable, unless disturbed by erratic changes in the growth of the money supply.

The great debate in economics has been one of Keynesian versus Monetarist views on how the economy should be managed. Although Keynesian views are much less to the fore than a generation ago, empirical experience has shown that the most successful economies have applied macroeconomic policies that encompass both types of approach.

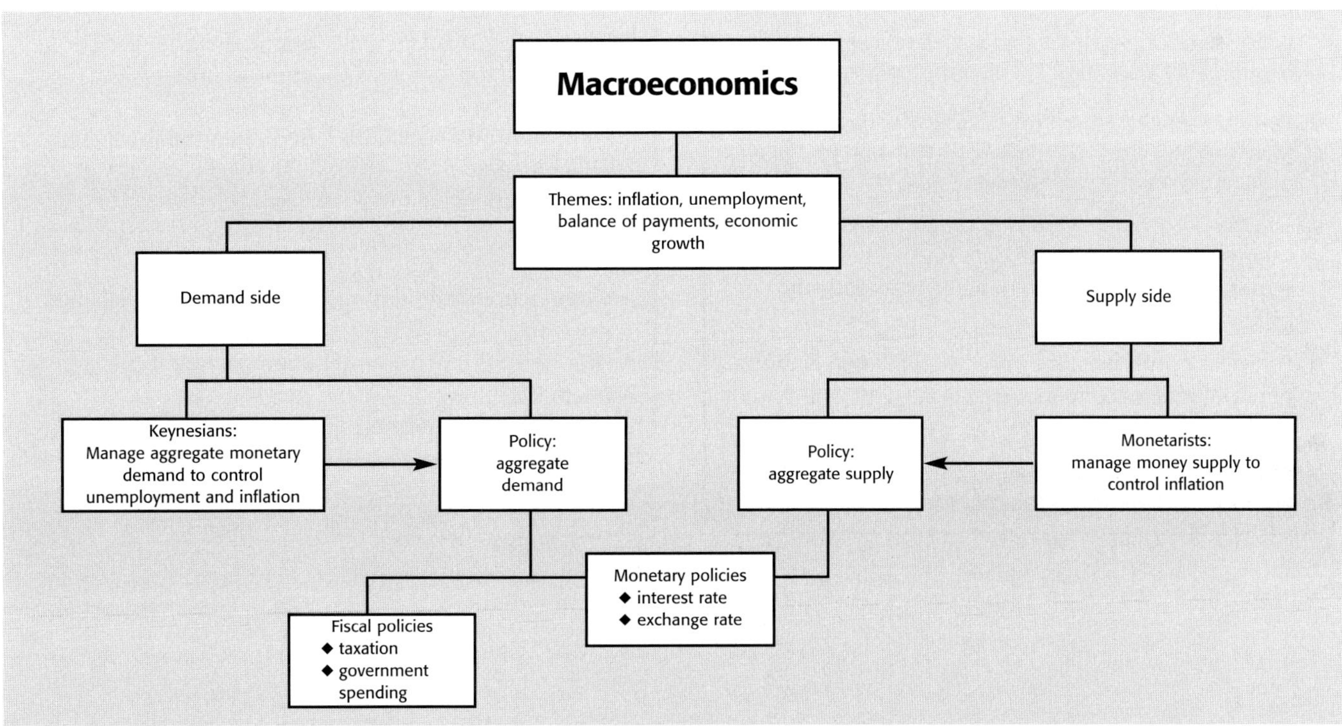

Figure 9.1 Major macroeconomic issues

Self-assessment tasks

The following short answer questions have been set in recent CAPE examinations, 2003–2005.

1 (a) Explain TWO of the following macroeconomic variables
- balance of payments accounts,
- the exchange rate,
- inflation. (4 marks)

(b) State ONE way in which inflation is measured. (CAPE, 2006) (2 marks)

(Total 6 marks)

2 (a) Explain TWO of the following macroeconomic variables:
- unemployment,
- economic growth,
- interest rate. (4 marks)

(b) State ONE way in which unemployment is measured. (2 marks)

(Total 6 marks)

3 (a) State how:
- Keynesian economists,
- Monetarists,

would seek to resolve a problem of inflation in the macroeconomy. (4 marks)

How might they know if their policies had been successful? (2 marks)

(Total 6 marks)

Summary

In this chapter it has been shown that:

- Macroeconomics is concerned with the study of a wide range of problems and issues relating to the economy as a whole.
- In any economy, developed or developing, governments are concerned with managing a range of macroeconomic variables.
- The main economic variables can be measured in a variety of ways; the use of data is essential for the government to be able to manage the economy effectively.
- For most economies, the control of inflation is the principal macroeconomic objective.
- Economists hold different views on how these objectives should be managed; the main approaches are those of the Keynesian and Monetarist Schools.

Key words

Definitions of Key words can be found in the Glossary.

balance of payments
balance of trade
capital account
current account
exchange rate
financial account
fiscal deficit
inflation
international investment position
Keynesians
Monetarists
new classical economists
nominal exchange rate
nominal interest rate
price index
rate of unemployment
real effective exchange rate
real exchange rate
real interest rate
trade weighted exchange rate
unemployment
weights

10 National income

This chapter covers unit 2, module 1, topic 2.
On completion of this chapter, you should be able to:

- explain the different ways of deriving the national accounts and do related calculations
- explain the importance of national income accounting for analysing the economy as a whole
- explain the limitations of GDP and GNP as measures of net economic welfare

National income statistics

Use of national income statistics

Governments measure the total output of the country in order to assess the performance of the economy. An economy is usually considered to be doing well if its output is growing at a high and sustainable rate.

Governments use a variety of measures of the country's output. These are collectively known as **national income** statistics. This is because the total output of the country is equal to total income (and total expenditure).

The most widely used measure of national income is known as **Gross Domestic Product** (GDP). Gross means total, domestic refers to the home economy and product means output. So, for example, Pakistan's GDP is a measure of the total output by the factors of production based in Pakistan. GDP is calculated by adding up consumers' spending, government spending on goods and services, total investment, changes in stocks and the difference between exports and imports.

From GDP, a number of other measures of national income can be found. GDP plus **net property income from abroad** gives **Gross National Product** (GNP). Net property income from abroad is the income which the country's residents earn on their physical assets (such as factories and leisure parks) owned abroad, and foreign financial assets (such as shares and bank loans) minus the returns on assets held in the country but owned by foreigners. So GNP gives a measure of the income of the country's residents.

GNP minus capital consumption gives **Net National Product** (NNP). This can also be referred to as national income. Capital consumption can also be called depreciation or replacement investment as it covers investment undertaken to replace worn out and out-of-date capital. GDP minus capital consumption gives **Net Domestic Product** (NDP). So gross measures include all investment whilst net measures only include investment which *adds* to the capital stock.

GDP is first measured at market prices, that is, the prices charged for goods and services in shops. However, all the measures are recorded in terms of both market prices and factor cost. The latter is the value of output excluding indirect taxes and subsidies. So, to convert a measure from market prices to factor costs, indirect taxes are deducted and subsidies are added.

The ways of measuring GDP

There are three ways of calculating GDP. These are the output, income and expenditure methods. They should give the same total because they all measure the flow of income produced in an economy. Figure 10.1 illustrates

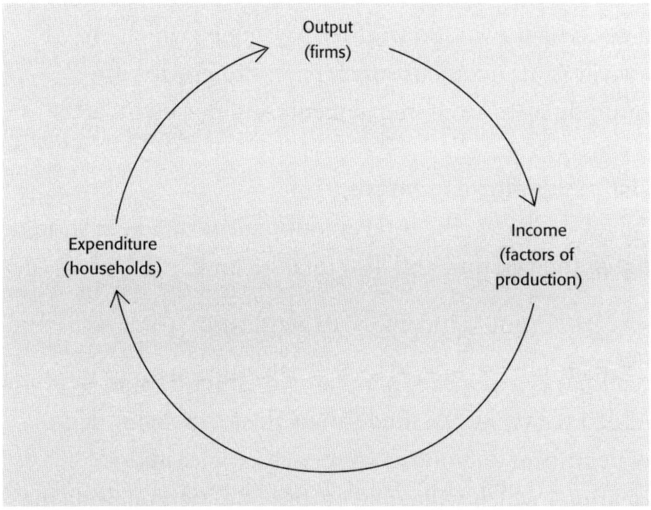

Figure 10.1 The circular flow of income in a simple economy

the **circular flow of income** in a simplified model of the economy.

The value of output is equal to the incomes which it generates, that is wages, rent, profit and interest. If it is assumed that all incomes are spent, expenditure will, by definition, equal income.

The output measure

The output method measures the value of output produced by industries including, for example, the output of the manufacturing, construction, distributive, hotel and catering and agricultural industries.

In using this measure it is important to avoid counting the same output twice. For example, if the value of cars sold by car manufacturers is added to the value of output of tyre firms, double counting will occur. Value added is the difference between the sales revenue received and the cost of raw materials used. It is equal to the payments made to the factors of production in return for producing the good or service. So, if a sugar manufacturing company purchases raw cane for \$20,000 and processes this into refined sugar that sells for \$50,000, it has added \$30,000 to output. It is this \$50,000 that will be included in the measure of output.

The income measure

The value of output produced is based on the costs involved in producing that output. These costs include wages, rent, interest and profits. All these payments represent income paid to factors of production. For instance, workers receive wages and entrepreneurs receive profits. In using this measure it is important to include only payments received in return for providing a good or service. So transfer payments, which are transfers of income from taxpayers to groups of individuals for welfare payments, are not included.

The expenditure measure

As stated above, the total amount spent in a year should equal total output and also total income:

Output = Income = Expenditure

What is produced in a year will either be sold or added to stocks. So, if additions to stocks are added to expenditure on goods and services, a measure is obtained which will equal output and income. In using this method it is necessary to add expenditure on exports and deduct expenditure on imports. This is because the sale of exports represents the country's output and creates income in the country, whereas expenditure on imports is spending on goods and services made in foreign countries and creates income for people in those countries. It is also necessary to deduct indirect taxes and add subsidies in order to get a value which corresponds to the income generated in the production of the output.

Self-assessment task

Which of the following should be included in measuring GDP by the income method?

- government subsidies to farmers,
- the pay of civil servants,
- the pay of nurses,
- supernormal profits,
- state pensions.

Money and real GDP

Money (or nominal) GDP is GDP measured in terms of the prices operating in the year in which the output is produced. It is sometimes referred to as GDP at current prices and is a measure which has not been adjusted for inflation.

Money GDP may give a misleading impression of how well a country is performing. This is because the value of money GDP may rise not because more goods and services are being produced but merely because prices have risen. For example, if 100 million products are produced at an average price of \$5, GDP will be \$500 million. If in the next year the same output of 100 million products is produced but the average price rises to \$6, money GDP will rise to \$600 million. So to get a truer picture of what is happening to output, economists convert money into real GDP. They do this by measuring GDP at constant prices, that is, at the prices operating in a selected base year. By doing this they remove the distorting effect of inflation. For example, in 2001 a country's GDP is \$800 billion and the price index is 100. Then in 2002, money GDP rises to \$864 billion and the price index is 105.

$$\text{Real GDP is money GDP} \times \frac{\text{price index in base year}}{\text{price index in current year}}$$

So: $\$864\text{bn} \times \frac{100}{105} = \$822.86\text{bn}$

The price index used to convert money into real GDP is the **GDP deflator**, which measures the prices of products produced rather than consumed in a country. So it includes the prices of capital as well as consumer products and includes the prices of exports but excludes the prices of imports.

Self-assessment task

In 2002 a country's GDP is $1,000bn. In 2003 nominal GDP rises to $1,092bn and the price index increases by 4 per cent. Calculate:

(a) real GDP;
(b) the percentage increase in real GDP.

Comparison of economic growth over time and between countries

Changes in real GDP are used to calculate economic growth rates. So, for example, if the real GDP of Zimbabwe grows from Z$50bn in 2001 to Z$52bn, the economic growth rate for 2002 is 4 per cent. Table 10.1 shows the economic growth rate of a range of countries during the year 2000.

In comparing economic growth rates over time and between countries, care has to be taken over a number of issues. One of these is that the official real GDP figures may understate the true change in output. This is because of the existence of, and changes in, what is called the hidden, informal or shadow economy. These terms refer to undeclared economic activity. People may not declare to the authorities the incomes they earn for two main reasons. One is that they are seeking to evade paying tax. For example, a plumber may receive payment for undertaking jobs in his spare time and not declare the income he receives to the tax authorities. So some of the services he produces will not be included in GDP. Another reason for not declaring economic activity is that the activity is itself illegal, for example smuggling goods.

Some idea of the size of the shadow economy can be found by measuring any gap between GDP as measured by the expenditure and income methods. This is because people will be spending income they have not declared!

If the size of the hidden economy is relatively constant, the rate of economic growth may be calculated reasonably accurately. However, even a stable-sized hidden economy can make international comparisons of economic growth rates difficult. This is because the size of the hidden economy varies between economies. It is influenced by the marginal rates of taxation, the penalties imposed for illegal activity and tax evasion, the risk of being caught and social attitudes towards, for example, different illegal activities. Figure 10.2 shows a comparison between the size of the hidden economy in a number of industrial countries. Greece had the highest percentage of unmeasured economic activity, 29 per cent, and Switzerland the lowest, 8 per cent. The size of the hidden economy grew between 1989 and 1999 in each of the countries shown. In most developing economies this statistic is likely to be high.

Official GDP figures may also not provide an accurate measure of output and changes in output because of low levels of literacy, non-marketed goods and services and the difficulties of measuring government spending.

In countries with low levels of literacy, it will be difficult for government officials to gather information about *all* economic activity. Some people will be unable to fill out tax forms and others will fill them out

	GDP (% change real GDP)		
Country	%	Country	%
Argentina	0.0	Jamaica	–0.4
Barbados	2.9	Japan	1.4
Brazil	4.0	Malaysia	8.7
Chile	5.6	Philippines	3.9
China	8.0	Poland	4.5
Colombia	3.0	Russia	7.0
Czech Republic	2.7	Singapore	9.9
Egypt	5.2	South Africa	3.0
France	3.0	South Korea	9.2
Germany	2.8	Trinidad & Tobago	4.1
Hungary	5.3	Turkey	6.0
India	6.1	UK	3.0
Indonesia	4.5	USA	5.2
Israel	5.1	Venezuela	3.1

Table 10.1 Comparison of economic growth rates in a selected number of countries in 2000
Source: *The Economist*, 27 January 2001.

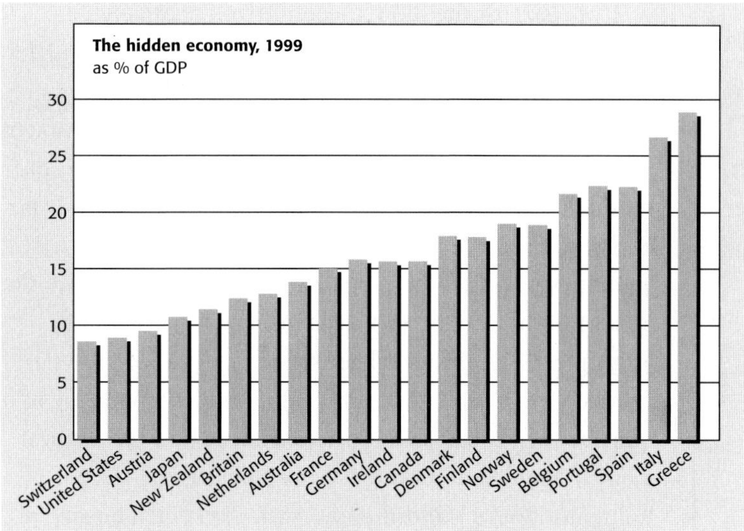

Figure 10.2 The hidden economy in selected developed economies
Source: Dr Friedrich Schneider, University of Linz.

inaccurately. So estimates will have to made for some output. This is a particular problem in Pakistan, which has a male illiteracy rate of 42 per cent and a female illiteracy rate of 71 per cent.

Estimates also have to be made for non-marketed goods and services. The GDP figures only include marketed goods and services, that is goods and services which are bought and sold and so have a price attached to them. Goods and services which are produced and which are either not traded or which are exchanged without money changing hands go unrecorded. For example, domestic services provided by homeowners, painting and repairs undertaken by homeowners and voluntary work are not included in the official figures. The proportion of goods and services which people produce for themselves and the amount of voluntary work undertaken vary over time and between countries.

It is also difficult to value the output of government goods and services which are not sold, such as defence. In the past in the UK the output was valued at cost, normally in terms of the value of inputs. This gave a somewhat distorted view of what was happening to output. For instance, if productivity increased in the fire service, fewer firemen and women might have been needed. This would have reduced the cost of providing the fire service. Output as officially recorded would have fallen, although the level of service provided might have been unchanged or may even have increased. To overcome this problem, in 1998 the Office for National Statistics (ONS) in the UK developed a

Trees killed by acid rain. One tree is resistant to acidity
Source: Mark Edwards, Still Pictures.

system for measuring government outputs of services other than through the value of inputs. This method covers education, health and social security – around 50 per cent of the public sector – and uses a variety of key performance indicators (such as student numbers for education and claimant numbers for social security) in order to estimate output.

Comparison of living standards over time

Real GDP per head figures have traditionally been used as one of the main indicators of living standards. If a country's real GDP per head is higher this year than last year, it is generally expected that the country's inhabitants will be enjoying higher living standards. This is indeed often the case but it is not always so.

Real GDP per head is found by dividing total real GDP by the country's population to give an average. However, real GDP is not actually evenly distributed. It is possible that, whilst real GDP per head rises, some people may not experience rises in income and some may even suffer reductions in their income. For instance, in the mid 1990s the Indian economy grew at 7.5 per cent a year but the proportion of Indians living in poverty dropped just 1 per cent to 34 per cent.

The change in real GDP figures may also not reflect the true change in the quantity of goods and services that consumers can enjoy if the level of undeclared economic activity changes over time. A rise in the hidden economy may mean that people are experiencing a higher standard of living than first appears to be the case (see above).

To assess changes in living standards, consideration has to be given not only to the changes in the quantity of products produced but also to changes in the *type* of products produced and the ways in which they are made. Indeed a rise in real GDP does not guarantee a rise in living standards. During a war, output may rise because more weapons are being produced but not many people will say that the quality of their lives is improving. The recruitment of more police to cope with more crime will again increase real GDP but will be unlikely to cause people to feel better off.

The type of products which raise people's living standards are consumer goods and services, such as housing, food and clothing. A shift of resources from consumer products to capital goods will enable more consumer products to be produced and enjoyed in the future. However, in the short run if the economy is operating at the frontier of its production possibility curve such a move will cause people to enjoy fewer consumer products (see chapter 1).

Even if people are able to enjoy more consumer goods and services it does not necessarily mean that they will be happier. As access to more and higher-quality products rises, the desire for even more and better products may increase at an even faster rate. For example, people who do not have a car are happy when they buy their first car but often within a short space of time they want a better model.

Real GDP measures the quantity of output produced but not the quality. Output could rise but if the quality of what is produced declines, the quality of people's lives is likely to fall. In practice, though, the quality of output tends to rise over time, largely due to technical change.

Working conditions also tend to improve over time and working hours usually fall. If real GDP per head stays constant from one year to the next but working conditions rise and/or working hours fall, people's living standards will rise.

However, whilst workers tend to enjoy improved conditions over time, the quality of the environment in some countries declines as a result of pollution and, for example, deforestation. A decline in environmental conditions will lower living standards but not real GDP. Indeed, if more resources have to be devoted to cleaning up the environment, real GDP will increase whilst living standards decline.

Figure 10.3 shows a comparison of the quality of life in a number of the world's cities. It is based on a survey by William M. Mercer which ranks cities on the basis of 39 criteria of the quality of life, ranging from recreational and transport facilities to crime and education.

Comparison of living standards between countries

The citizens of a country with a higher real GDP per head are likely to enjoy higher living standards than people living in a country with a lower real GDP per head, but again this is not necessarily the case.

Real GDP figures may give a misleading impression of a country's output because of the same problems of measurement as stated earlier in comparing living standards over time.

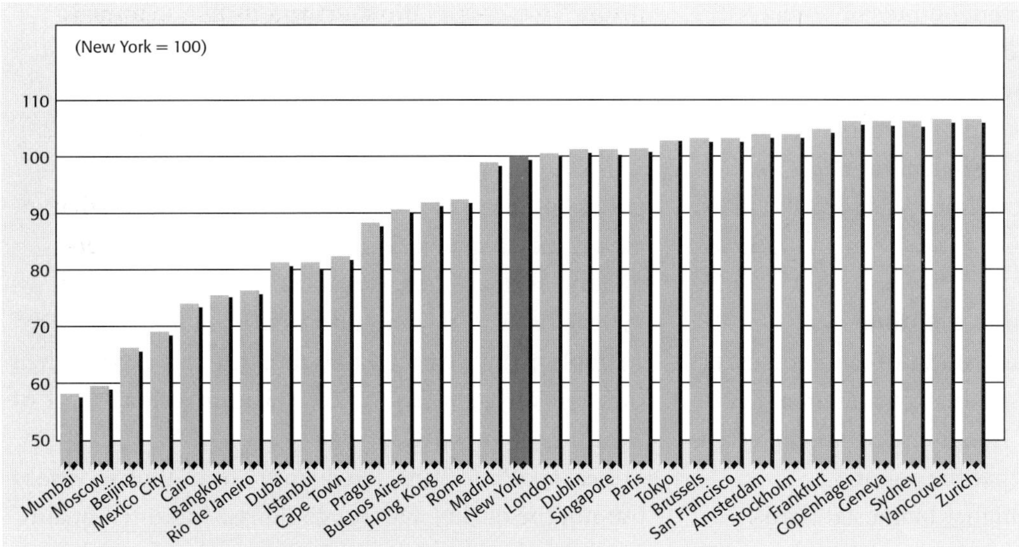

Figure 10.3 The quality of life in selected world cities in 2000
Source: William M. Mercer.

To compare living standards between countries it is necessary to convert the real GDP per capita into a common currency. To avoid the comparison being distorted by exchange rate changes, economists usually adjust exchange rates to take into account their purchasing power parities. For example, suppose the exchange rate is 6 Malaysian ringgits = $1 and the USA has a real GDP per head of $25,000 whilst Malaysia has a real GDP per head of 6,000 ringgits. From this information it might appear that, when Malaysia's real GDP per head is converted into dollars ($1,000), people in the USA are, on average, 25 times better off than people in Malaysia. However, if $1 can buy more goods and services in the USA than in Malaysia, then using the exchange rate to convert ringgits into dollars will exaggerate Malaysia's output. In terms of ability to buy products (purchasing parities), 12 ringgits may be worth $1. Using this as the basis for converting Malaysia's output into dollars would show that people in the USA are 50 times better off than people in Malaysia.

Self-assessment tasks

Read the article below and then tackle the exercises that follow.

The Economist's Big Mac Index offers a light-hearted guide to whether currencies are at their correct levels, according to the notion of 'purchasing power parity'. Under PPP, exchange rates should adjust to equalise the price of a basket of goods and services across all countries; the Big Mac PPP is the exchange rate at which hamburgers would cost the same in America as in other countries. Dividing the price in shekels of a Big Mac in Israel by the price in dollars of an American Big Mac produces a Big Mac PPP of 5.68 shekels to the dollar. Since the market rate is 4.13, this suggests the shekel is 38% overvalued. At the other extreme, the Philippine peso is almost 60% undervalued; the market rate is 51 to the dollar, against a Big Mac PPP of 21.

Source: 'Burgernomics, *The Economist*, 13 January 2001 (adapted).

1 Explain what is meant by purchasing power parity.
2 Explain what effect using an undervalued exchange rate for the Philippine peso would have when comparing the GDP of the Philippines with that of the USA.

Even if a country is found to have a higher real GDP per head than another country, using purchasing power parities, it does not necessarily mean that its inhabitants will enjoy higher living standards. For example, Kuwait has a very high real GDP per head but some immigrant workers in the country receive relatively low wages. Where income is very unevenly distributed, only a small number of households may benefit from a high average income.

As with making comparisons over time, in assessing living standards consideration has to be taken of factors not measured in real GDP per head. One difference is in working hours. A study by UBS, a Swiss bank, published in 2000 found that the world's hardest working population lives in Santiago, Chile. Measured across a range of professions, the average worker in Santiago worked 2,244 hours a year. Work rates were also high across Asia and Latin America – for example, 2,200 hours in Kuala Lumpar and 2,150 hours in Mexico. Working hours were lower in the USA and Europe with people in Paris, for instance, only working an average of 1,600 hours. Other factors which are not measured in real GDP per head include working conditions, political freedoms, fear of crime and the quality of the environment. The type and quality of products produced also has to be taken into account.

Other indicators of living standards and economic development

In assessing living standards, economists can use a wide range of indicators including, for example, the number of televisions per household, infant mortality rates and energy use per capita. What they normally do, however, is to use composite indicators. These include a number of indicators of living standards. For example, two American economists, William Nordhaus and James Tobin in 1972 developed a new measure of economic welfare. They called this Net Economic Welfare (NEW), although it is now sometimes also referred to as Measurable Economic Welfare (MEW). This measure seeks to give a fuller picture of living standards by adjusting GDP figures to take into account other factors which have an impact on the quality of people's lives. Factors which improve living standards such as increased leisure hours are added to the GDP figure, whilst factors which reduce living standards, including rising crime and pollution levels, are deducted. Of course, in practice, it is difficult and expensive to measure the value of non-marketed economic 'goods' and 'bads'.

Economic development involves a wider meaning of living standards as it encompasses an improvement in people's welfare, including an increase in their choices

	Life expectancy at birth (years)	Adult literacy rate age 15 and above (%)	Combined primary, secondary and tertiary gross enrolment ratio (%)	GDP per capita (PPPUS$)	HDI value	HDI ranking
Canada	79.1	99.0	100	23,582	0.935	1
Norway	78.3	99.0	97	26,342	0.934	2
United States	76.8	99.0	94	29,605	0.929	3
Australia	78.3	99.0	114	22,452	0.929	4
Iceland	79.1	99.0	89	25,110	0.927	5
Sweden	78.7	99.0	102	20,659	0.926	6
Belgium	77.3	99.0	106	23,223	0.925	7
Netherlands	78.0	99.0	99	22,176	0.925	8
Japan	80.0	99.0	85	23,257	0.924	9
UK	77.3	99.0	105	20,336	0.918	10

Table 10.2 Human Development Index 1998
Source: *Human Development Report*, United Nations, Oxford University Press, 2000.

and abilities. The most well-known measure of economic development is the United Nations Human Development Index (HDI) which has been published since 1990. The index is a composite one, taking into account real GDP per head (PPP$), life expectancy at birth and educational attainment as measured by adult literacy and combined primary, secondary and tertiary enrolment ratio. These are included as it is thought that people's welfare is influenced not only by the goods and services available to them but also by their ability to lead a long and healthy life and to acquire knowledge.

The HDI value for a country shows the distance a country has to make up to reach the maximum value of 1. Table 10.2 shows the top ten countries ranked by their HDI indexes in 1998.

As table 10.3 shows, a country's ranking by HDI does not always match its ranking in terms of real GDP per capita. Indeed, in some cases there are marked differences. Table 10.3 shows three pairs of countries with similar HDI values but noticeably different GDP per capita figures.

Country	HDI value	GDP per capita (PPPUS$)
Luxembourg	0.908	33,505
Ireland	0.907	21,482
Saudi Arabia	0.747	10,158
Thailand	0.745	5,456
South Africa	0.697	8,488
El Salvador	0.696	4,036

Table 10.3 Examples of countries with similar HDI values but different incomes, 1998
Source: *Human Development Report*, United Nations, Oxford University Press, 2000.

Self-assessment tasks

Study the data below on some key indicators for CARICOM economies and then tackle the questions that follow.

	Gross national income per head (PPP) US$,2004	Life expectancy at birth, 2003per capita Male	Female	CO_2 emissions m tonnes, 2000
Antigua & Barbuda	10,360	73	78	4.9
Bahamas	16,140	66	74	5.9
Barbados	15,060	72	77	4.4
Belize	6,510	70	73	3.1
Dominica	5,250	75	79	1.4
Grenada	7,000	70	76	2.1
Guyana	4,110	58	67	2.1
Haiti	1,680	50	54	0.2
Jamaica	3,630	74	78	4.2
St Kitts & Nevis	11,190	69	74	2.4
St Lucia	5,560	72	76	2.1
St Vincent & The Grenadines	6,250	70	76	1.4
Suriname	n.a.	68	73	5.0
Trinidad & Tobago	11,180	70	74	20.5

Source: World Development Report, 2006.

1 Describe the variations in Gross National Income per head and comment on the extent to which these variations might be a true reflection of variations in living standards.

2 Suppose that Gross National Income per head and CO_2 emissions per head can be used to produce a crude measure of net economic welfare. Show how this might produce rather different variations between countries when compared with using Gross National Income per head data only.

3 Discuss what other variables you might use in order to produce a more accurate measure of net economic welfare.

Self-assessment task

On completion of this chapter, you should be able to answer the following question taken from CAPE examinations, 2005.

1 The table below lists Econland's transactions in 2003.

Items	Amount ($)
Wages paid to labour	800,000
Consumption expenditure	600,000
Taxes	250,000
Transfer payments	50,000
Profits	200,000
Investment	250,000
Government purchases	200,000
Exports	300,000
Imports	300,000
Savings	250,000

(a) Calculate Econland's Gross Domestic Product using the expenditure method. (10 marks)

(b) Based on the information in the table above, state whether the income approach can be used to calculate the Gross Domestic Product. Explain your answer. (10 marks)

(c) State with reasons, which of the transactions listed below will NOT be counted in the Gross Domestic Product:

- a meat processing company builds a new plant,
- a drug dealer sells $5,000 worth of illegal drugs,
- a clothing factory produces $1 million worth of dress shirts,
- a student purchases a used text book,
- company A launches a hostile takeover of Company B and purchases its stocks,
- a public utility company installs new turbines and cooling equipment. (21 marks)

(d) Explain what is meant by 'double counting'. Illustrate your answer with the use of an example. (9 marks)

(Total 50 marks)

Summary

In this chapter it has been shown that:

- The GDP in an economy can be measured in three ways – by the output, income and expenditure methods.
- Real GDP is a more accurate measure of output since it is adjusted for inflation.
- In developing economies especially, the quality of data available on living standards may be unreliable due to the large hidden economy and the value of non-marketed goods and services.
- An increase in real GDP per head is likely to mean higher living standards, although not necessarily an increase in net economic welfare.

Key words

Definitions of Key words can be found in the Glossary.

circular flow of income
Gross Domestic Product
Gross National Product
national income
net domestic product
net national product
net property income from abroad

11 Classical models of the macroeconomy

This chapter covers unit 2, module 1, topic 3.
On completion of this chapter, you should be able to:

- explain why, within the classical model, all unemployment is voluntary
- explain the role of wage and interest rate flexibility in restoring full employment
- explain the factors that influence aggregate demand and aggregate supply
- explain price determination within the classical model
- use the classical aggregate demand and supply model to show changes in the price level and employment

Classical theory of unemployment

The contemporary view of unemployment was defined earlier in chapter 9 and is that it refers to those who are actively looking for work but who are without a job. There are many causes of unemployment. In Caribbean economies, for example, some unemployment is seasonal due to fluctuations in the labour demands of agriculture and tourism. Such unemployment is involuntary and is usually corrected in the short term as the next season occurs. Other more serious forms of unemployment are due to the cyclical nature of economic activity, the effects of exogenous events such as world political crises or longer-term structural change in an economy.

The classical theory of unemployment does not recognise these causes. The only cause in its view is that unemployment is the result of real wages being too high, resulting in employers not being willing to employ as many workers that would like to work at a wage rate above the equilibrium point. This is shown in figure 11.1. The principles are broadly the same as those stated in chapter 7 and are:

- The demand for labour in the economy is a function of the marginal physical product of labour. This decreases as more workers enter the labour market.
- The supply of labour increases as wages rise. This is a reflection of the unpleasant nature of most types of work, resulting in more workers being willing to enter the labour market as wages rise.

A young girl in Dubique, Dominica on the Atlantic coast. Unemployment in the village of tin roofed wooden houses is high since the decline of the nearby Stowe Estate which used to produce bananas, limes, mangoes, poultry and meat and where many of the villagers worked
Source: Alamy.

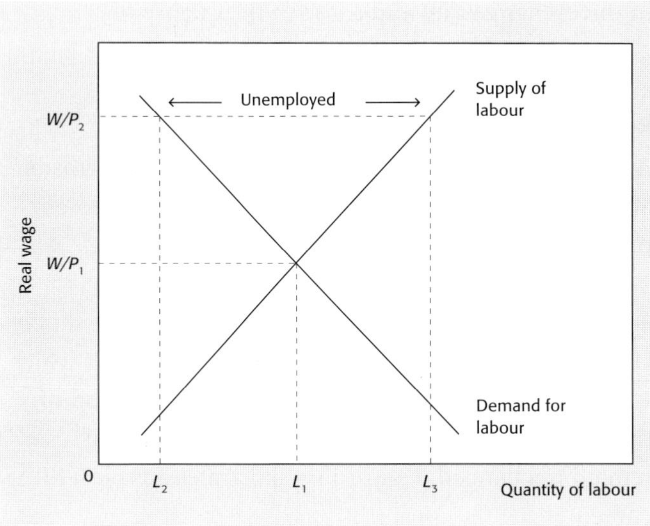

Figure 11.1 Classical unemployment

Returning to figure 11.1, the equilibrium real wage rate is W/P_1. Unemployment occurs when wages are too high. So, at wage W/P_2, employers are only willing to hire L_2 workers; the number able and willing to work is L_3. So, the difference, L_3–L_2, are unemployed. This **real wage unemployment**, as it is sometimes known, is voluntary since these workers are refusing to work for less than W/P_2. There is a natural tendency for the market to move towards the equilibrium real wage. So, as the unemployed workers obtain jobs, wages will be forced downwards to the equilibrium point.

Through this process the demand for labour will increase from L_2 to L_1 and the number of people willing to work at the equilibrium wage will fall from L_3 to L_1. Real wage rates therefore need to be flexible for this to occur.

In the classical model it is also possible to show how a change in the interest rate can be used to increase employment. The underlying assumption is that the demand for loanable funds is a direct function of the interest rate in the economy. So, if interest rates fall, entrepreneurs will demand more loans from their banks as the real cost of borrowing will have fallen. This in turn will result in a fall in unemployment as firms increase their capital stock and recruit more workers.

Aggregate demand

Aggregate demand is the total spending on goods and services in an economy. It consists of four components. These are:

- **Consumer spending** (*C*). This is the amount that consumers spend on goods and services. In all economies, it is the largest component of aggregate demand and is heavily dependent upon the level of disposable income. In general, as disposable income increases, so too does consumer spending on a wide range of items.
- Investment (*I*). This refers to expenditure by private sector firms and other businesses on capital goods such as new machinery, new buildings and other similar assets that are of long-term value. As referred to earlier in this module, this type of investment is likely to be affected by interest rates. Other factors influencing investment include business expectations on future economic prospects and technological change.
- **Government spending** (*G*). This covers both current and capital spending on a whole range of public services such as defence, police, social services, transport, health and so on. Its relevance in relation to aggregate demand depends to some extent on the organisation of the economy – where there is a strong public sector, then government spending is likely to be a higher proportion of aggregate demand than in a market economy that is heavily dependent on the private sector.

- **Net exports** (*X–M*). This is the difference between exports and imports of goods and services in an economy. For the UK, exports of goods and services are less than imports and therefore net exports make a negative contribution to aggregate demand. This is often true for developing economies, particularly when the terms of trade are working against their interests.

More details on these components will be included in the next three topics.

In terms of a formula, aggregate demand (*AD*) is

$$AD = C + I + G + (X–M).$$

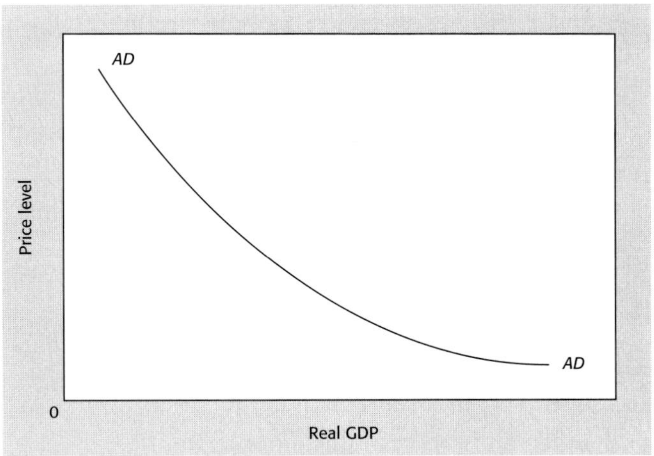

Figure 11.2 The aggregate demand curve

Figure 11.2 shows a typical aggregate demand curve.

It slopes down from left to right because a lower price will:

- raise demand for net exports because the country's goods and services will have become more price competitive;
- increase the purchasing power of households with savings in the form of bank and building society deposits and other financial assets because their wealth will enable them to buy more;
- reduce the rate of interest and so stimulate consumption and investment.

A change in the price level causes a movement along the AD curve. If, however, any of the components of AD change for reasons other than a change in the price level, the AD curve will shift. Figure 11.3 illustrates an increase in aggregate demand. This could occur because of, for example, a rise in expectations about the future, a cut in direct tax, an increase in the money supply, a fall in the exchange rate and a rise in the quality of domestically produced products.

Aggregate supply

Aggregate supply (AS) is the total output that firms in an economy are willing and able to supply at different price levels in a given period of time.

It is possible to distinguish between short-run aggregate supply (SRAS) and long-run aggregate supply (LRAS). Short-run aggregate supply is the output which will be supplied at different price levels in a period of time when the prices of the factors of production remain unchanged. Figure 11.4 illustrates a typical SRAS curve.

It slopes up from left to right. This is because a higher price level will enable firms to meet any extra unit costs in the form of, for example, overtime payments, and to enjoy higher profit margins.

The SRAS curve will shift if productivity or the payments to factors of production change. For example, an increase in wage rates, not matched by an increase in productivity, will shift the SRAS curve to the left, as illustrated in figure 11.5.

Long-run aggregate supply is the output which firms would produce after the price level and factor prices have fully adjusted after any shift in aggregate demand. Keynesians often illustrate the LRAS curve as perfectly elastic at low levels of output, then upward sloping over a range of output and finally perfectly inelastic. This is to emphasise their view that in the long run the economy can operate at any level of output and not necessarily at its full capacity. Figure 11.6 shows that from Q to Q_1, output can be raised without increasing

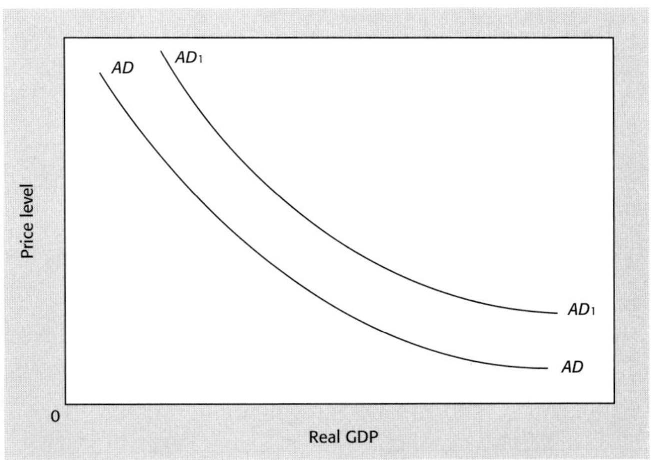

Figure 11.3 An increase in aggregate demand

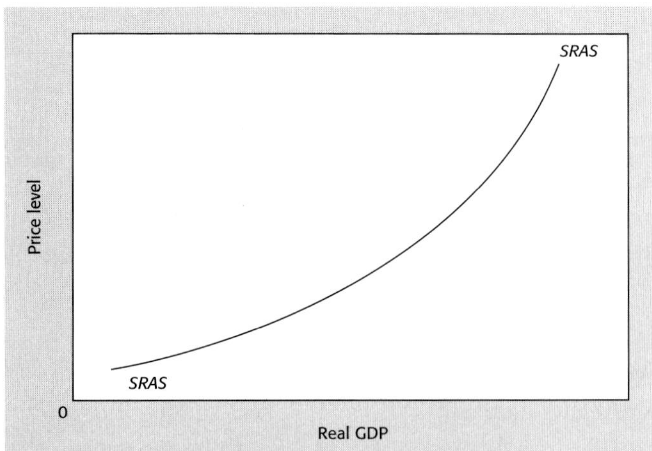

Figure 11.4 The short-run aggregate supply curve

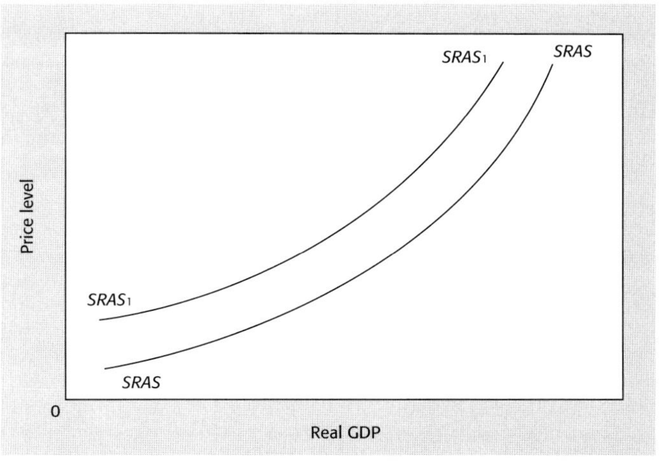

Figure 11.5 A reduction in aggregate supply

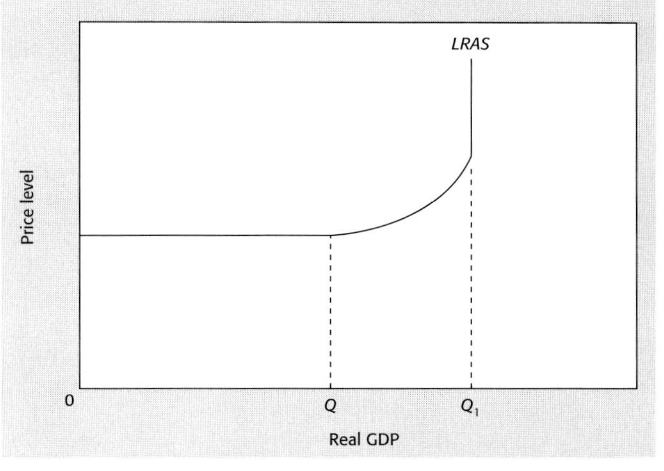

Figure 11.6 The long-run aggregate supply curve

the price level. When output and hence employment are low, firms can attract more resources without raising their prices. As output rises from Q_1 to Q_2, firms begin to experience shortages of resources and bid up wages and the cost of land and capital equipment. When output hits Q_2, the economy reaches the maximum output it can make with existing resources.

New classical economists illustrate the LRAS curve as a vertical line because they believe that, in the long run, the economy will operate at full capacity. This version of the LRAS curve is shown in figure 11.7.

Both Keynesian and new classical economists agree that the factors which will shift the vertical part of the LRAS curve are changes in the quantity and quality of resources as these will affect the productive capacity of the country.

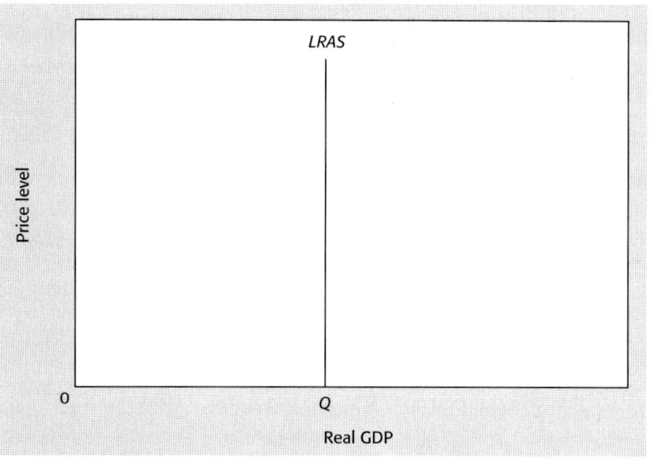

Figure 11.7 A vertical long-run aggregate supply curve

The LRAS curve will shift to the right if there is an increase in the quantity and/or quality of resources. For example, improvements in training will raise the quality of the labour force and an increase in investment will increase the quantity and, possibly, the quality of capital goods. Both of these changes will increase the maximum amount of output the country can produce. Other causes of changes in LRAS include changes in technology, the quality of education and net immigration.

Interaction of aggregate demand and supply

The equilibrium level of output and the price level are determined when aggregate demand and aggregate supply intersect, as shown in figure 11.8.

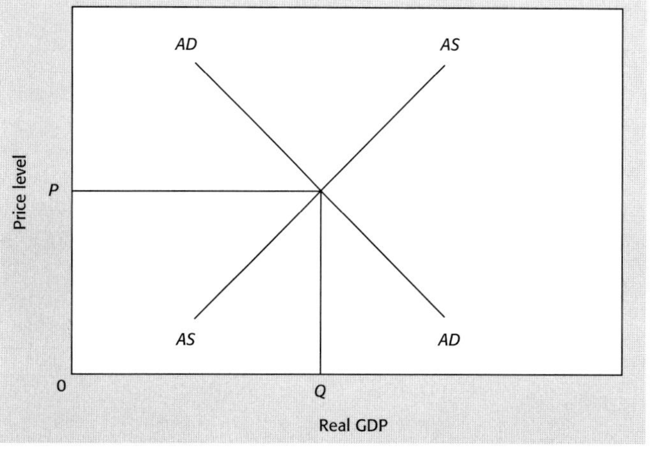

Figure 11.8 The interaction of aggregate demand and aggregate supply

Self-assessment tasks

Read the article below and then tackle the exercises that follow.

In December 2000 Mexico was experiencing a shortage of skilled labour. This had begun to create bottlenecks to increased growth and pushed up wage rates. For example, in Chihuahua, a northern border state, a centre for assembly-for-exports plants, real wages had risen by 32 per cent over the year. The government was seeking to raise productivity, in the short run, by introducing more flexible labour laws and, in the long run, by improving education and training.

1 Using a Keynesian LRAS curve, explain at what position on the curve the Mexican economy was seemingly operating in December 2000?

2 Illustrate, and explain, the effect of:
- a rise in wage rates on the SRAS curve,
- improved education and training on the LRAS curve.

If the price level was initially below *P*, the excess demand would push the price level back to the equilibrium level. Whereas, if price was above *P*, some goods and services would not be sold and suppliers would have to cut their prices.

An increase in aggregate demand resulting from, for example, an increase in government spending is likely to increase output and raise the price level, at least in the short run. This outcome is illustrated in figure 11.9.

An increase in aggregate supply will also be likely to raise output and so lower the price level, as shown in figure 11.10.

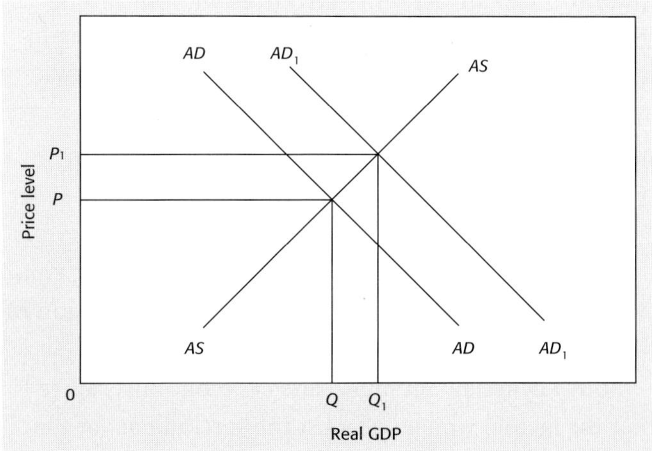

Figure 11.9 The effect on output and the price level of an increase in aggregate demand

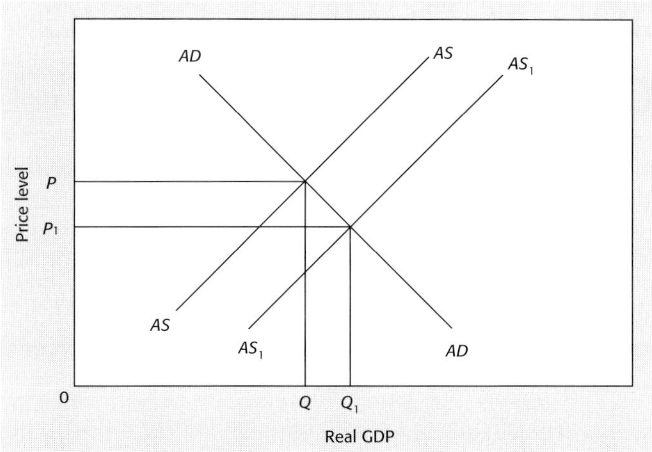

Figure 11.10 The effect on output and the price level of an increase in aggregate supply

Self-assessment task

Identify the effects of the following on aggregate demand, aggregate supply, output and the price level:

- a reduction in the rate of interest,
- an increase in government spending on health care,
- advances in information technology,
- an increase in the quality of training,
- a cut in income tax,
- an increase in wealth.

Self-assessment task

The following question was set in the 2006 CAPE examinations.

1 (a) Explain the meaning of the following terms:

- aggregate demand,
- aggregate demand curve,
- aggregate supply,
- aggregate supply curve,
- equilibrium price level. (15 marks)

(b) Using aggregate demand and aggregate supply curves to illustrate your points, discuss the impacts of the following events on the price level (*P*) and equilibrium GDP(*Y*) in the short run:

- a tax cut holding government purchases constant, with the economy operating at near full capacity;
- an increase in the money supply during a period of high unemployment and excess industrial capacity;
- an increase in the price of oil caused by war in the Middle East, assuming that the government attempts to keep interest rates constant by accommodating inflation. (27 marks)

(c) Investment is usually regarded as the most unstable component of aggregate spending. Several factors contribute to such instability. Explain how the variability of profits and expectations contribute to the instability of investment. (8 marks)

(Total 50 marks)

Summary

In this chapter it has been shown that:

- In the classical model, all unemployment is voluntary and restricted only to those who are unwilling to work for the market wage rate.
- Aggregate demand, the total spending on goods and services in an economy, consists of consumer spending, investment, government spending and net exports.
- Aggregate supply is the total output that firms are willing to supply at different price levels in a given time period.
- The interaction of aggregate demand and aggregate supply determines the level of output and price level in an economy.

Key words

Definitions of Key words can be found in the Glossary.

aggregate demand
aggregate supply
consumer spending
government spending
net exports
real wage unemployment

12 The consumption function, basic Keynesian models and investment

This chapter covers unit 2, module 1, topics 4, 5 and 6.
On completion of this chapter, you should be able to:

- explain the nature and purpose of the consumption function
- explain the multiplier process in the closed and open economy
- calculate the multiplier
- explain the different approaches to consumption and the reasons for the divergent views on the subject
- explain the relationship between saving and consumption and the importance of each for economic growth and stability in the economy of territories in the region
- explain the relationship between saving and investment
- explain inflationary and deflationary gaps
- explain the Keynesian equilibrium level of national income
- explain the accelerator theory
- identify the factors that account for the volatility of investment

The circular flow of income

When governments spend more than they raise in taxation, they add to the circular flow of income. Figure 12.1 shows another version of the circular flow diagram contained in figure 10.1.

The inner circle shows the real flow of products and factor services and the outer circle the money flow of spending and incomes. This figure is a simplified diagram; it assumes that all income is spent and that households and firms are the only sectors involved in economic activity. In practice, some income is saved, some is taxed and some is spent on imports. Some expenditure is also additional to the spending which comes from the incomes generated by domestic output. These extra items of spending are investment, government spending and spending by foreigners on the country's exports. A diagram can be drawn showing how some income and some expenditure 'leaks' out of the circular flow in the form of saving, taxation and imports whilst other spending is 'injected' into the circular flow in the form of investment, government spending and exports. This is shown in figure 12.2.

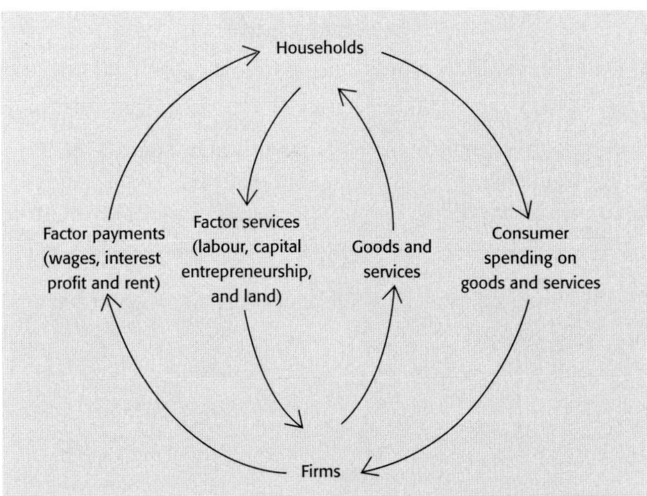

Figure 12.1 The circular flow of income in a closed economy

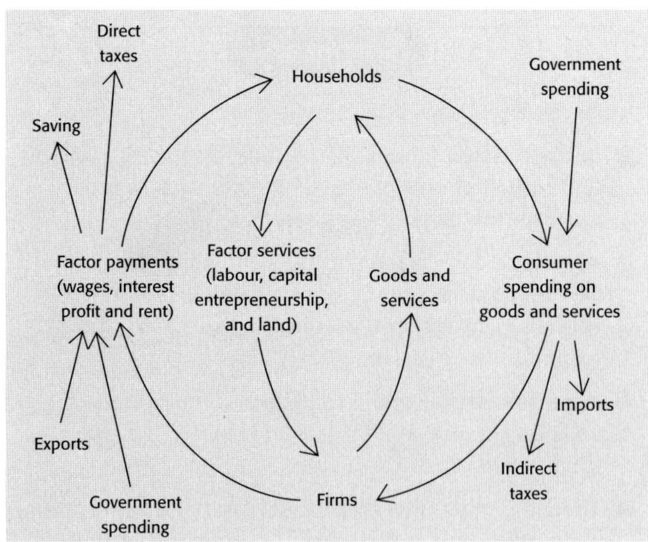

Figure 12.2 The circular flow of income in an open economy

Aggregate expenditure

Aggregate expenditure is the total amount which will be spent at different levels of income in a given time period. This total spending is made up of consumption (C), investment (I), government spending (G) and net exports, that is exports minus imports ($X - M$).

Consumption Consumption or consumer spending is spending by households on goods and services to satisfy current wants, for example, spending on food, clothes, travel and entertainment. The main influence on consumption is the level of disposable income (income minus direct taxes plus state benefits). When income rises, total spending also usually rises. Rich people spend more than the poor.

However, whilst total spending rises with income, the proportion of disposable income which is spent tends to fall. Economists refer to this proportion as the **average propensity to consume** (apc).

$$\text{apc} = \frac{\text{consumption}}{\text{income}} = \frac{C}{Y}$$

When a person, or country, is poor most if not all disposable income has to be spent to meet current needs. Indeed, consumption may exceed income with people or countries drawing on past savings or borrowing. This situation can be referred to as **dissaving**. However, when income rises some of it can be saved. **Saving** is defined as disposable income minus consumption. The **average propensity to save** (aps) is the proportion of disposable income which is saved and is equivalent to 1 minus apc. As saving rises, the actual amount saved and aps tend to increase. The rich tend to have a lower apc and a higher aps than the poor.

The rich also have a lower **marginal propensity to consume** (mpc) and a higher **marginal propensity to save** (mps) than the poor. The mpc is the proportion of extra income which is spent:

$$\text{mpc} = \frac{\text{change in consumption}}{\text{change in income}} = \frac{\Delta C}{\Delta Y}$$

1 – mpc gives mps which can also be calculated by:

$$\frac{\text{change in saving}}{\text{change in income}} = \frac{\Delta S}{\Delta Y}$$

The relationships between consumption and income and saving and income can also be investigated by using the consumption and saving functions. The **consumption function** indicates how much will be spent at different levels of income. It is given by the equation: $C = a + bY$, where C is consumption, a is autonomous consumption (that is, the amount spent even when income is 0 and which does not vary with income), b is the marginal propensity to consume and Y is disposable income; bY can also be defined as income-induced consumption, because it is spending which is dependent on income. For example, if $C = \$100 + 0.8Y$ and income is \$1,000, the amount spent will be $\$100 + 0.8 \times \$1{,}000 = \$900$.

The **saving function** is, in effect, the reverse of the consumption function and is given by the equation: $S = -a + sY$, where S is saving, s is the marginal propensity to save, Y is income and a is autonomous dissaving (that is, how much of their savings people will draw on when their income is 0; this amount does not change as income changes). The figure sY is induced saving – that is, saving which is determined by the level of income. The saving function can be used to work out how much and what proportion households will save at different income levels. For instance, if $S = -\$200 + 0.2Y$ and income is \$4,000, then:

$$S = -\$200 + 0.2 \times \$4{,}000 = \$600.$$

The average propensity to save will be \$600/\$4,000 = 0.15. This will also mean that apc is 1 – 0.15 = 0.85.

A number of factors, other than income, influence consumption. These include the distribution of income, the rate of interest, the availability of credit, expectations and wealth. If income becomes more evenly distributed, due to, for instance, an increase in direct tax rates and state benefits, consumption is likely to rise. This is because the rich have a lower mpc than the poor. When they lose income they are unlikely to cut back on their spending significantly, whilst the poor who gain more income will spend most of the extra.

Households will also usually spend more when interest rates are low. This is because the return from saving will be reduced, buying goods on credit will be cheaper and households who have borrowed before to buy, for example, a house, will have more money to spend. If it becomes easier to obtain loans it is likely that total spending will increase. However, people are unlikely to borrow and to raise their spending if they are pessimistic about the future. Indeed, expectations about future economic prospects are thought to be a significant influence on consumption. When people become more optimistic that their future jobs are secure and that their incomes will rise, they are likely to raise their spending. An increase in wealth, which may result, for example, from a rise in the value of houses or the price of shares, will also probably increase consumption.

Banana crop ravaged by hurricane

The permanent income/life cycle hypothesis

The Keynesian consumption function described above assumes that there is a regular linear relationship between consumption and disposable income. This view has been increasingly questioned by economists from an empirical standpoint. Two important qualifications can be made.

The first is known as the **life cycle** hypothesis. The basis of this is that incomes vary predictably over people's lives. Young students, for example, have low incomes. Once educated and in employment income should rise, and, as one's career path develops, then disposable income also increases and is likely to peak at some point towards the end of working life. On retirement, normally 65 years of age for men, income falls sharply depending on whether the individual has contributed to a meaningful pension scheme. This pattern of income variation is called the life cycle.

The life cycle hypothesis needs qualification since people borrow and save over their lives to smooth out life cycle changes in their incomes. Younger people tend to borrow more than those who are older; middle-aged people on the other hand are invariably in a better position to save more of their income.

The second qualification centres around **permanent income** and **transitory income**. The former is quite simply a household's typical normal income that determines its ability to consume on a month-by-month, year-by-year basis. For those on a fixed salary, their income is stable and can be assured whilst they are in employment. This is not true for many families. In the Caribbean, the income of farmers and those who rely on tips and commission is likely to vary from one year to the next. In the case of farmers, their household income can fluctuate wildly depending on their harvest. If the banana crops of farmers in say Dominica are ravaged by a hurricane, then their income will be adversely affected; farmers elsewhere in the Caribbean who may not have experienced the hurricane are likely to benefit from higher market prices due to less supply from Dominica. In situations like this, people will borrow and save to cover these eventualities and so smooth out fluctuations in transitory income.

So the consumption function assumes that there is a linear relationship between consumption and income and that any change in consumption as a result of a change in disposable income is income induced. This is not necessarily the case in reality as explained by the life cycle and permanent income hypotheses.

Investment Investment is spending by firms on capital goods, such as factories, offices, machinery and delivery vehicles. The amount of investment undertaken is influenced by changes in consumer demand, the rate of interest, changes in technology, the cost of capital goods, expectations and government policy.

If consumer demand rises, firms are likely to want to buy more capital equipment to expand their capacity. Similarly, a fall in the rate of interest is likely to stimulate a rise in investment. This is for two key reasons. One is that the cost of investment will fall. Firms which borrow to buy capital goods will find it cheaper and firms which use retained profits will find that the opportunity cost of investment will fall. The second reason is that a lower interest rate is likely to raise consumer demand.

Advances in technology will raise the productivity of capital goods and so will probably stimulate more investment. Similarly, a fall in the price of capital equipment and/or cost of installation of capital goods is likely to raise investment.

As with consumption, expectations can play a key role in determining investment. When firms are optimistic that economic conditions are improving and demand for their products will rise, they will be encouraged to raise their investment. Governments can also seek to increase private sector investment by cutting corporation tax (the tax on company profits) and by providing investment subsidies.

Government spending This covers spending on items such as the wages of teachers in state schools, medicines used in state hospitals and government investment in, for example, new roads and new hospitals. The amount of government spending which is undertaken in any period is influenced by government policy, tax revenue and other factors, including demographic changes. If a government wants to raise economic activity it may decide to raise its spending. Higher government tax revenues will enable a government to spend more, without resorting to borrowing. Pressure for a rise in government spending may come from an increase in the number of children (education) and/or an increase in the number of elderly people (health care and state pensions).

Net exports The level of net exports is influenced by the country's GDP, other countries' GDP, the relative price and quality competitiveness of the country's products and its exchange rate. When a country's GDP rises, demand for imports usually increases. Whereas when incomes rise abroad, demand for the country's exports is likely to increase. A rise in exports may also result from an improvement in the competitiveness of the country's products, due for example to a rise in productivity or improved marketing.

The level of the exchange rate can be a key influence on net exports. If the exchange rate falls in value, the country's exports will become cheaper and imports will become more expensive. If demand for exports and imports is elastic, export revenue will rise whilst import expenditure will fall, causing net exports to fall.

Self-assessment tasks

Read the short case study below and then tackle the exercises that follow.

The economy in Singapore grew by nearly 10 per cent in 2000. It is predicted to grow by less than half that rate in 2001. This is largely because the growth of Singapore's exports is expected to fall due to lower global electronics demand, the US economic slowdown and weaker growth in Asia. Such a decline in the growth of its exports would have a significant impact on the country because it has such an open economy.

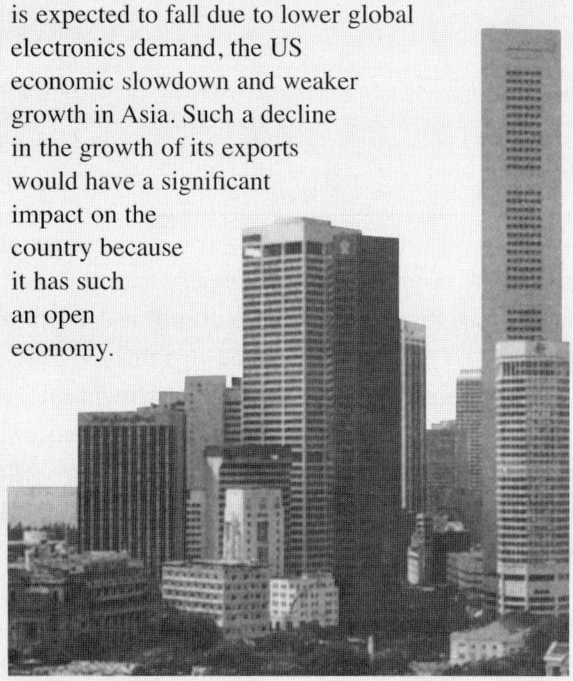

1 What is meant by an open economy?
2 Explain how 'lower global electronics demand, the US economic slowdown and weaker growth in Asia' would be likely to reduce the growth of exports from Singapore.
3 Discuss two factors which could increase another component of Singapore's aggregate expenditure.

Income determination

The level of income in an economy is determined where aggregate expenditure is equal to output. If aggregate expenditure exceeds current output, firms will seek to produce more. They will employ more factors of production and so will cause GDP to rise. Whereas if aggregate expenditure is below current output, firms will reduce production. So output will change until it matches aggregate expenditure, as shown in figure 12.3.

This diagram is often referred to as a Keynesian 45° diagram. It measures money GDP on the horizontal axis and aggregate expenditure on the vertical axis. The 45°

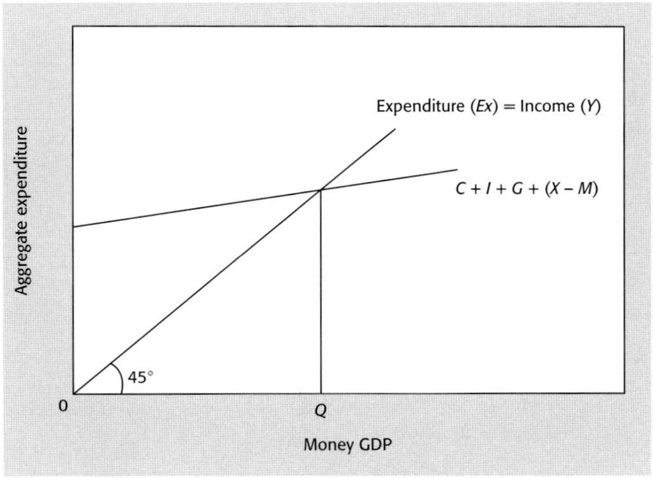

Figure 12.3 The Keynsian 45° diagram

line shows the points at which aggregate expenditure equals national income (GDP). So output is determined where the $C + I + G + (X - M)$ line cuts this 45° line.

If, for example, consumption and investment increase because consumers and entrepreneurs become more optimistic about the future, aggregate expenditure will rise and output will increase from Q to Q_1. Figure 12.4 illustrates this increase in GDP.

Withdrawals and injections

For income to be in equilibrium it is also necessary for **injections** of extra spending into the circular flow of income to equal **withdrawals** (also called **leakages**) from the circular flow. As noted earlier, possible injections into the circular flow are investment, government spending and exports, whilst the possible withdrawals are saving, taxation and imports. Figure

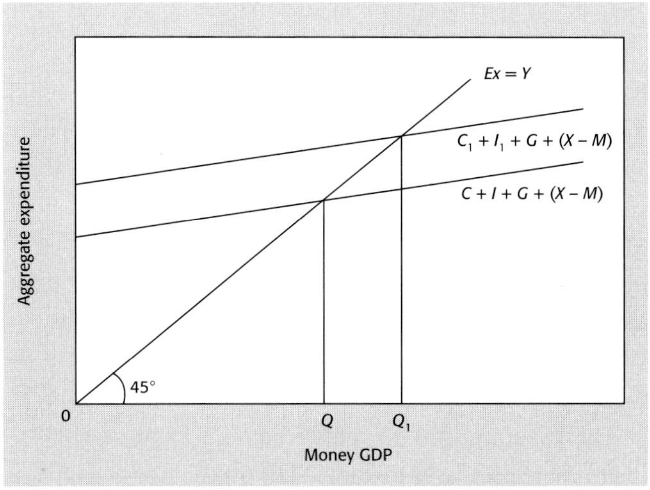

Figure 12.4 Impact of a rise in aggregate expenditure

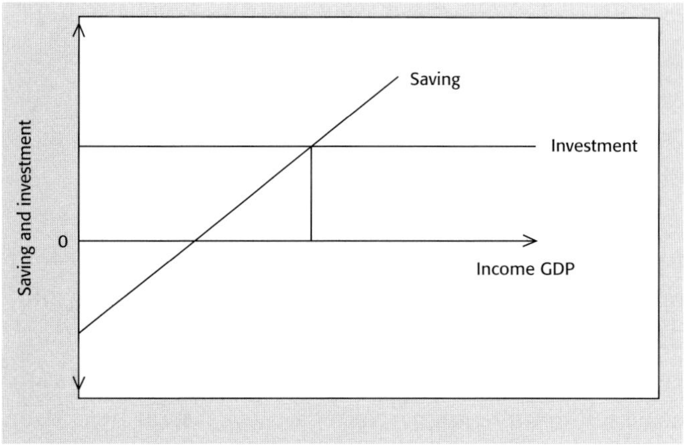

Figure 12.5 Equilibrium income in a simple economy

12.5 shows equilibrium income in a two-sector economy (households and firms).

A rise in investment would in turn cause a rise in GDP. This is as shown in figure 12.6.

A fall in saving would have a similar effect. Figure 12.7 shows equilibrium income where $I + G + X = S + T + M$ in a four-sector economy (households, firms, the government and the foreign trade sector).

If, for example, tax rates should rise without any change in government spending, GDP will fall as shown in figure 12.8.

A rise in saving will also cause GDP to fall. Indeed, a decision by households to save more can result in them saving less. This is because higher saving can reduce income and hence the ability of households to save. This is referred to as the **paradox of thrift.**

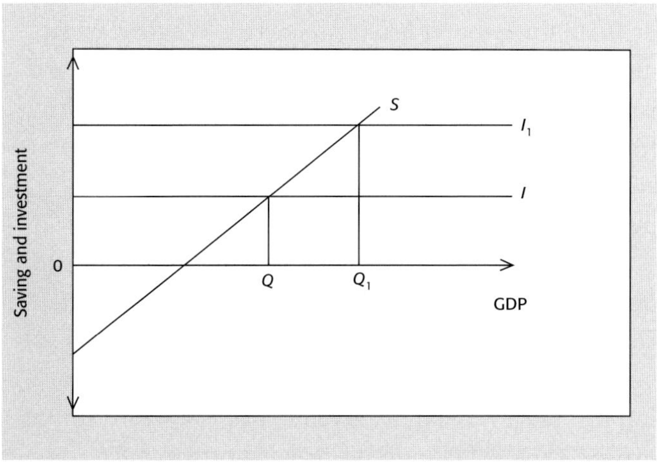

Figure 12.6 A rise in investment in a simple economy

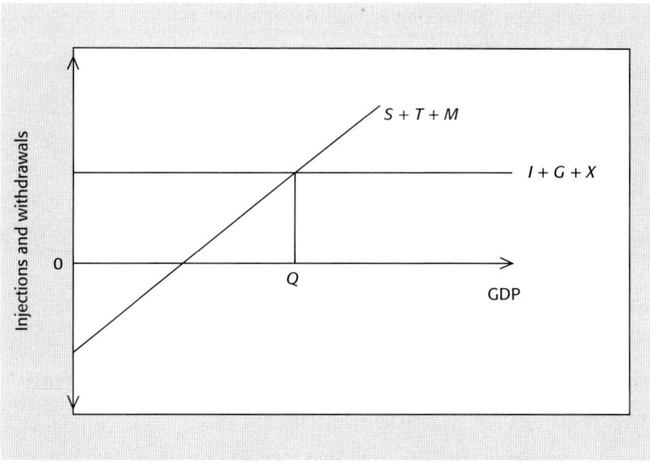

Figure 12.7 Equilibrium income in an open economy

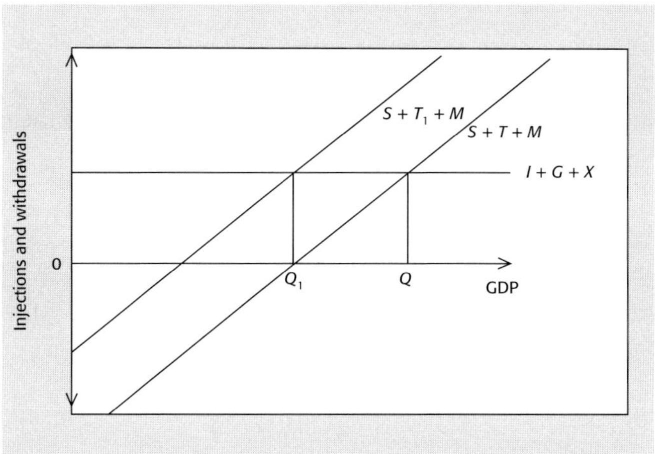

Figure 12.8 Impact of a rise in taxation on equilibrium income

Inflationary and deflationary gaps

In the short run, and Keynesians argue also possibly in the long run, an economy may not achieve full employment. An **inflationary gap** will occur if aggregate expenditure exceeds the potential output of the economy. In such a situation not all demand can be met, as there are not enough resources. As a result the excess demand drives up the price level. Figure 12.9 shows that the economy is in equilibrium at a GDP of Q, which is above the level of output, X, that could be achieved with the full employment of resources. The distance ab represents the inflationary gap.

A government may seek to reduce an inflationary gap by cutting its own spending and/or by raising taxation in order to cut consumption.

Figure 12.10 shows a reduction in government spending moving the economy back to the full employment level.

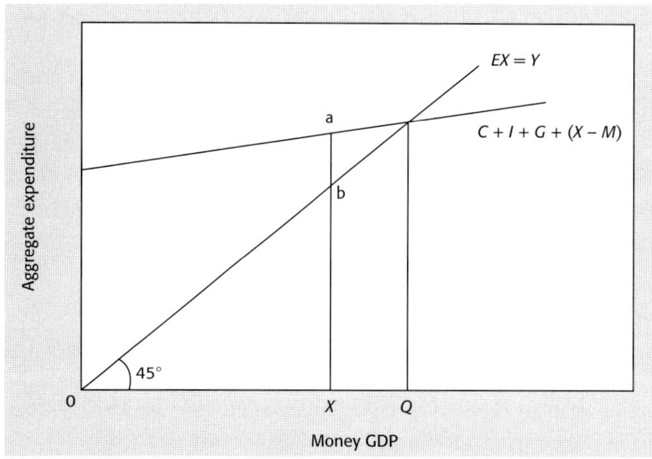

Figure 12.9 An inflationary gap

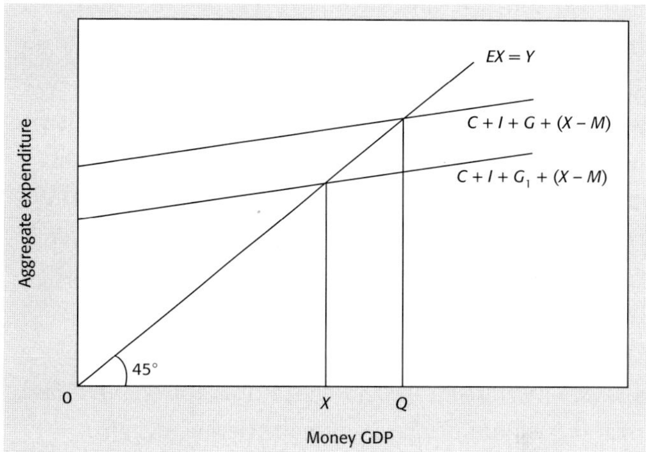

Figure 12.10 Impact of a cut in government spending

The equilibrium level of GDP may also be below the full employment level. In this case there is said to be a **deflationary gap**. Figure 12.11 shows that the lack of

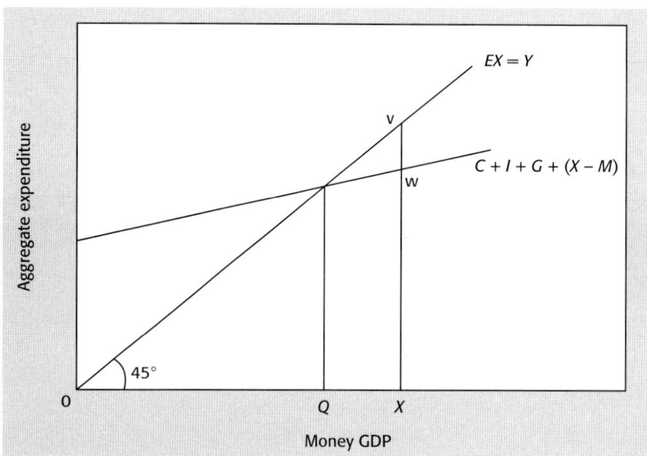

Figure 12.11 A deflationary gap

aggregate expenditure results in an equilibrium level at a GDP of *Q*, below the full employment level of *X*. There is a deflationary gap of vw.

The Keynesian solution to a deflationary gap is increased government spending financed by borrowing. Figure 12.15 shows an increase in government spending eliminating the deflationary gap.

The multiplier

Figures 12.10 and 12.12 show that a change in government spending (or taxation) results in a change in GDP of greater magnitude. This tendency for a change in aggregate expenditure to result in a greater rise in GDP is known as the **multiplier** effect. This effect occurs because a rise in expenditure will create incomes, some of which will, in turn, be spent and thereby create more incomes. For example, if people spend 80 per cent of any extra income, an increase of government spending of $200m will cause a final rise in GDP of $1,000m. This is because the initial $200m spent will create higher incomes. People will spend $160m of these incomes thereby generating a further rise in incomes. Of the $160m, $128m will be spent. This process will continue until incomes increase to $1,000m and the change in injections is matched by a change in withdrawals. In the example above, GDP rises until the $200m of extra government spending is matched by an extra $200m of saving.

The value of the multiplier can be found after the change in income has occurred by using the formula:

$$\frac{\text{change in income}}{\text{change in injection}} = \frac{\Delta Y}{\Delta J}$$

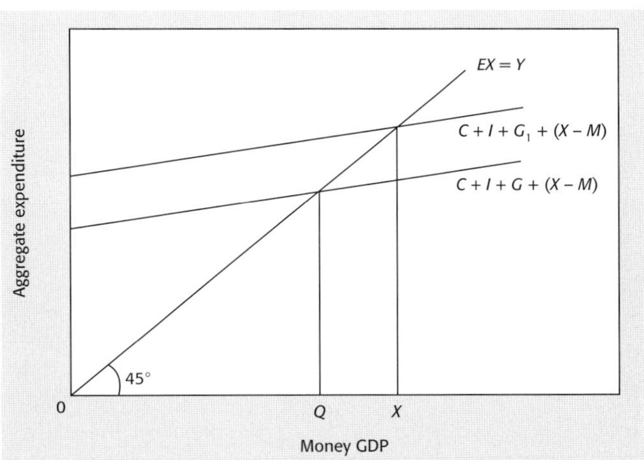

Figure 12.12 Impact of an increase in government spending

In the example above, the multiplier is

$$\frac{\$1{,}000\text{m}}{\$200\text{m}} = 5$$

The multiplier can also be estimated in advance of the change by using the formula:

$$\frac{1}{\text{marginal propensity to withdraw}}$$

The multiplier and equilibrium income in two-, three- and four-sector economic models

As we saw with the circular flow, economists often seek to explain their analysis first in a simplified form and then go on to include more variables. This is also the case with the multiplier where economists start with a simple model of the economy which only includes two sectors and then move on to a model which includes three sectors and then finally one which includes all four sectors.

Two-sector economy In a two-sector economy (households and firms) there is only one withdrawal, saving, and one injection, investment. In such an economy the multiplier can be found by using the formula:

$$\frac{1}{\text{mps}}$$

where mps is the marginal propensity to save. Because in this model income is either spent or saved, it can also be calculated by using the formula:

$$\frac{1}{1 - \text{mpc}}$$

Equilibrium income will occur where aggregate expenditure equals output, which in this case is where $C + I = Y$ and injections equal withdrawals, $I = S$.

A two-sector economy is sometimes referred to as a closed economy (that is one which does not engage in international trade) without a government sector.

Three-sector economy The additional sector is the government sector. So the model is still based on a closed economy but there is now an additional sector, the government, and so an extra injection, *G*, and an extra withdrawal, *T* (taxation). The multiplier is now:

$$\frac{1}{\text{mps} + \text{mrt}}$$

where mrt is the marginal rate of taxation (the proportion of extra income which is taxed). Equilibrium income is achieved where aggregate expenditure equals output, $C + I + G = Y$, and injections equal withdrawals, $I + G = S + T$.

Four-sector economy This is the most realistic model as it includes all four possible sectors and is an open economy: households, firms, the government and the foreign trade sector. Again equilibrium income is where aggregate expenditure equals output, but this is now where $C + I + G + (X - M) = Y$, and injections equal withdrawals, which is now where $I + G + X = S + T + M$. The multiplier is now:

$$\frac{1}{\text{mps} + \text{mrt} + \text{mpm}}$$

where mpm is the marginal propensity to import (the proportion of extra income which is spent on imports).

Self-assessment task

In an economy, mps is 0.1, mrt is 0.1 and mpm is 0.2. GDP is \$300bn. The government raises its spending by \$6bn in a bid to close a deflationary gap of \$20bn. Calculate:

- the value of the multiplier,
- the increase in GDP,
- whether the injection of extra government spending is sufficient, too high or too low to close the deflationary gap.

Autonomous and induced investment

Investment can rise or fall by significant amounts and it interacts with changes in income to cause significant changes in economic activity.

Investment which is undertaken independently of changes in income is known as **autonomous investment**. For example, a firm may buy more capital goods because it is more optimistic about the future or because the rate of interest has fallen. In this case, the aggregate expenditure line will shift upwards as shown on figure 12.13. As a result of an increase in investment from I to I_1, GDP rises by a multiple amount, from Q to Q_1.

In contrast to autonomous investment, **induced investment** is illustrated by a movement along the expenditure line. This is because induced investment is investment which is influenced by changes in income.

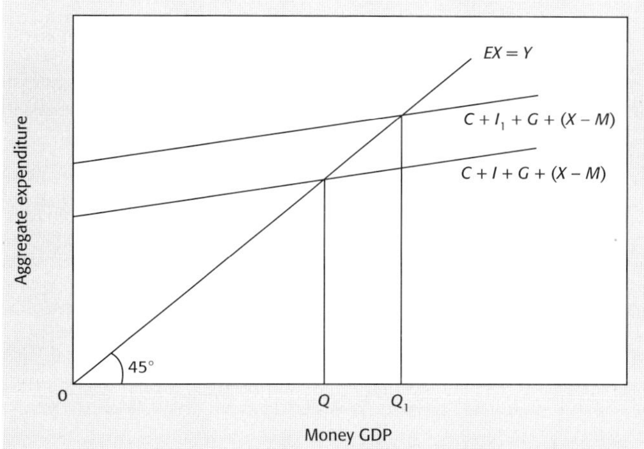

Figure 12.13 An increase in autonomous investment

If income and hence demand increases firms will be likely to buy more capital equipment. However, they will only continue to add to their capital stock if GDP continues to rise.

The accelerator

The **accelerator** theory focuses on induced investment and emphasises the volatility of investment. It states that investment depends on the rate of change in income (and hence consumer demand, and that a change in income will cause a greater proportionate change in investment. If a £1 million increase in GDP causes induced investment to rise by £3 million, the accelerator co-efficient is said to be 3.

If GDP is rising but at a constant rate, induced investment will not change. This is because firms can continue to buy the same number of machines each year to expand capacity. However, a change in the rate of growth of income can have a very significant influence on investment. An example may help to show this.

In table 12.1 it is assumed that the firm starts the period with eight machines, that one machine wears out each year and that each machine can produce 100 units of output per year.

The table shows that when demand for consumer goods rises by 25 per cent (from 800 to 1,000) in the second year, demand for capital goods rises by 200 per cent (from 1 to 3). When the rate of growth of demand for consumer goods slows in year 4, demand for capital goods falls. In the last year when demand for consumer goods falls, investment falls to zero with the worn out

Year	Consumer demand	No. of machines at start of period	No. of machines required	Replacement investment	Induced investment	Total investment
1	800	8	8	1	0	1
2	1,000	8	10	1	2	3
3	1,600	10	16	1	6	7
4	1,800	16	18	1	2	3
5	1,800	18	18	1	0	1
6	1,700	18	17	0	0	0

Table 12.1 Changes in investment

machine not being replaced, and hence productive capacity is reduced.

However, an increase in demand for consumer goods does not always result in a greater percentage change in demand for capital goods. For instance, firms will not buy more capital goods if they have spare capacity or if they do not expect the rise in consumer demand to last. It may also not be possible for firms to buy as many capital goods as they wish if the capital goods industries are working close to full capacity. In addition, with advances in technology, the capital output ratio may change with fewer machines being needed to produce a given output.

The marginal efficiency of capital

In deciding whether to invest in capital goods such as new machinery and equipment, firms must take into account the rate of return they might expect from their investment. Although this is in some respects a microeconomic concept, it has macroeconomic relevance since it can be used to explain why investment in an economy increases or decreases and what the overall effect will be on GDP.

The **marginal efficiency of capital** is a measure of the productivity of an additional unit of capital employed by a firm. It is calculated by dividing the value of additional output resulting from an extra unit of capital by the value of that unit of capital. It is therefore expressed as a percentage. Figure 12.14 shows the marginal efficiency of capital (MEC) curve or put more simply, a firm's demand curve for capital.

Various points can be noted from this figure:

- The MEC has a negative slope, indicating that the rate of return declines as successive units of capital are used. (The shape is a consequence of the law of diminishing returns.)
- Firms are likely to invest in those projects that give the highest rates of return, but only up to the point where the rate of return is equal to the market interest rate.
- A fall in the market rate of interest will see further capital projects become profitable, encouraging the firm to increase its investments. So, as the rate of interest falls from r_1 to r_2, capital investment increases from k_1 to k_2.

Another way of looking at the marginal efficiency of capital is that it is the highest interest rate at which a particular investment project might be expected to break even. In practice some allowance needs to be

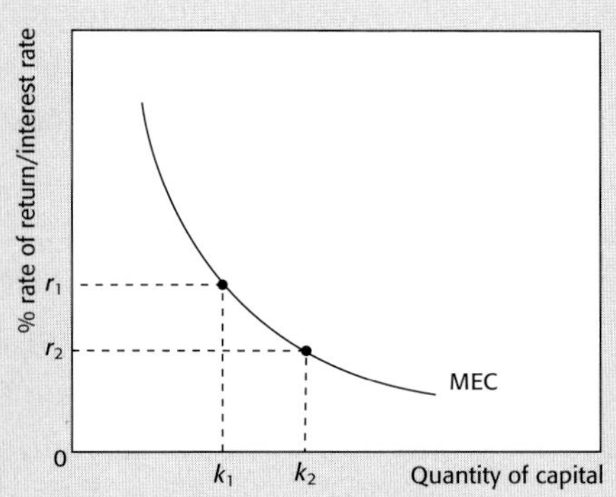

Figure 12.14 The marginal efficiency of capital

made for risk since the returns from any project are subject to much uncertainty, especially where large sums are involved.

From a macroeconomic standpoint, once all firms' demand curves for capital have been obtained, they can be aggregated to produce the total demand for capital funds at different market rates of interest. The conditions that affect the decision to invest though are not just confined to the rate of interest. As economies grow and through globalisation, new investment opportunities abound. It is therefore fair to assume that over time the MEC curve will shift to the right. This is shown in figure 12.15.

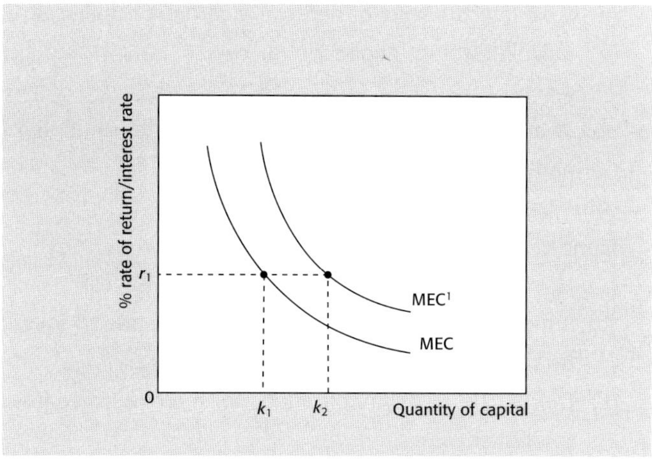

Figure 12.15 An increase in investment opportunities

The shift to the right of the MEC curve indicates that at any market interest rate, the quantity of capital invested will increase. So in figure 12.15, at rate r_1 the quantity that firms are willing to invest increases from k_1 to k_2. Various factors cause this including:

- an increase in business confidence and expectations,
- advances in technology,
- government incentives to encourage new investment,
- an increase in the cost of labour relative to the cost of capital.

Self-assessment tasks

1 On completion of this chapter you should be able to answer the following questions taken from CAPE examinations, 2005.

(a) Define the following terms:
- marginal propensity to consume,
- multiplier,
- actual investment,
- planned investment. (8 marks)

(b) Explain the relationship between the following:
- marginal propensity to consume and multiplier,
- actual investment and planned investment. (8 marks)

2 You are given the following information about Country Z:
- consumption function: $C = 200 + 0.8\,y$
- investment function: $I = 100$
- aggregate expenditure (AE) = Consumption + Investment ($C + I$)
- aggregate expenditure (AE) = National Income (y)

(a) Determine the following:
- marginal propensity to consume, (4 marks)
- marginal propensity to save. (4 marks)

(b) Using a 45° line diagram, plot the aggregate expenditure function. (Use the graph sheet provided to answer this question.) (12 marks)

(c) Indicate the equilibrium point on the graph drawn in (b) above. (4 marks)

(d) Calculate the level of national income at equilibrium. (6 marks)
(e) Calculate the multiplier. (4 marks)
(Total 50 marks)

3 Below are recent estimates of the value of the multiplier for three economies in 2005:

Germany	1.13
UK	1.42
Japan	1.76

(a) How might you explain the above differences? (6 marks)
(b) Suppose the respective governments decide to invest $100m in a new motorway project. What will be the final effects on GDP in each country? (6 marks)
(c) Discuss the policy implications for the respective governments arising out of differences in the multiplier values. (13 marks)
(Total 25 marks)

4 (a) What factors might cause the marginal efficiency of capital curve in an economy to shift to the left? Use a diagram in your answer. (10 marks)
(b) Discuss the extent to which the accelerator and marginal efficiency of capital theories can be used to explain the volume of investment in a Caribbean island of your choice. (15 marks)
(Total 25 marks)

Summary

In this chapter it has been shown that:

- The consumption function indicates how much will be spent at different levels of income.
- The traditional view of a linear consumption function has been questioned through the permanent income and life cycle hypotheses.
- Equilibrium national income is achieved when aggregate expenditure equals output.
- An inflationary gap occurs if aggregate expenditure exceeds the full employment level of output; a deflationary gap exists if aggregate expenditure is below the full employment level of output.
- Any change in injections or leakages into the circular flow of income will have a multiplier effect on GDP.
- The accelerator theory demonstrates that investment is volatile; it states that changes in GDP create greater percentage changes in investment.
- The level of investment in the economy can also be explained through the marginal efficiency of capital; this theory assumes that the rate of interest is the only determinant of the quantity of capital that is invested in an economy.

Key words

Definitions of Key words can be found in the Glossary.

accelerator
aggregate expenditure
autonomous investment
average propensity to consume
average propensity to save
consumption function
deflationary gap
dissaving
induced investment
inflationary gap
injections
leakages
life cycle
marginal efficiency of capital
marginal propensity to consume
marginal propensity to save
multiplier
permanent income
saving
saving function
transitory income
withdrawals

Module 2

Macroeconomic policy analysis

On completion of this module you should be able to:

understand the underlying principles of money demand and supply

appreciate the role of the central bank in the economy

understand monetary and fiscal policy and their applications

understand the nature and burden of the national debt

13 Demand and supply of money

This chapter covers unit 2, module 2, topic 1.
On completion of this chapter, you should be able to:

- define the functions of money
- explain money demand
- explain why money demand may respond to interest rates and income
- describe the relationship between money demand, velocity of circulation and economic activity
- explain how the money supply is determined and the various techniques used by central banks to regulate this sector
- explain how commercial banks create money
- give reasons why residents may substitute foreign currency for domestic money

Money: its functions and characteristics

Money is something that virtually all of us take for granted in so far as we need it to carry out our daily lives. Riding on a bus, purchasing a soft drink or an ice cream are simple yet very frequent examples of when we hand over a few coins or a note to whoever is providing these things for us. The process is so simple in fact that we have no need to even think about it. Having said that, all of us (except possibly for Bill Gates of Microsoft!) would like more money, but that is a different matter as we saw earlier.

Bill Gates of Microsoft
Source: Photo by Popperfoto/Reuters.

The money we hand over for purchases is usually our national currency, such as dollars, pounds, euros, ringgits, rupees and so on. The coins and paper notes themselves have little or no intrinsic value – their value to us stems directly from the fact that sellers have complete confidence in the money we are giving to them and so exchange it for the goods and services we require. This confidence in turn enables them to buy supplies for their shop or petrol for their bus and so on. In the simple way described above, we have shown the functions of money.

The practice of using money is absolutely essential for the smooth operation of businesses and international transactions in the modern global economy. In the absence of the sort of money we know, people would have to rely on **barter**, the term used to mean the direct exchange of one good or service for another. Where this is the only way of exchange (as was the case in some former Russian republics quite recently) then the whole process of meeting ones needs is slow, cumbersome, time consuming and very impractical. There must be what is called **double coincidence of wants**, whereby two people have to have the appropriate goods or services which each other wants. Money therefore makes the whole process of exchange and trade so much easier and simpler.

Just what makes up the money supply is explained a little later. For the time being, bearing in mind what has already been said, money is anything that is regularly

used to buy goods and services. Normally, of course, this is coins, notes, cheques, credit cards and debit cards. It could though be a valuable commodity (such as gold and silver) or even chocolate and Levi jeans, both of which were scarce and widely accepted as payment in the former Soviet Union in the 1980s, when people were losing confidence in the Russian rouble. Implicit in the above are the characteristics of money; money is anything which is generally acceptable, durable, portable, scarce and divisible into small units.

From the economist's standpoint, money has three necessary functions. Let us look at each briefly.

First, money is a **medium of exchange**. The function was amplified earlier in recognising that money is the 'medium' that buyers use for purchases and that sellers are willing to accept in 'exchange' for these purchases. By physically handing over money, there is a common and automatic acceptance of money fulfilling its function as a medium of exchange.

Money's second function is as a **unit of account**. As such, money is used as the 'unit' by which prices are established in dollars and cents, pounds and pence and so on. This function applies for both current and projected transactions, for example when banks agree to lend a certain sum of money to a borrower and also agree on how much interest has to be paid by the borrower to the bank for this service. The 'account' aspect stems from money units being accountable, in the sense that the value of the money can be recorded and summed. It is also a means by which the relationships between various units of a currency are established, for example 100 cents equalling $1.

The third function of money is that of a **store of value**. Here, it is recognised that money can be held or 'stored' for a period of time before it is used, or it can be accumulated (if you are fortunate enough) to provide a source of wealth. As with the medium of exchange function, the holder of the money is confident that money will retain its value compared to when it was received. Not only coins and notes but bank deposits, bonds, stocks and other forms of holding money can be used as the basis for storage over time. In all cases, this accumulation of money can be realised in monetary terms in the future.

These three functions of money are very important and necessary for the smooth working of all economies except for subsistence economies. If any of these functions break down and cannot be met, people lose confidence in money. When this occurs, economic collapse is the only outcome. There is therefore an important need for government economic policy to ensure that this does not happen. The most obvious sign when this is the case is that money fails to act as a store of value at times of hyperinflation and, in a short time, people can no longer have confidence in money as a medium of exchange.

Discounts everywhere

A general decline in retail and wholesale prices in Japan has led to a mushrooming of budget shops. Products with their prices slashed include:

- Half-price burgers at fast-food outlets.
- Cut-price gyudon (beef bowl) at food stalls.
- Marked-down lunch boxes at 24-hour convenience stores.
- Low-priced garments at discount stores.
- Factory over-runs going at fire-sale prices at American-style malls.

But lower prices have not necessarily led to smaller profits for many companies.

When the Matsuya chain slashed the price of its gyudon to 290 yen (US$4.35) last September, it enjoyed a 30 per cent jump in customers.

McDonald's Japan, which sparked off the country's fast-food price war last year with its half-price basic hamburgers, has also seen its earnings go up.

Source: Kwan Weng Kin, Singapore, 3 June 2001.

The Quantity Theory of Money

The high levels of inflation that have been recorded by some countries over the time period shown in table 9.1 have led to considerable interest amongst economists as to the causes of inflation. Let us identify in a simple way what these causes are.

A good starting point is to note what the well-known US economist Milton Friedman had to say about inflation. He said that 'inflation is always and everywhere a monetary phenomenon'. In other words, periods of inflation coincide with increases in the money supply. So

$\uparrow$ money supply $\longrightarrow$ $\uparrow$ rate of inflation

There is though an important qualification; namely, that this will only occur if the rate of growth of the money supply is greater than the increase in the level of output in the economy, so forcing up prices. This has been an obvious cause of inflation for some of the economies shown in table 9.1. It is in many respects an example in the macroeconomy of supply being greater than demand. This can be shown diagrammatically in figure 13.1. This figure shows that:

- the demand curve for money is like any other demand curve – people want to hold a larger quantity of money when the value falls as they need more money to buy their particular purchases;
- the supply curve for money is vertical since it is fixed by the central bank;
- at the initial equilibrium (*X*), the demand for money and supply of money are balanced – the value of money is at *p* and the price level at 2*p*;

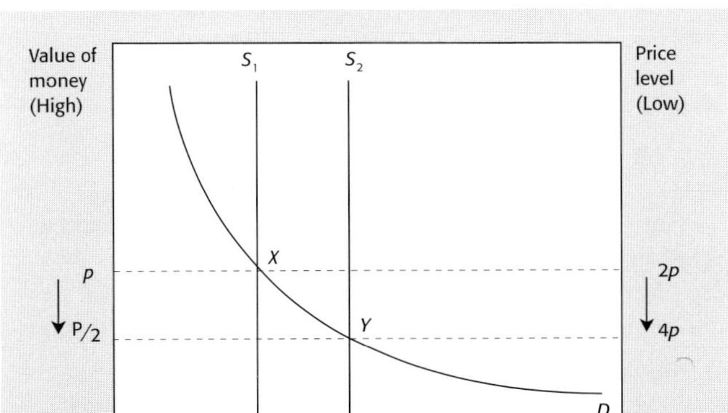

Figure 13.1 The effects of an increase in the money supply

- an increase in the supply of money (for example by printing more notes) shifts the supply of money from S_1 to S_2;
- the outcome is that there is a new equilibrium position at *Y* where the value of money has fallen and the price level increased pro-rata.

In taking the above line, monetarists such as Milton Friedman make use of the so-called **Quantity Theory of Money**. This theory is based on an interpretation of the equation

$$MV = PT$$

where *M* is the money supply, *V* is the number of times money changes hands, *P* is the price level and *T* is the output or transactions in the economy.

This equation (or Fisher equation as it sometimes known) has to be true since both sides represent total expenditure in the economy. By holding *V* and *T* constant, as they are unaffected by changes in the money supply, it follows that a change in the money supply causes an equal percentage change in the price level.

This is a highly simplified representation of what is a most complex situation, but it can be used to show quite clearly how the reckless printing of money can result in an increase in the general level of prices. This has clearly happened where governments have sought to get out of debt and finance their own spending by simply printing more money. It is by no means the only reason – where there is war, political upheaval and civil unrest, high inflation can result as people panic and lose confidence in the money supply, preferring to hold their assets in physical rather than monetary forms (see below).

Therefore, monetarists believe that changes in the money supply can have a significant impact on the price level of a country. They assume that changes in V and T are determined independently of the money supply. So they believe that a change in the money supply will cause an equal proportionate change in the price level. For example, if $M = 100$, $V = 5$, $P = 2$ and $T = 250$, then with a constant *V* and *T*, a rise in the money supply of 50 per cent to 150 will cause the price level to rise by 50 per cent to 3.

However, Keynesians dispute the validity of the quantity theory. They argue that a change in the money supply can affect any or all of the other three variables and so it is not possible to predict what will happen when the money supply changes. For example, *M* could rise by 50 per cent but if *T* also rises by 50 per cent, *P* will not change.

Self-assessment tasks

Study the table below and then tackle the exercises that follow.

Country	Narrow money supply (annual % change)	Consumer prices (annual % change)
Australia	9.3	5.8
Britain	4.8	2.9
Canada	14.2	3.2
Japan	4.3	−0.2
Sweden	1.9	1.4
Switzerland	−2.6	1.5
USA	−3.0	3.4

Source: *The Economist*, 3 February 2001.

1 Distinguish between narrow and broad measures of the money supply.
2 Analyse the relationship between changes in the money supply and inflation rates shown in the data.
3 Discuss whether an increase in the money supply will necessarily cause inflation.

Interest rate determination Monetarists and Keynesians also disagree over how the rate of interest is determined. Most monetarists support the **loanable funds theory**. This states that the rate of interest is determined by the demand and supply of loanable funds, as shown in figure 13.2.

The demand for loanable funds comes from firms wanting to invest, households wanting to (say) buy a car on credit and from the government seeking to fund a budget deficit. Government demand for loanable funds is not very sensitive to a change in the rate of interest but a rise in the rate of interest will lower firms' and households' demand. So the demand for loanable funds curve slopes down from left to right. The supply of loanable funds comes from savings. A higher rate of interest will increase the return from savings and so the supply curve is upward sloping.

An increase in the supply of savings will lower the rate of interest and cause an extension in demand for loanable funds, as illustrated in figure 13.3.

In contrast, Keynesians argue that the rate of interest is determined not by the demand and supply of loanable funds but by the demand and supply of money. It is assumed that the supply of money is determined by the monetary authorities and is fixed in the short run.

Keynes developed the **liquidity preference** theory to explain the demand for money. He identified three main motives why households and firms may decide to hold part of their wealth in a money form. The motive most people will be familiar with is the **transactions motive**. This is the desire to hold money to make everyday purchases and meet everyday payments. How much is held by a household or firm is influenced by the income received and the frequency of the income payments. Generally the more income received and the more infrequently the payments are received, the higher the amount which will be held.

Firms and households also usually hold rather more of their wealth in a money form than they anticipate they will spend. This is so that they can meet unexpected expenses, and take advantage of unforeseen bargains. The name given to this motive is the **precautionary motive**. Money resources held for the transactions and precautionary motives are sometimes

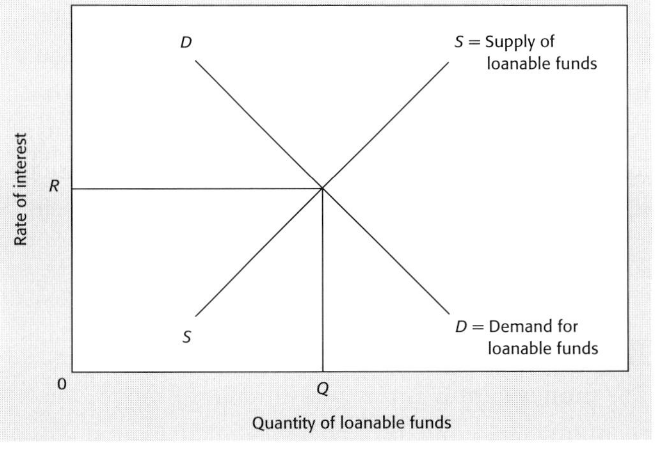

Figure 13.2 Interest rate determination

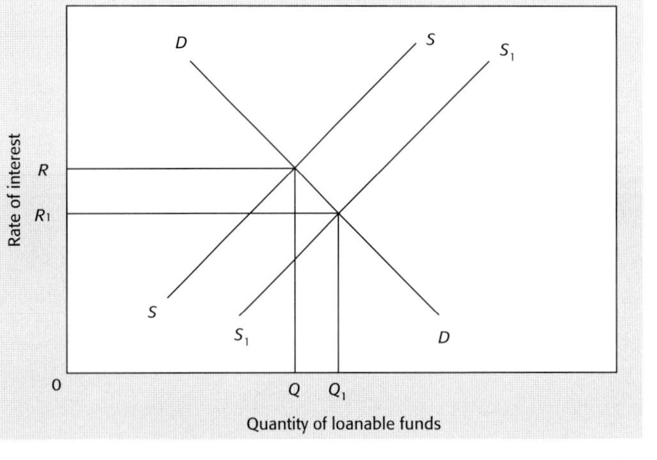

Figure 13.3 The effect of an increase in savings on the rate of interest

referred to as **active balances** as they are likely to be spent in the near future. They are relatively interest inelastic so that, for example, a rise in the rate of interest will not result in households and firms significantly cutting back on their holdings of money for transactions and precautionary reasons.

In contrast, the third motive for holding money balances, the **speculative motive**, is interest elastic. Households and firms will hold what are sometimes called **idle balances** when they believe that the returns from holding financial assets are low. One financial asset which firms and households may decide to hold is government bonds. These are government securities which represent loans to the government. The price of government bonds and the rate of interest (in percentage terms) move in opposite directions. For example, a government bond with a face value of £500 may carry a fixed interest rate of 5 per cent of its issue price. If the price of the bond rises to £1,000 the interest paid will now represent 2.5 per cent of the price of the bond. Households and firms are likely to hold money when the price of bonds is high and expected to fall. This is because they will not be forgoing much interest and because they will be afraid of making a capital loss. Whereas, the speculative demand for money will be low when the price of bonds is low and the rate of interest high.

Figure 13.4 shows the combined transactions, precautionary and speculative motives for holding money in the form of liquidity preference (or demand) for money. The rate of interest is at *R* since this is where the liquidity preference curve intersects the supply of money curve.

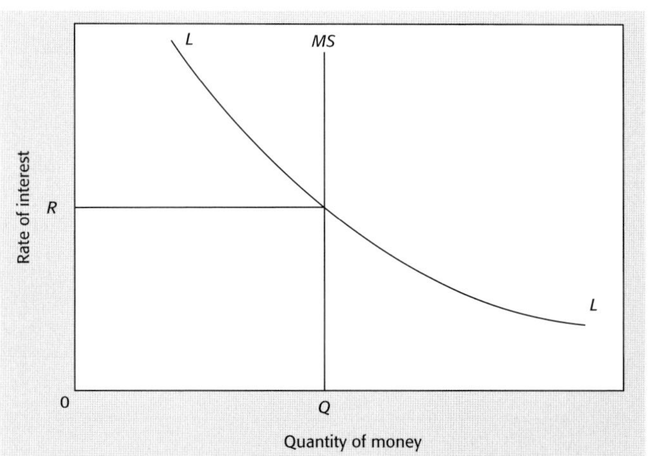

Figure 13.4 The liquidity preference theory of interest rate determination

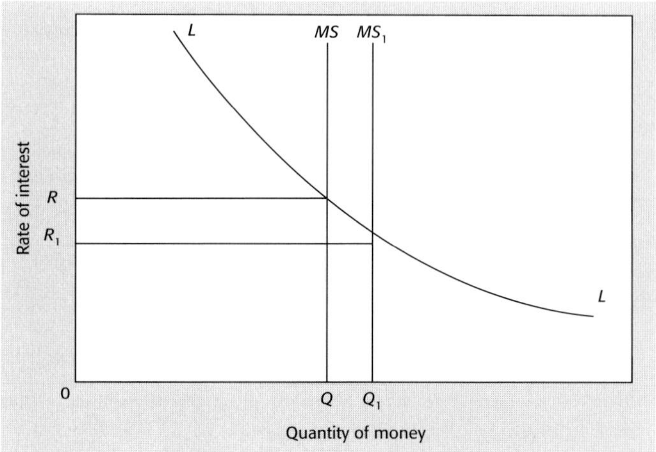

Figure 13.5 An increase in the money supply and a fall in the rate of interest

An increase in the money supply will cause a fall in the rate of interest, as illustrated in Figure 13.5.

The rate of interest falls because the rise in the money supply will result in some households and firms having higher money balances than they want to hold. As a result they will use some to buy financial assets. A rise in demand for government bonds will cause the price of bonds to rise and so the rate of interest to fall.

The liquidity trap Although it is expected that an increase in the money supply will cause the rate of interest to fall, Keynes described a situation where it would not be possible to drive down the rate of interest by increasing the money supply. He described this situation as the **liquidity trap** and thought it could occur when the rate of interest is very low and the price of bonds very high. In this case he thought that speculators would expect the price of bonds to fall in the future. So if the money supply was to be increased they would hold all the extra money. They would not buy bonds for fear of making a capital loss and because the return from holding such securities would be low. Figure 13.6 shows that at a rate of interest of *R*, demand for money becomes perfectly elastic and the increase in the money supply has no effect on the rate of interest.

The money supply

The **money supply** is the total amount of money in an economy. This consists of currency in circulation plus relevant deposits. Governments measure the money

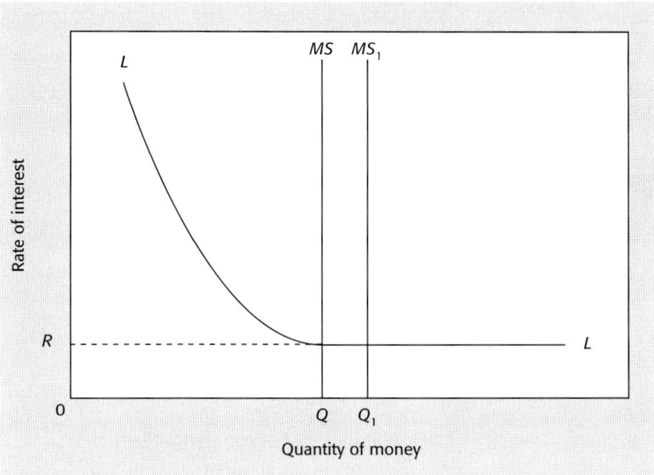

Figure 13.6 The liquidity trap

supply to gain information about trends in aggregate demand, the state of financial markets and to help them in determining the direction of monetary policy (see next chapter).

Measuring the money supply is not as easy as it might appear from the above definition. This is because it is difficult to decide what to include in any measure of money – it is further complicated by governments in different economies using different measures of their money supply.

Economists define items as money if they fulfil the functions of money described earlier in this topic. However, the extent to which items carry out these functions varies and can change over time. As a result governments use a variety of measures of the money

Self-assessment tasks

Read the article below and then tackle the exercises that follow.

Japan's gesture

When Masaru Hayami was appointed governor of the newly independent Bank of Japan two years ago, he had a reputation for stubborness. Now he has demonstrated that trait with a vengeance.

In recent weeks he has faced a barrage of calls for him to stick with the Bank's ultra-loose monetary policy which has kept overnight rates at about zero by flooding the markets with liquidity. But on Friday Mr. Hayami persuaded the Bank's policy board to raise the overnight money rate to 0.25 per cent. For the first time in 10 years, Japanese interest rates moved up rather than down.

The immediate economic effects of ending the zero interest rate policy instituted in February 1999 may be modest.

As Bank of Japan officials point out, Friday's decision in itself is hardly likely to tip Japan's economy into recession. A rise of 0.25 per cent is small, and still leaves interest rates at remarkably low levels.

Nor will it necessarily translate into an immediate rise in borrowing costs for all companies. Corporate loans are pegged not only to overnight market rates but also to the official discount rate, which remains at 0.5 per cent. Economists estimate that typical corporate lending rates might rise by just 0.1 per cent.

Japan has for many years looked like John Maynard Keynes' description of an economic slump in which businesses become so fearful that there is nothing monetary policy can do to persuade them to spend. Cutting interest rates in those conditions is as useless as 'pushing on a string'. But if cutting rates in Japan had little impact, then raising them may turn out to be considerably more significant.

Source: Gillian Tett and Ed Crooks, *Financial Times*, 14 August 2000 (adapted).

1 Define liquidity.
2 Explain why 'flooding the markets with liquidity' would be expected to keep interest rates low.
3 Discuss the possible effect that the rise in Japanese corporate lending rates may have on investment.
4 Explain why cutting interest rates can be 'as useless as "pushing on a string"'.

supply which are occasionally altered to reflect developments in the roles carried out by particular items.

Notwithstanding, the measures of money supply can be divided into two main ones. These are:

- **narrow money** – this is money which is used as a medium of exchange and consists of notes and coins in circulation and cash held in banks and in balances held by banks at the central bank. This is sometimes referred to as the **monetary base.**
- **broad money** – this consists of the above plus a range of items that are commensurate with money's function as a store of value.

Within the Caribbean, the control of the money supply lies with the various central banks such as the Central Bank of Barbados and the Bank of Jamaica. The standard measures of money supply used are shown in table 13.1

Table 13.2 shows the money supply for Barbados at the end of December 2005. The control of M1 and M2 is particularly important.

Due to an increasing quarterly inflation rate in 2005, M1 has consistently increased on a month-by-month basis. More specifically, in July and December especially, the Bank found it necessary to increase the total value of notes in circulation due to increased seasonal demand. The change in M2 has been less consistent, with falls recorded in five months of 2005 as the Bank sought to control the amount of lending by commercial banks in order to reduce the rate of inflation.

Measure	Definition
M0	Currency in the hands of the public plus reserves held on behalf of commercial banks.
M1	Notes and coins outside the banking system plus current account balances.
M2	M1 plus short-term time and savings deposits, foreign currency transferable deposits, certificates of deposit and repurchase agreements.
M3	M2 plus travellers cheques, short-term bank notes, long-term foreign currency time deposits and money market mutual funds.
M4	M3 plus treasury bills, negotiable bonds and pension funds.

Table 13.1 Standard measures of the money supply

Notes in circulation	532,824
Coins in circulation	43,038
Less Treasury and bank cash	127,296
Total currency with public (M1)	448,566
Demand deposits	2,738,895
Total money supply (M2)	3,187,461

Table 13.2 Money supply in Barbados (BDS $000)
Source: Central Bank of Barbados.

Instruments of monetary control

In theory there are several instruments of monetary control that central banks can use. These include:

- **open market operations** – this is where the central bank buys or sells government securities in order to influence lending by commercial banks. If the central bank wants to reduce bank loans, it will sell government securities. This causes the commercial bank's liquid assets to fall, so restricting their ability to lend.
- **discount rates** – this is the rate at which the central bank discounts treasury bills that are issued on behalf of the government to finance their current expenditure. They are short term and if a

central bank wishes to increase the money supply, it will increase this rate in order to encourage commercial banks to purchase treasury bills.

- financing fiscal deficits – governments invariably have to borrow money to cover fiscal deficits. This involves long-term debt, which is likely to be bought by the non-banking sector. The government's debt is managed by the central bank.
- setting of reserve requirements – banks are required to keep a certain proportion of their assets in a particular form such as cash. By increasing the reserve requirement, the ability of commercial banks to create credit is reduced.
- **moral suasion** – this is a situation where the government uses all sorts of pressure to get the central bank to operate in a way that is in line with the government's macroeconomic requirements for managing the economy.

In practice, central banks tend to have their own variant on the above general instruments of monetary control. In Jamaica, for example, the Bank of Jamaica employs two approaches. These are shown in the accompanying box (see p. 194).

The role of commercial banks in creating money

Commercial banks can increase the money supply through their own lending policies. When a bank gives a loan to one of its clients, the borrower's account is credited with the amount that is borrowed. In this way every loan creates a deposit. Commercial banks are therefore in a powerful position to create money since they can create more deposits than they have cash and other liquid assets (items that can be quickly converted into cash).

From experience, banks have found that only a small proportion of deposits are cashed. When people make payments, especially large payments, they tend to make use of cheques, credit cards and direct debits. These means of payment involve a transfer of money using

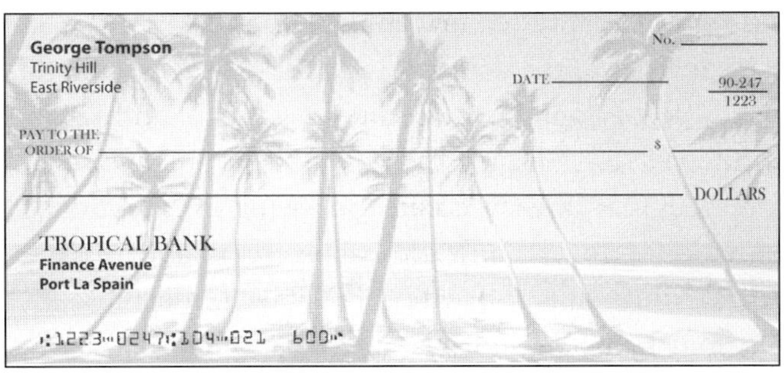

entries in the records that banks keep of their customers' deposits rather than by paying out cash. So, banks can create more deposits than they have liquid assets.

Nevertheless, they have to be careful when calculating what **liquidity ratio** (the proportion of liquid assets to total liabilities, that is deposits) to keep. The lower they keep the ratio, the more they can lend. However, they have to be able to meet their customers' demands for cash. If they miscalculate and keep too low a ratio or if people suddenly start to cash more of their deposits, there is a risk of a run on the banking system. Indeed, banking is based on confidence. Customers have to believe there is enough cash and liquid assets to pay out all their deposits even though, in practice, this is not the case.

By estimating what liquidity ratio to keep, a bank will be able to calculate its **credit multiplier**. This can also be referred to as a bank or credit creation multiplier, and shows by how much additional liquid assets will enable banks to increase their liabilities. It is given by the formula

$$\frac{\text{total value of new deposits created}}{\text{value of change in liquid assets}}$$

For example, if total deposits rise by \$600m as a result of a new cash deposit of \$100m, the credit multiplier is \$600m/\$100m = 6. It is also possible to calculate the credit multiplier by using the formula

$$\frac{100}{\text{liquidity ratio}}$$

If a bank keeps a liquidity ratio of 10 per cent, the credit multiplier will be 100/10 = 10. Knowing this enables a bank to calculate how much it can lend. It first works out the possible increase in its total liabilities. This is found by multiplying the change in liquid assets by the credit multiplier. So, if the credit multiplier is 10 and liquid assets rise by \$40m, total deposits will rise by \$40m × 10 = \$400m.

To work out the change in loans (advances), the change in liquid assets is deducted from the change in liabilities. This is because the change in liabilities will include deposits given to those putting in the liquid assets. In the example, the change in loans will be \$400m – \$40m = \$360m.

Instruments of monetary policy

The Bank of Jamaica's (BOJ) two main operational tools in the management of the monetary base are open market operations and reserve requirements. Management of the monetary base focuses on the balance sheet of the Bank of Jamaica, in particular its net domestic assets (NDA) and net international reserves (NIR). The Bank's balance sheet is represented by the following identity:

MB = NDA + NIR

Where MB, the monetary base, is the sum of notes and coins issued by the central bank and commercial bank cash reserves.

The operational tools, open market operations and reserve requirements, are used to influence financial activities of institutions over which the BOJ has supervisory responsibilities.

- **Open market operations** (OMO) are the most important monetary policy tool and determinant of changes in the monetary base, the main source of fluctuation in the money supply. This relationship between the money supply and the monetary base is expressed below:

  $M^* = k$ **MB**

  Where k is the money multiplier and M^* is the money supply.

  OMO constitute an indirect instrument of monetary policy and involve short-term agreements to purchase or sell the Bank's holdings of government securities. In addition, the issuing of the Bank's own certificates of deposits are also used to influence the level of liquidity in the financial system, the volume of credit and the level of interest rates. In practice, open market purchases of government securities or certificates of deposits from the market will expand the Bank's monetary base, thereby raising the money supply through the multiplier process. On the other hand, an open market sale contracts the monetary base, lowering the money supply.
- Reserve requirements is the only direct policy tool within the operational framework of the Bank. Reserve requirements are the portion of deposits that financial institutions have to keep on hand or hold on deposit at the Bank of Jamaica. By law, the central bank requires that for every dollar deposit at the financial institutions, a fraction must be held on deposit at the Bank of Jamaica. Reserve requirements therefore define a limit on the amount of credit that a financial institution can extend. The cash reserve requirement stipulates that a certain proportion of the deposits of the institution are held on deposit at the banks in the form of cash. Changes in the cash reserve requirement affect the money supply by causing the multiplier to change. A decline in the requirements leads to an expansion of the money supply because more multiple deposit creation can take place while an increase in the reserve requirement reduces the money supply. Currently, the Bank of Jamaica is in the process of steadily reducing this requirement.

The Bank also controls liquidity through its intervention (direct sales/purchases) in the foreign exchange market. The efficient management of the flexible exchange rate system requires that the Bank intervenes in the market from time to time to smooth out supply conditions and to ensure the relative stability of the exchange rate. Thus, the Bank uses its monetary policy tools to influence the flow of foreign currency and any pressures emanating in the foreign exchange market.

Source: Bank of Jamaica, 2005.

In practice, however, a bank may not lend as much as the credit multiplier implies it can. This is because there may be a lack of households and firms wanting to borrow or a lack of creditworthy borrowers.

A bank may also change its liquidity ratio if people alter the proportion of the deposits they cash, if other banks alter their lending policies or if the country's central bank requires banks to keep a set liquidity ratio.

Currency substitution and money hoarding

The analysis of the demand and supply of money in this topic can be applied to all economies where normal economic relationships and mechanisms are operating, irrespective of the level of development. In exceptional situations – for example Zimbabwe (see chapter 9), the former Russian republics and possibly even Jamaica in the mid 1990s – people lose confidence in money and instead resort to barter and other physical means of exchange.

In other situations, where interest rates are zero or pitifully low, there seems little or no point in people keeping money in commercial banks, especially if prices are falling. This was the case in Japan in 2000 (see above) and Hong Kong in 2004 when business confidence was very low. An obvious thing to do in these circumstances is for people to substitute goods and assets, particularly property, for money. There is also a tendency to hoard money in anticipation of falling prices, making many goods cheaper in the future. An alternative might be to purchase foreign currency such as $US or euros in the hope that these worldwide currencies would be more able to hold their value.

Self-assessment tasks

On completion of this chapter, you should be able to answer the following question taken from CAPE examinations, 2005.

1 (a) Discuss the following:
- Two advantages of paper money,
- Two advantages of cheques as compared with commodity money,
- Two disadvantages of commodity money. (18 marks)

(b) Currency and chequable deposits have no intrinsic value and they are not backed by gold or other precious metals, yet they are regarded as money. Discuss the role of acceptability and fiat or law in determining the value of money. (12 marks)

2 (a) Discuss the basic determinant of the transactions demand for money and the speculative demand for money.

(b) Assume that the money market is initially in equilibrium and that the money supply is increased. With the use of a diagram, explain the adjustments toward a new equilibrium interest rate. (20 marks)

(Total 50 marks)

Summary

In this chapter it has been shown that:

- Money has three functions: acting as a medium of exchange, a unit of account and a store of value.
- The quantity theory of money can be used to show that an increase in the money supply will lead to a proportionate increase in the price level.
- The loanable funds theory states that the rate of interest is determined by the demand and supply of loanable funds.
- Keynesians use liquidity preference theory and the supply of money to explain the rate of interest.
- The money supply in any economy consists of narrow money and broad money.
- Central banks have various instruments of monetary control in order to influence the ability of commercial banks to create money.
- The credit multiplier can be used to explain how much money banks are able to create.

Key words

Definitions of Key words can be found in the Glossary.

active balances
barter
broad money
credit creation multiplier
discount rates
double coincidence of wants
idle balances
liquidity preference theory
liquidity rates
liquidity trap
loanable funds theory
medium of exchange
monetary base
money supply
moral suasion
narrow money
open market operations
precautionary motive
Quantity Theory of Money
speculative motive
store of value
transactions motive
unit of account

14 Monetary policy and fiscal policy

This chapter covers unit 2, module 2, topics 2 and 3.
On completion of this chapter, you should be able to:

- define monetary policy
- describe the effects of monetary policy on aggregate demand
- evaluate the potency of monetary policy
- describe the effects of interest rates and money supply on national income
- evaluate ways of controlling the money supply
- define fiscal policy
- describe the effects of fiscal policy on aggregate demand
- evaluate the potency of fiscal policy
- define the budget, budget deficit, budget surplus, balanced budget and the balanced budget multiplier
- describe methods of financing budget deficits

Introduction

Figure 9.1 in the first topic of this unit was a broad representation of the means by which governments are able to manage their economies. Traditionally, **monetary policy** and **fiscal policy** have been used in virtually all types of economy to manage aggregate demand in order to achieve the government's macroeconomic objectives. This is still the case, although particularly in developed economies like the UK, supply-side policies have been increasingly used to meet longer-term objectives such as sustained economic growth.

Monetary policy refers to any measures that are used by the government to bring about changes in the supply of money or interest rates. (Some economists would also include policies that change the exchange rate.) Increasingly though, experience has shown that the control of interest rates rather than the money supply is the most effective way of regulating aggregate demand. This is now the main policy that is used by central banks and governments for the short-term management of the economy in for example the UK, the eurozone and the Caribbean.

Fiscal policy is the way in which governments manage aggregate demand by making changes to taxation and their own expenditure. This is the traditional Keynesian approach and like monetary policy, has been widely practised in all types of economy. Like monetary policy, fiscal policy is used to 'fine tune' the economy from a short-term perspective.

Monetary policy and fiscal policy do not operate in isolation; they work together in affecting aggregate demand at any one time – although one may well have rather more importance than the other. (This is a very valid reason for considering both topics in this chapter.)

The effects of monetary and fiscal policies on aggregate demand are shown in table 14.1. This also indicates the reasons why these policies are applied and some of the difficulties that might arise. As the table shows, using monetary and fiscal policies is by no means straightforward and the outcomes are by no means guaranteed as will be explained later.

The budget

Managing the economy is a complex task. The annual **budget** is eagerly awaited and attracts much media attention as the overall outcome is a very clear indicator of the state of the economy. In this statement, the Finance Minister or Chancellor of the Exchequer (as the person is known in the UK), outlines the government's spending and taxation plans for the year ahead. The direction taken in the budget should give a clear indication of the government's macroeconomic priorities.

Problem	Short-term policy: Monetary	Short-term policy: Fiscal	Difficulties
↓ Unemployment	↓ rate of interest ↑ MS	↓ indirect taxes ↑ government spending	Higher inflation in short term. Could increase national debt.
	→ Shift to right of AD		
↓ Rate of inflation	↑ rate of interest ↓ MS	↑ direct taxes ↓ government spending	Increased unemployment and lower output. Unpopular with voters.
	→ Shift to left of AD		
Current account deficit on Balance of Payments	↑ rate of interest (depreciate exchange rate)	↑ taxation	Effectiveness depends on price elasticity of demand for imports and exports.
	→ Shift to left of AD		

Key: , ↓ – decrease, ↑ – increase, → – leading to

Table 14.1 Monetary and fiscal policy options

In principle, there are three types of budget. These are:

- **budget deficit** – in this situation, projected government spending exceeds projected revenue from the many forms of taxation. This is where the government sees the need to reflate the economy by increasing aggregate demand. Normally this is in response to a situation where there is a need to expand the economy in order to create more jobs and income.
- **budget surplus** – in contrast, this describes a budget where government revenue from taxation exceeds the projected expenditure by the government on social protection, health care, education, transport and so on. Here the government has identified a need to deflate the economy by cutting back aggregate demand. This is normally in response to a situation where the rate of inflation in the economy is higher than the government feels to be appropriate. It could also be in response to a deteriorating deficit on the balance of trade.
- **balanced budget** – as its name suggests, this is a neutral situation where projected revenue and government spending are equal. Within the budget though there is likely to be some re-allocation of taxation and expenditure.

In this last situation, the re-allocation process could in itself create an expansion or contraction in aggregate demand, depending upon the size of the **balanced budget multiplier**. At first sight this may seem odd given that the overall budget remains balanced.

The reason for this is due to the differential effects of various fiscal policy measures. Suppose the government spends an additional \$1m. As a result, aggregate demand will rise by \$1m. On the other hand, if the government increases the total income tax bill by \$1m, households do not cut their expenditure by \$1m because some of what they pay in new taxes would otherwise have been saved. The net effect therefore is an increase in aggregate demand by the amount that would otherwise have been saved. So, if the mps is 0.1 and the mpc is 0.9, the net effect of these changes is a cut in consumption of \$0.9m, a rise in government spending of \$1m and an increase in aggregate demand of \$0.1m. In turn, this increase in net spending will create new employment and income through the normal multiplier process described earlier in module 1.

Within the budget, governments may use **discretionary fiscal policies** (sometimes called active fiscal policies) to alter aggregate demand through changes in government spending and taxation. These policies are discretionary in the sense that it is the government's decision as to whether the changes should be made. As will be explained below, when aggregate demand is low, the government boosts demand by cutting taxes or increasing its own expenditure. Specifically how this is done – that is exactly what combination of measures will be used – is invariably taken with one eye on the political ramifications.

In contrast, **automatic stabilisers** are incorporated into the budget. These are the revenue received from certain types of taxes and expenditure on certain forms of government spending and that change automatically with fluctuations in real GDP. For example, if real GDP increases, the government will automatically receive increased tax revenue from income tax and purchase taxes due to the rise in incomes. It is also likely to experience a fall in spending due to an increase in the number of people in employment. Alternatively, a fall in real GDP will result in less tax revenue for the government and the need for additional expenditure to support those who have been thrown out of work. In both cases, the effects of the multiplier processes have been reduced. Fiscal policy therefore acts as a type of shock absorber, helping to stabilise aggregate demand and output.

If the government is using a deficit budget to promote an expansion in real GDP, this is likely to mean that more borrowing has to take place. In turn, the **national debt** will increase unless the deficit can be funded from accumulated surpluses from previous years. For many economies this is highly unlikely. With the increase in real GDP and hence aggregate demand, an expansionary budget should lead to a rise in real incomes and, hence, tax revenue. This will in part offset some of the projected borrowing requirement.

Where economies have experienced strong economic growth, tax revenue has invariably grown and resulted in governments being able to repay debt. In the UK, for example, the so-called 'Golden Rule' or Code of Fiscal Stability has been applied since 1999. In simple terms, this works on the principle that over the medium term the government should only borrow to invest, not to

Barbados PM delivers long-awaited budget

After postponing his budget statement on two occasions, Prime Minister Owen Arthur has delivered news that will bring some relief to low and middle income earners. He has also proposed a major initiative to reduce energy costs in a plan that could save BD $65m to $90m.

The main features of the Economic and Financial Statement are:

- an increase in the National Insurance Scheme contributory pensions;
- personal allowance for low income earners to increase from BD$20,000 to £22,500;
- marginal tax rate to fall from 37.5 per cent to 35 per cent.

With respect to energy saving measures:

- import duty on energy-saving systems to be waived, 5 per cent tax on fluorescent light bulbs and fittings to be introduced;
- taxi owners and operators of vehicles used for tourism must purchase diesel-powered vehicles with an engine capacity of 1600 cc's or more in order to be exempt from import duty;
- a flat rate excise tax of 20 per cent to be levied on energy-efficient vehicles, including those using alternative energy sources;

- financial incentives for farmers growing fuel cane;

and significantly:

- an increase in the import tax on goods from outside the Caribbean region from 3 to 6 per cent. Food and special health care products to be taxed at former rate.

Source: Caribbean Net News, 19 January 2006 (adaptation).

fund current spending. So, debt accumulation in the long run will be accompanied by higher output and tax revenue without needing a change in tax rates. The challenge that is facing the government is to stick to this principle, particularly with respect to keeping public spending under control (see self-assessment task). If public borrowing increases beyond recognised limits, then the only option, if the rule is to remain, is for taxes to increase.

The issue of public debt for Caribbean economies will by analysed in detail in chapter 15.

Self-assessment tasks

Study the two pie charts below for the UK's Budget in 2006 and then tackle the questions that follow:

Where taxpayers' money is spent

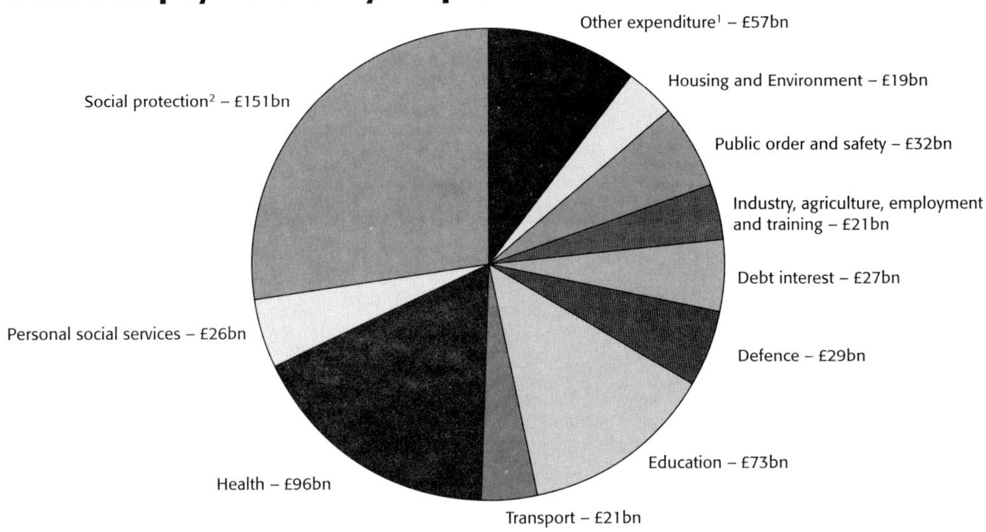

Total managed expenditure – £552 billion

[1] Other expenditure includes spending on general public services; recreation, culture, media and sport, international co-operation and development; public service pensions; plus spending yet to be allocated and some accounting adjustments.
[2] Social protection includes tax credit payments in excess of an individual's tax liability.
Source: HM Treasury, 2006–07 near cash projections.
Figures may not sum due to rounding.

Where taxes come from

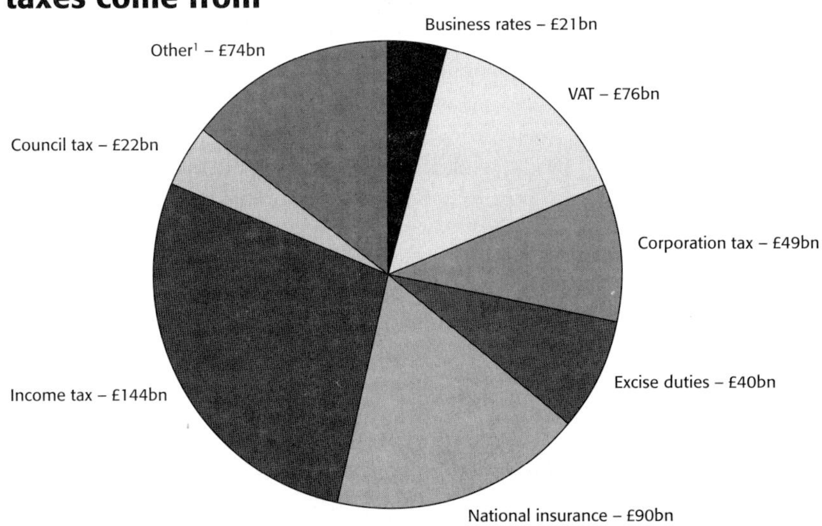

Total receipts – £516 billion

[1] Other includes capital taxes, stamp duties, vehicle excise duties, and some other tax and non-tax receipts (e.g. interest and dividends).
Source: HM Treasury, 2006–07 projections.
Figures may not sum to total due to rounding.

1 Was the UK's budget a deficit budget or surplus budget in 2006? Justify your answer.
2 Describe the composition of government spending and tax revenue in 2006.
3 How might the government use the budget to:
   - help families on low incomes,
   - enhance longer-term economic prospects.

Monetary policy, fiscal policy and unemployment

If an economy has high unemployment, or if there is a substantial risk of unemployment increasing, the obvious monetary policy response is to cut interest rates. The response to this action is that:

- firms may increase investment as the cost of borrowing has fallen,
- consumers may save less and spend more as the return from holding money in commercial banks has been reduced,
- consumers may also decide to borrow more money for financing large purchases such as a new house or car,
- the exchange rate may depreciate, leading to a rise in exports.

Reflationary fiscal policy can also be used to reduce unemployment. Various possibilities include:

- a reduction in indirect or direct taxation to increase people's purchasing power and disposable income,

Self-assessment tasks

Read the article below and then tackle the exercises that follow:

Interest rate cut to zero as Japanese tighten their belt

Japan returned to zero interest rates yesterday in a desperate move to stave off recession and a deflationary spiral.

The decision came as President George W Bush and the Japanese Prime Minister, Yoshiro Mori, met in Washington to compare notes on the economic downturn.

Recent dramatic stock market falls around the world have been triggered by worries about an American slowdown and fears over Japan's fragile financial sector.

Mr Mori said he believed that the interest rate cut would have a 'positive effect' on the Japanese economy and called for America to take measures to increase growth.

The Japanese return to zero interest rates comes only seven months after it abandoned the policy. The Bank of Japan was responding to intense political pressure to steady plunging share prices amid worrying signs that Japan's economy is failing to pull out of a 10-year slump.

There are fears that the interest rate cut can do little to help the world's second largest economy. The rate was already a phenomenally low 0.15 per cent, leaving the bank with little leverage compared with America and Britain, where rates are far higher.

Economists fear that the change will not deal with Japan's fundamental problems. Many Japanese have already deserted the banking system. Rather than spending the cash they withdraw, most are keeping money at home, generating a boom in the sale of home safes.

Sceptics about the benefits of lowering interest rates include Masaru Hayami, the governor of the bank. He argued that the economy would recover only if firms restructured and banks were forced to write off their huge bad loans.

For much of the past 10 years, the ruling Liberal Democratic Party's response to recession has been to throw money at vast public works projects of little economic value.

In an economy characterised by falling prices, many consumers have learnt to wait for goods to get cheaper. Others fear the future so much that they would rather hoard their cash for a rainy day than spend it now.

Japan's 10 years of stagnation is sometimes called a 'golden recession' because its adverse effects have not been immediately apparent. Tokyo's shopping districts are packed at the weekends with expensively dressed young people.

But such impressions obscure real change and genuine hardship. Unemployment and bankruptcies have led to homeless people becoming a feature of urban life in Japan. Some make a living from collecting discard adult *manga* comics and reselling them at a discount. The fact that Japanese now buy the second-hand magazines is itself remarkable. In an image-conscious society, people would once have been embarrassed to be seen buying a used comic.

Source: *Daily Telegraph*, 20 March 2001 (adapted).

1 Why are interest rates normally well above 0 per cent?

2 Using material in the article and your knowledge of Economics, explain the effects of 0 per cent interest rates on:
- consumers,
- businesses,
- the banking system.

3 What other policies could Japan try to get out of this so-called 'golden recession'?

- a cut in the profits tax on firms in order to stimulate new investment,
- an increase in government spending, in particular current spending.

Taken together these responses are designed to increase the level of aggregate demand. The extent of any of these changes will depend on the size of the multiplier and many other factors such as the extent of the changes, the response from consumers and firms and the general level of confidence in the economy. Figure 14.1 shows the effect of the increase in aggregate demand. As this shows, aggregate demand shifts from AD to AD_1 and real GDP increases from Y to Y_1. Provided the economy is operating on the horizontal part of its long-run AS curve, the price level will remain at P. The difficulty, as table 14.1 indicated, is that the increase in aggregate demand might fuel inflation. If this happens, the shift in AD_1 will cross the $LRAS$ curve at some point on its vertical section, indicating that the full employment level of real GDP has been reached at that time.

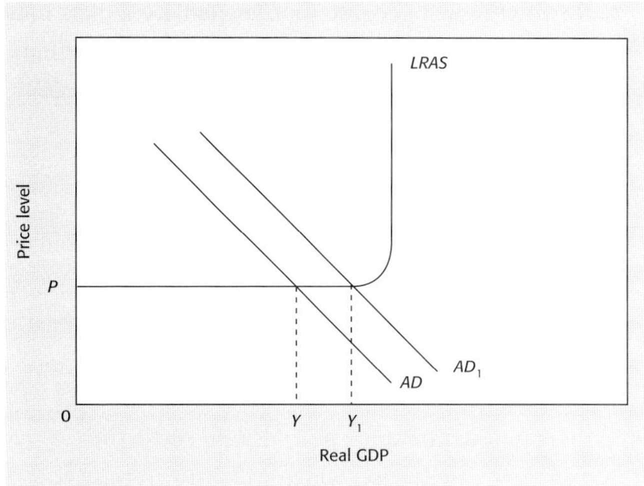

Figure 14.1 An increase in aggregate demand

Monetary policy, fiscal policy and inflation

In theory, monetary policy and fiscal policy can be used to control a problem of inflation through lowering aggregate demand. In practice, monetary policy is now more widely applied for this purpose, in particular through a rise in the rate of interest (see box, p.202). This should reduce inflationary pressures as:

St. Georges, Grenada. Borrowing from the IMF and interregional borrowing (e.g. from Trinidad) is high for Grenada
Source: Still Pictures.

- Borrowing will become more expensive. Firms may cut back on their investment plans and individuals may defer large-scale purchases as their real cost has increased.
- Savings will be increased. At the same time, those with bank loans will have to pay more for the money they have borrowed, reducing disposable income.
- Firms will begin to shed labour, putting pressure on wage demands to be reduced.
- 'Hot money' will flow into the economy. The increased demand for pounds will cause the exchange rate to rise, which in turn will raise the price of exports. This loss of price competitiveness is likely to lead to a reduction in earnings from visible exports.

Deflationary fiscal policies may also be used to reduce aggregate demand. Such policies involve:

- raising direct taxation in order to cut back on the disposable income of consumers or increasing indirect taxes on products such as alcohol, tobacco, petrol and purchase taxes so as to reduce spending power,
- cutting back on various forms of government spending – this is a direct means of reducing aggregate demand.

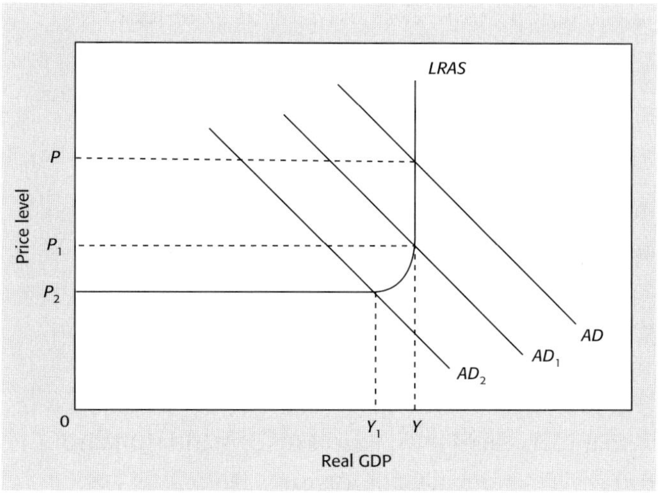

Figure 14.2 A reduction in aggregate demand

Figure 14.2 shows how reducing aggregate demand can achieve the objective of reducing inflation. As aggregate demand falls from *AD* to AD_1, as a consequence of one or more of the means described above, the price level falls

Economy drives further rate rises

The Bank of England is charged by the government with keeping inflation under control, with a target rate of 2%. So it is not surprising that with inflation now hovering around 2.5%, the Bank decided to act.

At its monthly meeting today, the Monetary Policy Committee increased the Bank of England's base rate to 5%, the highest level for five years.

Interest rates have been rising in many countries around the world as banks try to curb inflationary expectations as economic growth accelerates.

In the UK, economic growth has been running ahead of the Chancellor's forecast for some months, although it recently slowed to a year-on-year rate of 2.6%.

Additionally, house prices are continuing to rise strongly in most parts of the country, with prices increasing at an annual rate of more than 8%.

The Bank has been concerned that higher house prices encourage people to borrow and spend more, thus boosting inflation.

In addition, the Bank is worried that higher wages will boost inflation.

Wages are rising in the UK by around 4.2% annually, just below the Bank's informal target rate of 4.5%.

So far two things have helped keep wages and prices in check.

Higher immigration from Eastern Europe may have lowered inflationary pressures on wages despite relatively high employment rates.

And cheap prices on imported goods, particularly from China, have kept the lid on High Street prices despite the strong demand.

Both of these factors may have less significance in the future, if the rate of immigration slows, as the government wants, and if China is forced to revalue its currency and raise the price of its exports.

The Bank believes that, in an uncertain world, it is better to err on the side of caution and raise rates – rather than embed inflation in the system, where it is very hard to get rid of later.

Some economists believe that the current round of rate rises will significantly slow the UK economy next year.

However, decisions on future government spending – and borrowing – will also affect the Bank's thinking.

So far, the government is running a large, and larger-than-planned, budget deficit of nearly 3.4% of gross domestic product, and the extra state spending has helped stimulate growth but also added to inflationary pressures.

Source: BBC News, 9 November 2006 (adaptation).

from P to P_1. The level of real GDP remains unchanged at Y. The reality of reducing aggregate demand is that the final effect of any measure is uncertain. So, it could be that aggregate demand is reduced too much, resulting in real GDP falling below Y. This is shown when aggregate demand falls from AD to AD_2, the cost being more unemployment. The skill in managing the economy in this situation is to control aggregate demand so that it is at the full employment level.

Monetary policy, fiscal policy and the balance of payments

Fiscal policy measures can be effective where an economy is experiencing a deficit on the current account of its balance of payments. (The most likely reason for the deficit is that imports of visible goods exceed the exports of such goods.) Two main ways are possible. These are:

- Expenditure-dampening measures that aim to reduce total expenditure by consumers and firms on imported goods. A rise in income tax, for example, will reduce disposable income, leaving less income for consumers to spend on imported as well as home-produced goods. A cut in government spending, particularly where this involves imported goods, could also be used.
- Measures that result in domestic consumers substituting home-produced goods for imported goods. An obvious way to achieve this is by imposing a tariff or increasing the tariff that is levied on imported goods. (In CARICOM the tariff could only be imposed on imported goods from non-members.) Such a measure works more effectively where home-produced substitutes are readily available. A second measure could be to provide subsidies for home producers – this would reduce the price of domestically produced goods relative to similar imported products.

Monetary policy is unlikely to be used in this context. It may even worsen a current account deficit since a rise in interest rates could lead to an increase in the value of a currency, making imported goods even cheaper.

Overall the potential for using fiscal policy to correct a balance of payments problem is short term. For most economies, supply side weaknesses underpin adverse balance of payments situations.

The problem of time lags

It might appear from the analysis so far that in applying monetary and fiscal policies, governments can be certain that their actions will produce a more or less immediate solution to the problem. This is by no means the case. In particular, **time lags** occur in so far as there is a delay between the government announcing a particular policy measure and this policy having the desired effect on the economy.

Some policies can be applied more speedily than others. For example, increases and decreases in indirect taxes can be made very quickly, sometimes overnight. This is not so for direct taxes, as any changes to tax rates or thresholds will take time to be implemented. Changes to government spending will also take time to have an effect. This is particularly so in the case of capital projects such as road building and investing in new schools. In the case of monetary policies, although such changes may eventually be effective, there can be a considerable time lag between a change in the rate of interest and the final change in aggregate demand.

Underpinning the problem of time lags are the multiplier effects of any fiscal and monetary policies. These take place over time and it is by no means easy to determine just how long it will take for the multiplier process stemming from a policy change to work its way through the economy. So, all in all, forecasting the final effects of fiscal and monetary policy changes on the economy is by no means straightforward.

The potency of monetary policy and fiscal policy

There is little argument that monetary and fiscal policies are powerful tools that are available for the effective management of the economy. If proof were needed, it comes in the extent to which they have been used and remain in use in all types of economy, developed or developing, where there is some form of market function in operation. Over time, they have had different levels of importance and influence.

In the UK, for example, over the past decade governments have taken the view that monetary policy is the best means of controlling aggregate demand, avoiding the 'boom–bust' cycle experienced when fiscal policy was the dominant means of economic management. (See box on the Monetary Policy

Committee, p. 202). In Caribbean economies, fiscal policies arguably have a greater role to play in managing the economy, mainly because of the nature of these economies due to their stage of economic development (see box on Barbados budget, p. 198).

For any country though, the short-term management of the economy invariably involves the use of both fiscal and monetary policies in order to regulate aggregate demand. The role of government is therefore one of deciding on the policies that best allow it to meet its stated objectives, and to take such decisions within the much broader context of its underlying political ideology. Managing the economy therefore cannot be entirely set apart from political reality.

It is necessary, however, to appreciate that as policy tools, the effectiveness of fiscal policy and monetary policy is limited. Some limitations are summarised in Table 14.2.

A more general problem facing any government is that of a lack of up-to-date, accurate information on the present state of the economy and forecasts of future prospects. This is particularly acute in most developing economies, where the quality of statistical information available to the government is not what it is in most developed economies. Although the quality has much improved in recent years through the efforts of the World Bank and in the Caribbean area, CARICOM, it remains an obstacle to more-effective economic management. A further obstacle that affects all economies is that of uncertainty brought about by external shocks to the global economy. Events such as the Asian financial crisis of the mid 1990s, the aftermath of 9/11 and conflicts in the Middle East have had profound effects on some economies. 9/11, for example, has posed many more unforeseen problems for the smaller economies of the Caribbean than for the larger developed economies of the European Union.

Monetary policy	Fiscal policy
◆ A rise in interest rates is likely to cause new unemployment. ◆ A rise in interest rates will benefit savers at the expense of borrowers. The converse applies when interest rates fall. ◆ Changes in interest rates will only be effective if businesses and consumers match the government's confidence in future economic prospects. ◆ 'Hot money' flows are likely to be influenced by interest rates.	◆ It can take a long time to implement major changes to the tax structure in an economy. ◆ There are long time lags in making changes to most types of government spending. ◆ Increases in some forms of direct taxation can have a disincentive effect on working and on the investment plans of firms. ◆ Some fiscal measures have side effects, for example an increase in purchase taxes to reduce inflation will increase the cost of living.

Table 14.2 Limitations of monetary policy and fiscal policy

Self-assessment tasks

On completion of this chapter you should be able to answer the question below that is taken from the CAPE 2006 examinations.

1 Fiscal policy is one of two policy channels through which the government can affect the macroeconomy. Discretionary fiscal policy and automatic stabilizers are two important fiscal policy measures.
   (a) Differentiate between 'discretionary fiscal policy' and 'automatic stabilizers'.
   (b) Using examples, explain how discretionary fiscal policy and automatic stabilizers work during periods of recession or inflation in an economy. (12 marks)

2 Suppose that as Chief Economic Adviser, the Minister of Finance calls you into his office and says the following:

'Unemployment is too high. We need to lower it by increasing both output and income. Right now the equilibrium level of income/output is $900 billion, but perhaps an acceptable unemployment rate could be achieved if aggregate output increases to say, $1,100 billion. Note, however, that the marginal propensity to consume is 0.75, and taxes must remain at the present levels. So, adjusting taxes (*T*) is out of the question.'

(a) Under the circumstances outlined above, explain how the government can use fiscal policy – taxing and spending – to increase the equilibrium level of output from $900 billion to $1,100 billion.

(b) Using a 45° line diagram, graph the original situation and the solution you gave in (a) above. (18 marks)

3 Suppose that instead of keeping taxes (*T*) constant, the Minister of Finance decided to finance the increase in government spending with an equal increase in taxes so as to maintain a balanced budget. Explain what happens to aggregate spending as a result of a rise in both taxes and government spending. (10 marks)

4 How much a balanced-budget increase in government spending (*G*) and taxes (*T*) will raise output depends on the balanced budget multiplier.

(a) What is the balanced budget multiplier?

(b) Referring to the solution given in 3 above, how large is the balanced budget multiplier? Explain you answer. (10 marks)

(Total 50 marks)

Summary

In this chapter it has been shown that:

- Monetary policy refers to any measures that bring about changes in the rate of interest and the supply of money.
- Fiscal policy is the term used to describe how governments use taxation and government spending to manage the economy.
- Monetary policy and fiscal policy are widely used by governments to manage economic performance, namely to control inflation, the level of unemployment and the current balance of the balance of payments.
- When used, changes in monetary policy and fiscal policy affect the level of aggregate demand and hence real GDP.
- The budget is an annual statement prepared by a government in which its expenditure and taxation intentions are published. Various types of budget can be produced, depending on macroeconomic priorities.
- Time lags have to be taken into account when governments make changes to monetary policies and fiscal policies.
- The limitations of monetary policies and fiscal policies should be evaluated by governments prior to making any policy changes.

Key words

Definitions of Key words can be found in the Glossary.

automatic stabilizers
balanced budget
balanced budget multiplier
budget
budget deficit
budget surplus
discretionary fiscal policies
fiscal policy
monetary policy
national debt
time lags

15 Public debt

This chapter covers unit 2, module 2, topic 4.
On completion of this chapter, you should be able to:

- define the national debt
- analyse the effects of the national debt on the economy
- explain the burden on the national debt
- evaluate ways of reducing the debt burden
- calculate and interpret the debt service ratio

Measures of indebtedness

In simple terms the national debt is the debt of a country's government. This may be owed to residents or to foreign lenders. When owed to residents, the debt tends to be repayable in local currency; with foreign-owned debt this is not the case, resulting in the interest and redemption payments making claims on the foreign exchange and financial resources of the country.

Fundamentally, the national debt and **public debt** are the same. Within Caribbean economies though virtually all of the national debt is owed to foreigner creditors by the respective governments. This type of debt is sometimes referred to as **external public debt** by organisations such as the Caribbean Development Bank.

Another important measure is the **debt service ratio**. This is defined as loans due for repayment (amortisation) plus interest payments as a proportion of the total exports of goods and services in an economy. Trends in this ratio are a good measure of external financial solvency. If the ratio is rising, then an increasing proportion of foreign earnings has to be set aside to meet the debt service burden. This is not good news for an economy since it will lead to balance of payments difficulties. Although all economists may not agree, a ratio of 15–20 per cent is considered the limit beyond which debtor countries will experience severe difficulties in meeting their obligation to service their debts. A debt service ratio above this limit would also mean that unpopular domestic measures have to be taken to ensure that repayments are made.

Public debt in Caribbean economies

No present-day study of the recent macroeconomic performance of Caribbean economies can ignore the problem of public debt accumulation. This has been an on-going problem since the mid-1990s and has intensified in the early years of the twenty-first century (see box). The position is that most economies are heavily in debt and the burden of this debt has been a substantial influence on their domestic budgetary policies.

The gap between annual government revenue and expenditure, sometimes called the **fiscal balance**, has widened. As a result, public debt, and hence interest costs, has risen. In 2005/06, debt servicing costs were around 17 per cent of government expenditure in Trinidad and Tobago and 24 per cent for Jamaica. Moreover in the case of Jamaica, accumulated debt is substantially more than their annual GDP.

Figure 15.1 shows that the Caribbean countries are among the most indebted market economies in the world. Seven are among the top ten, 14 are among the top 30 in terms of debt to GDP ratio. Guyana has the unenviable distinction of being the most indebted country in these terms, with public sector debt of around two years' GDP at the end of 2002.

Table 15.1 lists the countries according to their primary fiscal balance and public debt to GDP ratio in 2003. According to the IMF, when the latter measure is over 50–60 per cent then this is considered to be serious. In these terms, only three countries – the Bahamas, Suriname and the Dominican Republic – had low debt in 2003. Seven countries had debt beyond 90 per cent, with four countries between these extremes.

A shadow on the beach – the party is over for the Caribbean's spendthrift governments

Since Said Musa became Prime Minister of Belize in 1998, public debt has increased from 41% of GDP to 93%, much of it borrowed at commercial interest rates. The economy has grown, but much of the cash was poorly spent. Critics point to half-empty state housing projects and chaotic lending by the government. Belize's government though are by no means the only Caribbean spendthrifts.

The borrowing binge is a recent affair. On average, the public debt of Caribbean countries has risen by two-thirds since 1998. Unlike Latin American governments whom are recidivist bad debtors, Caribbean countries, with stable currencies and democracies, until recently looked good risks. So borrowing has been all too easy. Caribbean banks, not least in energy-rich Trinidad, are awash with cash and have been eager to lend – provided there's a government guarantee.

Across CARICOM, fiscal deficits have ballooned since the late 1990s. This was partly a result of more frequent hurricane damage, and other disasters (including the slowdown in tourism after 11th September 2001). More recently, high oil prices forced some governments to cut fuel taxes. But policy has also been lax. Caribbeans expect governments to be big spenders. In Antigua, the Bird family held power for most of the past half century until an election in March; they abolished income tax but brought almost half the workforce on to the government payroll. Antigua's debt soared to 114% of GDP.

For the debtor governments, the long beach party may finally be over. Rising interest rates will make new borrowing more expensive. In Jamaica, interest payments already eat up over half of government revenue. Even well-managed Barbados was downgraded this month by Standard & Poor's, a credit-rating agency, because of its rising debt.

Ratna Sahay, of the IMF's Western Hemisphere Department, concluded in a recent paper that a continuation of current policies would endanger the Caribbean's macroeconomic stability. Merely to stabilise public debt at its current levels will require aggressive fiscal tightening in several countries. Antigua has begun a painful clean-up – the government is mulling over new taxes.

Source: *The Economist*, 26 August 2004 (adaptation).

The beaches of Ambergris Caye, Belize, often have less-than-immaculate sand
Source: AP Photo/Vicki Smith.

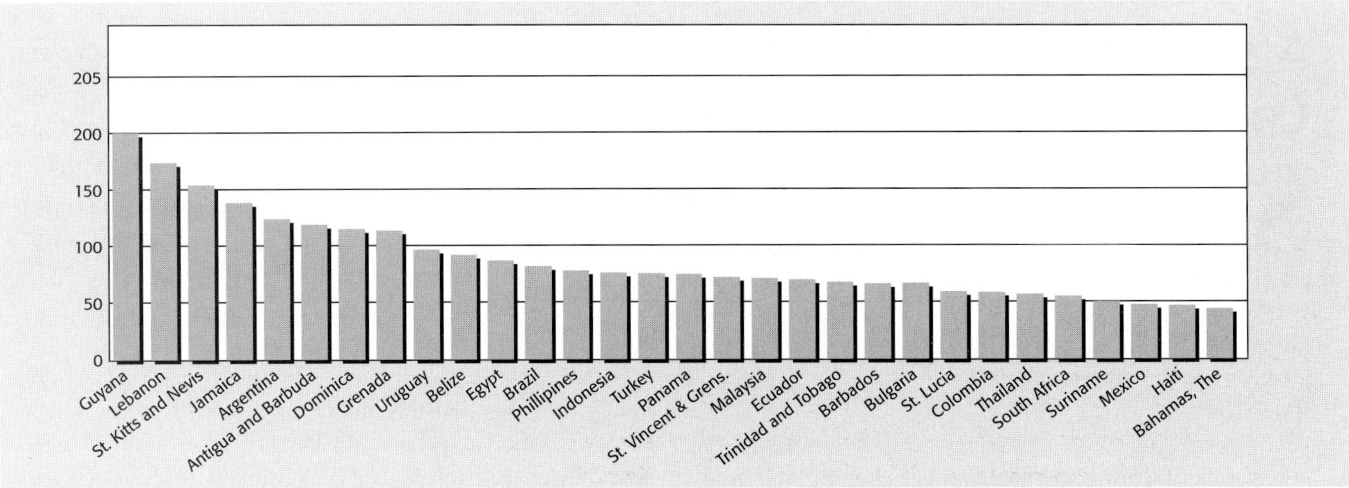

Figure 15.1 The Caribbean: ranking among top 30 most indebted emerging market countries (public sector debt-to-GDP ratio, end 2002)
Source: IMF, World Economic Outlook; country authorities; and IMF staff estimates.

	Public debt		
Primary fiscal balance	**Low to medium (0 – 50%)**	**High (50 – 90%)**	**Very High (>90%)**
Higher than 5%			Jamaica
0 – 5%	The Bahamas	Trinidad and Tobago	Dominica, Grenada
Less than 0%	Suriname	Barbados	Antigua and Barbuda
		Dominican Republic	Belize
		St Lucia	Guyana
		St Vincent and the Grenadines	St Kitts and Nevis

Note: [1] the fiscal balance but excluding interest payments.

Table 15.1 Public debt and primary fiscal balances[1] in 2003 (%GDP)
Source: IMF Working Paper WP/05/26.

Table 15.1 also indicates that nine of the 15 countries had primary fiscal balances of less than 0 per cent. In other words they were operating with budget deficits which would result in debt levels rising. This is the opposite of what is needed to bring down debt levels. For countries with a serious debt level, primary budget surpluses are required in order to prevent a further increase in the debt stock. It is though not quite as simple as this in so far as the surpluses needed will increase with interest rates and the size of the accumulated debt. The surplus can be reduced through real exchange rate appreciation and real GDP growth. Looking back at table 15.1, it might appear that Jamaica is successfully applying domestic macroeconomic policies to reduce debt. Unfortunately this is not so as public debt has continued to rise because of high interest costs and low economic growth.

The scale of the change in indebtedness is shown in table 15.2. Since 1999, the experience of CARICOM countries has been variable. Trinidad and Tobago, with its extensive oil and gas reserves, has reduced its debt; so too has Guyana. Of the remaining countries, St Kitts and Nevis and Jamaica have recorded poor macroeconomic performances over the period shown and this is further evidenced in the large increase in their external debts.

Republic day, Guyana. Guyana has reduced its debt
Source: Still Pictures.

Figure 15.2 shows the debt ratios and debt service ratios for Jamaica over the same time period as table 15.2. The ratios for Jamaica have been volatile. The tourism sector was badly affected following 9/11. Earnings in 2003 were substantially less than in 2002 and this is shown by a steep rise in the debt to exports ratio and the debt service ratio. The latter improved in 2004 but remained at a very high level.

Country	1999	2004	% change
Antigua and Barbuda	401.5	519.9	+ 29.5
Bahamas	404.1	563.0	+ 39.3
Barbados	388.5	666.3	+ 71.5
Belize	257.5	955.6	+ 271.1
Dominica	114.4	186.7	+ 63.2
Grenada	109.8	330.4	+ 200.9
Guyana	1,210.9	1,078.7	– 10.9
Jamaica	3,024.1	5,120.4	+ 69.3
St Kitts and Nevis	149.3	304.4	+ 103.9
St Lucia	161.2	308.6	+ 91.4
St Vincent and the Grenadines	160.5	170.1	+ 6.0
Suriname	n.a	n.a	
Trinidad and Tobago	1,584.8	1,350.6	– 14.8

Table 15.2 External debt outstanding, 1999–2004 (US$M)
Source: Caribbean Development Bank, 2005.

Causes of the increasing public debt problem

A recent study by the IMF has identified two main causes of the increasing level of public debt described above. These are:

- a deterioration in the primary fiscal balance (see table 15.1),
- exogenous shocks that have had a negatively profound effect on most Caribbean economies.

The significance of these lies to some extent in that Caribbean governments can in principle manage their economies in a seemingly responsible way to avoid a deterioration in the primary fiscal balance; there is though very little or nothing that they can do to prepare for unanticipated shocks, some of which affect all economies.

The IMF's research has shown that St Kitts and Nevis had the highest public debt to GDP rates of 160 per cent at the end of 2003. In Grenada, the ratio rose most rapidly in the IMF's study period of 1997–2003. These countries, along with Antigua and Barbuda, Belize and Dominica, consistently operated with primary fiscal deficits, with the result that public debt accumulation persisted. In the case of Jamaica, although it operated with primary fiscal surpluses, a sharp increase in its interest payments on outstanding loans was the most important factor for the rapid public debt accumulation. An obvious conclusion to be drawn is that, except for Jamaica, the other Caribbean countries referred to could have used more expedient internal budgetary policies to reduce public debt accumulation.

In the late 1990s and early years of this century, the global economy has been affected by a whole series of unexpected events. Although difficult to quantify, these have had a bearing on the problems faced by Caribbean economies.

The IMF have recognised the

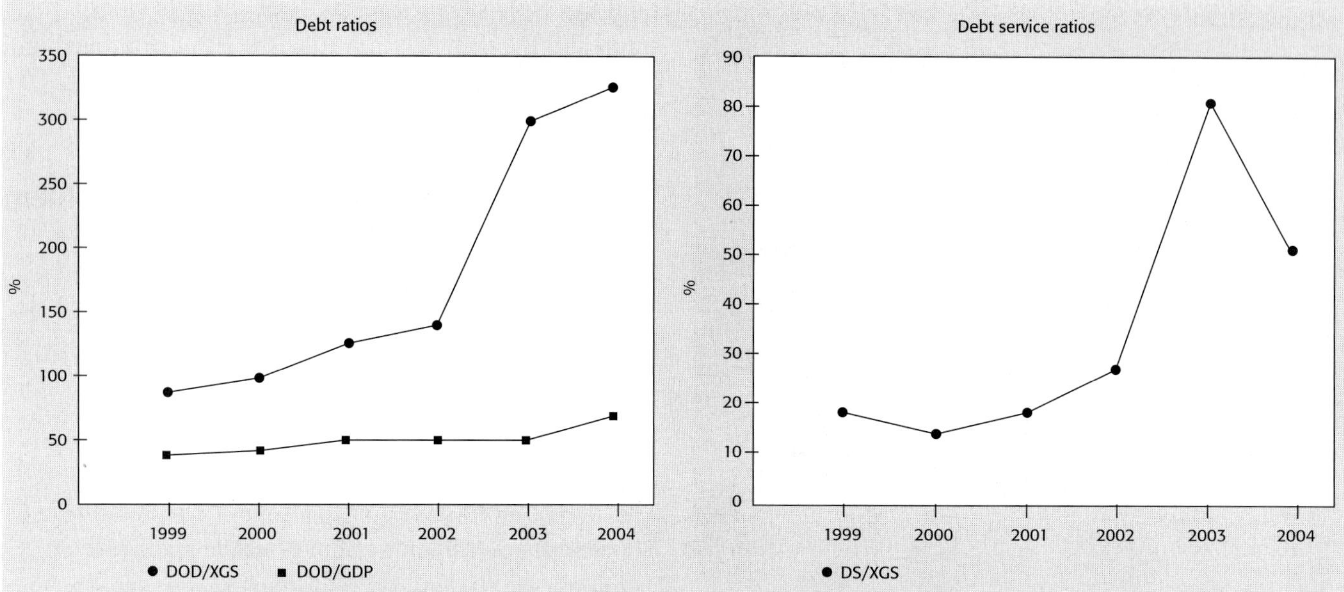

Notes: DOD – disbursed outstanding debt.
XGS – exports of goods and services.
DS – debt service payments.

Figure 15.2 Debt ratios and debt service ratios for Jamaica, 1999–2004
Source: Caribbean Development Bank, 2005.

following:

- a rise in global interest rates, raising the annual payments that indebted economies have to make;
- large increases in world oil prices, which slowed down economic growth and forced some Caribbean governments to step in with increased subsidies, so reducing government revenue;
- a slow down in global economic growth, which has had an adverse effect on tourism in the Caribbean area. The US market, the most important tourism generator, has been hit at various times by the slow down in the economy, in particular following 9/11;
- a deterioration in the terms of trade (see next module) for staple Caribbean products such as bananas, sugar and cotton. The effects have been to decrease economic growth and government revenue;
- natural disasters in the form of hurricanes and floods.

In their conclusions, the IMF believe that Caribbean governments could have done more to plan for some of these shocks, in particular those that could have been anticipated, for example the deterioration in the terms of trade and natural disasters. In contrast, unanticipated shocks such as 9/11 defy any form of advance economic planning.

Effects of public debt on the economy

Assessing the effects of public debt on the economy is not an easy task. Although some general effects can be identified, the overall impact of debt accumulation depends upon various factors including the debt service ratio, the speed of public debt accumulation, the total value of the debt and the general macroeconomic stability of the country in question.

Some general effects though can be recognised. These include:

- The opportunity cost of funding debt repayments. Payments made to overseas governments and financial institutions are taking away valuable resources that could otherwise be used to very positive effect. The opportunity cost stems from the fact that less domestic funding is available for new hospitals, schools, roads and so on.
- Domestic taxation on income and profits and purchase taxes especially, will need to be at a higher level in order to help governments make amortisation and interest repayments. This burden invariably falls on those who can least afford it in most Caribbean economies. One notable exception is in Trinidad and Tobago, where around half of the government's annual tax receipts are generated from the income and profits of multinational oil companies.

Natural Gas Plant, Trinidad. When the international companies were rooting around for oil off the coasts of Trinidad and Tobago, they cursed whenever they struck natural gas. Now oil prices have fallen and the country's oil reserves are expected to run out while proven natural gas could last another 60 years

- Imported goods will in the main be heavily taxed not only to reduce their consumption but also to retain valuable foreign currency for debt repayments.
- Politically, governments will be under pressure to not run budget surpluses, although, economically, a serious debt position should require it. A budget surplus would usually result in a situation where the burden of total debt could be reduced.
- There is a clear need to ensure that borrowed funds are used in a positive way to assist future economic development. This is by no means always the case (see box article on Belize on p. 207 for example). The tragedy is that no economic return has been generated yet and debt repayments have to be made over many years. A sensible way for governments to use borrowed funds is on capital projects that produce a long-term gain rather than to fund short-term revenue deficits.
- Some short-term deficits have been funded domestically by public commercial banks and government social security schemes. This is a dangerous strategy.
- The rate of economic growth is likely to suffer in economies with serious debt problems. Hence future living standards are being compromised.
- Unless governments manage their finances in a responsible way, the public debt problem could become so serious that it generates a financial crisis. One has only to look at Argentina and Brazil during the 1990s to see what effect macroeconomic mismanagement can have. That is why organisations such as the IMF, World Bank and the UK's Department for International Development have sought to provide their assistance to Caribbean economies in order to avoid financial meltdown.

Reducing the debt burden

It should be clear from what has been described so far in this topic that reducing public debt should be a key macroeconomic objective for all Caribbean economies. Although the scale of the debt burden varies, a common feature has been a deteriorating fiscal position.

According to the IMF, there are five key elements to successfully reducing public debt to more sustainable

Economist concerned about regional debt

KINGSTOWN, St Vincent: A regional economist has expressed concerns about the size of public debts across the region and said that at the end of 2005 only Trinidad and Tobago and Jamaica had a higher credit rating than in 1999.

'And that speaks volumes to the problems of economic performance and high levels of economic risk taken by a number of these countries', said Jwala Rambarran, Chief Economist at Caribbean Money Market Brokers (CMMB).

Rambarran, a Trinidadian national, during a review of the St Vincent and the Grenadines budget in Kingstown, said the Caribbean was 'slipping' when ranked with what was taking place economically worldwide.

'We are becoming higher risk economies and this shows up tremendously when we look at the Caribbean public debt profile. At the moment we have seven Caribbean countries that rank among the highest indebted emerging markets in the world', he said.

'The Caribbean becomes, and is now perceived as, very risky by the international investor community. And that is of concern to investors. If you want these guys to invest here ... it helps to meet some of your financial needs', Rambarran added.

He said the Cricket World Cup, which will be held in the Caribbean next year, would be a 'defining moment' since many countries were doing much spending in anticipation of 'legacy returns' of visitors.

Rambarran further said only three countries across the region have met the European Union criterion of keeping public debt at 50 per cent of Gross Domestic Product (GDP). He said if the region is to 'get protection from the international community this is where you are going to have to hang your hat'.

'Across the Eastern Caribbean, countries have already realised that they face tremendous fiscal and debt challenges and they have started very largely with considerable delay to try and address the situation.'

The CMMB chief economist noted that Dominica has been under an International Monetary Fund (IMF) programme for the past four years, while Grenada was 'riding out pretty good recovery' after the devastating Hurricane Ivan of September 2004.

Source: Caribbean Net News, 14 February 2006 .

levels and so help Caribbean economies achieve their growth potential. These are:

- **Fiscal consolidation**. This involves reducing the current level of fiscal deficits and hence interest payments. In the short term, this will require expenditure to be cut back and brought more in line with revenue. The longer-term benefit of this is that the credibility of economic reform packages will be enhanced, raising internal and external business confidence. When this happens more foreign investors should be attracted and the rate of economic growth will increase. The IMF believe that present economic policies are not allowing most Caribbean economies to fully exploit their growth potential.
- **Debt management.** The aim here is to manage public debt in a more effective way through debt restructuring. A typical instance would be for countries to negotiate a longer maturity period for debt, so reducing the overall annual servicing costs. This usually involves replacing high interest short-term debt with lower interest long-term debt. St Lucia and St Kitts and Nevis, for example have applied this approach. Guyana, which has more serious problems, managed to obtain debt forgiveness in 2004 under the IMF – World Bank initiative for heavily indebted poor countries (HIPC)
- Privatisation and asset sales. This is an obvious way of raising funds, provided there are appropriate assets that can be sold off by the public sector. Unlike when this occurred in the UK, there is only modest potential for such sales in most Caribbean economies.
- Reduction in vulnerability to adverse exogenous shocks. Natural disasters such as hurricanes, floods and crop diseases have had a profound effect on all Caribbean economies. In addition, the region is very susceptible to the external global environment, particularly when the US economy is adversely affected. Disaster mitigation and better economic contingency planning could reduce the impact of such unforeseen events.
- Structural reforms. Here, various supply-side policies could be implemented, including labour market reforms, reducing employment in the public sector, improved regional economic

co-operation and reforms in the financial sector. There is also a case for assessing whether the fixed exchange rate regime that is in place is working in the best interests of Caribbean economies.

Compared with many parts of the world, the Caribbean region has the potential natural and human resources to grow faster. The standard of living, with minor exceptions, compares well with other developing economies. The challenge the governments face is to overcome the economic weaknesses that are the result of public debt accumulation. With firm, decisive policy actions on several fronts, the Caribbean region can achieve its true economic potential.

Self-assessment tasks

On completion of this chapter you should be able to answer the following questions.

1 (a) Define the term 'public debt'. (5 marks)

(b) With the use of examples, outline two ways in which public debt can be measured. (10 marks)

2 Explain how government borrowing to finance a large budget deficit will affect domestic interest rates and domestic investment. (15 marks)

3 With reference to Caribbean examples, discuss some of the problems that governments face when seeking to reduce their indebtedness. (20 marks)

(Total 50 marks)

Summary

In this chapter it has been shown that:

- The national debt and public debt are fundamentally the same.
- All Caribbean economies have a serious problem of public debt accumulation; in most, public debt has increased significantly in the early years of the twenty-first century.
- The debt service ratio is a useful way of looking at the annual debt repayment obligations of an economy.
- There are many causes of the increase in public debt; some are internal, whereas others are the result of exogenous stocks.
- Public debt places a strain on the government's finances and results in country's not achieving their potential rate of economic growth.
- The debt burden can be reduced in various ways, but only with firm decisive polices and positive macroeconomic management.

Key words

Definitions of Key words can be found in the Glossary.

debt forgiveness
debt management
debt ratio
debt service ratio
external public debt
fiscal balance
fiscal consolidation
primary fiscal balance
public debt

Module 3

Growth and development and international economic relations

On completion of this module you should be able to:

- understand the basic concepts of growth and development
- understand the characteristics of developing economies in general and Caribbean economies in particular
- understand the impact of imports and exports on the macroeconomy
- appreciate the arguments for and against protection
- appreciate the costs and benefits of economic integration and be aware of the different types of economic integration
- appreciate the benefits and costs derived from current integration arrangements such as CARICOM, FTAA and the EU
- understand the balance of payments accounts and determine the causes and consequences of balance of payments crises
- understand the factors that determine exchange rates and assess the impact of changes in the exchange rate on the economy
- understand the role and functions of international economic institutions
- understand the advantages and disadvantages of foreign direct investment
- develop awareness of the factors underlying the process of globalisation and assess the implications of globalisation for developing countries

16 Growth and development

This chapter covers unit 2, module 3, topic 1.
On completion of this chapter, you should be able to:

- distinguish between growth and development
- outline the basic issues related to growth
- outline the basic issues related to development
- explain the concept of human development
- describe the structural characteristics of Caribbean economies and the implications of these characteristics for economic development in the region

Economic growth and development

Economic growth

As explained earlier, economic growth occurs when an economy achieves an increase in its national income, measured by Gross National Product (GNP), in excess of its rate of population growth. This will lead to an increase in GNP per capita. For many years it was assumed that the existence of poverty in many of the world's poorer economies could be eradicated if these countries managed to sustain economic growth over a period of time. As a result, economic growth was seen as synonymous with economic development. If economies grew they would also experience development. It was assumed that increased availability of goods and services in an economy would lead to a 'trickle down' effect which would have an impact upon all, including the poorer members of society, in terms of jobs and other economic benefits. In reality however, despite the fact that in recent years many developing countries have achieved quite high growth rates, it has been observed that, although economic growth has resulted in benefits for poorer members of society in some countries, in others the levels of living of the mass of the population remained unchanged. In some cases this level may even have deteriorated. As a result a wider perception of economic development is now accepted which is related to, but distinct from, economic growth.

Wyclef-Jean hugs a Haitian fan at his concert in Jacmel, Haiti. The concert sponsored by Jean's Yele Haiti charity promotes music and the arts as a development tool for the impoverished Caribbean nation
Source: AP Photo/Ariana Cubillos.

Economic development

In it's 'World Development Report' of 1991 the World Bank offered the following view of development,

Economic growth in Jamaica

In December 2005, the Planning Institute of Jamaica estimated the growth of the Jamaican economy in the July–September quarter to have been a massive 2.7 per cent. This contrasted with negative growth and almost zero growth in the previous four quarters. The Institute's estimates for future growth in 2006 ranged from 1 to 2.9 per cent per quarter.

Growth in the Jamaican economy like all in the Caribbean area, is heavily dependent on what is happening in the economies of its main trading partners. This is particularly true for exports of bauxite and alumina and for tourism. More worrying though was the general downturn in agricultural prices and the appreciation of the local currency which further damaged the export performance of this sector. The Institute also believed that growth was stymied by two active hurricanes and the effects of rising oil prices on production costs.

The main sources of growth were in the 'goods producing sectors', including agriculture, manufacturing and construction. Mining and quarrying and construction contributed most to overall growth. The agricultural sector rallied after four consecutive quarters of negative growth but future prospects remain highly uncertain. In contrast, the growth performance of the service sector was flat, with a downturn in the hotels, restaurants and clubs sector where future prospects, like those for agriculture, are a cause for concern.

Source: Economic update and outlook, Planning Institute of Jamaica, Vol 10 No. 2, 2005.

Bauxite Mines, Jamaica
Source: Still Pictures.

The challenge of development... is to improve the quality of life. Especially in the world's poor countries, a better quality of life generally calls for higher incomes – but it involves much more. It encompasses as ends in themselves better education, higher standards of health and nutrition, less poverty, a cleaner environment, more equality of opportunity, greater individual freedom, and a richer cultural life.

Although this statement acknowledges that economic growth is important it makes it clear that higher income in itself is not sufficient to ensure that there is a rise in the quality of life for the citizens of a country. This is a much broader view of development than one confined purely to increases in GNP. It is one that provides a different focus for those responsible for development policy planning, and moves away from measures designed purely to increase and maintain an economic growth target. Todaro states that development must be seen as a multi-dimensional process.

> Development...must represent the whole gamut of change by which an entire social system, tuned to the diverse basic needs and desires of individuals and social groups within that system, moves away from a condition of life widely perceived as unsatisfactory toward a situation or condition of life regarded as materially and spiritually better.
>
> (M. P. Todaro, *Economic Development*, 1995)

According to Todaro and others, the movement to a better life can be analysed and measured against three core values:

SUSTENANCE: The ability to meet basic needs

SELF-ESTEEM: To be a person

FREEDOM FROM SERVITUDE: To be able to choose

Indicators of comparative development

Classification according to levels of income The simplest way in which economies can be classified is according to the value of their Gross National Product (GNP) per capita. Every economy can be classified as low income, middle income (subdivided into lower and upper middle), or high income. Low-income and middle-income economies are sometimes known as **developing economies.** Classifying economies in this way is convenient, but as we have seen the level of development of a country goes beyond relative levels of income. It can also be misleading if it is assumed that all countries classed as 'developing' are at the same stage of development. In fact economies grouped together in terms of income may well be at completely different stages of development. Nevertheless, categorising economies according to their levels of income provides a simple and measurable way of grouping economies.

The income groups were categorised as follows in 2000:

LOW INCOME	$755 or less
MIDDLE INCOME	$756 to $2,995 (lower middle) $2,996 to $9,265 (upper middle)
HIGH INCOME	$9,266 or above

The thresholds between the categories are updated each year to account for international rates of inflation. As a result the thresholds are constant in real terms over time.

Classification according to levels of indebtedness
Sometimes it is useful to classify developing economies according to the degree of their indebtedness. These categories are: severely (or highly) indebted, moderately indebted and less indebted. The categorisation depends upon a number of measures of international indebtedness, the most important of which is the proportion of GNP which is devoted to servicing the debt. The fact that such a categorisation is used is a reflection of the extent to which international indebtedness is an obstacle to economic development.

The characteristics of developing economies The term 'developing economy' is used to describe a great variety of different countries and there are many differences between them, so in some ways it is wrong to think of them as a distinct group with the same characteristics. Very often the differences which exist between them are related to the geographical area in which the countries are located. This also means that developing countries located in the same region are usually affected by the same types of problem. The development problems of developing countries in Sub-Saharan Africa may, for example, be quite distinct from those of developing countries in Asia. In this sense there is no such thing as a 'typical developing country', and policies to foster economic development may need to be country specific. The policies that are appropriate for one may not be appropriate for all. Nevertheless, for some purposes it is necessary to treat developing countries as a group and it is useful to identify their shared characteristics. Very often the characteristics that they share generate the similar problems that they have to face. The following is a brief description of the shared characteristics of developing economies. Recognising the differences between developing countries while identifying the characteristics that they have in common can be characterised as '*UNITY IN DIVERSITY*'.

Economic structure Economic activity can be placed in the following sectors:-

1 The Primary Sector. This includes agriculture and the extractive industries, such as oil extraction and coal mining.
2 The Secondary Sector. This is all manufacturing industries and the construction sector.
3 The Tertiary Sector. This is also known as the service sector.

Developing countries typically have a high dependency upon the primary sector. In those economies classified as low-income economies, agriculture contributed between 30 per cent and 60 per cent of output in the 1990s. This high dependency on agricultural output makes developing countries vulnerable to the forces of nature. In those economies in which agricultural output is mainly for subsistence a drought can swiftly lead to famine. In those developing economies that are dependent upon agricultural products for their exports the drought can wipe out their foreign currency earnings. In contrast to this, in high-income economies the average figure for agricultural production was only 5 per cent or less of GDP.

Population growth and population structure World population in mid 2000 was estimated to be 6.06 billion and growing by 75 million people each year. More than 95 per cent of this growth is taking place in developing countries.

Many observers suggest that the theories of Malthus can be applied to the current population problems of the developing countries. Writing as long ago as 1798 the Reverend Thomas Malthus offered a quite pessimistic view of population growth. The essence of his view was that a country's population had a tendency to grow in geometric progression over time. However, food supplies had a tendency to increase only in arithmetic progression:

population grows in geometric progression 1, 2, 4, 8, 16, 32, 64...
food supplies grow in arithmetic progression 1, 2, 3, 4, 5, 6, 7...

This was because the quantity of land was in relatively fixed supply (the fixed factor), and, as increasing quantities of ever-more readily available labour (the variable factor) were added in production, diminishing returns would set in. The tendency over time therefore was that population increases would outstrip increases in food supplies. This would cause a number of 'checks' to population growth so that the population would fall to a level sustainable by the available food supplies. These checks included famines brought on by the overpopulation, diseases and epidemics caused by malnourishment, and wars as countries, increasingly desperate to feed their growing populations, fight over dwindling resources.

This Malthusian view of population growth can be challenged on a number of grounds. The main weakness is that it fails to recognise the impact of changes in technology upon food production and distribution. Malthus could not have been aware of the huge changes that have occurred in agricultural production, such as mechanisation, the application of more effective fertilisers and insecticides and the introduction of new high yield seeds such as the 'miracle' strains of rice introduced in Japan, Taiwan and South Korea. These changes mean that food supplies have increased to a level capable of supporting a much higher level of world population. Nevertheless, malnourishment and famine remain depressing features of many developing countries. However, these problems are more likely to be caused by a wider range of factors than an overall Malthusian analysis would suggest. These include factors such as the uneven distribution of resources in the world, poor management of agricultural sectors, vulnerability to sudden shocks, such as floods and drought, and an inability to respond to these. As we shall see the crippling impact of international debt in developing countries also creates conditions in which human miseries, including hunger and famines, can flourish.

The fact that developing countries have much higher birth rates than the developed economies does not only lead to greater increases in the total population of developing countries but all the attendant problems which this brings. It also has an impact upon the population structure of these countries. It means that when the age composition of developing countries is considered it is seen that they tend to have a large number of very young people. This creates a high proportion of dependent, non-productive members of the population. They are said to have very high **dependency ratios**. This means that a proportionally small working population has to produce enough goods and services to sustain not only themselves but also a large number of young people who are economically dependent upon them. This will give rise to conditions of poverty and in addition create pressures to force the young into the workforce. The Human Development Report 2000 illuminates the problem of child labour. It estimated that there are now 100 million children who live or work on the streets. Developed countries also

A retiring nation

Italy has far more pensioners than it can afford

Italy's greying population and falling birth rate put the country on course for a debacle over its pension system. One of Italy's leading experts on pensions, Giuliano Cazzola, points to an array of figures that, unless other trends are reversed within a decade or so, will spell doom for the country's pensioners.

Italians now get a state pension at the age of 56, or after 35 years of work, whichever comes first; this is gradually being scaled up to the age of 62, or 37 years in work, by 2006. Those who retire after fewer years in work get smaller pensions. Various governments since 1990 have tinkered with the system, but the savings will take time to come through.

At present, 60% of Italy's welfare pot is gobbled up by pensions, against an EU average of 45%. Until the new arrangements kick in, some public-sector workers can collect a pension – and will go on collecting it – after only 20 years' work. Many of them have two or more state pensions.

The number of pensioners is rising inexorably, partly because the average age of the population is being pushed up by the low birth rate, partly because people are living longer, and partly because Italians retire ridiculously early. On current trends, Professor Cazzola reckons, by 2030 some 42% of Italians will be pensioners – the highest proportion in Europe. If nothing is done, he says, the average Italian's pension package, now typically amounting to 54% of final salary and indexed for inflation, by 2050 will drop to less than 30%.

The best bet, most experts reckon, is to get more people into private pension schemes to top up their state pensions, and to raise the retirement age still further. So far, only 1.8m out of about 20m workers have joined private schemes. Yet in the run-up to the recent general election, the subject was barely mentioned.

They won't be sitting pretty forever
Source: Stephanie Haze, Corbis.

Source: *The Economist*, 7 July 2001.

tend to have problems with the age structure of their populations. Here the problem is different because the birth rate is so low and below the rate required to replace the present population. The result is that the population is actually ageing. In Britain, for example, it is estimated that the number of people aged 40 or below will fall by 2.7 million by the year 2030. In the European Union as a whole by 2050 it is estimated that two-thirds of the population will be over 65 and therefore considered 'not economically active'. Again, dependency ratios are high and this brings problems, but this time because of the high number of old people who are reliant upon the productive proportion of the population for support.

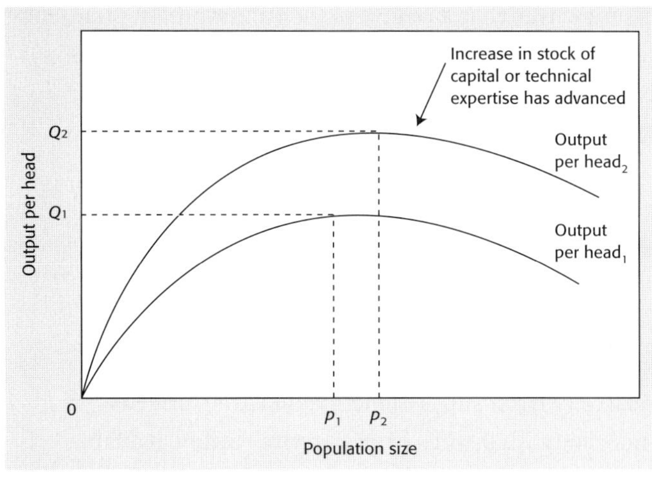

Figure 16.1 Optimum population

The concept of optimum population The concept of the optimum is useful when considering the idea of overpopulation and underpopulation. The **optimum population** is said to exist when output per head is the greatest, given existing quantities of the other factors of production and the current state of technical knowledge (see figure 16.1). As the population grows it can make better use of the stock of the other factors of production such as land and capital. This is because increasing returns are enjoyed as the population grows. If, as the population increases the output per head continues to grow, we could consider the country to be underpopulated. As the population continues to grow we would expect the output per head to eventually peak and then decline as decreasing returns are experienced.

At this stage the population has gone beyond the optimum and the country is considered to be overpopulated. In the real world, of course the situation is more dynamic and the state of technical knowledge is constantly improving. The quantity of the other factors also continuously changes so that the optimum population for a country is not a fixed entity. In addition the criteria for assessing under- or overpopulation are purely economic and may be disputed by conservationists.

Income distribution It is a general characteristic of developing countries that income is unevenly distributed. This is partly because income-generating assets, especially land, are owned by the few. As a result there are great extremes of rich and poor. In 1998 for example World Bank figures show that in Peru the poorest 20 per cent of the population had only 4.4 per cent of total household income, while the richest 20 per cent had 51.3 per cent of total household income. In Brazil the inequality is even greater, with the poorest 20 per cent having only 2.5 per cent and the richest 20 per cent having 63.4 per cent of total household income. The transition of Eastern European countries from centrally planned to market economies has, not unsurprisingly, increased inequality. In the Russian Federation and in Ukraine inequality increased so rapidly in the 1990s that the distribution of income is now more unequal than in the rich and established economies of the Organisation for Economic Co-operation and Development (OECD). The great extremes of rich and poor in developing economies means that deprivation is common.

Employment Developing countries tend to suffer from higher levels of unemployment and underemployment than developed countries. Unemployment tends to be high because in countries with surplus populations the supply of labour tends to exceed the supply of the other factors of production. Typically, developing economies suffer from shortages in capital and entrepreneurial skills but in addition there is pressure on the supply of land suitable for the production process.

External trade The foreign trade of many developing countries tends to show a great reliance upon the export of primary produce. When considering manufactured goods as a proportion of an economy's exports, it is clear that generally speaking developing countries depend upon primary products and developed economies depend upon manufactured goods. For example when considering the forty-five countries included in the High Human Development category of the HDI, manufactures made up 80 per cent of merchandise exports in 1997. This average fell to 58 per cent when considering the ninety-four countries categorised as Medium Human Development. Very few countries categorised as Low Human Development had any significant manufacturing exports at all. This is unsurprising since many of the population live at the margins of subsistence.

The significance of these data is that those developing countries that participate in international trade become reliant upon primary exports for foreign currency earnings. This makes them vulnerable in their trading relationships because of the demand and supply conditions in the markets for primary products. The demand for primary products tends to be price inelastic. Similarly, the supply of primary products tends to be price inelastic. The supply of some are also subject to frequent shifts depending for example on the size of the harvest. This means that the market for primary products is subject to frequent and severe fluctuations in price.

These fluctuations in price can de-stabilise the economies of developing countries. In addition, the demand for many primary products especially foodstuffs is income inelastic. This means that as world incomes rise there is little impact upon the demand for primary products as most of the higher incomes are spent on manufactured goods. Over time there is a tendency for the terms of trade of primary goods to decline compared to manufactured goods. Therefore those developing countries that are dependent upon primary products are receiving relatively lower prices for their exports of primary products and paying relatively higher prices for imports of manufactured goods. It should be noted, however, that there has been a decline in the number of developing countries that are heavily reliant upon primary products as manufacturing sectors are established in some developing countries. In others, principally in Sub-Saharan Africa, there remains a heavy reliance upon a narrow range of primary exports.

Self-assessment tasks

Study the data below and then tackle the questions that follow:

Country	GNP per head PPP $US	Employed labour force (%) 2001 Agric	Ind	Services	Life Expectancy (years)	Adult Literacy %
Antigua & Barbuda	10,360	4.0	5.6	90.4	71.9	89
Bahamas	16,140	3.8	5.4	90.8	65.5	96
Barbados	15,060	4.2	7.1	88.7	72.6	99
Belize	6,510	20.2	9.6	70.2	68.4	77
Dominica	5,250	21.0	10.1	68.1	74.6	94
Grenada	7,000	13.8	7.6	78.6	64.5	96
Guyana	4,110	23.1	18.8	58.1	65.5	99
Jamaica	3,630	19.9	8.1	71.7	73.3	89
St Kitts/Nevis	11,190	14.7	7.9	77.4	72.2	98
St Lucia	5,560	20.8	9.8	69.4	73.6	90
St Vincent & the Grenadines	6,250	24.9	8.7	66.4	73.6	96
Suriname	n.a.	13.0	11.7	75.4	68.9	88
Trinidad and Tobago	11,180	7.8	13.5	78.7	66.7	99

Selected indicators of development for CARICOM member states, 2004
Sources: CARICOM, World Bank.

1 On the basis of GNP per head, it might be concluded that living standards in Barbados are about four times higher than those in Jamaica. Do you agree?
2 Explain the variations in the employment structure of CARICOM economies and discuss any implications for the economic development of the region.
3 What correlation (if any) is there between
   - GNP per head and life expectancy,
   - GNP per head and adult literacy.
4 Comment upon the extent to which CARICOM member states are developing economies.

Urbanisation Developing economies still have high proportions of their populations living in rural areas. On average over half of the population of developing countries are classified as rural. Nevertheless, developing economies show very rapid rates of rural–urban migration. High-income countries already have the majority of their populations living in urban areas. As a result there is little growth in the urban population of developed countries. The rural–urban migration in developing countries can cause extra pressure on resources in already overcrowded urban areas. There is pressure on the infrastructure, with housing, roads and schools incapable of coping with the extra demand. The 1999/2000 World Development Report for example shows that from 1980 to 1998 the urban population of Bangladesh grew from 11 per cent to 20 per cent but only around 41 per cent of this growing urban population had access to sanitation.

Technology The gap between developed and developing countries in terms of the application of new technology is deep and widening. This covers a wide range of applications including new production techniques, new, more efficient means of communication and the electronic storage and retrieval of information. Only 5 per cent of the world's computers are located in

Off to the city

Government eases the rules

It was one of Mao Zedong's many big ideas, and thus far one of his most enduring. In the late 1950s, at the time of the 'great leap forward', China established its *hukou*, or household registration system, which required people to live and work only where they were officially permitted to. For a government intent on running its economy according to a strict central plan, it was well to have people stay where they were told. For China's hundreds of millions of rural dwellers it made leaving their village nearly as difficult as leaving the country.

Over the past 20 years China has moved steadily further from central planning, and workers have moved in huge numbers away from the nation's economically backward countryside to its far more vibrant cities. According to official estimates, China's migrant labour force now numbers somewhere around 100m. The government expects another 46m to come looking for jobs in the cities in the next five years as the number of surplus rural workers swells to 150m.

In light of such numbers, China's announcement on August 16th that it plans to revamp the registration system seems a bit like closing the barn door after the horse has escaped. But if the government carries through with its plan to abolish restrictions on labour mobility, it will in fact make a huge difference to the lives of those migrants.

While that is clearly true, it has also helped avert an outcome that many of China's urban dwellers dread: an unrestrained influx into the cities of people from the countryside. While city people are glad to have enough migrants to handle the jobs they themselves do not want, they fear that too many will put unbearable strain on housing, communications and other resources. Some municipal governments have already tinkered with existing rules to admit only 'desirable' outsiders. The cities of Shenzhen and Zhuhai offer residency to those who can buy property, and Beijing grants documentation to technical workers with senior qualifications.

Now to move in
Source: PA Photos.

Source: *The Economist*, 1 September 2001.

developing countries. Although the application of the internet to commerce will increase efficiency, especially in distribution, it will widen the technology gap for those developing countries that lack the technical skills and the infrastructure to participate effectively.

A well-known development economist has summarised the common problems that stem from these common characteristics as follows:

> widespread and chronic absolute poverty, high and rising levels of unemployment and underemployment, wide and growing disparities in the distribution of income, low and stagnating levels of agricultural productivity, sizeable and growing imbalances between urban and rural levels of living and economic opportunities, serious and worsening environmental decay, antiquated and inappropriate educational and health systems, severe balance of payments and international debt problems, and substantial and increasing dependence on foreign and often inappropriate technologies, institutions and value systems.

The concept of human development

As shown earlier, a good starting point for measuring living standards is GNP or GDP per capita, particularly where the information is in terms of purchasing power parity. The concept of living standards, and in turn the level of economic development, is rather broader since it encompasses an improvement in people's welfare. It is therefore appropriate to consider a range of information when investigating the question of human development and the extent to which people in some countries are better off than others.

A well-known and widely used measure for this purpose is the United Nations' (UN) *Human*

Development Index (HDI). The index was developed in 1990 by a Pakistani economist, Haq, and has been used annually since then by the UN to assess the progress or otherwise of the world's economies. In particular it is used to distinguish whether a country is developed or developing and is a standard means of measuring well-being, particularly child welfare.

The HDI is compiled using three basic aspects of human development:

- a decent standard of living, measured by GDP per capita at purchasing power parity;
- a long and healthy life expectancy, measured by life expectancy at birth;
- educational attainment as measured by the adult literacy rate (two-thirds weight) and the combined gross enrolment rate for primary, secondary and tertiary schools (one-third weight).

Each of these three components has equal weight in the final HDI calculation. The index has a maximum value of 1. The value for any country shows the gap that has to be made up to reach this maximum. In the 2006 calculations, based on 2004 data, Norway was top with an HDI value of 0.965. It held top place also in 2005. Ireland and Japan had made most progress since the 2005 edition, rising four ranks to 4 and 7 respectively. The US was ranked 8 and the UK, 18. The highest ranked Caribbean economy was Barbados at 31.

The HDI index can be used to segment countries:

- 0.8 and above – high human development,
- 0.5 but less than 0.8 – medium human development,
- below 0.5, low human development.

Table 16.1 shows the HDI values for Caribbean economies in rank order, based on 2004 data. As this shows, all are classified as having medium human development or above. In these terms, Barbados compares favourably with emerging European economies such as Slovenia, Cyprus, the Czech Republic and Hungary. Except for Haiti (HDI value 0.482), all countries that have low human development are in Africa.

Economic growth and developing economies

Introduction

The production possibility curve as described in unit 1 can be used to explain the important distinction between changes in the *actual* output of goods and services and changes in the *potential* output of goods and services.

A change in the actual output of goods and services

Country	Rank	HDI	Life Expectancy at birth	Adult Literacy	Enrolment ratio	GDP per head
Barbados	31	0.879	75.3	n.a.	89	15,720
St Kitts/Nevis	51	0.825	70.0	97.8	80	12,702
Bahamas	52	0.825	70.2	n.a.	66	17,843
Trinidad & Tobago	57	0.809	69.8	n.a.	67	12,182
Antigua	59	0.808	73.9	85.8	69	12,586
Dominica	68	0.793	75.6	88.0	83	5,643
St Lucia	77	0.790	72.6	94.8	76	6,324
Grenada	85	0.762	65.3	96.6	73	8,021
St Vincent & the Grenadines	88	0.759	71.3	88.1	68	6,398
Suriname	89	0.759	69.3	89.6	72	n.a.
Dominican Republic	94	0.751	67.5	87.0	74	7,449
Belize	95	0.751	71.8	75.1	81	6,747
Guyana	103	0.725	63.6	96.5	76	4,439
Jamaica	104	0.724	70.7	79.9	77	4,163

Table 16.1 Human Development Index, 2004
Source: Human Development Report, 2006.

could be achieved by the better utilisation of existing factors of production. In figure 16.2 assume the economy is currently producing at point *X*. This is a point well within the production frontier shown by the production possibility curve. Production at this point might be caused by a lack of aggregate demand in the economy. The movement from point *X* to point *Y* on the curve could be achieved for example by increasing demand through fiscal and/or monetary policy. This would lead to an increase in the output of both goods and services. In turn it would certainly lead to an increase in Gross Domestic Product and be considered as actual economic growth. In the long run, however, further increases in output could only be achieved if the potential output of the economy was to grow. This would be represented by a shift in the production possibility curve itself. In the above diagram the shift of the curve from PPC_1 to PPC_2 represents a growth in the potential output of this economy. In the long run therefore explanations of economic growth need to focus upon those factors which increase the potential output of an economy.

Factors contributing to economic growth

The position of the production possibility curve is determined by an economy's production function. This shows the maximum output that can be produced by an economy given the current endowment of factors of production and the current state of technical expertise.

In order to achieve economic growth which can be sustained over time it is necessary to:

- *Increase the quantity of resources at the disposal of the economy.* All of the factors of production could potentially be increased. Clearly, given the growth in population in developing countries it would seem that the supply of labour would grow through the natural increase in population. If there is a positive net migration the population will also grow as the number of immigrants exceeds the number of emigrants. An increase in the labour force will not create a great impact upon production possibilities, however, without an increase in the other factors. Capital goods can only be increased if investment takes place. Enterprise can be increased through training and government policies that encourage risk-taking in the economy. Land can only really be increased through conquest. Any land gained through reclamation schemes should really be considered as a type of capital because it needs investment before it becomes available.
- *Increase the quality of resources at the disposal of the economy.* Improvements in the quality of resources will increase the productivity of the factor inputs. The quality of labour can be improved through education and training. This is known as *investment in human capital.* This term can also be applied to any development of the factor enterprise. The quality of capital goods is improved through time as technology improves. The quality of capital goods used in developing countries improves as these countries participate in international trade. The quality of land for agricultural use can be improved through the application of fertiliser, and through irrigation and drainage schemes.

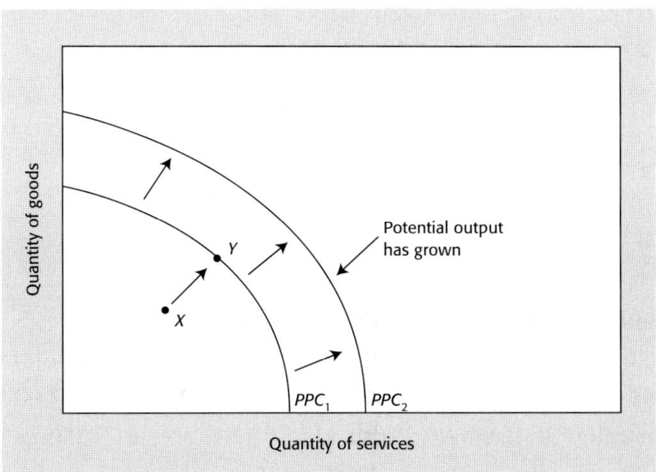

Figure 16.2 An increase in the potential output of an economy

The main obstacle to increases in the quantity and quality of resources in developing countries is of course the opportunity cost of diverting resources away from their current use. Although labour may well be in abundance it is difficult to improve its quality. Many young people are deprived of education because of a shortage of schools, teachers and textbooks. Devoting more resources to education means they have to be diverted from some other use. In addition, many children are required to work to support family incomes. Capital goods are created through the process of investment. Because many developing countries are barely above the subsistence level it is impossible for them to divert resources away from current consumption without creating a decline in living standards below that required for survival. The opportunity cost is too high. Very often the only way in which capital goods can be acquired in such circumstances is for the necessary resources to be provided from abroad in the form of loans or aid. As we have seen, many developing countries have acquired a large debt problem which has necessitated the transfer of funds in the form of debt repayments from themselves to the richer countries. This again diverts much needed resources away from development projects and poverty alleviation in the developing countries. The provision of development aid might be considered to be the answer to the difficulties of providing sufficient funds for development.

One important factor necessary for growth is to improve the state of technical expertise utilised in the economy. The high rates of growth experienced by the developed countries in the industrial era have been sustained by the application of technological innovations to mass production. This could only be achieved through extensive research and development into new techniques of production.

Again the concept of opportunity cost can be used to illustrate the problems faced by the developing countries. Research and development is expensive and has a high opportunity cost in the developing countries who can ill afford to divert scarce resources into this use. The benefits to the economy will only be experienced in the medium to long term. Today over 90 per cent of the world's research and development expenditure takes place in the countries of the developed world. This allows the developed economies to maintain their dominance of world markets in manufactured goods. In addition the new technology developed in the richer countries has been developed to be applied to rich countries' problems. For example, rich countries tend to use capital-intensive production methods. They try to economise on the use of highly skilled and expensive labour which is in short supply in the rich countries. They also produce for the mass market, so the scale of production is large. The developing countries have large supplies of unskilled labour and often produce for much smaller markets. As we have seen they cannot afford to divert resources to the production of capital goods which are capable of utilising the new technologies. As a result the new technologies cannot be easily transferred from the developed countries to the developing countries. The technology transfer which might be considered necessary to allow the developing countries to progress is seen as inappropriate.

Improving the quantity and quality of the components of an economy's production function, together with the level of technical expertise in an economy, will certainly result in an increase in the potential output of an economy. Changes that lead to such improvements can be considered as the sources of growth. An example might be an increase in the savings ratio in an economy. This might lead to the diversion of resources from consumption to investment in the economy and an increase in capital accumulation. We have seen, however, the difficulties faced by the developing countries in accessing the sources of growth. We now need to consider the difficulties that result from an over-reliance upon foreign loans.

The impact of indebtedness on economic growth and development

As stated earlier, a further categorisation of developing economies considers the extent of their indebtedness. Some are categorised as heavily indebted poor countries (HIPC). This means that one of two key debt ratios is exceeded. The first ratio is the relationship between the debt service ratio and the GNP. The second is the relationship between the present value of debt service to exports. If either the proportion of debt service exceeds 80 per cent of GNP or the present value of debt service is 220 per cent of exports then the country is considered to be heavily indebted. If either of the two ratios exceeds 60 per cent of the critical level then the country is said to be moderately indebted. The presence of debt on such a scale diverts resources to debt repayment and away from spending on health and education, on infrastructure and poverty relief. Such debt provides a very real obstacle to development.

Jubilee 2000 The London-based organisation Jubilee 2000 was established in 1996. It became a coalition of 100 voluntary groups and ran a high profile four-year campaign to cancel the debts of fifty-two HIPCs. These countries have a total combined debt in the region of

$375 billion. In 1998 it cost them $23.4 billion to service this debt. Most of the debt is owed to government departments in OECD countries, the World Bank, the IMF and international aid agencies. The campaign gathered huge support and produced the world's largest petition signed by 24 million people in 166 countries. Despite this the campaign has fallen short of its objective. Campaigners criticise the slow pace of progress on debt reduction and also point out the limited extent of the debt relief so far achieved. Campaigners place blame for their failure upon the World Bank and the IMF, which jointly administer the main debt relief vehicle, the HIPC initiative. So far of the fifty-two HIPCs only twenty-two countries meet the criteria for debt relief set by the World Bank and the IMF. To qualify for debt relief HIPCs must have poverty reduction strategies in place that meet World Bank/IMF criteria. Only one country, Uganda, has satisfied the criteria sufficiently to have its debts cancelled. Twenty-one other HIPCs gained agreement for debt service levels to be reduced in December 2000. It may be several years however before their poverty reduction strategies satisfy the World Bank/IMF sufficiently to have their debts cancelled. In the meantime sixteen of these countries will still be spending more on debt than on health. Mauritania, for example, despite the reduction agreed, will be paying $63 million on servicing its debt and only $51 million on education and $17 million on health. Tanzania will pay out $168 million on debt servicing compared to $87 million on health. In addition to the slow progress, the debt relief so far achieved covers only twenty-two of the fifty-two HIPCs. Their total combined population is 205 million, but the combined population of all the HIPCs is 1,030 million, so that only 20 per cent of those living in an HIPC will benefit from any kind of debt reduction in the near future. Despite such limited successes what the campaign has done is to place debt on the international agenda. The pressure for relief from debt burden for the world's most indebted countries goes on, and a

Economic performance of Caribbean economies

It is very clear from published data that there are substantial differences in real growth rates between Caribbean economies. The highest rates of GDP growth over many years have been recorded by the likes of St Lucia, St Kitts & Nevis, St Vincent and the Grenadines and Bahamas. The lowest rates of growth, usually 1 per cent or less, have been for Jamaica, Trinidad and Tobago, Guyana and Suriname. The obvious question to ask is why is this so.

Most Caribbean states are small by conventional economic standards. As such they face constraints as a consequence of size – they are also vulnerable to external shocks, particularly from natural disasters and the vagaries arising from the state of the US economy. The better performance of the smaller or microstates has been partly attributed to the high degree of openness of their economies, with international tourism and offshore finance being particularly significant generators of growth. Significantly, these economies do not have substantial agricultural sectors.

Economic structure is not the only reason. Endogenous growth theory has been used to try to explain growth variations. The argument is that growth is very much determined by policies that originate *within* an economy – a country's government and its institutions can be fundamental in increasing the rate of economic growth. Equally, it follows that actions by a country's population and decision-makers may actually stifle growth.

The following factors have been identified as explaining good economic performance amongst Caribbean economies:

- exploitation of natural resources
- political stability
- cultural and social cohesion
- GDP per head/HDI rank
- openness
- economic structure

Endogenous variables therefore can be very important in explaining variations in the economic growth of Caribbean economies.

Source: R. Rankissoon, Senior Economist, Republic Bank Ltd, Trinidad and Tobago, 2002 (adaptation).

successor to Jubilee 2000, Jubilee Plus, is planned.

Benefits and costs of economic growth

Benefits

The main benefit of economic growth is the increase in goods and services which become available for the country's citizens to enjoy. This raises their material living standards. If you have difficulty in believing this, ask your parents what life was like when they were your age!

Economic growth also makes it easier to help the poor. Without any increase in output and income, the only way in which the living standards of the poor can be raised is by taking income and hence goods and services from higher income groups. Whereas if economic growth occurs at least some of the extra income can be given to the poor in the form of higher benefits, thereby enabling them to enjoy more goods and services.

A stable level of economic growth increases firms' and consumers' confidence. This makes planning easier and encourages investment. Economic growth may also increase a country's international prestige and power. For example, China's rapid growth in the early 1990s increased its status in world politics.

Costs

Economic growth may bring with it a number of costs. If the economy is operating at the full employment level there will be an opportunity cost involved in achieving economic growth. To produce more capital goods, in order to increase the country's productive capacity, some resources will have to be moved from producing consumer goods to producing capital goods. So current consumption of goods and services will have to be reduced. However, this will only be a short-run cost since in the long run the increased investment will increase the output of consumer goods and services.

Economic growth may also bring increased stress and anxiety. A growing economy is a dynamic economy that also undergoes structural changes. Workers may have to learn new skills and may have to change their occupation and/or where they live. Some workers may find this difficult to cope with. Economic growth may also be accompanied by increased working hours and pressure to come up with new ideas and improvements. When Japan was growing rapidly in the 1980s some workers put in very long hours and students felt under considerable pressure to pass examinations.

Economic growth may also be accompanied by the depletion of natural resources and damage to the environment. Higher output may, for example, involve firms using more oil, building on green field sites and creating more pollution. However, this does not have to be the case. Output can be increased in ways which do not damage the environment.

Sustainable economic growth

Very rapid growth may be achieved but this may be at the expense of the living standards of future generations if it results from the reckless use of resources. Countries are now becoming more concerned to achieve **sustainable economic growth**. This occurs when output increases in a way which does not compromise the

Recycling paper – a sustainable activity

Freight 'cancelling out' warming curbs

International trade growth, with more use of aircraft and lorries, is making a mockery of attempts by world leaders to curb global warming, according to economists.

A report published today reveals uncontrolled growth of greenhouse gas emissions from international freight. According to the report, entitled Collision Course, emissions from the transport sector will cancel out the benefits of reducing green house gas emissions by more efficient use of fossil fuels elsewhere.

The report comes out two days before 160 nations meet in the Hague to negotiate reductions in greenhouse gas emissions, and in the same week that the Chancellor cut fuel duty to buy off lorry drivers.

The report says that greenhouse gas emissions from transport are among the fastest growing contributors to climate change. Road freight and aviation, the most polluting methods of moving freight, are increasing dramatically.

The situation is worse in the EU, where demand for more freight is growing faster than the economy, and railways, inland waterways and coastal shipping are losing out to road transport and air freight. Just-in-time deliveries mean more lorries running empty – in fact, up to 30% of all journeys.

Andrew Simms, co-author of the report, says the world economy is hooked on fossil fuels, an addiction that is taking a heavy toll on the environment. 'Just like normal addicts, our politicians and economists construct elaborate excuses to justify their destructive addiction,' said Mr Simms. 'We have to return to a scale of economic activity that is humanly and environmentally sustainable.'

He added: 'If the projected 70% rise in international freight transport materialises by 2004 the resulting increase in greenhouse gas emissions will make a mockery of both the reduction targets set for industrialised countries and the current exclusion of international freight from climate controls.'

Waste

Kiwifruit Carried by plane from New Zealand to Europe; 5kg of carbon dioxide pumped into the atmosphere for every 1kg of fruit carried.

Asparagus 1kg of asparagus from California uses 4kg of aviation fuel. If grown in Europe, 900 times less energy would be used.

Apples Importing South African apples rather than growing them within 20 miles of the selling point causes 600 times as much nitrogen oxide pollution.

Strawberry yoghurt Delivering full glasses of yoghurt to Germany involved a total journey of 5,000 miles for the ingredients.

Orange juice 80% of orange juice drunk in Europe comes from Brazil. For every tonne consumed at least 25 tonnes of materials are used up. Blackcurrant juice produced in Europe would be just as nutritional.

Source: Paul Brown, *The Guardian*, 11 November 2000.

needs of future generations. Materials such as aluminium, paper and glass can be recycled. More use could be made of renewable energy resources in preference to non-renewable resources, and improvements in technology may both increase output and reduce pollution.

International comparisons of living standards

There are many problems when interpreting data on comparative living standards between countries. This equally applies to Caribbean comparisons, where most countries are at a similar stage of development, as well as to comparisons between countries that differ more significantly in their relative levels of development. Problems include:

- fluctuations in the exchange rate against the $US – large movements can affect the GNP per head measure;
- measuring purchasing power, particular in economies where prices are not well known;
- no allowance is made for the size of the subsistence sector. This can be large in emerging and less developed economies;
- the shadow or informal economy is not included. In the UK this is estimated to be up to 25% of GDP. In less developed economies it is likely to be at least this figure;
- no allowance is made in GNP per head for the distribution of income;
- countries with a high GNP per head may have achieved this through the serious denigration of their physical environments or through excessive expenditure on defence;
- traditional measures do not take into account variables such as social justice and political freedom.

Self-assessment tasks

1 Using the data in table 16.1, comment upon the extent to which the HDI rankings are correlated with GDP per head. Use examples from the table to support your answer.

2 Discuss why an increase in a country's GNP might not result in an improvement in well-being for all of its citizens.

Summary

In this chapter it has been shown that:

- Economic development refers to the processes through which countries seek to raise their living standards.
- Broadly speaking, economies can be classified on the basis of GNP per capita.
- The characteristics of developing economies are diverse.
- The Human Development Index is a useful statistical measure for classifying economies.
- Economic growth occurs when there is an increase or shift outwards of the PPC and can occur through an increase in the quantity and quality of resources available.
- Not all growth is beneficial; the costs of growth and the extent to which growth is sustainable should be taken into account.

Key words

Definitions of Key words can be found in the Glossary.

dependency ratio
economic development
Human Development Index
optimum population
sustainable economic growth

17 International trade

This chapter covers unit 2, module 3, topic 2.
On completion of this chapter, you should be able to:

- explain why exports are critical for generating domestic income, while imports generate income for foreigners
- outline the factors which influence exports and imports
- explain the importance of exports and imports for the level of economic activity in the small open economy
- explain the gains from trade
- evaluate the arguments for trade liberation
- describe the methods of trade protection
- define and calculate the commodity terms of trade

The global economy of the twenty-first century

International trade is the lifeblood of virtually all modern developed and developing economies. As such, it involves the buying and selling of goods and services across national frontiers. At a personal level this is clearly seen through the many imported items that can be found in supermarkets and other retail stores. Products such as Coca Cola, Fuji film, Nike trainers and Nescafé coffee are global brands and are widely available throughout the world.

Increasingly, through international trade, economies have become more and more economically dependent upon each other. For example, the well-being of the US economy affects the well-being of many other economies in Central and South America, Europe, Asia and Africa. Similarly, the South East Asian currency crisis of 1996 had knock-on effects throughout the world. This dependency can crudely be shown by the respective contributions of **exports** and **imports** to a country's Gross Domestic Product (GDP). For the UK, in 2004, these were approximately 29 per cent and 32 per cent respectively. In other economies, this percentage was even greater.

Coca Cola: a much traded product of the global economy

Trade provides an important link between developed and developing economies. From a very general standpoint, the developed economies provide a range of consumer goods, capital equipment and financial services in exchange for raw materials, certain types of agricultural products and, increasingly, for a range of manufactured goods from the developing economies. Also included in international trade are the ever-increasing global receipts from international tourism. These are of very substantial importance, both domestically and as a source of foreign exchange, for many developing economies in the Caribbean, East Africa and Asia.

On the surface, it may seem best if we 'buy local'. After all this promotes sales of home-produced goods and restricts the drain on foreign currency reserves caused by the need to pay for imports. But if all countries followed this strategy, there would be very little international trade except for certain essentials that could not be produced in the home market. As we shall see below, this state of affairs is very wasteful and the world economy as a whole would be poorer as a consequence.

Trade permits countries to specialise in products and commodities which they can produce relatively efficiently. The reasons for this specialisation are many and include the availability of particular factors of production. Economies which have naturally occurring resources, such as oil or copper, can exploit these and trade them on the world market. Alternatively, the climate or soils of a country may make it a good source of certain types of food product or a good destination for international tourists. Other economies may have a highly skilled workforce or have unit labour costs below that of others so enabling them to competitively produce clothing, electrical goods or vehicles. These examples are a very clear link to the factors of production identified in unit 1.

From an accounting standpoint, the balance of payments in an economy is a financial record of all such international transactions. In principle, receipts from exports of goods and services can be used to pay for imports which cannot be produced as efficiently or which cannot be produced at all. The nature of the global economy though is that this is not as simple an exchange process as might be indicated. Some economies, such as Germany, Japan and China, have traditionally had export surpluses. In contrast, others, such as the UK, the US and many developing economies, have spent more on imports than exports. Although by definition the world economy's trade flows balance, for individual countries this may not happen. If the imbalance is other than marginal, corrective action has to take place (see topic 4).

Self-assessment task

Think about the main types of goods

- imported into your country,
- exported by your country.

Make a list of these and see if you can come up with a simple explanation as to why this is so. Make reference to the factors of production in your explanation.

Export revenue

Exports, particularly of primary products, provide an important source of income for virtually all Caribbean economies. Traditional export crops are sugar cane, bananas, coffee, pineapples and cocoa. These are largely traded on the international market to the USA and EU member states, the UK especially. Other short-term crops such as sweet potatoes, yams and vegetables tend to be traded more on an intra-regional basis. The significance of export revenue is that it is an injection into the circular flow of income and, in turn, produces a multiplier effect throughout the entire economy. When export revenue falls, due to less production or a fall in prices, there is a negatively profound effect on the producing economies. Table 17.1 provides a profile of exports for five Caribbean economies.

Country	Total exports (US $m)	% primary products[1]	Total exports as percentage GDP
Barbados	334.8	58.1	n.a.
Belize	214.9	82.8	n.a.
Guyana	379.1	73.6	95
Jamaica	1,084.3	36.0	41
Trinidad & Tobago	5,364.5	64.1	60

Table 17.1 Composition of exports for selected Caribbean countries, 2003
Note: 1 includes mineral products.
Source: Annual Statistical Yearbook of Latin America & the Caribbean, 2005.

The export revenue of all Caribbean primary producing countries is though volatile. In particular, it is subject to serious dislocation due to hurricane damage. In 2005, Hurricanes Dennis and Emily caused very serious damage to the agricultural sector of Jamaica. As a result, the sugar cane crop was wiped out, production of bananas was reduced by 60 per cent and coffee production was down by almost 100 per cent on 2004 levels. The result was one of serious concern to the agricultural community and for the economy as a whole.

Total export revenue for primary agricultural products depends on a whole range of factors, most of which can be anticipated but not with any degree of certainty. These factors include:

- *The price of exports.* World commodity prices for some Caribbean exports are subject to major changes, most of which are downward. This is particularly true of banana prices that rose to US$ 1,015 per tonne in September 2005, a 40 per cent increase on the 2004 price, yet 30 per cent down on prices earlier that year. Sugar prices in contrast are relatively stable.

- *The exchange rate.* When exports are sold, the Caribbean suppliers require payment in local currency or maybe US$. Just what they receive will depend upon the relevant exchange rate at the time of sale.
- *Availability of substitutes.* The demand for some agricultural products is affected by the price and availability of substitutes. For products such as bananas and sugar, there are other producing countries competing for the business of Caribbean producers (see self-assessment task).
- *Unforeseen factors.* Hurricanes, for example, can wipe out production of some crops overnight. This has a devastating effect on local economies and usually requires government support to put producers back on to a basis where they can resume their businesses.

Most economies in the Caribbean area are dependent on international tourism as a vital source of export revenue. Table 17.2 shows total tourism receipts (US$m) in 2000. (These data are illustrative as later information is not available for all economies.)

International tourism income comes from two types of visitor, those who require accommodation and who stay over and cruise arrivals who usually stay for less than 24 hours and have a much lower average spend per person.

The international tourism market, like that for primary products, is by no means stable. In particular the value of tourism exports in Caribbean economies is vulnerable to outside factors including:

Country	Total tourism Receipts (US$M)	As % GDP	% Cruise arrivals
St Lucia	276.7	55	62
Antigua & Barbuda	290.1	49	64
Barbados	718.5	36	50
St Kitts & Nevis	58.2	31	69
Grenada	70.2	28	58
St Vincent & the Grenadines	75.3	28	54
Jamaica	1,333.0	25	41
Trinidad and Tobago	212.8	19[1]	17

Note: [1] – estimate.

Table 17.2
Source: Caribbean Tourism Organisation, 2004.

- The state of the economy in tourist-generating countries, in particular the USA, the UK, and Germany. When these economies are growing and disposable incomes are rising then this represents a positive state of affairs for the Caribbean attractors. In recent years, sluggish growth in the USA especially has been to blame for some of the problems in this market.
- The development of alternative destinations. For European tourists, there has been tremendous growth in tourism to China and other parts of South East Asia. For US tourists, parts of central and Latin America are relatively new markets. Such developments put pressure on the Caribbean tourist industry to increase its levels of service and invest more extensively in tourist infrastructure.
- Changes in the cruising industry, notably bigger vessels that require extensive port facilities and are capable of serving other destinations.
- A rise in the cost of long haul air travel in particular brought about by rising oil prices. Although marginal at present, there is growing concerns in Europe over the sustainability of this form of travel.
- Safety and security issues, in particular post 9/11.

All of these factors can have an effect on international tourism receipts.

The principles of international trade

The economic logic which has underpinned the development of international trade has its origins over 200 years ago in the writings of classical economists who firmly advocated what we now refer to as **multi-lateral free trade**. Their principles of absolute and, particularly, of comparative advantage have modern relevance in the objectives of the World Trade Organisation (WTO), which exists to promote free trade amongst all countries in the world economy.

The simple economic principles involved are summarised below. These show that trade will take place when countries have a clear-cut or **absolute advantage** over other countries. If we look at the UK's position for example:

- India has a clear-cut advantage over the UK in the production of tea;

Self-assessment tasks

1 The letters below were published in the *Daily Telegraph* on 3 March 2006 in response to an earlier article on the relative merits of cane and beet sugar. Read them and then tackle the questions that follow.

Cost of cane and benefits of beet

SIR – As Europe's main cane sugar refiner (Rose Prince: 'Buying sugar is as much a moral choice as a hazard to our waistlines', Weekend, February 25), Tate & Lyle acts as the most important bridge to Europe for African, Caribbean, Pacific and least developed countries.

This access is independent of EU market demand, but commands an EU price, giving suppliers between £250 million and £300 million more for their sugar than would otherwise be the case. Last year this meant that 300,000 direct employees in some of the world's poorer economies benefited from additional income for their raw sugar, compared with what they would have received by selling in the world market, competing with producers such as Brazil, Australia and Thailand. These funds are vital to sustaining their economies and employment.

Robert Gibber
Tate & Lyle
London

SIR – Rose Prince indulged in the nation's favourite pastime – farmer bashing. Yes, beet pulp from refining is used for animal feed, but what is wrong with that? It ensures there is no waste and it is not a 'foul smelling mass', just innocuous, sweet smelling shreds.

Beet farming does not have a 'corrosive effect' on the soil; it has its place in the crop rotation and uses no more pesticides than other crops. Subsidies help with the higher cost of European production. Most cane sugar is grown on farms in the Caribbean and South America, subsidised by very low wages, long working hours and a disregard for health and safety conditions, not just by small farmers seeking fair trade.

Beet sugar is produced, refined and consumed in this country, so demands no unnecessary food miles – something Rose Prince has applauded in previous articles.

Helen Bletcher
Appleby, Lincs.

Tate and Lyle sugar refinery
Source: Fiona Hanson/PA Archive/PA Photos.

(a) Using information from the Tate & Lyle letter, explain how the multiplier process can be used to analyse the effects of the increased export earnings that is paid to sugar cane farmers

(b) Comment upon the arguments put forward for producing sugar beet in the UK.

2 Try to obtain information on recent trends in international tourism for a Caribbean country of your choice. Explain the likely factors that might be responsible for the trends you observe.

- the Windward Islands can produce bananas, which the UK cannot produce;
- France has an obvious advantage in producing wine for export to the UK.

A list like this can be quite extensive; we could also compile a similar list of items for the trade of any economy.

What is obvious is that, under certain circumstances, trade can also be beneficial where a country may not have such clear-cut advantage. Provided it has a relative or **comparative advantage** in the production of a particular good over another country, trade can produce gains for both partners.

Summary of the principles of absolute and comparative advantage

The following assumptions are made:

- there are just two countries involved in trade;
- each can produce just two products (say, cloth and cheese);
- productivity differs between them, so varying quantities of each are produced;
- production costs and opportunity costs are constant for each product.

The production possibilities are shown in figure 17.1.

If each country was self-sufficient and devoted half of its resources to each product then the situation would be as shown at points A and B on these production possibility frontiers.

India is clearly better at cloth production, France is better at producing cheese. India is said to have an absolute advantage in cloth, France in cheese. If, however, they subsequently specialised, concentrating on those products where they had absolute advantage, each country would actually be better off as a result of trade taking place (see table 17.3).

India could now import 200 units of cheese from France, an overall gain of 150 units, without losing any cloth production. France can similarly benefit from buying cloth from India.

The above situation, sometimes called reciprocal absolute advantage, means that one country is better at producing one product, the other is superior in the production of the other. This rather obvious situation can be developed a stage further through the principle of comparative advantage – this states that trade between two countries should still take place and be mutually beneficial provided the domestic opportunity costs of production differ.

Going back to our earlier example, let us assume that India has a clear-cut advantage over France in the production of both cloth and cheese (somewhat unlikely, but remember this is no more than a simple model!). Factor endowments, including more advanced machinery, good pasture land and a more productive workforce, could provide this advantage. On the

	Cloth (units)		Cheese (units)
India	400	or	100
France	100	or	400

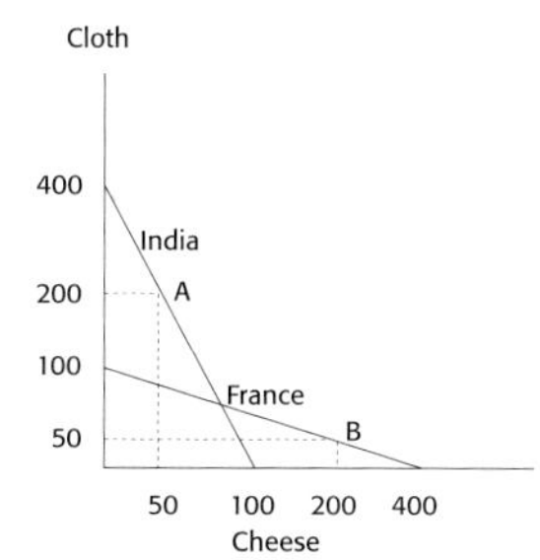

Figure 17.1 Production possibilities – absolute advantage

	Before trade (half of all resources to each industry)		After trade (all resources to chosen industry)	
	Cloth (units)	**Cheese (units)**	**Cloth (units)**	**Cheese (units)**
India	200	50	400	0
France	50	200	0	400
Total world production	**250**	**250**	**400**	**400**

Table 17.3 The gains from trade under absolute advantage

surface, there may seem little point in the two countries trading because India has the edge in producing both cloth and cheese. This situation is shown in figure 17.2.

If India decided not to trade at all, opting for self-sufficiency, each time it wanted more cloth, say, it would have to divert resources from cheese production. This trade-off, applying the concept of opportunity cost, can be illustrated by a movement on the production possibility frontier from *X* to *Y*. As India gained 100 units of cloth, it had to sacrifice fifty units of cheese production – the opportunity cost being that each unit of cloth gained resulted in a loss of half a unit of cheese. A reverse movement would produce a gain of one unit of cheese for every two units of cloth sacrificed. In the case of France, to gain an extra unit of cheese, there would be an opportunity cost of four units of cloth whereas each additional unit of cloth produced would result in a loss of a quarter of a unit of cheese.

The outcome of this principle is that countries should specialise in those goods in which they have the greatest relative efficiency over their trading partners. So, using the data above, India should concentrate on producing cheese, France on cloth. If this were to happen, and all resources were re-allocated in this way, total production would increase. This is shown in table 17.4.

The simple principles explained above are based on several assumptions. These are:

- The production possibility frontiers are linear.
- The exchange rate operating for international transactions must be between the respective domestic opportunity cost ratios. Otherwise trade will not be mutually beneficial. Indeed, where the differences between these opportunity costs are widest, then the potential for trade is greatest.
- No transport costs are charged. In today's global economy, this is very unrealistic, but it does reinforce the point made immediately above. There will be a gain from trade if the production benefit is greater than the transport costs.
- The two-country, two-product assumption is again a long way from reality in the twenty-first century. Countries might specialise in narrowly defined product areas, for example, high-quality woollen cloth, not cloth in general, and there are many potential trading partners in the global economy.
- Production costs are most unlikely to be constant. As countries specialise, for example, then they are likely to benefit from economies of scale as specialisation proceeds. They may also experience diseconomies of scale if specialisation goes too far.
- There are no restrictions on free trade between those countries which possess absolute and comparative advantage. This is clearly a very unrealistic assumption that has to be made.

	Cloth (units)		Cheese (units)
India	500	or	250
France	400	or	100
	900		350

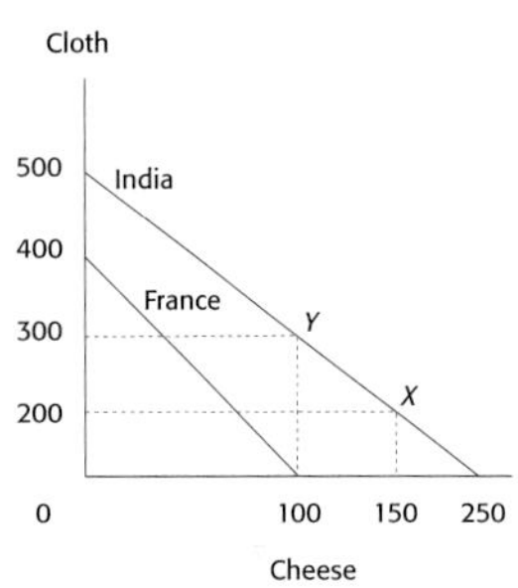

Figure 17.2 Production possibilities with one country having absolute advantage in both products

	Cloth (units)	Cheese (units)	
India	0	500	Total production has increased by 50 units
France	800	0	
	800	500	

Table 17.4 The gains from trade under comparative advantage

Notwithstanding these assumptions, there are clear gains from international trade as the principles of absolute and comparative advantage indicate. These principles are extendable of course to any number of countries and any number of products – the more of each, the greater the total gains from trade, as long as the principle of comparative advantage is followed.

Multilateral free trade is therefore beneficial for the overall well-being of the world economy. It ensures that goods are produced in those countries that are most efficient, minimising the waste of scarce resources. Conversely, it is clear that restrictions on trade will reduce the gains that free trade can produce. In the interests of economic efficiency tariff barriers and any other measures which protect the free movement of goods are to be frowned on.

Types of protection and their effects

Since free trade leads to a rise in world economic welfare, why should any country adopt policies which prevent free trade? Sometimes policies are adopted which distort market forces in order to give a competitive advantage to the domestic industry of an economy. Such policies are called **protectionist policies** because they provide some degree of protection from foreign competition. There are various methods of protecting domestic industry.

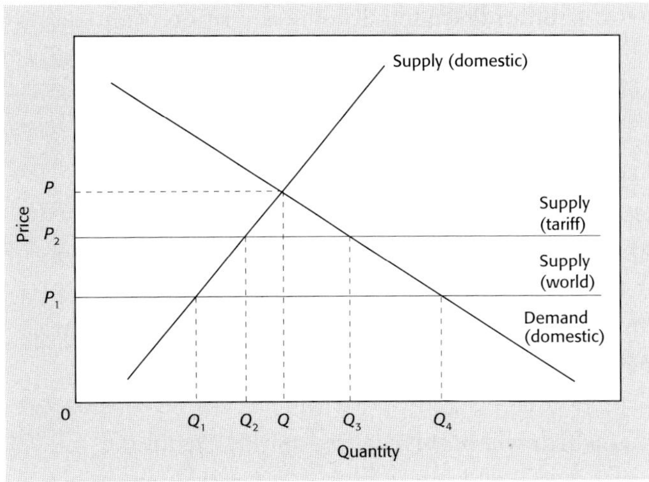

Figure 17.3 The effects of a tariff

Tariffs

A **tariff** is a tax on imports. It can be either specific, that is so much per unit, or *ad valorem*, which is a percentage of the price. Like all indirect taxes, tariffs have the impact of reducing the supply and raising the equilibrium price of the import. This gives a competitive advantage to home-produced goods and services, which become more attractive to consumers, resulting in a fall in imports.

Consider the economy in figure 17.3. If it did not engage in world trade, consumers would pay price *P* and consume quantity *Q*. This would be determined by the domestic supply and demand for the commodity. If the economy engaged in international trade, then consumers would benefit from international specialisation. World supply is shown as supply (world). Under these circumstances prices would fall to P_1. Consumption of the good would rise from *Q* to Q_4. At this price, however, only Q_1 would be supplied by the domestic producers. This means that domestic production has fallen from *Q* to Q_1. Lower-cost overseas producers have free access to the market, which has benefited consumers, but domestic producers have suffered, leading to a fall in employment in the industry. The imposition of a tariff, like all indirect taxes, would shift the supply curve upwards. This would increase the price to domestic consumers from P_1 to P_2. Production by domestic producers would increase from Q_1 to Q_2. Some jobs in the domestic economy would be saved.

Clearly, tariffs distort market forces and prevent consumers from benefiting from all the advantages of international specialisation and trade.

Container ship
Source: Alamy.

Quotas

Quotas are restrictions on the maximum quantity of imports. Their effect is to reduce the supply of imports on the domestic market. This will lead to a higher equilibrium price than would occur in a free market. Just as with tariffs the impact is to prevent the domestic consumer from benefiting from all the advantages of international trade. One difference is that whereas the government gains revenue as a result of tariffs, with quotas the increased price paid by consumers results in the foreign firm which supplied the imports earning higher profits. One answer might be for the government to sell licences to foreign firms to allow them to sell some allocation of the quota on the domestic market. The prospect of raised profits would ensure a market for the import licences.

Exchange control

One way of preventing excessive spending on imports is to set legal limits on the dealings in foreign currency that a country's citizens can make. If importers are limited in their access to foreign currency, they cannot pay for imports to the full extent of the domestic demand that exists. Imports will fall to a level below that which will occur in a free market. Again the consumer would suffer. **Exchange controls** existed in the UK before 1979 and there have been periods when there was a limit to the amount of foreign exchange that British citizens could take on overseas holidays. In 1979, all exchange controls were abandoned by the newly elected Conservative government. All member states of the European Union abandoned exchange controls in 1993.

Export subsidies

We have defined 'protectionism' in terms of any policy that distorts market forces to give competitive advantage to domestic industry. Sometimes, this is achieved through direct subsidies on exports. The impact of an export subsidy is to increase the supply of an industry's exports on the world market, which will have the impact of reducing price below that determined in a free market. Foreign consumers will enjoy an increase in their economic welfare as the price of the good falls. Those employed in the domestic market might also benefit as production increases to match demand for the lower-priced goods. They might enjoy higher wages and their jobs might be more secure but only as long as the subsidy lasts. Those who lose are the taxpayers who have to pay for the subsidy. In addition, as firms divert output to the overseas market, the supply of goods may fall in the domestic market, leading to rising prices and reduced welfare for domestic consumers.

The methods of protectionism described so far are all quite clear and obvious ways in which domestic industries can be given a competitive advantage over foreign industry in order to reduce imports and/or boost exports. Because these methods so obviously distort international market forces in pursuit of the more narrow national interest, they are all generally forbidden, except under very limiting circumstances, under the terms of international trading agreements such as the former General Agreement on Tariffs and Trade (GATT).

Protectionist policies are sometimes called *expenditure-switching* policies because their aim is clearly to switch expenditure, both domestic and foreign, to the output of goods and services of the domestic economy (see chapter 14 also).

An assessment of the arguments in favour of protectionism

International specialisation and free trade are justified because they lead to an optimal allocation of resources on a world scale and to a rise in the economic welfare of consumers. Any arguments advanced in justification of protectionist policies can only be assessed if the impact on world resource allocation and consumer welfare is considered.

It is often argued that protectionism is justified:

- *To safeguard employment in the home economy.* An examination of the UK's trade accounts over the last few years will reveal the extent to which imports of manufactured goods have increased. The import penetration ratio is the proportion of the domestic sales of a product which is taken up by imports. For example, in 1968 the import penetration ratio in textiles was 16 per cent. This means that out of every £100 spent on textiles in Britain, £16 was spent on imported textiles. By 1997 the figure had risen to 53 per cent. In the category radio, television and communications equipment, the import penetration ratio was as high as 98 per cent in 1997. As import penetration rises, domestic firms come under increasing pressure to maintain sales and the less successful will have to lay off workers and some may close down completely. This can result in considerable structural unemployment and can lead to calls for some degree of protection from imports. Very often interest groups, such as trade unions, will call for tariffs when faced with a flood of cheap imports from abroad. Any argument in favour of import controls to protect jobs can only be justified on social grounds. To maximise economic welfare, labour should be considered as a resource that must be swiftly allocated and reallocated to its best use. This process can be aided by any measures to improve the occupational and geographical mobility of labour. Looked at in this way 'a flood of cheap imports' should be welcomed as a benefit to the consumer rather than seen as a threat to jobs.

- *To correct balance of payments disequilibria.* Typical policies include raising income taxes and interest rates to prevent consumers purchasing imports. These policies were sometimes known as *expenditure-dampening policies.* In addition to preventing imports, such policies also reduce consumer spending on the output of domestic industry, so the side effect is a rise in unemployment. This results in a call for expenditure switching policies as an alternative way of protecting the balance of payments and the exchange rate.
- *To prevent the exploitation of labour in developing economies.* Very often when cheap goods are imported into a market there are claims that the goods are cheap because labour in the exporting countries is paid a very low wage. It is claimed that the labour is exploited and as a result imports should be

Self-assessment tasks

Read the newspaper editorial below and then tackle the exercises that follow.

Free trade is fair

'Fair trade, not free trade' is the banner carried by protestors outside the World Trade Organisation conference. It is code for quotas, tariffs and prohibitions. So when Britain's man in Seattle blathers approvingly about 'fair trade', it matters. By adopting the language of the protectionists, Stephen Byers, the DTI Secretary, advertised before the hard bargaining had even started that this Government will not exert leadership to defeat obscurantism. Nor will President Clinton, who is backing away from America's commitment to free trade in order to appease the rioters and their friends in the media. If the two powers that built the world's open trading system – and are still seen as its custodians, even if Britain has surrendered trade policy to the EU – do not have the gumption to face down Dyke Action and the Raging Grannies, God help us.

Free trade does not happen of its own accord. The natural condition of the world is protectionist: the gains of increased commerce are spread widely, and to some degree invisibly, while the losses are concentrated heavily in sectors that mobilise quickly for political action – as French farmers and Detroit's motor industry have shown in their time. Trade barriers are rarely reduced without a Herculean effort by far-sighted leaders, acting in concert, at grand summits like this one in Seattle. So far, it looks as if the current generation of leaders is incapable of making such an effort.

The European Union is seeking to do little more than protect its ruinous system of farm subsidies, while suggesting otherwise with disingenuous demands for a comprehensive agenda. President Clinton – already electioneering for Al Gore – has abruptly changed US trade policy in a sop to the trade unions, calling for the WTO to extend its power into the area of labour rights. Mr Clinton is making emotive noises about 'child labour', but the real issue is cheap labour, which is the one competitive advantage left to poor countries. The gambit is rightly regarded as an invidious form of rich world protectionism by most of the WTO's 134 members. If pressed, it will wreck the meeting.

It is lamentable that the governments of the world's richest countries cannot find the political will – in the easiest of conditions, at the height of a long economic boom – to uphold the system that made them so rich. The best that can now be expected from this miserable summit is a fudge that does no damage.

Source: Daily Telegraph, 3 December 1999.

1 What is meant by 'fair trade'?

2 Discuss why the EU is reluctant to reduce its quotas, tariffs and prohibitions on trade with developing economies.

prevented. This results in a call for import controls on moral grounds but also often on the grounds that firms in the importing country cannot compete with the cheap imports because they have to pay higher wages. This argument in favour of import controls is often combined with the argument that they are required in order to protect jobs. Such arguments in favour of import controls have no economic justification whatsoever. If labour is cheap in an economy this is a reflection of that economy's factor endowment. A large supply of unskilled labour will lead to low wages and usually low priced products. The law of comparative advantage suggests that this will lead to increased economic welfare as those economies with cheap labour specialise in those products in which they have the lowest opportunity costs. This will be in those products which are highly labour intensive. It should be noted that there may well be moral arguments to justify protectionism in this case, but it should also be considered that any measures which reduce imports from such countries are likely to make the problem of low wages worse. This is because any fall in demand for imports from such economies will reduce the demand for labour further and make wage rates fall even lower.

- *To prevent dumping.*
  Dumping is a term in economics which describes the process of selling goods in an overseas market at a price below the cost of production. This is a form of price discrimination because consumers in the home market will pay a higher price than those in the overseas market. The purpose of dumping might be to destroy existing competition in the overseas market or to prevent new firms in the overseas market from becoming established. Dumping can be achieved through export subsidies provided by the home government or through ensuring that consumers in the home market pay a sufficiently high price to cover total costs. Alternatively, firms might be prepared to suffer losses in the short term if this allows them to destroy competition and create a monopoly, increasing excess profits in the long term. Clearly, if dumping leads to anti-competitive behaviour in the long run and prevents the emergence of comparative advantage, then import controls on products dumped in a market can be justified. It should be noted, however, that firms which face competition through cheap imports will often claim that goods are being dumped, when in reality the low prices of such goods are merely a reflection of the greater efficiency of the exporting firm. Whether a good is truly being dumped on a market needs careful investigation before import controls can be justified.
- *To safeguard infant industries.*
  As shifts in comparative advantage occur, conditions for the location of industries in particular economies can become favourable. Establishing a fledgling industry can be quite difficult in the early years, however, especially if the new industry faces competition from a long-established company. The **infant industry** with only a small part of the market will not be able to benefit from all potential economies of scale and will be unable to compete in the market. It will be in the interests of the established firm to try to drive the new industry out of business and it might cut prices fiercely to retain its market. If the infant industry does have the potential to develop into an efficient producer in line with comparative advantage, then import controls may well be justified in this case. It should be noted, however, that many industries call for protection in their fledgling state but they then develop a vested interest in maintaining this protection once they have become established. Interest groups develop to lobby politicians to prevent import controls from being removed.

The terms of trade

The simple principles of international trade explained above assume that the exchange rate that operates for such transactions lies somewhere between the respective domestic opportunity cost ratios. In practice, this exchange rate is referred to as the **terms of trade** or commodity terms of trade in the case of countries that are primarily exporters of primary commodities. It measures the rate at which one country can exchange its goods for those from other countries.

Arithmetically the terms of trade, expressed in index form, can be calculated for a single year or over a period of time by means of the following formula:

$$\text{Terms of trade index} = \frac{\text{Index of export prices}}{\text{Index of import prices}} \times 100\%$$

In practice, calculating the terms of trade for a particular economy is a difficult task since the index has to take into account the average prices of all commodities and goods that are exported and imported. These prices are then weighted by the relative importance of each item, usually on a value basis. So, the more complex and developed the economy, the more difficult it is to make an accurate estimate.

Official statistics show the terms of trade as a single index in relation to a base year of 100. So, if in one year after this base year the terms of trade index is 102.6, this means that on average the country concerned is receiving relatively better prices for its exports than it is having to pay for its imports. In this situation, it is said that the terms of trade have improved. On the other hand, if the terms of trade index had fallen to 98.4, this means that the country was having to pay relatively more for its imports than it was receiving for its exports. Here, the terms of trade are said to have deteriorated.

Relatively minor annual changes are not particularly significant. On a longer-term basis though the time trend is very important and can have a marked impact on the economy. Globally, the main trends over the last decade or so have been:

- a progressive deterioration in the terms of trade for primary exporting countries,
- some volatility in the terms of trade for fuel exporters but a substantial improvement since 1999,
- minor changes for most developed economies, mainly as a consequence of changes in the price of imported items, notably fuel. The general trend though has been one of improvement.

Table 17.5 shows the terms of trade indexes for selected countries in Latin America from 1995 to 2004. For Chile, there was a large favourable increase in its terms of trade from 2003 to 2004 due to an increase in the world prices of copper and copper ores, the country's principal exports. In the case of Argentina, fuel exports account for the recent improvement in its terms of trade. Elsewhere, and for other countries not shown in table 17.5, the terms of trade have deteriorated due entirely to the fall in typical commodity prices for agricultural goods. Although reliable data are not available, this is also true for all Caribbean agricultural exporting countries. For Trinidad and Tobago, an exporter of petroleum products and natural gas, the terms of trade will have improved due to large price increases since 2003. The same is true for Barbados with respect to its exports of aluminium. Some benefit from rising commodity prices will have been lost through the increased prices for manufactured imports. A crude indication of these price trends is shown in table 17.6 for selected typical Caribbean export products.

Country	1995	2000	2001	2002	2003	2004
Argentina	96.0	100	99.3	98.7	107.2	109.2
Brazil	107.6	100	99.6	98.4	97.0	97.9
Chile	102.1	100	93.3	97.2	102.8	124.9
Costa Rica	103.1	100	98.4	96.9	95.5	91.9
Ecuador	72.7	100	84.6	86.8	89.8	91.5
Mexico	83.1	100	97.4	97.9	98.8	101.6
Latin America Area	89.7	100	96.3	96.6	98.7	104.0

Table 17.5 Terms of trade index, 1995–2004 (2000 = 100)
Source: Annual statistics of Latin America and the Caribbean, CEPAL, 2005.

Product	1995	2000	2001	2002	2003	2004
Bananas	104.7	100	138.8	125.5	89.4	125.1
Sugar	162.4	100	105.6	84.2	86.7	87.6
Coffee	154.3	100	70.4	63.6	65.6	82.0
Aluminium	116.6	100	93.2	87.1	92.4	110.7
Crude Oil	61.1	100	77.3	85.9	102.5	127.9
Natural Gas	40.0	100	91.8	77.9	127.2	136.8

Table 17.6 Price indexes for export commodities, 1995–2004 (2000 = 100)
Source: Annual Statistics of Latin America and the Caribbean, CEPAL, 2005.

In 2004 a World Bank study on the Caribbean area made it clear that for the region as a whole, in some years the annual increase in GDP was being sacrificed due to a deterioration in the terms of trade. The general findings are shown in table 17.7.

	2001	2002	2003	2004[1]	2005[1]
GDP growth rate in Caribbean area	3.1	3.0	0.9	2.4	4.1
Terms of trade/ GDP growth rate	−0.2	0.1	−0.4	0.1	−0.7

Note : [1] – forecast

Table 17.7 GDP growth and the terms of trade, 2001–2005
Source: Perry G. for World Bank, 2004.

Self-assessment tasks

1. Discuss the case for Caribbean economies increasing protection on imports of manufactured goods such as mobile phones and television.
2. How might this case differ if protection increased on agricultural products.

Summary

In this chapter it has been shown that:

- Exports produce a positive income stream for an economy; in contrast imports benefit the economies of the countries that produce them.
- The determinants of demand for exports and imports consist of a range of price and non-price factors.
- The gains from trade can be explained through the principles of absolute and comparative advantage; trade produces a more efficient allocation of resources since total production has increased compared with a no trade situation.
- These arguments underpin the quest for reducing the barriers to free trade in the global economy.
- Economies, developed as well as developing, continue to apply various methods of trade protection.
- The terms of trade is an index of the ratio of export prices to import prices.

Key words

Definitions of Key words can be found in the Glossary.

absolute advantage
comparative advantage
dumping
exchange controls
exports
imports
infant industry
protectionist policies
quota
tariff

18 Economic integration

This chapter covers unit 2, module 3, topic 3.
On completion of this chapter, you should be able to:

- define a free trade area, customs union, common market and economic union
- identify the costs and benefits of economic integration
- outline the objectives of Caribbean integration
- analyse the implications of integration arrangements such as FTAA and EU for Caribbean economies

Meaning of economic integration and types of integration arrangements

Despite the work of the WTO, the structure of international trade in the twenty-first century is such that the benefits are being realised, not so much on a global scale, but through the increasing role of 'regional' trading blocs. Much of world trade takes place within these blocs, although the WTO continues to press for greater exchange between the blocs and developing countries.

There are four main organisations. These are:

- The European Union (EU) – 27 member states in Western Europe and recently enlarged through the accession of countries in Central and Eastern Europe.
- The North American Free Trade Agreement (NAFTA) – this includes the USA, Canada and Mexico.
- Latin America Free Trade Area (LAFTA) – 20 various members in Central and South America.
- The association of South East Asian Nations (ASEAN) – principally Australia, New Zealand, China, Hong Kong, Japan, Taiwan and South Korea plus NAFTA members.

Geographically, the most recent development has been the participation of the powerful NAFTA countries in the FTAA and APEC organisations. The latter especially provides a substantial counterveiling force to the EU, the world's largest trading bloc with an internal market of 470 million consumers.

The process by which these trading blocs have been established is referred to as **economic integration**. It refers to deliberate ways in which national economies agree to merge their economic affairs into a single economic organisation. Consequently, there is a 'blurring' of their boundaries as their economies become more closely linked to each other. Table 18.1 shows the four main forms of organisation.

More specifically, the four main forms of organisation are:

- **Free trade area** – the loosest form of organisation involving the systematic removal of trade restrictions between members. In practice, this may be for just a selected range of commodity types, such as manufactured goods. The sensitive nature of trade in agricultural goods has meant that they have been either excluded or partially excluded from all groups except for EU internal trade.
- **Customs union** – the crucial feature is that members agree to erect a common external tariff on trade with non-members. This tariff may be on all trade or, as is the case with the EU, mainly on imported goods that member states are able to adequately produce themselves. Agriculture has always been a very sensitive issue in the EU, with policy being to very clearly protect the interests of EU member states. Consequently, developing countries are highly critical of this policy, despite preferential access for the agricultural products from some such countries.
- **Common market** – the free movement of factors of production, which allows workers and businesses to move between members, is necessary for there to be a common market. In the case of the EU, the move to the Single European Market

Type of organisation	Characteristics	Comments
Free trade area	Removal of tariffs and quotas on internal trade (some or all product types).	Members are free to determine their own external trade policies towards non-members. NAFTA, FTAA and APEC are at this stage.
Customs union	As above but with agreement on a common external tariff on trade with non-members.	Protective of members in so far as some trade is diverted from outside to within the customs union. Southern African Customs Union is only pure example.
Common market	Removal of restrictions on movement of labour and capital between member states; removal of non-tariff barriers that hinder trade; some common policies.	Seeks to make the internal market more competitive and therefore leads to benefits for members. CARICOM, COMESA and CACM are good examples.
Economic union	As above but with more centralised control over economic policies.	EU now has single currency and common interest rate for 12 members. Only real example.

Table 18.1 Main forms of economic integration

was a difficult one, involving the removal of hundreds of non-tariff barriers. There must also be at least one common policy for a common market to be recognised.

- **Economic union** – as the name implies, macroeconomic policy harmonisation and co-ordination are required with the subsequent loss of economic sovereignty that is involved. In its strongest form, there is a single currency and exchange rate as is the case with the eurozone.

The costs and benefits of economic integration

In assessing the costs and benefits of economic integration, it is necessary to ascertain the type of organisation that is being considered. In the case of a free trade area the benefits are broadly those that were recognised when discussing the principles of absolute and comparative advantage. The costs are largely in terms of a loss of productive capacity and employment in sectors of the economy where a country has a relative disadvantage.

The position with a customs union is more complex and involves the concepts of **trade creation** and **trade diversion.**

Trade creation refers to the way in which high cost domestic production of a good or commodity is replaced by imported products that are from a more efficient source within the customs union. The effect therefore is that countries in the customs union engage in more trade with each other. In the case of the UK, this has meant that an increasing range of manufactured goods and agricultural products have been imported from lower cost producers in the rest of the EU. The cost has been one of a loss of business for many UK firms and considerable unemployment. From a wider perspective though, UK consumers are better off since the products will be available at a lower price, increasing consumer surplus. Overall there has been a net efficiency gain for the economy and, hence, an increase in economic welfare.

Trade diversion is rather different. This occurs when membership of a customs union causes trade to be diverted from a low-cost supplier outside the customs union to within. The cause of this is the effect of the external tariff, which makes imported products far more expensive within the customs union. This aspect of customs union theory is particularly controversial in the case of the UK, whereby now higher cost food and agricultural products have been replaced by products from within the customs union. The most recent geographical enlargement of the EU, for example, has opened up the UK's market to low-cost producers from Poland and other central European countries.

Figure 18.1 shows this effect in theoretical terms. Prior to joining the customs union, the average world price for food products was P_w. At this price, domestic demand was Q_{dd} and a small amount, Q_{ds}, was supplied by domestic producers. On joining the customs union, the common external tariff on food products raises the price that has to be paid by domestic consumers to P_t. This results in a fall in domestic demand, depending on the price elasticity of demand. There is also an increase in supply from previously higher-cost producers based within the customs union. Although there is revenue from the tariff (see box *T*), there is a loss of consumer welfare. This is represented by the two deadweight loss triangles.

Trade creation and trade diversion are sometimes referred to as the **static effects** of a customs union. The overall effect depends upon their relative strength. Most empirical studies show that the gain in consumer welfare from trade creation exceeds the loss in consumer welfare from trade diversion, usually by a factor of up to 4:1 for the customs union as a whole. For individual member states the extent of the gain or loss is dependent upon their general pattern of trade.

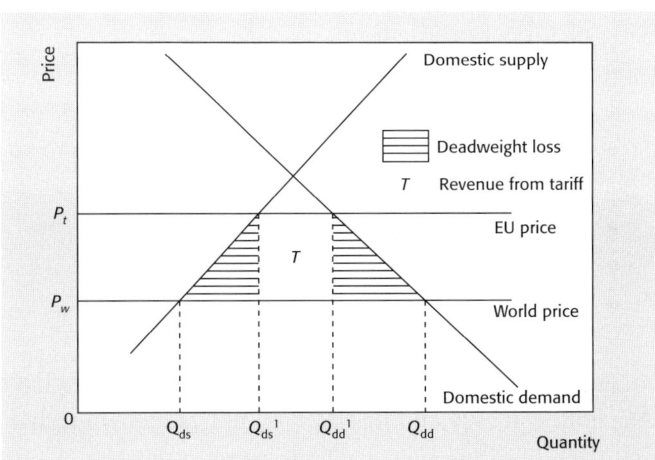

Figure 18.1 The impact of imposing an import tariff

Other important consequences occur as a result of the formation of a customs union. These take place over a longer period of time and are referred to as **dynamic effects**. These include:

- *Economies of scale and the reorganisation of productive capacity.* The removal of trade restrictions expands the size of the internal market providing more opportunities for firms to expand their scale of operations. A likely consequence could be the nationalisation of production and its concentration on a single site.
- *An increase in competition and less threat of monopoly power.* The enlarged market creates a more competitive business environment, making it more difficult for monopolies to abuse their power, particularly if there is an agreed competition policy in place.
- *A change in economic potential.* This is more of a cost than a benefit in so far as business locations in the geographical core of a customs union tend to be preferred locations, particularly for FDI (see later). In contrast, peripheral areas invariably lose out due to their higher costs.
- *Abuse of market power.* This is another cost and can arise where producers within a customs union agree to collude, for example, on prices. Although illegal, price-fixing cartels could be established, resulting in a loss of consumer welfare.

Finally, in a common market, there are effects that are a consequence of **factor market integration**. These effects provide both benefits and costs arising from the free movement of labour and firms.

For labour, the common market provides opportunities for workers to move freely between member states. In the EU, for example, the most recent geographical enlargement to include new member states in Central and Eastern Europe has led to large numbers of workers migrating to richer countries in search of work. Since May 2004, over 160,000 Polish workers have left home – around 50,000 have moved to the UK. The benefit to the UK economy is that these workers have filled a 'skills gap' or labour shortage for builders, plumbers, electricians, truck drivers, pharmacists, nurses and dentists. Unskilled workers have also migrated. The costs to their home economy though should not be overlooked, not least as they represent a serious drain on productive capacity. For CARICOM countries, the most

Polish job-seekers line up to enter a job fair in Warsaw, Poland, where they hope to find work in Ireland
Source: Czarek Sokolowski/AP/PA Photos.

likely migration is for workers to move from poorer member states to where there are employment opportunities in the extractive industries and tourism or from rural areas to the capital cities in search of work.

For capital, the common market results in businesses being free to rationalise and expand their operations. In the EU, this has resulted in manufacturers such as vehicle producers and food processing companies as well as retailers and logistics providers becoming pan-European organisations. A particular benefit is that they can obtain economies of scale and source more cheaply in the expanded market. Strategically, such moves allow European companies to remain competitive in the wider global market. The cost is that rationalisation negatively affects the well-being of manufacturing in the less attractive regions of the EU.

CARICOM

CARICOM, the Caribbean Community, was established by the Treaty of Chaguaramas in 1973. Initially, there were four members, Barbados, Jamaica, Guyana and Trinidad and Tobago. CARICOM replaced the former Caribbean Free Trade Association. Eight further members joined in 1974. At present, there are 15 full members and five associate members (see figure 18.2), although not all have signed up to the CARICOM Single Market Economy (CSME) treaty that was ratified in 2006.

The original objectives of CARICOM were:

- to improve standards of living and work;
- to achieve full employment of labour and other factors of production;
- to accelerate, co-ordinate and sustain economic development and convergence;
- to expand trade and economic relations with third party states;
- to enhance international competitiveness;
- to increase production and productivity;
- to enhance co-ordination in the foreign and foreign economic policies of member states.

As with the EU, the realisation of the above objectives has not been easy and has been complicated by internal political divisions and problems surrounding the controversial membership of Haiti. In 2006, after initial

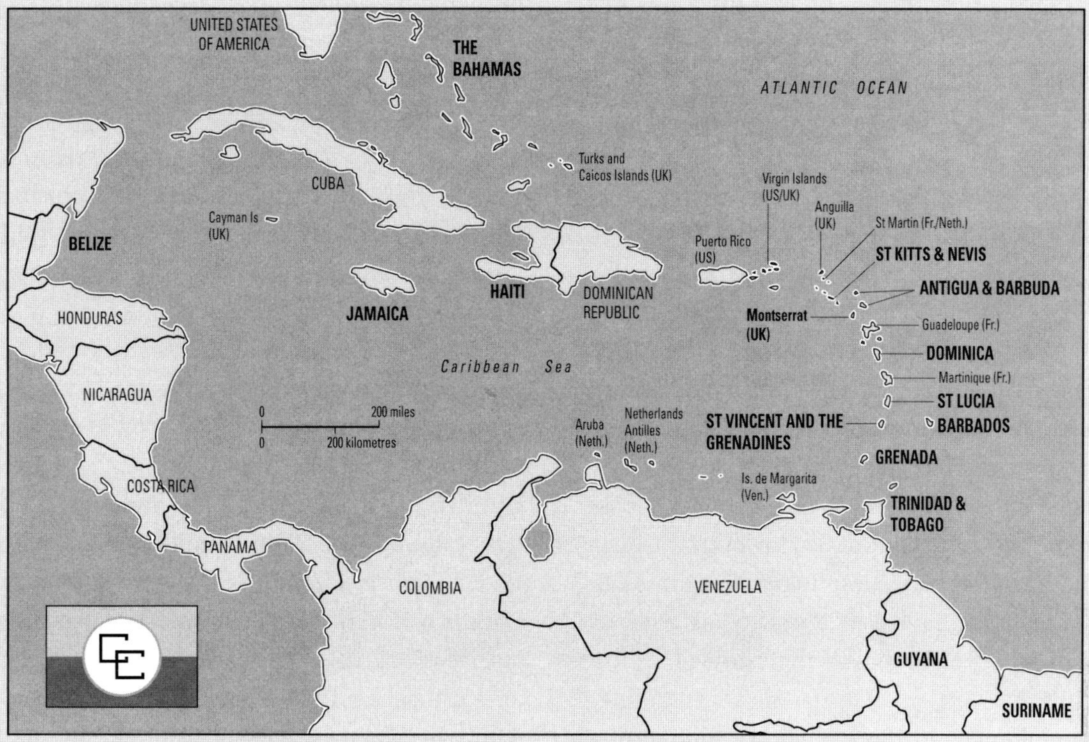

Full members:

Antigua and Barbada	Dominica	Jamaica	Saint Vincent & the Grenadines
The Bahamas	Grenada	Montserrat	Suriname
Barbados	Guyana	Saint Kitts & Nevis	Trinidad & Tobago
Belize	Haiti	Saint Lucia	

Figure 18.2 CARICOM, the Caribbean Community

legislative difficulties, the new CSME treaty finally came into effect. The initial signatories were the three largest economies, Barbados, Jamaica and Trinidad and Tobago, plus Belize, Guyana and Suriname. A little later, Antigua and Barbuda, Dominica, Grenada, St Kitts and Nevis, St Lucia and St Vincent and the Grenadines became full members. The CSME is designed to accelerate and deepen integration between member states. The objectives remain similar to those from 1973 but the features of CSME clearly indicate that functionally it really is a common market. The key elements are:

- free movement of goods and services, through eliminating non-tariff barriers that hinder intra-regional trade;
- a common external tariff;
- to permit CARICOM-owned businesses to set up anywhere in the CSME without restrictions;
- free movement of capital – various measures will be needed for this to happen;
- free movement of labour – various measures to ease the flow;
- a common trade policy relating to internal and external trade.

As with the EU and the realisation of the Single European Market, with CARICOM, the moves to set up the CSME were largely prompted by a feeling of frustration that more could be achieved though the greater integration of Caribbean economies. This is happening but it is a long-haul process. It is also likely to be a difficult process as not all economic benefits will necessarily apply to Caribbean economies in the same way that they have applied to the developed economies of say the EU.

Caribbean economies and the EU and the FTAA

Over the years, the EU has given preferential access into its market for a range of agricultural products, raw materials and a limited range of manufactured goods from the African, Caribbean and Pacific (ACP) group of developing economies. This agreement, under various Lomé Conventions and the current Cotonou Agreement, has also provided special forms of aid and technical assistance.

Typical products include cocoa, coffee, bananas, wood, iron ore, sisal, cotton, rubber and tea. Most of these are products that the EU is unable to produce for itself for climate reasons. It is a further feature of the ACP strategy that the EU does not require preferential access for its own exports into ACP markets. This leaves Caribbean economies (say) free to get the best deals available on world markets.

Superficially, this might seem to be a good arrangement for the ACP countries. However, various criticisms can be made. First, despite preferential access, the export performance of the ACP group has been disappointing. Table 18.2 indicates that the ACP group's share of EU trade is very small. It has also been falling. Secondly, developing countries outside the ACP group such as India, Bangladesh and Pakistan and many countries in North Africa and Central America, are not given preferential access. Most are poorer than the ACP group and can claim with some justification that the EU's policy is discriminative.

As well as trade, the EU has provided substantial community aid assistance to ACP countries for a wide range of structural and infrastructure programmes. Jamaica, for example, has received grant aid to improve the competitiveness of its banana producing industry. The EU is currently supporting a range of infrastructure projects, trade promotion programmes and various human development initiatives. In St Vincent and the Grenadines, EU support has been received for projects to develop tourism, improve youth training and to provide assistance for small businesses.

CARICOM's relationship with the Free Trade Area of the Americas (**FTAA**) is much more problematic. The FTAA is a proposed agreement to remove trade barriers among all countries in the American continents (except for Cuba, Venezuela and Bolivia). As such it is a geographical extension of the North American Free Trade Agreement involving the USA, Canada and Mexico.

At present, although bilateral trade agreements are operating between CARICOM members and other countries in the Americas, discussions to form a FTAA have faltered. The main stumbling block has been the issue of subsidies and free trade in agricultural goods. On the one hand, the USA especially wishes to continue to give subsidies to its farmers to produce a range of agricultural goods. The poorer developing economies, led by Brazil, insist that this is unfair and uncompetitive and restricts their ability to trade in products for which they have a comparative advantage. Freeing trade in manufactured goods is less of an issue, although poorer countries fear that their economies will be swamped by tariff-free imports from the USA and emerging manufacturing countries.

The proposed FTAA also has political critics, notably in Venezuela, where it is seen as an attempt by the USA to exert its economic influence to exploit Latin America. Other moderate politicians, particularly in Brazil, are willing to lend support provided the US eliminates the subsidies it gives to agriculture. CARICOM's position is that it remains concerned about the present position and the extent to which FTAA is becoming increasingly marginalised. At the same time, MERCOSUR, the South American common market, is proactive in wanting to consolidate its trade relations with the Caribbean Community. In turn, CARICOM are openly considering free trade agreements with Venezuela and Cuba.

Product group	% imports into EU	% share of EU total imports	% exports from EU	% share of EU total exports
Mineral fuels	26.4	4.1	5.6	5.3
Food & live animals	24.4	13.3	10.8	8.5
Manufactured goods	16.7	4.4	11.7	2.5
Crude materials	11.9	8.0	1.6	2.5
Machinery & transport equipment	8.6	0.7	45.0	2.7
Beverages & tobacco	2.4	12.1	2.6	4.6
Other	8.3	2.0	20.5	2.0
TOTAL	100	2.8	100	2.7

Table 18.2 EU trade with ACP countries in 2004
Source: Eurostat (DG Trade), 2006.

Self-assessment task

The following question was set in the 2006 CAPE examinations.

1 (a) Using appropriate examples, explain EACH of the following terms:
- free-trade area,
- customs union,
- common market. (12 marks)

(b) Describe, briefly, EACH of the following:
- CARICOM,
- CSME,
- FTAA. (9 marks)

(c) Outline THREE objectives of Caribbean integration. (9 marks)

(d) Discuss FOUR advantages to CARICOM member states arising from the free movement of factors of production – goods, services, capital and people – under the CSME. (20 marks)

(Total 50 marks)

Summary

In this chapter it has been shown that:
- The characteristics of a free trade area, customs union, common market and economic union differ.
- There is trade creation and trade diversion within the context of a customs union or higher type of integrated organisation.
- The costs and benefits of economic integration from a dynamic standpoint.
- The objectives of CARICOM and the economic logic that underpins it.
- Caribbean economies interact with the EU.
- There have been difficulties in trying to set up the FTAA.

Key words

Definitions of Key words can be found in the Glossary.

CARICOM
common market
customs union
dynamic effects
economic integration
economic union
factor market integration
free trade area
FTAA
static effects
trade creation
trade diversion

19 Balance of payments

This chapter covers unit 2, module 3, topic 4.
On completion of this chapter, you should be able to:

- define the balance of payments
- distinguish between the current account and the capital account
- describe balance of payments accounting principles
- analyse the causes and consequences of balance of payments disequilibria
- outline the policy measures for correcting balance of payments disequilibria

Introduction

Basic aspects of the balance of payments were introduced in chapter 9. It is a good idea for you to remind yourself of these before starting this chapter where the emphasis will be on the causes and consequences of disequilibria in the balance of payments and the policy response from governments in such situations.

For the purpose of the balance of payments:

- **Credits** are receipts from abroad. They represent an inflow of foreign currency into an economy and add to foreign currency reserves.
- **Debits** represent outflows of money abroad. These involve payments in a foreign currency and decrease the foreign currency reserves of a country.

Table 19.1 gives typical credits and debits for Caribbean economies.

Table 19.2 provides a summary of the current accounts of the balance of payments for CARICOM members in 2004. As this indicates, 11 out of the 14 members shown (Haiti is excepted) have deficits on their merchandise trade. In other words, the value of their imports of goods and services is greater than the value of such exports. The countries in credit owe this to their exports of minerals and energy products. In contrast, all except Montserrat and Suriname had surpluses on the service section of the current account. More specifically the net receipts from the travel account, which includes international tourism receipts, were in credit for all except Guyana. Although some part of the deficits on merchandise trade is to pay for imports for the tourist industry, this table provides overwhelming proof of the economic significance of international tourism for the well being of the whole of the CARICOM area. This benefit cannot be understated.

Credits (+)	Debits (-)
◆ Exports of agricultural commodities, minerals and energy products ◆ Investment by foreign multinationals in all sectors of the economy ◆ Receipts from international tourism ◆ International aid ◆ Private transfers from Caribbean residents abroad.	◆ Imports of consumer goods and producer goods, including energy ◆ Profits distributed by foreign multinationals abroad ◆ Payments made for travel on foreign airlines.

Table 19.1 Typical credits and debits for Caribbean economies

Country	Balance of Merchandise trade	Balance of Services	of which	Travel Account
Antigua & Barbuda	−323.6	277.1		300.2
Bahamas	−1,427.5	1,011.0		1,568.9
Barbados	−999.9	668.2		667.8
Belize	787.7	85.8		91.8
Dominica	−84.9	41.2		51.5
Grenada	−201.9	63.0		74.1
Guyana	−14.1	8.1		−3.3
Jamaica	−1,944.6	571.7		1,151.5
Montserrat	−20.5	−8.3		7.1
St Kitts/Nevis	−118.0	53.0		93.7
St Lucia	−275.5	214.4		288.8
St Vincent & the Grenadines	−159.7	72.0		81.3
Suriname	42.1	−129.7		2.6
Trinidad & Tobago	1,508.7	479.5		245.6
CARICOM	−3,231.6	3,407.1		4,621.5

Note: The value of transport services, commercial services and government services are also included in the balance of services.

Table 19.2 Summary of current account of the balance of payments for CARICOM member states, 2004 (US$m)
Source: CARICOM.

Balance of payments problems

Introduction

The structure of the balance of payments was outlined in chapter 9. In principle, the overall deficits and surpluses for any economy should balance – this is a function of the way in which the accounts are drawn up and how the inclusion of a balancing item (net errors and omissions) produces an outcome which is seemingly in equilibrium. The same is true on an international scale. A surplus on the balance of payments for one country for example, is offset by a deficit or deficits elsewhere. So, if this is the case, why are economists concerned about balance of payments problems?

In order to answer this question it is necessary to distinguish between equilibrium and disequilibrium in the balance of payments. In this context, equilibrium has a rather different meaning to the way the term was introduced in unit 1. Here, equilibrium refers to a situation where manageable deficits are cancelled out by modest surpluses over a period of time. Under such circumstances there is no particular tendency for the exchange rate to change (see below). So, on a short-term basis it does *not* necessarily mean that a deficit is bad and a surplus is good.

Two situations of equilibrium might be:

1 *Where the imports of goods and services exceeds exports but where this is offset by an inflow of foreign direct investment.* In other words, a current account deficit is counterbalanced by a financial account surplus. The UK economy is a good example of this.
2 *Where the exports of goods and services exceed imports but where there is substantial investment abroad by companies and residents.* Here, a current account surplus is recorded, but matched by a deficit on the financial account.

It is difficult to put a time period on this – the crucial thing is not to look at the balance of payments of an economy on a one year only basis.

Disequilibrium occurs when, over a particular period of time, a country is recording persistent deficits or surpluses in its balance of payments. As a consequence, it has to be recognised that the exchange rate is either overvalued or undervalued on the foreign exchange market. In such situations, particularly in the case of a deficit, corrective action is required in order to prevent the economy draining its foreign currency reserves or ending hopelessly in debt (see figure 19.1 below).

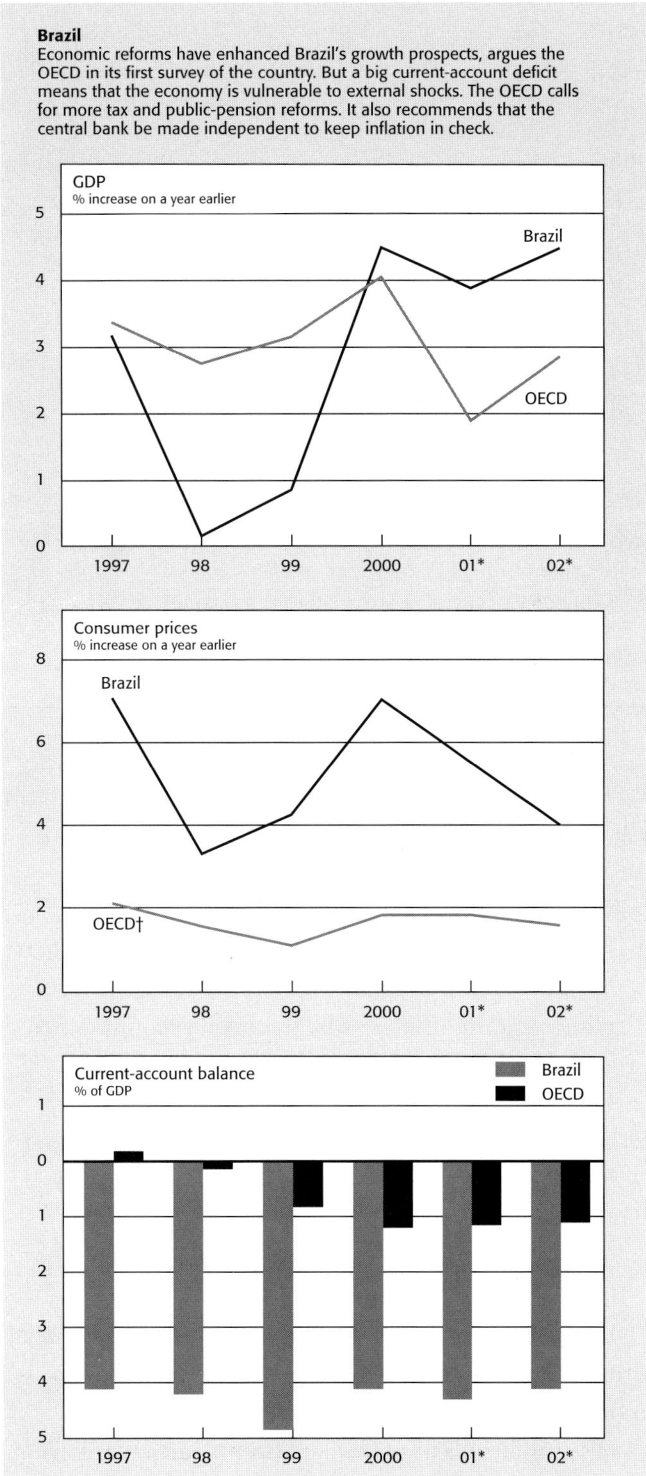

Figure 19.1 *Forecast. †Private-consumption deflator, excluding Hungary, Mexico, Poland and Turkey
Sources: OECD.
The Economist, 17 June 2001 (adapted).

The problem of debt was described in chapter 15. The significance for the balance of payments of many developing economies is that large sums of capital were borrowed from commercial banks in the 1970s and early 1980s to fund development projects from which it was expected future income streams would be generated. Many such projects have turned out to be very poor investments; in other cases the money has been spent on other things or has been used corruptly by recipients. The legacy is one of chronic balance of payments deficits. The problem for many countries is that a very substantial part of their export earnings has to be paid annually in order to service this debt.

With this in mind, disequilibrium in the balance of payments can arise where:

1. The imports of goods and services exceed exports and the financial account is in deficit.
2. Exports of goods and services may just exceed imports but there is a persistent deficit on the financial account.
3. Exceptionally, there is a large surplus on the current account, generating an overall balance of payments surplus. A pertinent example of an economy in this situation for many years has been the case of Japan.

Current account contrasts in emerging economies

Some of the largest South East Asian economies are still running big trade surpluses. For example, in the year to May 2001, China's surplus was \$21.1bn, South Korea's \$15bn and Taiwan's \$11.4bn. All had similar surpluses on the current account of their balance of payments (see table 19.3).

	Trade balance (\$bn)	Current account (\$bn)
China	+21.1	+20.5
Hong Kong	−11.9	+8.8
Indonesia	+26.1	+5.5
Malaysia	+15.6	+8.4
Philippines	+7.3	+9.5
Singapore	+4.2	+21.8
South Korea	+15.0	+14.0
Taiwan	+11.4	+12.0
Thailand	+3.1	+6.9

Table 19.3 Current account contrasts in SE Asia, 2000–2001

In contrast, emerging economies in central and South America and in cental Europe (Venezuela and Russia excepted) had worrying deficits on both (see table 19.4).

The particular case of Brazil (figure 19.1) clearly shows the economic problems that can result from persistent trade and current account deficits.

	Trade balance ($bn)	Current account ($bn)
Argentina	+1.6	−9.4
Brazil	+34.7	−26.6
Mexico	−9.5	−17.8
Venezuela	+17.5	+12.5
Czech Republic	−3.6	−2.7
Hungary	−2.4	−1.7
Poland	−10.0	−8.8
Russia	+60.7	+45.9

Table 19.4 Current account contrasts in emerging economies, 2000–2001

Causes of balance of payments disequilibrium

Let us assume that the disequilibrium is that referred to above in the first two situations. This type of problem can be experienced by all types of economies. Three main causes of the disequilibrium can be identified. They are:

1 The economy has a high propensity to import goods. Consequently, substantial deficits are recorded annually on the trading account. The UK is typical – the balance of trade in goods for all recent years except for 1997 has been in deficit, particularly with respect to trade with the rest of the EU. UK citizens like to purchase imported cars, clothing, footwear, food, drink, electrical goods and so on, even though all of these items can be produced in the UK. The perception of many people is that 'British is not best'. There are similar problems in developing economies. The cause though is different – such countries have very limited domestic production and have to rely on imported goods for much of their consumer demand. As far as exports are concerned, developing economies often rely heavily for their export revenue on sales of primary products on world markets. As shown in chapter 17, the terms of trade are often unfavourable, meaning that they have to continually export a greater volume of goods for the same export revenue. It is therefore easy to see why many have trading deficits on their trading accounts.

2 There may be lack of confidence in a particular economy, resulting in few capital inflows. There may even be a situation of an exodus of capital from the economy. The determinants of the level of confidence are very difficult to explain in simple terms. It is a complex phenomenon related to the macroeconomic variables referred to in chapter 9, often set within a political context. Confidence may also be severely affected by one particular event, again often of a political rather than of an economic origin, and this may well deter foreign investors.

3 From a shorter-term standpoint, a period of expansion in the macroeconomy, leading to increased consumer spending power, could produce a situation where much of this is spent on imported rather than locally produced goods. Imports are therefore 'sucked in' to the economy, with potentially serious problems for the overall balance of payments.

Self-assessment task

Using data you have collected, decide whether the balance of payments of your country is in equilibrium or disequilibrium. Can you explain why this is so?

Cosmopolitan Singapore offers superb eating as well as world-class shopping

Consequences of balance of payments disequilibrium

There are consequences of disequilibrium in the balance of payments for

- the domestic economy,
- the external economy.

For the domestic economy, the consequence is that there will be a pressing need for corrective action (see below). This need will be evidenced through a domestic economy which is characterised as having a very narrow type of economic structure and still heavily dependent on agriculture in the case of developing countries. For the UK it is shown through the closure of many types of manufacturing firms. Vast sectors of industry have suffered de-industrialisation, so increasing the demand for imported goods. Long-term unemployment therefore is an obvious consequence.

A second domestic consequence is that because of low business confidence, foreign investors are increasingly reluctant to invest in an economy with a balance of payments disequilibrium because of the risks that are involved. Economic prospects will be uncertain and there is a likely possibility that the currency may be devalued (see below). A situation like this hardly encourages new foreign investors to invest in an economy.

A third consequence is that for consumers there is likely to be fewer stocks of certain exotic imported consumer goods (for example, perfume, designer clothes) and the general range will be restricted, often to products not produced domestically. Imports are also likely to have a higher rate of tax imposed on them in order to restrict consumption.

For the external economy, it is often the case that disequilibrium in the balance of payments will put pressure on the government to introduce or upgrade some of the methods of protection described earlier in chapter 17.

A second consequence is shown in figure 19.2. Suppose the economy starts from the disequilibrium position shown in diagram (a) where at r_1 the total demand for foreign currency exceeds the supply of foreign currency by $0Q_1 - 0Q_2$. This is a consequence of imports of goods and services exceeding exports, but with a balanced capital inflow and outflow (see diagrams (b) and (c) respectively). As will be elaborated below, the corrective action that is needed is for the exchange rate to be devalued. This results in overall equilibrium (at r_2, Q_3) in diagram (a), with a reduced current account deficit and a financial account surplus.

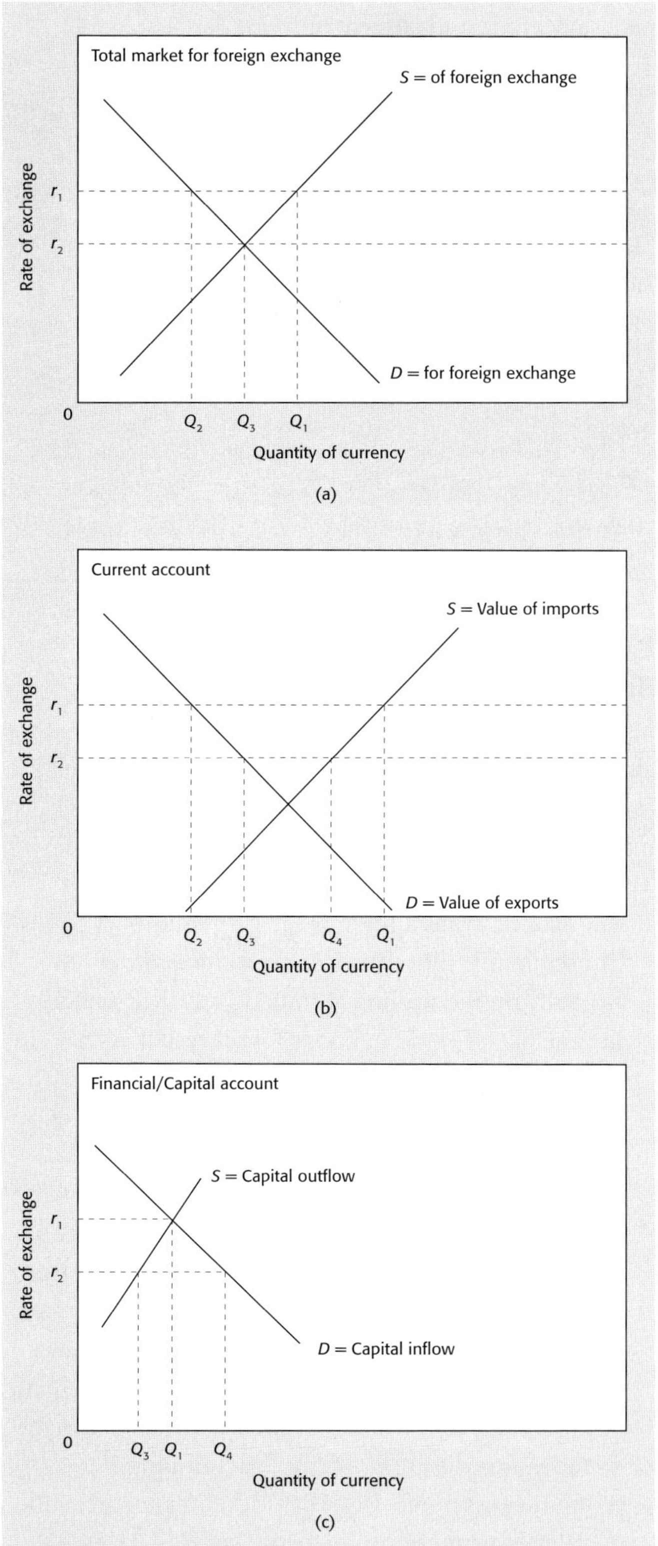

Figure 19.2 Disequilibrium and equilibrium in the balance of payments

In turn though, the consequences for the domestic economy should be recognised. For example:

- import prices will rise, in turn increasing the cost of living and fuelling cost-push inflation;
- export prices will fall – depending on the products involved, revenue may increase, as indeed will employment;
- confidence in the economy might be affected in the short term, possibly due to the fear of a further devaluation.

Policy measures for correcting balance of payments disequilibria

As will be explained in the next topic, when managed exchange rate systems are in operation, intervention in the foreign exchange market to maintain the rate must take place on a daily basis. In addition, governments will need to take remedial action to correct the balance of payments deficit which gave rise to the downward pressure on the exchange rate in the first place. This is because the automatic adjustment mechanism, which occurs in a freely floating exchange rate system, is absent when exchange rates are pegged. The exchange rate will not automatically decline to restore competitiveness. So, without adjustment to export and import prices brought about by exchange rate changes, the balance of payments deficit may well persist. Given that a country's reserves are not limitless, measures must be taken to remove the deficit or the reserves will eventually run out and the country will find it impossible to keep the exchange rate pegged at the agreed value. Policies to remove the balance of payments deficit can be categorised as follows.

Expenditure-switching policies

An expenditure-switching policy is any action taken by a government which is designed to persuade purchasers of goods and services both at home and abroad to purchase more of that country's goods and services and less of the goods and services produced by others. Effectively this would include any policies designed to persuade domestic purchasers to purchase home-produced goods and services rather than imports. It would also include any policies designed to persuade foreign purchasers to buy more exports from your economy. These policies are not designed to reduce the total amount of spending in a country but to re-direct or 'switch' spending to your country's products rather than those produced in another country. The impact should be a fall in import expenditure and a rise in export earnings. The former will lead to a fall in the supply of a country's currency on the foreign exchange market and the latter will lead to a rise in the demand for the country's currency on the market. Both will lead to upward pressure on the exchange rate.

Expenditure-switching policies include the following measures:

- tariffs,
- quotas,
- exchange controls,
- export subsidies.

These have been described in chapter 17. Along with embargoes and voluntary export restraints, all have the disadvantage that they interfere with market forces and prevent the consumer from benefiting from the effects of specialisation and trade. In addition, a government's ability to resort to expenditure-switching policies is limited by membership of the WTO (formerly the GATT). As a result they may be forced to resort to expenditure dampening policies.

Expenditure-dampening policies

An expenditure-dampening policy is any action taken by a government that is designed to reduce the total level of spending in an economy. This will have two principal effects. First, a reduction in spending will mean that there will be fewer purchases of imported goods and services. Secondly, domestic producers will find that their domestic market is 'dampened' and is more difficult to sell in. As a result they may try to make up for the decrease in sales domestically with increases in sales abroad. The overall impact therefore should be a fall in imports and a rise in exports. Expenditure dampening policies include:

- *Deflationary fiscal policy*. This means raising taxes and reducing government expenditure. Raising taxes will reduce disposable incomes meaning that less will be available to spend on imports. In addition, the reduced government spending will lead to a downward multiplier effect which will depress incomes further. The extent of the reduction in import spending will depend upon the **marginal propensity to import**. This measures the change in import spending as disposable incomes change. A high marginal propensity to import will mean that a fall in disposable incomes will have a great impact upon import spending, and taxes may not have to be raised by much to reduce import spending by the required amount. Alternatively, if the marginal propensity to import is low, it will require a large increase in taxes to bring about the necessary reduction in import spending.

- *Deflationary monetary policy.* This means raising interest rates and reducing the money supply. In addition to attracting inflows of foreign capital that will increase the demand for the currency on the foreign exchange market, increases in the rate of interest will reduce the money supply and deflate the economy. This is because the higher interest rate will reduce the demand for loans for consumption and investment and lead to a fall in aggregate monetary demand.

A major disadvantage of a managed exchange rate system is that it creates a deflationary situation when there is downward pressure on the exchange rate as a result of a balance of payments deficit. The deflationary outcome will have the intended effect of reducing spending on imports, but it will also have the additional unintended effect of reducing spending on home produced products. This means that unemployment will rise in the domestic economy.

The maintenance of a pegged rate in times of balance of payments deficit requires exchange market intervention on a daily basis together with expenditure-switching and expenditure-dampening policies with the resulting negative side effects. If the problem persists then it is clear that the deflationary pressure will cause the economy to operate at less than full capacity, with all the waste in terms of lost output that this implies. Under these circumstances there may be a case for a **devaluation** of the currency. This means that the government announces that it will peg the exchange rate at a new lower value. This has the same effect as a depreciation of the currency. It alters the relative price of imports and exports to restore competitiveness. If the economy continues to suffer from inflation however, devaluation will become increasingly frequent and the benefits of a pegged exchange rate will be lost.

Gold bullion in the vaults at the Bank of England
Source: Bank of England.

The long-term answer to the difficulties associated with a persistent balance of payments deficit is to improve the quantity and quality of goods and services produced in the economy. As a result governments have increasingly adopted supply-side policies to improve the underlying competitiveness of the economy so that persistent deficits do not arise. Only in this way can economies enjoy full employment and the full benefits of international trade. A persistent balance of payments surplus can also create difficulties for an economy but under these circumstances the pressure on the government will not be so acute. This is because the government will be selling quantities of its own currency to prevent a rise in the rate. The effect is that the country's reserves of foreign exchange will be rising. Nevertheless if an economy suffers from a persistent surplus it may choose to undertake a **revaluation** of the currency to restore long-term equilibrium to the accounts.

Self-assessment tasks

Study the article below and then tackle the exercises that follow.

America's economic weakness?

	Current account balance ($bn)	As % of GDP
1997	−155	−1.9
1998	−215	−2.5
1999	−324	−3.6
2000	−370	−4.0
2001	−380(est)	−3.8(est)

On the surface, the United States has the strongest economy in the world. While other parts have been in turmoil, investors have been happy to pour their money into the US's booming markets. As a result, the current account deficit has ballooned. In 2001 it stood at an estimated 4 per cent of GDP.

The worry is that foreign investors will be concerned that the US is using their capital to finance low savings and a consumer spending boom rather than boost investment. As a result they will start to shift their money elsewhere – the dollar should therefore fall, boost US exports and slow import growth. A weaker dollar in turn will aggravate fears of inflation and a slow down in economic growth.

1 Refer back to the description of the balance of payments. Use these terms to explain the current account deficit of the US.

2 As well as currency depreciation, what other policies could the US use to reduce the current account deficit? And with what consequences?

Self-assessment task

The following question was set in the 2005 CAPE examinations. (You may need to read part of the next chapter in order to answer question 1 (a).)

1 (a) Explain the following terms:

- currency appreciation and depreciation,
- flexible and fixed exchange rates,
- balance of payments accounts. (18 marks)

Balance of payments of country X, 2001 (All figures are in billions of dollars)	
Merchandise exports	+40
Merchandise imports	−30
Services exports	+15
Services imports	−10
Investment income	−5
Net transfers	+10
Capital inflows	+10
Capital outflows	−40
Official reserves	+10

(b) Use the information in the table above to calculate the following for Country X (show all working).
- ◆ the balance of trade, (5 marks)
- ◆ the current account balance, (5 marks)
- ◆ the capital account balance. (5 marks)

(c) Does Country X have a balance of payments deficit OR surplus? (show all working). (5 marks)

(d) Explain the meaning of the plus (+) and minus (–) signs in the balance of payments account shown in the table above. (9 marks)

(e) Suggest ONE measure a country can take to bridge a current account deficit. (3 marks)

(Total 50 marks)

Summary

In this chapter it has been shown that:

- Developing economies such as those in CARICOM have typical currency inflows and outflows in their balance of payments that differ from those in more developed economies.
- International tourism receipts provide a major source of credit in the current account for most Caribbean Community economies.
- Disequilibrium in the balance of payments occurs when a country experiences persistent deficits or surpluses over a period of time; this can occur for various reasons connected with that country's trade or its exchange rate.
- Persistent deficits can have a detrimental effect on the domestic economy and the foreign exchange rate.
- Governments can apply expenditure-switching and expenditure-dampening policies to try to overcome the disequilibrium.

Key words

Definitions of Key words can be found in the Glossary.

- credits (in balance of payments)
- debits (in balance of payments)
- devaluation
- expenditure-dampening policies
- expenditure-switching policies
- marginal propensity to import
- revaluation

20 Exchange rates

This chapter covers unit 2, module 3, topic 5.
On completion of this chapter, you should be able to:

- define exchange rates
- explain exchange rate determination
- distinguish between fixed and floating exchange rate regimes
- describe the effects of exchange rate changes

Introduction

Chapter 9 introduced various exchange rate concepts. You will find it useful to remind yourself of what an exchange rate is and what types of exchange rate are used in Economics before progressing with this chapter.

Table 9.4 in chapter 9 gave a few examples of the various exchange rates for the East Caribbean dollar, the currency that is used in Antigua and Barbuda, Dominica, Grenada, St Kitts & Nevis and St Vincent and the Grenadines. This is just one of nine domestic currencies of CARICOM member sates. In global markets, these currencies are normally expressed in terms of US dollars, as in table 9.4. For intra-CARICOM trade, though, each currency has to be expressed in terms of each other – this means that for example, on 3 December 2006, 1 East Caribbean dollar was worth 24.5211 Jamaican dollars, 2.25688 Trinidad and Tobago dollars and 0.76226 Barbados dollars. This can make internal trade rather cumbersome; it also causes headaches for US cruise ship visitors who have to convert their American dollars into different local currencies on an almost daily basis.

Faced with similar problems, in 1999, 12 member states of the EU committed to a new single currency, the euro, from January 2001. (The UK, Denmark and Sweden continue to use their own currencies.) All new member states of the EU are not given a choice – they have to sign up in principle to replace their own currencies with the euro at some future date. Also, once in, the use of the single currency cannot be reversed.

The determination of exchange rates

The buying and selling of foreign exchange takes place on the foreign exchange market. Importers of goods into the UK will use pounds to buy the currency of the country from which they are purchasing the goods. This act provides a supply of pounds on to the foreign exchange market. Similarly, those who have bought products from the UK will be using their own currencies to purchase pounds – this action creates a demand for pounds.

The foreign exchange market does not exist in a single location but is made up of banks and other financial intermediaries that buy and sell foreign currency on behalf of their private and business customers. There is a continuous flow of currency through the market on a particular day. The price of the currency or exchange rate is determined by the relative strength of the supply and demand for the currency.

So far we have considered the supply and demand for pounds which arises from the export and import of goods into the UK. There are, however, other sources of the demand for and supply of pounds on the foreign exchange market.

Figure 20.1 shows the flows of currency on to the market. These are indicative of the structure of the balance of payments (see chapter 9). These flows are generated through trade in both goods and services and in addition short- and long-term capital flows that move between economies in search of the highest returns.

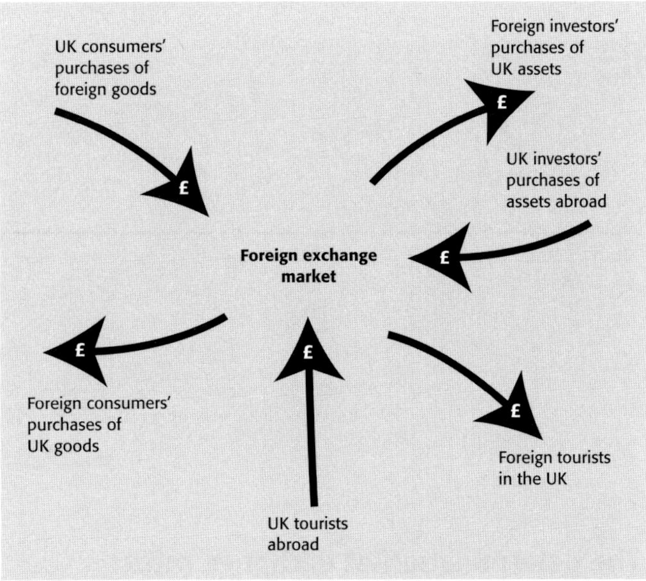

Figure 20.1 Currency flows on to the foreign exchange market

The determination of the equilibrium exchange rate in a free market

In a free market, the value of the exchange rate is determined solely by the forces of supply and demand. Figure 20.2 shows the supply and demand for pounds on the foreign exchange market. For simplicity we will illustrate this only with reference to the relationship between the pound and the dollar.

In this figure we see that the demand for pounds slopes down from left to right. This is because when the price of the pound in terms of dollars is high at P_3, then British goods and services are expensive to US consumers – they have to pay lots of dollars to gain pounds. As a result, the demand for British goods and services will be very low in the US and this means that few pounds are demanded on the foreign exchange market. As the value of the pound falls against the dollar however, US consumers can gain more pounds for their dollars and so more pounds are demanded on the foreign exchange market. The supply curve of pounds is shown to be upward sloping from left to right. This is because when the pound is very low against the dollar, for example, P_1, then US goods are very expensive in the UK. Few UK consumers will buy US goods and, as a result, few pounds will be supplied to the foreign exchange market. As the value of the pound against the dollar rises, US goods become more affordable to the UK consumers and more pounds are supplied to the market.

Now imagine that the price of the pound on the foreign exchange market is at P_3. Here the pound is overvalued because UK goods cannot sell in the US market. They are too expensive. The demand for pounds is very low but, because US goods are so cheap in the UK, British consumers are buying lots of US goods and services and supplying lots of pounds to the market. As we can see, at this exchange rate there is an excess of pounds on the market. Whenever there is an excess supply in a free market, market forces will result in a fall in price. The exchange rate of the pound will fall to an equilibrium rate at P_2 where supply equates to demand.

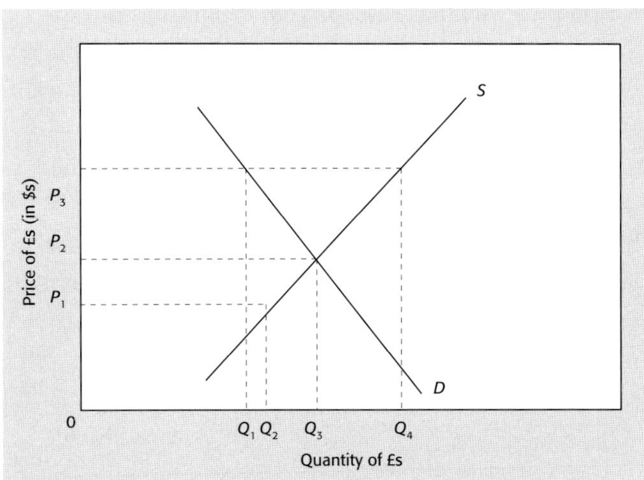

Figure 20.2 Exchange rate determination in a free market

Self-assessment tasks

1. With reference to figure 20.2 explain what would happen to the value of the pound if the rate was at P_1.
2. The explanation of exchange rate determination provided considers only the demand and supply of goods and services. Discuss whether the analysis would be different if the impact of the financial account of the balance of payments was included.

Causes of changes in the equilibrium exchange rate

Any change in supply or demand for a currency will cause a **depreciation** or **appreciation** in the exchange rate.

For illustration we will now consider the market for US dollars in terms of all other currencies.

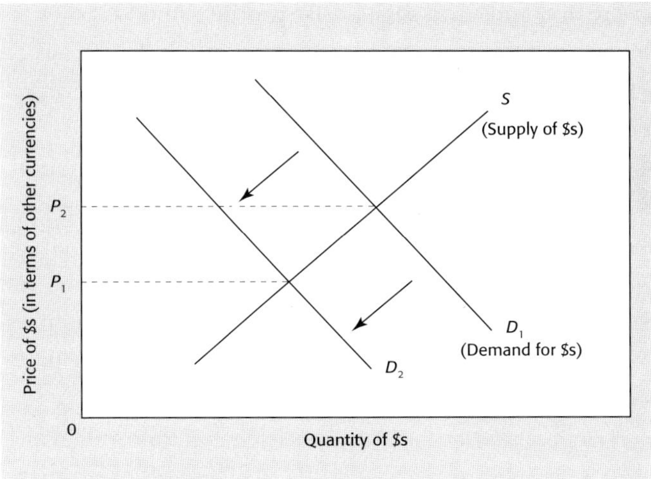

Figure 20.3 A depreciation in the dollar exchange rate

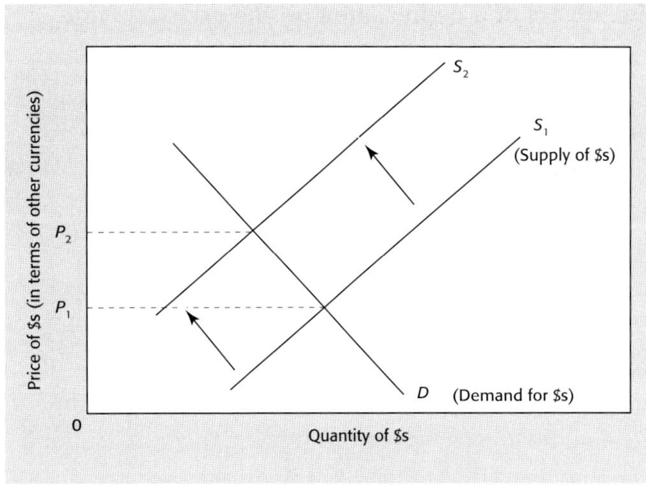

Figure 20.4 An appreciation in the dollar exchange rate

1 A depreciation in the exchange rate A depreciation in an exchange rate can occur, as shown in figure 20.3. Here there has been a fall in the demand for the dollar. This is represented by a shift of the demand curve to the left and could be caused, for example, by:

- *A reduction in the number of US goods and services sold abroad.* Importers of US goods and services are demanding fewer dollars to settle accounts with US firms. This could be caused, for example, by an increase in the price of US goods and services due to inflation or a longer-term decline in the quality of US goods and services.
- *A reduction in the number of international investors who wish to place their funds in the US economy.* This might be because interest rates in the US are lower than in other economies and, as a result, give a poorer return to investors.

2 An appreciation in the exchange rate An appreciation in the exchange rate can occur as shown in figure 20.4. Here there has been a decrease in the supply of the dollar. This is represented by a shift in the supply curve to the left and could be caused, for example, by:

- *A decrease in the number of foreign goods and services imported into the US.* US importers are using dollars to purchase foreign currency on the foreign exchange market. They provide a supply of dollars on to the market. The fall in the number of foreign goods purchased in the US could be caused by a rise in the price of foreign goods and services relative to those produced in the US, or perhaps there has been a decline in the quality of foreign goods and services.
- *A decrease in the number of US investors who want to place their funds in foreign economies.* Again, if interest rates fall abroad, then US investors will want to place their funds in US banks rather than abroad. They will now choose not to exchange their dollars for foreign currencies and the supply of dollars on the foreign exchange market will decrease.

Self-assessment task

Consider the impact of the following changes upon the value of the dollar. Provide a sketch for each change.

- a rise in interest rates in the US;
- a substantial current account deficit on the US balance of payments.

Effects of changing exchange rates on the economy

As stated earlier, if there is a change in the value of a country's currency against that of others it will change the transaction price of any goods and services which that country buys or sells in international markets.

- A fall or depreciation in the value of the exchange rate will mean that the price of imports into the country will rise and the price of the country's exports will fall.
- A rise or appreciation in the country's currency will mean the opposite, that is the price of imported goods will fall and the price of the country's exports will rise.

The impact of a depreciation on the exchange rate

As we have seen above, a balance of payments deficit will cause a depreciation in a country's currency, which will mean that import prices will rise. This will have a number of consequences. Domestic manufacturers who sell in the home market will find that their goods are now more competitive compared to imported manufacturers that have now become more expensive. They may find that there is an increase in demand for their products and they will try to expand production to meet this demand. There will be an increase in the demand for the factors of production, including labour. The impact of this will depend upon the level of employment in the economy. If there is a lot of spare capacity in the economy with lots of labour unemployed we would expect unemployment to fall. As full employment is approached however, labour becomes increasingly scarce and, as a result, we would expect labour to ask for higher wages. Because they are facing increased demand, manufacturers will be prepared to pay the higher wages and pass this on to the consumer in the form of higher prices. The extent to which cost increases can be passed on to consumers depends upon the price elasticity of demand for domestic manufactured goods. The higher the price elasticity of demand for domestically produced manufactured goods, the less domestic manufacturers will be able to raise prices. Nevertheless, we would expect some inflationary pressure because of increases in the demand for domestically produced goods when an economy's currency depreciates. Inflationary pressure will also arise from the supply side of production when a currency depreciates. This is because any imported raw materials will become more expensive when the exchange rate falls. If there are no domestic supplies of the raw material then manufacturers have no alternative but to pay the increased price if they wish to respond to the increase in domestic sales. Again they will try to pass the increase in cost on to the consumer so prices will tend to rise.

A depreciation of a country's exchange rate will also mean that its export prices will fall. This will mean that there will be an increase in the demand for that country's products in foreign markets. This in turn could be inflationary because exporting firms will be competing with other firms who are producing in a buoyant domestic market.

Despite the inflationary pressure we would expect the depreciation of the exchange rate to lead to a fall in imports and a rise in exports which will mean that the balance of payments deficit is replaced by a balance of payments surplus.

The impact of an appreciation in the exchange rate

When a country experiences a balance of payments surplus we have seen that this will cause a rise in that country's exchange rate. This will have a number of consequences. Import prices will fall and export prices

Self-assessment tasks

Calculate the impact of the following exchange rate changes upon transaction prices in the following cases: Assume that the nominal exchange rate of pound sterling to US dollars is £1 = $1.5. A cashmere sweater made in the UK and which sold for £200 would cost a US importer $300. Similarly a US car which sold for $12,000 would cost a UK importer £8,000.

1 Assume that the nominal exchange rate changes to £1 = $2.0:
   (a) Calculate the cost of the cashmere sweater to the US importer.
   (b) Calculate the cost of the US car to the UK importer.
   (c) What would you expect to happen to the volume of UK exports of cashmere sweaters and imports of US cars as a result of the new exchange rate?

2 Assume that the nominal exchange rate now changes to £1 = $1.0:
   (a) Re-calculate the cost of the cashmere sweater to the US importer.
   (b) Re-calculate the cost of the car to the UK importer.
   (c) What would you expect to happen to the volume of UK exports of cashmere sweaters and imports of US cars as a result of the new exchange rate?
   (d) As the exchange rate has changed it has changed the transaction prices of the trade in cashmere sweaters in the UK and the US. As a result we will expect the volumes of imports and exports to change. Explain what further information would be required to assess the impact of these changes in sales upon total spending on exports and imports.

will rise. Domestic consumers will switch to imported goods and services while foreign consumers will turn to their own country's products in preference to imports. As a result we would expect the volume of imports to rise and the volume of exports to fall. The extent of the volume change is determined by the price elasticity of demand for both imports and exports. There will be a decline in demand from both domestic and foreign purchasers of goods and services produced in the country with the appreciating currency, which may well lead to unemployment as producers face declining sales both at home and abroad.

The appreciation of the currency should have sufficient impact upon import and export spending that the balance of payments surplus is replaced by a balance of payments deficit.

Exchange rate regimes

In deciding upon their exchange rate policy, governments can choose between various types of exchange rate regime. Each have their respective strengths and weaknesses.

A **fixed exchange rate** regime is one where a government maintains a given exchange rate over a period of time. This could be for a few months or even years. In order to maintain the exchange rate at its stated level, the government is likely to find it necessary to use fiscal and monetary policy to control aggregate demand. So, when there is downward pressure on the exchange rate due to a high level of aggregate demand, the exchange rate can be protected through deflationary measures such as raising taxation, reducing government spending or raising the rate of interest. Alternatively, the government could use direct controls to restrict the outflow of currency.

Fixed exchange rates have certain advantages. For example, the risk and uncertainty of trade and promoting foreign direct investment is reduced. (In some respects a fixed exchange rate works here like a single currency.) It also reduces currency speculation and provides policy makers with less scope to manage the economy in a reckless manner. The downside is that experience has shown that protecting the exchange rate requires domestic economic polices to be frequently adjusted. In turn this can and does restrict economic growth. A further criticism is that the exchange rate may be fixed at the wrong rate – if this is too high, then balance of payments disequilibria will occur (see previous chapter). Over time, with a fixed exchange rate, it will be necessary to adjust it to take into account major macroeconomic changes in the economy. For example, an improvement in an economy's competitiveness that results in lower prices will not be fully passed on to export customers if the exchange rate remains unchanged. It is for these shortcomings that fixed exchange rates are now not favoured by the vast number of countries that trade in the global economy.

A **floating exchange rate** regime is where the rate of exchange is determined purely by the demand and supply of that currency on the foreign exchange market. This can lead to quite volatile changes in a currency (see below). As a result, many currencies are subject to a **managed float** whereby the currency is broadly determined by market forces but the government takes action to influence the rate of change in the exchange rate. For example, releasing reserves of currency can help support a currency when there is pressure on a currency to be depreciated. Caribbean currencies tend to be linked to the US dollar. Although they fluctuate against the dollar, the respective central banks tend to restrict the extent of any change in value of their currencies by having upper and lower exchange rate limits.

Floating exchange rate systems

When the value of a currency depreciates or appreciates purely as a result of market forces, that is, changes in demand and/or the supply of a currency, then the exchange rate is said to be freely floating. Under this system the exchange rate is determined purely by market forces. The major advantage of this is that since the government has no exchange rate target it is free to pursue other policy objectives, such as full employment. This means that where freely floating exchange rates are adopted there is considerable independence in economic policy making.

This can be explained as follows. If a country suffers inflation at a higher rate than its competitors in world trade, then the likely outcome is that this country's goods and services become uncompetitive in world markets. Domestic consumers will turn to lower-priced imports, and consumers in overseas markets will purchase their goods and services from low inflation countries. This is likely to lead to a deficit on the current account of the country's balance of payments. As we have seen, this leads to a fall in the exchange rate of that country's currency as an excess supply of the currency occurs in the foreign exchange market. A fall in the exchange rate will restore competitiveness of the economy's goods and services, because domestic consumers will now find that they have to pay more to obtain imports. Also foreign consumers now find that they have to give up less of their own currency to buy the exports of the country with the depreciating currency. The subsequent fall in imports and rise in exports should correct the balance of payments deficit.

This adjustment process does depend upon certain assumptions however, including the responsiveness of consumers to the price changes that result from the depreciating currency. In addition we have seen that one of the consequences of a declining currency is that inflationary pressures are created in the economy. This means that, as the currency depreciates to offset the inflation which has made the country's goods and services uncompetitive, it may well create further inflationary pressures within the economy which will mean that the goods and services remain uncompetitive and the cycle goes on. The inflationary pressure can become so bad that there is a complete loss of confidence in the currency in both the domestic and in foreign exchange markets. Nevertheless, as explained it is usually expected that given sufficient time it is likely that demand for exports and imports is sufficiently price elastic to ensure that the deficit is removed, despite the inflationary pressures that are created. This tendency for deficits (and surpluses) in the balance of payments to be removed through changes in the exchange rate with no need for government action is known as an automatic adjustment mechanism.

Despite the advantages of the self-regulating nature of floating exchange rates, most governments tend to favour some degree of intervention in foreign exchange markets. This is because of a number of serious disadvantages which freely floating regimes bring. These can be summarised as follows:

1 The fact that exchange rates fluctuate discourages trade. When contracts are signed to finance international trade in goods and services, entrepreneurs will assess the usual risks when considering whether a venture will result in profits being earned. They will consider their costs and revenue and this will allow them to estimate profit. In a floating exchange rate regime an extra risk is added to the transaction. A sudden fluctuation in the exchange rate might upset their calculations and wipe out estimated profit. It could, of course, result in severe losses if revenue falls below costs. There are several ways in which the risk of losses through currency fluctuation can be minimised, but the uncertainty which surrounds trade in floating exchange rate regimes remains a serious disadvantage of such a system.
2 It is suggested that the fact that a floating exchange rate system has a self-regulating mechanism to deal with balance of payments deficits means that governments do not face any pressure to exercise financial discipline in their policies. As we have seen, any inflation which results from lax economic policy-making is offset by a decline in the exchange rate. It is clear from the above analysis, however, that the decline in the exchange rate can itself cause prices to rise. As a result, it is claimed that floating exchange rates can be inflationary.

The disadvantages of floating exchange rates have encouraged governments to seek ways of intervening in the foreign exchange market to manage exchange rate change in order to provide stability and a favourable environment for growth in trade.

Managed exchange rate systems

If governments are to manage their exchange rates they need to intervene in the foreign exchange market. They can intervene directly by buying and selling currencies in order to offset upward or downward pressure on the exchange rate. This means that governments must have access to a large quantity of reserves of foreign exchange sufficient to influence the price in the market. They can also intervene indirectly through variations in the rate of interest. If, for example, there is downward pressure on the exchange rate because there is an excess supply of the currency on the foreign exchange market, a rise in domestic interest rates will attract inflows of capital in search of good returns. This will create an increase in the demand for the currency and offset the downward pressure. This means that the rate of interest is used as a tool to maintain the exchange rate.

Figure 20.5 shows the principles of a pegged exchange rate system, whereby the currency has a par value of $0P$, with an upper and a lower limit. If there is an increase in the supply of dollars, for example due to an increase in imports, then the supply curve shifts to S_1. This will reduce the value of the dollar in a free market to below its agreed lower limit. To maintain the currency at its lower limit, the demand for dollars has to shift to the right, an action requiring the use of foreign exchange reserves by the government. If it wishes to return the dollar to its par value, then even greater reserves are needed to bring it back to 0*P*. This is fine in theory but in practice can involve a massive drain on the foreign exchange reserves held by a country. (The UK's withdrawal from the Exchange Rate Mechanism in 1993 was a consequence of such actions failing to address the pound's fall in value.)

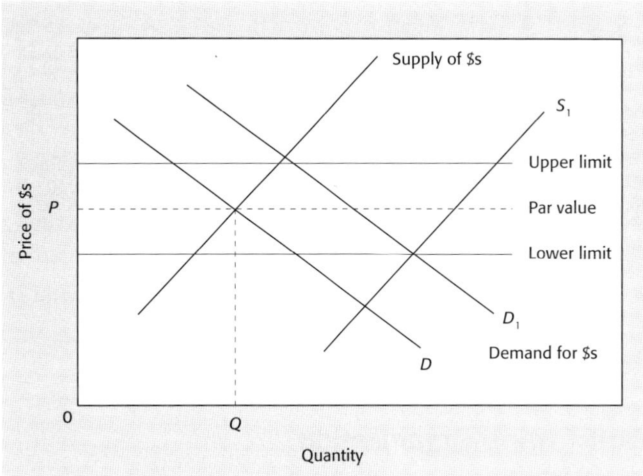

Figure 20.5 A managed exchange rate system

Self-assessment tasks

Comment on the likely effects on Caribbean economies of:

(a) a depreciation

(b) an appreciation

of the US dollar against that of Caribean currencies.

Summary

In this chapter it has been shown that:

- The exchange rate is the price of a currency in terms of one or more other currencies on the foreign exchange market.
- Various factors can cause the depreciation or appreciation of an exchange rate; these relate to the value of exports and imports at any time and to the confidence that foreign investors have in a particular economy.
- A fixed exchange rate regime is one whereby the exchange rate of a currency is pre-determined by the government.
- A floating exchange rate is one where the exchange rate is determined by market forces of demand and supply for that currency – some currencies such as those of Caribbean economies tend to be managed in the sense that they are linked to the $US.
- Exchange rate changes affect aggregate demand in the economy; in turn, the balance of payments, particularly on the current account, is affected.

Key words

Definitions of Key words can be found in the Glossary.

appreciation (of an exchange rate)
depreciation (of an exchange rate)
fixed exchange rate
floating exchange rate
managed float

21 International institutions

This chapter covers unit 2, module 3, topic 6.
On completion of this chapter, you should be able to:

- explain the role and functions of the World Trade Organisation (WTO)
- explain the role of international financial institutions (IFI's)

World Trade Organisation

The **World Trade Organisation** (WTO), with headquarters in Geneva, Switzerland, currently has 150 members. Vietnam was the latest country to be admitted in 2005. Significantly, after 15 years of tense negotiations, the People's Republic of China became a member in 2001.

The WTO's mission is a simple one. In its own words, it 'helps trade flow smoothly, freely, fairly and predictably'. In practice this should produce a trading system with the following characteristics:

- **Non-discrimination.** Two key principles are involved here. The first is known as the **most-favoured-nation treatment.** Under WTO Agreements, countries cannot grant a special favour (for example a lower rate of duty or duty free access) to one WTO member over another. In other words, all countries should be treated on an

Belize's Foreign Minister Godfrey Smith, left, and Mauritius' Agriculture Minister Arvin Boolell ponder during a press conference of the African, Caribbean and Pacific Group of States at the WTO ministerial conference in Hong Kong, Friday, 16 December 2005. Cotton, banana and sugar growing nations in Africa, the Caribbean and Pacific regions threatened to reject any global trade deal that eliminates safeguards for their farmers or their preferential access to European markets
Source: AP Photo/Kin Cheung.

equal basis. The second principle is called **national treatment**. This involves treating foreigners and locals equally. Under this agreement, imported and locally produced goods should be treated equally after goods have reached the domestic market. This does not prohibit a country imposing tariffs on imported goods – it does mean though that the goods then compete on the same basis thereafter. The principle also applies to services, so that foreign firms, for example, trying to set up in business elsewhere should be treated in exactly the same way as domestic firms wishing to expand their operations.

- Free trade. The most obvious way in which this can be done is by lowering trade barriers and tariff and non-tariff barriers. This will enable goods and services to flow more openly and fairly between members, providing the benefits of the gains from trade that were described in chapter 17.
- Predictability. The purpose of this objective is to 'bind' WTO members once they have agreed to open their markets. The rationale behind this is to provide a stable business environment whereby firms will feel secure that trade barriers will not be raised at some future date. This should create a business environment where investment is encouraged, jobs are created and consumers can enjoy the benefits of lower prices and more choice. It has particular relevance for businesses moving into emerging and developing economies, where inevitably there are likely to be concerns over future political stability and economic prospects.
- Promoting fair competition. The WTO system allows tariffs and in some circumstances, other forms of protection. Having said this, once a restriction has been imposed by a member, WTO agreements mean that thereafter there should be free and fair competition in the market. This must not be distorted by further constraints on foreign produced goods and foreign owned services.
- Special provision for developing countries. From the outset, the WTO has sought to assist the development of developing countries. This has not been easy given the stances taken by the USA and EU, for example, with respect to trade in certain agricultural products. Nevertheless, the WTO has sought to give such countries time and flexibility to implement various agreements. The agreements build upon the earlier GATT principles of providing special assistance and trade concessions for developing countries.

The Agreements

WTO agreements cover goods, services and intellectual property. They are often called the WTO's trade rules since the WTO is a rules-based system of agreements that have been negotiated by governments. The so-called Uruguay Round agreements are the basis of the current WTO system.

The Uruguay Round covered three main areas. These were:

- Tariff cuts. Developed country members of WTO agreed a 40 per cent cut in their tariffs on industrial products to be phased in over a five-year period from 1995. This agreement reduced the average tariff from 6.3 to 3.8 per cent. They also agreed that fewer imported products should be charged at higher duty rates. This was of particular benefit to developing countries, which saw the proportion of their exports faced with tariffs of 15 per cent and above in industrialised countries fall from 9 to 5 per cent of total products.
- More binding tariffs. This is the term used to denote a commitment by a member to not increase tariffs above the listed rate. Developed countries increased the number of 'bound' product lines to 99 per cent; developing countries increased their pledges to 73 per cent. The purpose behind these agreements is to provide rather more security for traders and other investors.
- Agriculture. Substantial progress was made to remove almost all import restrictions of a non-tariff form on agricultural products in world trade. Most of these physical restrictions were converted to tariffs, a process known as tariffication. At the same time, tariffs applying to products from developing countries have been progressively reduced and commitments have been received from developed countries to reduce domestic support and export subsidies for agricultural products. The Uruguay Round represents the first time that such agreement has been reached in principle.

Doha Round

The current round of negotiations started in November 2001 at the Fourth Ministerial Conference in Doha, Qatar. These have been extremely contentious and agreement on many issues has not yet been reached (see box).

Central to the Doha Round has been the determination of members to put the needs of developing countries at the heart of the WTO's work programme. In particular, there has been some commitment to assist the least developed countries through seeking to provide them with an increasing share of world trade as a means of assisting their economic development.

Some agreement though has been forthcoming. Countries have agreed to phase out all export subsidies by the end of 2013 and to terminate any cotton subsidies by the end of 2006. Other concessions to developing countries are known as the 'Everything But Arms' initiative – this is an agreement to introduce tariff free access for goods from least developed countries for 97 per cent of all products that are traded.

International Monetary Fund

The **International Monetary Fund** (IMF) was set up in 1945 at the Bretton Woods Conference to help promote the health of the world economy following the catastrophic damage caused by World War II. With headquarters in Washington DC, it currently has 184 members. Notable non-members are Cuba and North Korea.

Over the past 60 years of its operation, the IMF's purposes have remained unchanged, although its activities have evolved and developed in line with the emerging global economy. These purposes and responsibilities are:

No gains in global trade talks

Ministers from some 50 countries, around one third of the WTO membership, are under heavy pressure to approve deep cuts to farm subsidies and steeply lower tariffs in agriculture and manufacturing as they continue to thrash out their differences in a bid to achieve a new global trade deal.

Without a deal, the World Trade Organisation (WTO) will not be able to complete its so-called Doha round by its end of year deadline. For the past six months talks have stalled as the US and Europe defended calls for tariff and subsidy cuts. As well as demanding lower tariffs for manufactured goods, the EU also wants developing countries to free up their trade in services such as IT and finance. Ahead of the meeting, WTO chief Pascal Lamy called on the ministers to take urgent action.

'We need big political decisions to be taken now', he told the BBC.

But while Europe's trade minister Peter Mandelson has called for more to be done, he is currently standing firm, saying the EU will only improve its offer if 'others show a similar flexibility and willingness to go further'. Instead he insists the US must improve its offer to cut domestic farm subsidies.

Caribbean perspective

Caribbean and other developing countries had been demanding that the last talks in Hong Kong in December 2005 should have been a development round to address their concerns.

'We recognise the failures that we committed in the GATT/Uruguay round', says Evadne Coye, Jamaica's Ambassador to Brussels and Geneva.

'We therefore have to be arguing the ethical issues, the principles, and the justice issues', she told BBC Caribbean.

'In a world of giants, the only space we have is where people understand that there are differences and that there must be different rules', says Eamon Courtney, a former Foreign Trade Minister for Belize.

Sugar and other commodities lie at the heart of ACP objections.

Europe has been trying to change its special trade deals internally through reform of its agricultural subsidies and its external special trade deals through the Lomé and Cotonou agreements with African, Caribbean , and Pacific (ACP) states.

But the former European colonies of the ACP argue that it's not getting the same treatment as Europe's own farmers in being weaned off trade preferences.

'That spirit of Cotonou has not entered so far the negotiating mentality of the experts and the leadership of the European Commission', says Ambassador Coye.

Source: BBC Caribbean.com 28 June 2006.

- to promote international monetary co-operation,
- to facilitate the expansion and balanced growth of international trade,
- to provide exchange stability,
- to assist in setting up a multilateral system of payments,
- to make resources available to members experiencing balance of payments difficulties, provided adequate safeguards are provided.

These activities have been central to the development of global trade, since a stable system of international payments and exchange rates is necessary for trade to take place between two countries. In carrying out its responsibilities, the IMF has three main functions that are known as **surveillance**, **technical assistance** and **lending**. The first two are in line with its mission of promoting global growth and economic stability by encouraging countries to adopt sound economic policies. The third function is used where member countries experience difficulties in financing their balance of payments.

The surveillance function takes the form of IMF officers carrying out an annual in-depth appraisal of the economic situation in each member country. Following relevant statistical analysis and forecasts, there is a detailed discussion with a country's representatives on the policies that are seen by the IMF to be most conducive to achieving stable foreign exchange rates and economic growth. Most assessments are published. The IMF also combines information from individual country consultations to form assessments of regional and global prospects.

Technical assistance and training are offered by the IMF to help member countries design and implement effective economic policies. This assistance provides advice on fiscal, monetary and exchange rate policies especially. It has been widely taken up by emerging transition economies in Central and Eastern Europe and by some developing economies.

Many IMF members have experienced severe balance of payments problems over the past 60 years. In the twenty-first century, it is mainly developing economies that face fundamental disequilibria on their current accounts. In such circumstances, the IMF lends money to such countries to ease their immediate positions – it is though a necessary condition for such help that recipients work closely with the IMF to avoid similar, probably more serious problems in the future.

Not all aspects of the IMF's policy agenda receive universal acclaim. Anti-globalisation supporters, for example, condemn the IMF for favouring military dictatorships that are friendly towards US and EU multinational companies. They are also concerned about the IMF's attitude towards supporting economies where human rights and labour rights mean little. Other criticism comes from economists who are concerned at the IMF's pro-Keynesian approach for dealing with balance of payments disequilibria. They believe that supply-side policies rather then devaluation are the best way for alleviating structural imbalance.

There have also been situations where the IMF has been blamed for causing serious economic problems. In 2001 in Argentina, for example, it is generally believed that IMF-induced budget restrictions and the privatisation of important national resources were responsible for the catastrophic economic crises that ensued. As a consequence, the IMF is not well received in this part of the world and it has to be concluded that its record of success is rather limited.

World Bank

Like the IMF, the **World Bank** arose out of the Bretton Woods agreements; unlike the IMF though the World Bank's function is to provide financial support for internal investment projects such as building new roads, improving port infrastructure, constructing new health facilities and so on.

It is best described as the World Bank Group through the activities of its five constituent agencies. These are:

- International Bank for Reconstruction and Development (IBRD),
- International Finance Corporation (IFC),
- International Development Association (IDA),
- Multilateral Investment Guarantee Agency (MIGA),
- International Centre for Settlement of Investment Disputes (ICSID).

The IBRD and IDA provide low or no interest loans and grants to countries that do not have favourable access to international credit markets. Therefore, the focus of activities is very much on developing economies, including the emerging economies of Central and Eastern Europe and South East Asia. Grants are only provided to the world's poorest countries. Loans cover areas such as:

World Bank, Washington, DC
Source: EMPICS.

- health and education in order to enhance human development in a country – for improving sanitation and combating AIDS;
- agriculture and rural development – for irrigation programmes and water supply projects;
- environmental protection – for reducing pollution and for ensuring that there is compliance with pollution regulations;
- infrastructure – roads, railways, electricity;
- governance – for anti-corruption reasons.

Like the IMF, loans tend to be linked to conditions that involve wider-reaching changes being made to the economic policies of the recipient countries.

The World Bank has its critics. It has been accused of being a US/Western European dominated agency for supporting their economic and political interests. Through its strong advocy of free market reforms, its policies have been criticised as being harmful to the interests of some countries, particularly where the 'shock therapy' of reform has been introduced too quickly. Notwithstanding these and other criticisms, the World Bank has had a considerable impact in assisting the world's poorest economies.

Self-assessment task

With reference to examples of your choice, explain how:

- the World Trade Organisation,
- the International Monetary Fund,
- the World Bank

have assisted the economic development of the Caribbean area.

Summary

In this chapter it has been shown that:

- The World Trade Organisation seeks to promote the principles of multilateral free trade through obtaining agreement of its members to cut tariffs and other restrictions.
- The Doha Round of talks have been difficult, in particular with respect to farm subsidies and tariffs on agricultural products. Caribbean countries have been critical of the attitude of the US especially to reduce tariffs on agricultural imports.
- The International Monetary Fund provides various forms of assistance for countries experiencing fundamental disequilibria on their balance of payments.
- The World Bank's role is one of providing loans and grants to developing economies to assist their internal economic development.

Key words

Definitions of Key words can be found in the Glossary.

International Monetary Fund
lending
most-favoured-nation treatment
national treatment
non-discrimination
surveillance
technical assistance
World Bank
World Trade Organisation

22 Foreign direct investment and globalisation

This chapter covers unit 2, module 3, topics 7 and 8.
On completion of this chapter, you should be able to:

- define a multinational or transnational corporation
- explain the nature of foreign direct investment
- outline the potential benefits and disadvantages of foreign direct investment
- explain globalisation
- describe the factors responsible for globalisation
- describe the effects of globalisation on developing countries

Multinational corporations and foreign direct investment

A **multinational corporation** (MNC) or transnational corporation is defined as a firm that operates in more than one country. In other words, it is a business with a parent company based in one country but with production or service operations in at least one other country. The largest MNCs such as the Coca-Cola Corporation, Ford, Nestlé, McDonald's, Hilton Hotels and so on are worldwide operations, with manufacturing and retail outlets in many countries of the world.

Through their activities, MNCs provide **foreign direct investment** (FDI) to the economies in which they operate. This is investment that is necessary to produce or sell a good or service in a foreign country. FDI therefore involves capital flows between countries. It should not be confused with portfolio investment, which is the purchase of shares by foreign investors in businesses that are located in another country.

The activities of MNCs and the effects of foreign direct investment on the economies of recipient countries have been the subject of much debate and discussion by economists and politicians. In the Caribbean area, the impact of FDI from MNCs has been substantial (see below). It has been particularly significant in the bauxite, alumina, petroleum and natural gas industries. There has also been considerable FDI in sugar, tourism and utilities. US MNCs especially have been heavy investors in these businesses.

	Jamaica	Trinidad & Tobago	Bahamas
2003	250	0	550
2004	0	1,000	0
2005	259.7	1,200	0
2006	260	1,500	n.a.

Table 22.1 Estimated FDI in three Caribbean economies 2003–2006 ($USm)
Source: LOCO monitor, 2006.

	No. of projects	
Jamaica	Riu Hotels & Resort	2
	National Assets Recovery Services	1
	Verizon/International Teleservices	2
	Zim	1
Trinidad & Tobago	BP	3
	BHP Billiton	1
	Cirrus	1
	Essar Steel	1
	Alcoa	1
Bahamas	Derivatives Portfolio Management	1
	Everlast Productions	1
	Ferrell Schultz etc	1
	Gilead Sciences	1
	Kerzner International	1

Table 22.2 Top MNC's in three Caribbean economies since 2002
Source: LOCO monitor, 2006.

The US owned Sandals resort in the Bahamas
Source: Alamy.

Table 22.1 shows the estimated FDI for the three Caribbean economies that have received the largest flows since 2003. As this table indicates, these flows have been rather patchy. For Jamaica, except for 2004 when the country was badly affected by a financial crisis, recent levels of FDI have been stable and mainly in tourism and property. For Trinidad and Tobago, though, there has been increasing investment by MNCs in its extractive and energy industries. The case of the Bahamas is different again but with most FDI being in the business and financial services and tourism sectors.

The majority of MNCs shown in table 22.2 are US companies. This is true for FDI across the whole of the Caribbean area. Interestingly for Jamaica, Spanish companies have been major investors in recent years, particularly in tourism and property services (see self assessment task below). One of the reasons for this has been Spain's low rate of corporate taxation on overseas profits from MNCs. UK companies have been relatively modest but regular investors in each of the countries shown in table 22.2.

Benefits and costs of FDI

Although much depends on the scale and nature of the FDI in an economy, there are in principle many benefits to the receiving economy of investment by foreign-owned businesses. These include:

- *The impact of this new investment as an injection into the circular flow of income.* This leads to multiplier effects for the economy, in particular creating an addition to total expenditure and important employment creation. These jobs are initially an immediate result of the FDI but there are subsequent multiplier effects that create further employment throughout the economy. This effect should not be understated in economies that are emerging and where the opportunity for domestically funded investment is limited. Longer term, the injection of FDI increases the economy's potential output level.
- *Effects on the balance of payments.* FDI represents a credit item in the capital account of the balance of payments (see topic 4 above). This could be just a

St Kitts–Nevis attracts high foreign direct investment

St Kitts and Nevis' per capita income is over 70 percent higher than the average for the Eastern Caribbean Currency Union and ranked third worldwide, in attracting foreign direct investment. This was disclosed last week by St Kitts and Nevis Prime Minister and Minister of Finance, Dr Denzil Douglas, during an address to the annual National Consultation on the Economy.

He said that although the twin-island Federation is the smallest nation of the Western Hemisphere, 'we continue to rank among the most advanced countries of the world in respect of our social progress'. According to Dr Douglas the Federation's recent showing in the United Nations Human Development Index is testimony to this overwhelming fact and the major economic indications suggest that the St Kitts and Nevis economy has been among the strongest performers in the region for many years.

'For instance, our per capita income of US$8,889 or EC$24,000 is some 72% higher than the average for the Eastern Caribbean Currency Union as a whole, and although our population is only 8% of the population of the ECCU, our economy accounts for some 12.6% of the GDP of the ECCU', said Dr Douglas.

Dr Douglas said that during the period 1980 to 2003, St Kitts and Nevis experienced growth averaging 4.7 percent per year, the highest in the OECS for that 23-year period. He also said that the St Kitts and Nevis economy has also performed exceedingly well in terms of foreign direct investment which is an important measure of macroeconomic competitiveness. Prime Minister Douglas disclosed that during the 1980s foreign direct investment in St Kitts and Nevis amounted to 11.3 percent of GDP, 12.5 percent in the 1990's and 22.8 percent since 2000.

'Consequently in 2002, St Kitts and Nevis was ranked 3rd, after Luxembourg and Chad in the United Nations Index of Foreign Direct Investment performance. The OECS, as a whole, was ranked 20th in this important index', Dr Douglas disclosed.

Source: Caribbean Net News, 14 November 2005 (adaptation).

one-off short-term inflow, although it might be sustained once a business is established. In turn, further benefits could be created, for example, if the FDI establishes a manufacturing operation that subsequently exports some of its products. (This has been an important credit to the UK's current account as non-UK vehicle manufacturers have set up plants that produce for the wider EU market.) In the case of multinational hotel companies, their investment in Caribbean islands generates further income through increased flows of tourists and payments received by local carriers.

- *An increase in tax revenue for the government.* This comes about in two ways. First, those employed by the MNC contribute income tax receipts and, when spending their incomes, expenditure taxes on their purchases of goods and services. Secondly, the MNCs provide additional tax revenue through their purchase of local services and the corporation or profits taxes that they pay. For poor economies with a limited tax base, both provide an important additional source of government revenue.
- *Improved productivity.* This can come about as a result of pressure from an MNC on local suppliers to improve their efficiency.
- *Technology transfer and the acquisition of specialist equipment.* Developing economies receive the benefit of up-to-date technology and products that have been developed by MNCs in their home market.

At the same time it should also be recognised that there are various disadvantages and risks associated from FDI inflows. These include:

- The employment created may be only short term and could be less than expected. The reason for this is that MNCs invariably have little affinity to the overseas economies in which they have invested. Companies may pull out of a country, transferring production to another location. It could also be that MNCs employ workers from their own country in the top management jobs, with the result that employees from the host country are only recruited to fill lower-paid positions. US and Japanese companies in particular are well known for this approach.
- The net effects on the balance of payments may be less than anticipated. This could come about as profits earned in a host economy are repatriated and count as a debit item in the invisible section of the current account. Over time, the outflow of

such profits may well exceed the initial capital injection.

- Bearing in mind what was said about employment, the taxes received by the government may not be as great as might be expected. Account should also be taken of any subsidies that might have been given to MNCs in order to encourage them to set up in business in the first instance.
- Productivity gains and the technology transfer effects could be very limited depending on the type of FDI.
- There could be environmental costs associated with certain types of FDI, especially mineral extraction and natural gas production.

The net effect of an injection of FDI into an economy can therefore in some respects be a 'mixed blessing'. This is why not all governments welcome MNCs with open arms. For Caribbean economies, some limited research has been carried out into the impact of FDI. In 2003, for example, the Central Bank of Trinidad and Tobago carried out a form of cost–benefit study into the economic impact of the Atlantic Liquified Natural Gas project. This was a joint venture between BP, British Gas and local investors. The main results of the study were:

- marginal impact on GDP;
- temporary worsening of balance of trade, improved terms of trade, substantial foreign exchange generation;
- modest increase in employment (120 local workers) after construction stage;
- increased tax revenues.

Overall therefore not a glowing outcome. A similar picture emerges with respect to the benefits and costs of tourism growth, particularly where this growth is funded by MNCs (see self-assessment task).

Globalisation

It is very appropriate that the final topic in this macroeconomic unit is about **globalisation**. Having said this, globalisation is not easy to define since it is manifest in many different ways, two of which are:

- **Global brands**. Not only is the same brand label available in most national markets, the product is also standardised. Perhaps the best examples are Coca-Cola and McDonald's with its 'Big Mac'. Both are now available worldwide. These brands can be bought in Birmingham (UK), Berlin (Germany),

Self-assessment task

Study the article below and then tackle the questions that follow.

'Difficulties in paradise; the feasibility of sustainable tourism'

The Caribbean region is caught up on the tide of profound global changes. Unfortunately, it still depends on the export of a narrow range of primary commodities to the EU and the USA. The WTO's banana ruling and the EU's recent decision to open up its markets to 50 of the world's least developed countries increases the constraints facing Caribbean economies. These trends are likely to lead to an increased emphasis on the tourism industry, particularly in the short term. Longer term, the importance of sustainable tourism in the overall development of the Caribbean region remains a key issue.

Net earnings from tourism are subject to four substantial leakages. These are:

- imports of materials and equipment for construction,
- imports of consumer goods, food and drink especially repatriation of profits,
- overseas promotional expenditure,
- amortisation of external debt incurred in the development of hotels and resorts.

The foreign exchange leakage rates for four Caribbean economies were:

St Lucia	56%
Aruba	41%
Jamaica	40%
Antigua & Barbuda	25%

Source: G. Barnwell, *Caribbean Voice*, 2005 (adaptation).

1 Using information from the article, estimate the multiplier for the four Caribbean economies listed. (7 marks)

2 Account for the differences in the values of the multipliers you have calculated. (8 marks)

3 Discuss the importance of multiplier estimates such as these when governments are planning medium- to long-term growth strategies. (10 marks)

Budapest (Hungary), Buenos Aires (Argentina) as well as Bridgetown (Barbados). These are just two products sold by MNCs such as Nestlé, Kelloggs, IBM, Sony, Shell, Texaco, Ford, Microsoft and so on. Global brands are also to be found in the service sector, particularly through banks such as Bank of America and HSBC plc and hotel chains such as Hilton, Marriot and Holiday Inn.

- **Global sourcing**. This is much less obvious. It refers to the ways in which global companies have replaced 'local' sourcing for their operations through worldwide production. Some of the best examples are clothing and sportswear manufacturers such as Nike, Adidas and Reebok, electronics producers such as LG, Apple and Phillips and vehicle manufacturers like General

Motors, VW-Audi and Renault. In all cases, production has moved from domestic sources in the USA, Western Europe and Japan to lower cost countries in South East Asia (China especially), North Africa, Central and South Africa and Central and Eastern Europe.

Although there is no single definition of globalisation, the above examples provide plenty of evidence of what constitutes globalisation. To the economist though, globalisation is 'the ability to produce any good or service anywhere in the world, using raw materials, components, capital and technology from anywhere, sell the resulting output anywhere, and place profits anywhere' (BBC Economics Editor, 1996).

Factors responsible for globalisation

The factors responsible for globalisation are often specific to a particular MNC; in general terms the following have contributed to the process of globalisation:

- A reduction in protection in the world economy. As referred in chapters 17 and 21, the WTO has sought to reduce the overall degree of protection in world trade. High tariffs mean quotas and other trade curbing factors in the form of non-tariff barriers are inconsistent with globalisation. Although by no means a situation of multilateral free trade, as shown in chapter 18, the global economy is now characterised by a number of 'regional' trading blocs, many of which have established mutually beneficial links between one another.
- A reduction in international capital movement restrictions. This has been essential for business capital to flow freely within the global economy. Exchange control has been gradually dismantled, allowing FDI to flow between developed economies and from developed economies to those that are emerging and developing (see above).
- Developments in IT and falling communication costs. The pace of technological change over the past generation or so has been incredible. The ways in which businesses are able to communicate, via the internet and in handling data, has promoted global economic relations. Global supply chains, whereby businesses assemble, produce and sell their products, can be managed in a very effective way.
- A fall in real transport costs. Unit transport costs, particularly for sea transport, have been falling, making it increasingly viable for businesses to source on a global basis. The bulk distribution of products in containers by sea, and to a much lesser extent by air, has increased year on year. Economies of scale can also be gained as vessels and aircraft have increased in size and in terms of energy efficiency. In response, specialist US and European-owned global logistics carriers have played their part in facilitating the supply of goods between producers and customers worldwide.
- Liberalisation of domestic markets. In line with a reduction in protection, many of the world's emerging economies (China especially), have been much more positive and receptive to FDI from developed economies and in forming business partnerships with MNCs. These partnerships have taken various forms including joint ventures, licensing, franchising and supplier agreements. It has also been easier for MNCs to directly purchase businesses in other parts of the world.

Effects of globalisation

The main consequence of globalisation is that the world economy is now more integrated through the growth of trade and increasing dependency. Export trade as a percentage of world trade has grown steadily; in 2005 this was estimated to be around 25 per cent of GDP.

For developing economies such as those in the Caribbean area, globalisation has produced certain benefits. These include:

- higher living standards for more people,
- enjoyment of global brands,
- spreading best practice and technology transfer,
- improved medical supplies that could increase life expectancy.

Notwithstanding, globalisation has its critics. It is very clear that virtually all economies in the world are heavily dependent upon each other. This has been well evidenced following the Asian financial crisis of 1997/98, the 9/11 terrorist attack on New York and more recent political conflict in the Middle East. These events served to show how the world's economies, rich and poor, were inextricably linked, particularly to external shocks affecting the US. The impact on some developing economies has been relatively more severe

Self-assessment task

Study the article below and then tackle the questions that follow.

A Big Mac, fries and a green pea pie

In the late 1980s, executives at McDonald's, the world's biggest and best-known fast-food business, set about researching whether the time was right to open on the streets of mainland China. But Joseph Lau, the man assigned to the task, did not rely on management consultants or industry analysts to help him make the decision. Instead he wandered around the streets of Shanghai staring at people's footwear. The signs where that China was ready!

Now less than 20 years later, the Golden Arches, America's foremost symbol of capitalism, has over 770 outlets, with a target of at least 1,000 by the time of the 2008 Olympics. China has an emerging middle class, increasingly used to eating out. Unlike markets in some more developed countries, McDonald's sales are soaring in China – 58% increase in the last year alone.

Through a small side door inside one of Hong Kong's bustling MTR stations, McDonald's runs an innovation centre dedicated to dreaming up new products for its Asian customers. In mainland China, diners can choose from green pea pies, rice burgers and mint-flavoured soda alongside the staple Big Mac and regular fries.

The fast-food industry's *bete noire*, the health campaigners who accuse McDonald's of fuelling child obesity, is not a major headache in China. Of more concern is the threat from Starbuck's and Yum! Brands that owns KFC and Pizza Hut, both of which are fighting McDonald's for business from China's middle classes. In response, McDonald's has sought to upgrade its products, develop drive-in restaurants and very recently has negotiated an agreement with Sinopec, the state-owned oil company, to give it first refusal of locating its Golden Arches at any of the 30,000 filling stations it operates across China.

Is Starbucks a threat to McDonalds?

Source: *Daily Telegraph*, 24 November 2006 (adaptation).

1 Why does China provide a relatively new market opportunity for McDonald's?
2 Explain how McDonald's may benefit from economies of scale in the China market?
3 Discuss how McDonald's might compete with the other large fast food chains referred to in the article.

than in developed economies due to the latter's more robust structure that allows it to 'weather the storm' in a more effective way.

Further criticisms are more local. It is argued by anti-globalisation groups that globalisation is a new form of imperialism led by the US, that it accentuates the gap between rich and poor and leads to the exploitation of workers in developing countries. A good example of the latter is how some unscrupulous clothing manufacturers pay below the living wage for workers employed producing garments for retailers based in much more affluent countries.

To assess the impact of globalisation on the Caribbean area is far from easy. The costs and benefits require a very careful evaluation. A widely held view though is that CARICOM countries should forget their differences and work together in a more effective way to counter the more negative effects of globalisation on Caribbean economies (see self-assessment task).

Self-assessment task

Read the two short articles below and then tackle the question that follows.

CSME Answer to Globalisation

As the forces of globalisation continue to affect the region, Prime Minister Portia Simpson Miller, has said that the establishment of the CARICOM Single Market and Economy (CSME) provided a vehicle through which the region could successfully counter its effects.

She asserted that the region 'must now stand even more firmly as an economic bloc and devise and implement strategies based on each island's strengths and competitive advantages'. Mrs Simpson Miller was addressing a ceremony for the dedication of the new parliament building in Antigua and Barbuda on Monday (30 October).

The Prime Minister said that 'for the Single Economy to succeed, we must pool our collective energies at both the national and regional levels, we must build lasting partnerships, embracing the public sector, private sector and civil society'.

She added that, 'it is only in togetherness that we can promote the highest levels of efficiency in the production of goods and services. It is only in togetherness that we can speak with a strong and powerful voice around global bargaining tables.'

The Prime Minister further intimated that political differences should not be allowed to hamper the regional integration process and welcomed the introduction of dialogue between CARICOM heads and opposition leaders on issues of regional significance.

Source: *CARICOM News*, 1 November 2006 (adaptation).

Tourism in region to benefit from CARICOM/Spain Agreement

Regional tourism is expected to benefit from a 750,000 euro-grant in official aid from Spain, as part of a developmental assistance agreement between CARICOM and that European country.

At last week's three-day discussions, both parties agreed to place emphasis on human resources training in the tourism sector by initially strengthening the regional and national institutions linked to the sector. The Spanish delegation expressed interest in providing technical assistance and pledged commitment to developing the capacity of the Caribbean's tourism sector.

Meanwhile, a Regional Tourism School is expected to emerge from the CARICOM/Spain partnership. The school, which is to be established in Jamaica will promote the training of workers in the regional tourism sector in a manner that stimulates the productivity of the respective national industries.

Speaking with JIS News, Spanish Ambassador to Jamaica, Jesus Silva, said his country's interest in assisting CARICOM states to become more developed was wholly altruistic. He stressed that the aid to CARICOM was part of a partnership that would facilitate regional capacity building, which would be more beneficial than 'hand outs'.

Mr Silva noted that Spain had benefited from foreign aid, which fostered its rapid economic growth over the past ten years, and saw it fit to assist other countries, including Small Island Developing States (SIDS) along their development trajectory.

Source: *CARICOM News*, 24 October 2006.

1 Using the information above, and other local evidence, comment upon the various costs and benefits of globalisation for Caribbean economies.

Summary

In this chapter it has been shown that:

- A multinational corporation is one that operates in more than one country.
- Foreign direct investment involves the flow of capital between countries.
- There are various benefits and costs involved when MNCs operate in developing economies.
- Globalisation can take various forms and has been a powerful force in the world economy over the past generation; its impact seems quite likely to increase in the future.
- Globalisation has far-reaching consequences for developing economies such as those in CARICOM.

Key words

Definitions of Key words can be found in the Glossary.

foreign direct investment
multinational corporation
globalisation

Preparing for examinations

On completion of this section you should:

- ➤ know about the various skills and abilities that are assessed in the CAPE examinations
- ➤ know how to plan your preparation for examinations in an effective way
- ➤ feel confident in tackling CAPE examination questions and knowing what examiners expect when marking your script
- ➤ appreciate why some students do not succeed or perform to their true ability in examinations.

Introduction

The assessment processes in CAPE Economics are designed to test your skills and abilities to:

(i) recall, select and use economic theories, principles, concepts and methods;
(ii) identify and analyse economic problems and formulate solutions;
(iii) interpret and analyse economic data and draw logical conclusions;
(iv) analyse economic problems by using the models and concepts introduced in the course;
(v) develop structured and reasoned expositions on economic theory and policy.

The evidence on which this assessment of your skills and abilities in each unit is based comes from your performance in:

- ◆ two written examination papers;
- ◆ a project or, for private candidates, a case study paper.

(See Introduction to the book for more details.)

If you approach the assessment in a positive and meaningful way, then you ought to get the grade you are expecting, consistent with the time and effort you have devoted to your CAPE Economics studies. For some students though, for all sorts of reasons, the final grade may be a disappointment.

So, what should you do to be successful? There is no magic formula, but if you do the following, you are giving yourself every change of success:

- ◆ read both Units and all of the topics in this book and feel confident that you have understood the main subject content;
- ◆ complete all or most of the self-assessment tasks;
- ◆ where possible, understand how the various problems, concepts, theories and policies might be applied to Caribbean economies;
- ◆ know what to expect and how best to tackle the examination papers.

The seeds for success therefore are sown long before you enter the examination room. The key thing is to be prepared. In this respect, it is worth remembering what was posted on the dressing room wall of the formidable Australian cricket team that won the 2007 World Cup:

IF YOU FAIL TO PREPARE, YOU ARE PREPARING TO FAIL.

Why not put this on your wall? But if you do, remember to practise what it says.

A few hints on how to study

As a CAPE Student, study is something you do from the first day of your course. This involves the gradual accumulation of the knowledge and skills that constitute the subject you are studying. You should also see the regular review or revision of such knowledge and skills as part of this process. (This is where the self-assessment tasks in this book are a great help.) Revision therefore is not something that is only confined to the last week or so before an examination. So, 'make study a habit; make revision a habit'.

Managing your time in an effective way is crucial. There should be regular periods in the week when you have spare blocks of time that you can devote to studying CAPE Economics. Even if only 30 minutes, if this is spent effectively, it will be of value to you. You should also try to have set places where you can study, ideally free from distractions such as loud music, television noise and so on. This may not be easy but ... try to have set times and places for your study and stick to a routine.

A second important aspect of time management is planning. All students should try to do this by thinking ahead. This is particularly important where, as in the CAPE examinations, you are taking the examinations on a staged basis. (Paper 01 in each Unit is usually taken at the end of the first year of study.) Time is therefore limited between the start of teaching and when you have to take your first examinations.

Here are a few simple things that might help:

- Read through your class notes on a **daily** basis; follow this up by reading the relevant topic in this book.
- Make a **weekly** plan of what you have done; at the end of each week, go over the reading again and see if you can do the self-assessment tasks that are incorporated into the topic.
- When you have completed a topic, see if you can answer the specimen examination questions ... ideally without referring to your notes or to the book.

Think and plan ahead. Find out when you might have to do a 'mock' examination and above all, make sure you know when the actual examination will be taking place.

All of these simple things should help you feel relaxed and confident when you take the examinations. So, remember

IF YOU FAIL TO PREPARE, YOU ARE PREPARING TO FAIL.

A few hints on how to study effectively

Each of us has a preferred study environment where we can work in an effective and efficient way. For most of us it is likely to be a bedroom or a school library where the distractions going on around us can at least be shut off for an hour or two. The best time for study may also vary – much will depend upon your family circumstances and how you can arrange to study in relation to these and other commitments on your time.

Whatever the best time, the following advice should help you.

- Put yourself in a position where you can *concentrate on your work*. This is most unlikely to happen if there is your favourite television programme being broadcast in the same room. The *attention* span of most people is 40–60 minutes. After such a period, have a drink and a rest, maybe watch a short television programme before studying for a further period.
- When reading, *make notes* on what you have read and incorporate these into your class notes on a particular topic. You will also find it useful to do the self-assessment tasks in this book and work through sample examination questions on a topic. Writing and working in this way greatly enhances your understanding of a topic. *Do not just read material on its own* – the problem with this approach to study is that you will very quickly forget what you have read. The big advantage also of making notes is that they will be there for future revision when you need them.
- Once you have completed the study of a particular topic, condense your notes down on to a *revision card*, which you will find invaluable for use shortly before examinations. An example of such notes is shown in table 1.

Elasticity – responsiveness of quantity demanded to a change in price, income or prices of substitutes or complements

$$\text{PED} = \frac{\%\text{ change in qty demanded}}{\%\text{ change in price}}$$

— elastic >1, inelastic <1, unitary =1 — applies to all measures

$$\text{YED} = \frac{\%\text{ change in qty demanded}}{\%\text{ change in income}}$$

— +ve – normal goods; –ve – inferior goods

$$\text{XED} = \frac{\%\text{ change in qty demanded, good A}}{\%\text{ change in price, good B}}$$

— +ve – substitutes; –ve – complements

Use and applications: prediction of effects of price changes on quantity demanded
forecast effects of a change in income on demand
pricing strategies for firms in competition to producing complements

Examples:		
	low PED	– petrol, alcohol
	normal goods	– many consumer goods
	inferior goods	– cheap margarine, black and white TVs
	substitutes	– pork and chicken, car and bus travel
	complements	– bread and butter, petrol and car travel

Table 1 Example of revision card

So, it is not so much how long you study but how effective you are in your studying. Make sure you use your time effectively so that you *feel in control of your own learning experience.*

Examination questions

Types of question

There are four main types of question in CAPE examinations. These are:

- multiple choice questions,
- short answer questions,
- data response questions,
- essay questions.

All questions though draw upon the subject content of each of the two Units.

Let us look at each type in turn, as various skills are being examined in each of these forms of question.

Multiple choice questions are used to assess the extent to which you understand the full content of the syllabus. Typically, they take the form of a 'stem' followed by four possible answers. You are required to identify which of these so-called 'keys' is the correct answer. In most questions, one key is clearly wrong, two are temptingly correct, whilst one is the correct answer. So, beware! These questions are not as easy as they might appear.

With such questions, it is absolutely vital that you attempt all questions in the time available. If you are running out of time, make a guess. You have still a one in four chance of being correct.

With multiple choice examinations, practice is essential. Below is a strategy that you may find helpful:

- go through the question paper, answering those questions that you can answer quickly and with confidence that you know the correct key;
- leave any you find difficult or that require a lot of calculations;
- go back and attempt those questions requiring calculations;
- finally, return to those questions that you have found difficult;
- as the examination time runs out, make a guess at any questions you have not attempted.

If you take a 'mock' examination, find out all the correct keys – be sure you know how and why you got the right answer or why the key you selected was wrong. This point cannot be stressed too strongly.

Short answer questions are just what they are ... questions that require very short responses. The mark allocation is a very good indication as to how much writing is needed. The golden rule here is not write too much; the skill is to write just enough and spend just enough time to get all of the marks available.

This type of question assesses your knowledge and understanding of the subject matter. You must therefore be precise in the answers that you write.

Data response questions are more varied. In Paper 1, this type of question draws upon a relatively short, simple set of economic data. For Paper 2, they are derived from more varied stimulus material, for example graphs, diagrams, reports or textual prose, which may also contain data. The data handling skills you need to feel confident of when answering such questions are those contained in the Introduction and chapter 2.

When you come across a data response question for the first time:

- look at the title as it may give some clues about its content;
- read any table or column headings and see if you know what they mean;
- see if you can pick out the main patterns in the data using the 'eye balling' technique that was referred to in the Introduction;
- pick out any notable features of a chart or diagram.

Once you have done this you should feel comfortable with the information provided.

Data response questions require short answers. These can take three forms:

- questions that require no more than interpretation of the data provided – answers to such questions could be no more than a word or a number;
- questions that require your understanding of an economic concept that is contained in the data;
- questions where you are required to comment on some aspect or theme in the data.

The last two skills tend to be more prevalent in the data response questions for Paper 2 examinations. But do remember not to write more than you have to.

Essay questions require extended reading. This form of assessment is used in the Paper 2 question papers of CAPE examinations. All of the questions are 'structured', that is they consist of a number of parts. The number of parts varies a lot, but for each question you are expected to spend around a total of 50 minutes writing time.

General advice on how to write in an effective way was provided in the Introduction – why not go back and refresh yourself on the main points?

The wording of questions

A lot of care, thought and attention goes into the final production of all CAPE examination papers. So, when you sit an examination, it is important to appreciate that the questions which are on the examination paper have been set by an examiner who is requiring you to *answer these questions.* Put another way, examination papers never contain questions such as:

Write all you know about ...
or:
Write as much as you can remember about ...

Unfortunately, this point is not always appreciated by some students.

All examination questions contain two very important instructions. These are called:

Directive words – these words indicate what form the answer should take. For example, it could be in the form of a description, a discussion, an explanation or merely a statement. These words are there for a purpose, namely that they have been used by the examiners to say what they are looking for (in skill terms when you answer a particular question).

Content words – these are much more diverse in nature since they cover the whole of the subject area of the syllabus. Their aim is to make clear to you, the candidate, what is the focus of the question being set, and, indeed, what examiners expect you to write about.

Table 2 shows a list of key directive words that are most likely to occur in CAPE Economics examination questions. *You should study these carefully and understand what each means.* You will then appreciate that a question which asks:

'Define price elasticity of demand'

is not the same as:

'Explain what is meant by price elasticity of demand'

is not the same as:

'Discuss the relevance of price elasticity of demand in business'

A simple method for interpreting essay questions

The following question was set in a recent Paper 2 CAPE examination:

(a) Identify and discuss *three* sources of economic growth which may be present in any economy. (30 marks)

(b) (i) Outline the *major* features of globalisation. (5 marks)

(ii) Discuss *three* ways in which globalisation can affect Caribbean economies. (15 marks)

Directive word	What it means	Where you can expect it to be used
Calculate	Work out using the information provided	Usually in the early parts of data response questions, short answer, multiple choice questions and some structured essay questions
Define	Give the exact meaning	
Describe	Give a description of	
How	In what way or ways	
Identify	Give an example	
Illustrate	Give examples/diagram	
Outline	Describe without detail	
State	Make clear	
Summarise	Give main points, without detail	
What	State clearly	
Which	Give a clear example/state what	
Analyse	Set out the main points	In the later parts of data response questions, and structured essay questions
Apply	Use in a specific way	
Compare	Give similarities and differences	
Explain	Give clear reasons or make clear	
Account for	Give reasons for	
Consider	Give your thoughts about	
Assess	Show how important something is	In the final part of data response questions and in structured essay questions
Comment upon	Give your reasoned opinions on	
Criticise	Given an opinion, but support it with evidence	
Discuss	Give the important arguments, for and against	
Evaluate	Discuss the importance of, making some attempt to weight your opinions	

Table 2 Key directive words

The question is structured into three parts. The marks allocated are very varied – remember with 50 minutes per question, you should spend 30 minutes writing time on part (a) and 20 minutes on part (b). This is important.

Part (a) contains two directive words, 'identify' and 'discuss'. Table 2 provides information on each. The 'identify' word means no more than 'state/give an example of three sources of economic growth'.

So, if you refer back to chapter 16 you will recall that there are three key determinants of economic growth in any economy. These are capital accumulation, human capital and technological change. So, when writing your answer, you must make specific reference to each and try to give no more than a sentence of elaboration as to what each is.

The second directive word is 'discuss'. This requires you to look at how each of the three factors above can both contribute to economic growth and also be an obstacle to economic growth. In other words, to take an objective view.

Looking now at the content requirement, the key words here are 'sources of economic growth', in particular the word 'sources'. Your entire answer should be focussed on this aspect of economic growth. To do this effectively, you must avoid the temptation to write in a lot of detail about what is meant by economic growth.

Question (b)(i) requires an answer of no more than a few sentences in length. The directive word 'outline' means that you need to describe without much detail the major features of globalisation. Looking at chapter 22 you will see that these include global brands, global sourcing, foreign direct investment, the opening up of markets and so on. You need to spend only about five minutes describing these in outline.

Part (b)(ii) is more challenging. It contains the directive word 'discuss' and requires you to look at three ways in which globalisation can affect Caribbean economies. An applied answer is therefore needed. Looking at the question, the crucial word is 'affect'. In other words you need to write a two-sided answer on the pros and cons of the effects of globalisation on Caribbean economies. A good approach is clearly one which uses the three features outlined in part (i) and to take these in turn, considering their impact on Caribbean economies.

How to impress CAPE Economics examiners

Let us start with a few typical comments that CAPE examiners will write on some of the examination answers they read:

'Does not answer the question'
'Too vague'
'Misses point of question'
'No application'
'Commentary not made'
'Ignores second aspect of question'

These comments clearly indicate that the candidates have not done what was expected from them in the question. So, the first way to impress any examiner reading your examination scripts is:

To answer the question

In other words, produce an answer as directed by the question. The information above, in particular the simple method for dissecting various examination questions, should help you to write your answer in a clear, well-structured manner as directed by the question. This point cannot be emphasised too much!

There are various other ways with which you might impress an examiner. For example:

Diagrams – these are very important and a relevant means of economic explanation. Many of the topics you come across in Economics can be illustrated by a diagram or by means of an explanation supported by a diagram. You have only to glance at the topics in this book to see this. So, a relevant correctly drawn diagram, used effectively in your answer, will impress an examiner reading your examination script. An example of good technique is shown in figure 1.

The diagram shows how the price of tickets to watch cricket will be affected by the introduction of a subsidy. As this diagram indicates, the subsidy will lead to an increase in supply, shifting the supply curve downwards and to the right. The price which spectators will have to pay falls from P_1 to P_2 – it does not fall to P_3, as part of the subsidy (that shown between P_3 and P_2) will be retained by the ground owners to offset the higher costs incurred as a result of the increase in the number of spectators.

Current issues and problems. One of the reasons for

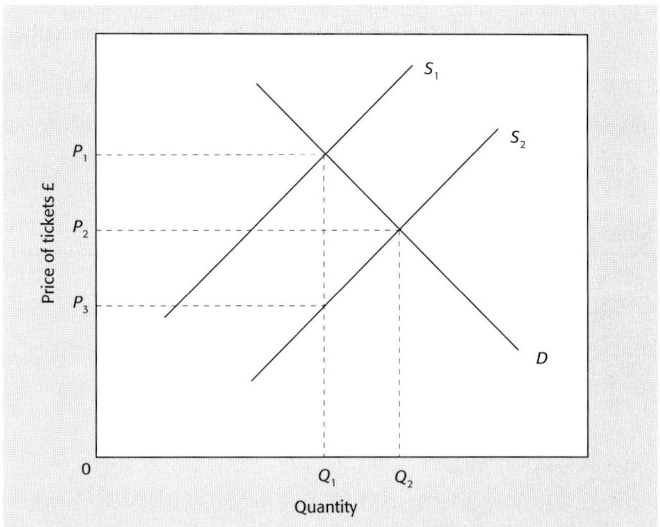

Figure 1 How to use a diagram effectively in your answers
Notes: D – Demand curve for cricket tickets
S_1 – Supply curve of cricket tickets
S_2 – Supply curve after introduction of subsidy

studying Economics is to help you understand some of the things that are taking place around you. So, when you get the opportunity, do so! For example, if you are answering a question on the negative externalities associated with environmental pollution, you might refer to a local Caribbean case which is known to you or something you have seen in a newspaper or magazine. Most of the topics in the syllabus can be supported by additional up-to-date material that is not always found in text books.

Refer to things you have read. It follows that there are instances where it would support your answer if you referred to this source material by name, for example an article, an example from a text book or the views of a particular economist.

Common mistakes made in CAPE Economics examinations

In addition to a failure to answer the question, the other main mistakes made by candidates are:

1 A failure to allocate writing time in an appropriate way.
2 Confusion over similar terms.
3 Meaningless, wrongly drawn diagrams or diagrams which add nothing to an answer.

Let us conclude this section by looking at each in turn.

1 The time available for each examination is relatively short. You must therefore make sure you allocate your time in the examination in a meaningful way.

Roughly speaking, allocate your writing time in direct proportion to the marks available.

Do not exceed the time you have allocated for each part.

If you cannot do a particular question, leave it and move on to the next part. (You can always return to it later on in the examination if time permits.) You will only get marks for the questions you answer – your script, though, will always be marked out of the total marks which are available.

2 A second problem in Economics examinations is that, on occasions, candidates sometimes confuse terms which are similar (in terms of content) or which have similar names (but mean something different). Table 3 contains a few common examples.

3 Finally, a common mistake which candidates often make is in the way in which they use diagrams in their answers. Common errors are:
- to label axes incorrectly or not to label them at all;
- to make diagrams too small;
- to draw lines and curves incorrectly, usually through being wrongly sloping;
- to fail to use a diagram in an answer when asked for one to be included;
- to include a diagram when one is not needed and where it does not enhance an answer at all.

Topic	Often confused with
elastic demand	inelastic demand
allocative efficiency	productive efficiency
prices	costs
merit goods	public goods
direct taxation	indirect taxation
external costs/benefits	social costs/benefits
real income	nominal income
rate of interest	exchange rates
fiscal policy measures	monetary policy measures
aggregate demand	aggregate supply
balance of trade	balance of payments
income	wealth
monopoly	monopolistic competition

Watch out also that you express formulae correctly – in particular elasticity formulae

Table 3 Common errors over terms and topics in the CAPE Economics syllabus

Self-assessment task

Three examples of badly drawn/incorrect diagrams are shown in figure 2. How many improvements can you make to them?

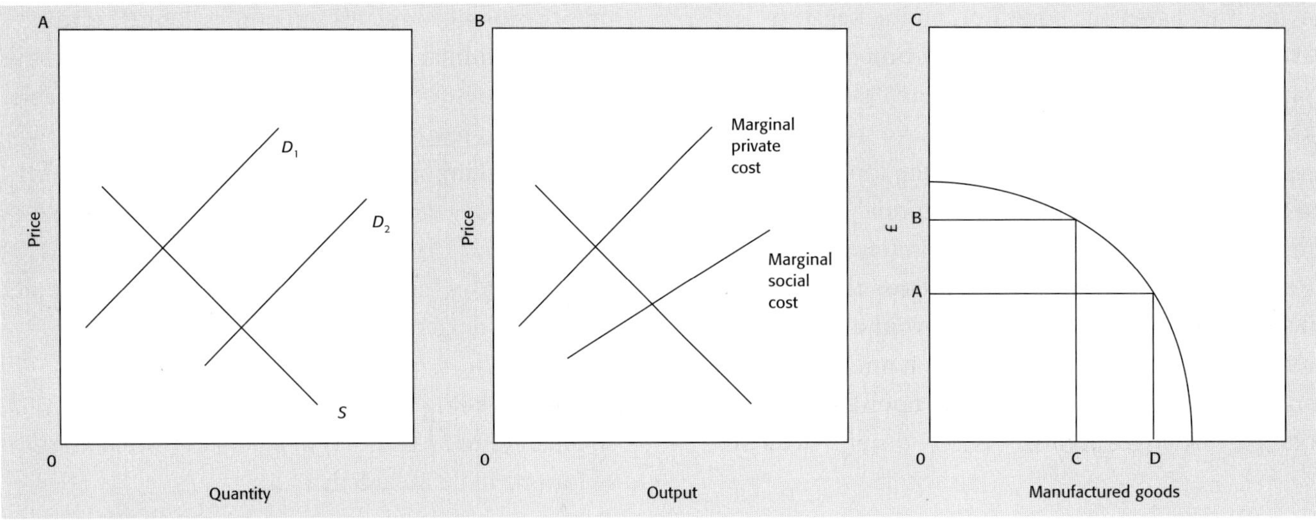

Figure 2 Examples of badly drawn diagrams

Summary

In this concluding section we have established that:

- It is very important for you to be well-organised and to be able to plan ahead if you are to succeed in CAPE Economics.
- Candidates who underperform in examinations have usually not been adequately briefed on the type and style of question.
- Revision should be an ongoing process, not just a last-minute activity you carry out just before a written examination.
- A lack of time and an inability to understand the relevance of directive words are the most common causes of underperformance.
- CAPE examinations contain a variety of forms of examination questions.

Glossary

The CAPE Economics syllabus contains many economic terms and concepts, some of which are set out in the learning outcomes and subject content of the syllabus document.

This glossary provides an alphabetical listing of these terms and concepts as well as many others that are included in the various topics in this book. When they first occur, the words and terms are reproduced in bold in the text and aggregated in a box at the end of each topic.

The definitions of terms and concepts in some cases are identical to what is contained in the text; for others, it differs slightly, mainly to aid your own understanding of the subject.

When writing essays or in examinations, it is good practice to use this vocabulary as much as you can.

abnormal profit – profits earned by a firm or an industry over and above normal profits; earned by a monopoly in the long run; in all other market structures, new firms will be attracted by such profits to enter the market

absolute advantage – in the context of international trade, for a given set of resources, one country is able to produce more of a particular good than another country

absolute poverty – a situation where a person or family is living at a level below what is regarded as the minimum level of consumption

accelerator – the process or model that links changes in investment to changes in output in the economy

active balances – the amount of money that is held by households and firms for possible use in the future

adverse selection – a situation of information failure, for example where an insurance company does not know the extent to which different customers are at risk and as a consequence charges all of them the same premium/price

aggregate demand – the total spending on goods and services produced in an economy. It is represented by $C + I + G + (X - M)$

aggregate expenditure – the total amount spent at different levels of income in a given time period in an economy

aggregate supply – the total output in an economy that producers are willing and able to supply at a given price level

allocative efficiency – this occurs where firms produce at the point where price is equal to the marginal cost of production; indicative that the appropriate quantity of resources is being used.

appreciation – where an exchange rate rises in relation to another currency or currencies; this results in exports becoming relatively more expensive, imports becoming relatively cheaper

asset price – the price that is paid for items such as land, buildings, capital equipment; can also apply to financial assets such as securities

asymmetric information – information that is not equally shared

automatic stabilisers – any form of taxation and government spending that reduces the intensity of economic fluctuations but where this is unprompted by any deliberate change in government fiscal policy

autonomous investment – investment that is not explained by changes in the level of output, for example investment that is determined by government policy

average propensity to consume – the proportion of disposable income that is spent on consumption

average propensity to save – the proportion of disposable income that is saved

average revenue – total revenue divided by the quantity that is sold

average total cost – total cost divided by the quantity that is produced

average product – total output divided by the number of workers employed; a simple measure of productivity in a firm

balance of payments – a record or statement of a country's transactions (trade and investment) with other countries; usually measured on an annual basis

balance of trade – the difference between the visible exports of goods and services and visible imports of goods and services

balanced budget – where government spending and receipts are equal

balanced budget multiplier – originated in Keynesian economics to describe a situation where a rise in government spending combined with an equal rise in taxation increases the level of national product by the exact amount that is spent

barriers to entry – any restriction that prevents new firms from entering a particular market

barter – a primitive form of trading involving the direct exchange of products

broad money – a measure of the money supply that includes interest-bearing deposits in financial institutions

budget – an annual statement of a government's plans for its own spending and tax revenue

budget constraint/budget line – a line that shows the combinations of two goods that a consumer can afford to buy with a given amount of income to spend

budget deficit – a situation where government spending exceeds tax revenue

budget surplus – a situation where tax revenue exceeds government spending

capital account – that part of the balance of payments showing transfers of financial assets between a country and elsewhere

capital consumption – the loss in value of capital equipment due to use over time; sometimes called depreciation

capital goods – man-made aids to production such as industrial machinery, equipment, factories

CARICOM – abbreviation of the Caribbean Community

cartel – a group of firms or producers who collude to fix prices or output in order to increase their profits

change in demand – any change in the determinants of demand other than the price of the product

choice – a situation where alternatives are available and where consumers, firms, governments and so on have to make an appropriate selection

circular flow of income – a simple model that is used to show how income flows between households and firms, taking into account leakages and injections

coefficient – a number that is part of an equation; usually has a constant value

collective bargaining – a situation where employers and trade unions get together to negotiate wages, hours and other conditions of work

command economy – a form of economy where decision-making is centralised and where market forces have little or no role in the allocation of resources

common market – a form of economic integration where there is the free movement of factors of production

comparative advantage – in the context of international trade, where a country is able to produce a good at a lower opportunity cost than other countries

complements – goods that are used together

concentration ratio – a measure of the proportion of sales or output that is produced by the '*x*' largest firms, where '*x*' can be 3, 4, or 5

constant – a value or set of conditions that does not change

consumer spending – the amount that is spent by consumers on goods and services

consumer surplus – the difference between the value a consumer places on units consumed and what is actually needed to purchase that product

consumption – the process by which goods and services are used by consumers to satisfy their wants

consumption function – the relationship between consumption and income; usually expressed in algebraic form

contestable market – a situation where there are no barriers to entry into a market and where, if abnormal profits are earned, there is a pool of potential entrants waiting to move into the market

credit creation multiplier – a numerical value of the extent to which banks are able to make loans on the basis of the deposits received

credits (in the balance of payments) – any item that has a positive entry

cross elasticity of demand – a numerical measure of the change in demand for one product following a change in price of another related product

current account (of the balance of payments) – a record of a country's trade in goods, services, income and current transfers

customs union – a form of economic integration where members agree to remove trade restrictions between themselves but where there is also a common external tariff on third party trade

debits (in the balance of payments) – any item that has a negative entry

debt forgiveness – a situation where some or all of a poor country's public debit is cancelled

debt management – the process by which a country's public debt is restructured in a more effective way to ease the problems of repayment

debt ratio – public debt as a proportion of GDP

debt service ratio – interest payments and loans due for repayment as a proportion of the total exports of goods and services

decreasing returns to scale – a situation where the ratio of output to inputs falls as inputs are increased

deflationary gap – the difference between the level of demand in the economy and that needed to achieve full employment

demand – the ability and willingness to buy a product

demand curve – this shows the relationship between the quantities demanded of a product and its price

demand schedule – the raw data that show the different quantities demanded at a range of prices

demerit goods – any good or activity that has negative externalities associated with it, that is seen by the government as being harmful and that is likely to be overconsumed if left to free market forces. Examples are excessive alcohol consumption and passive smoking

dependency ratio – the proportion of the population of a country that is non-productive

depreciation – where an exchange rate falls in relation to another currency; this results in exports becoming relatively cheaper and imports becoming relatively more expensive

deregulation – the removal of regulations that restrict competition in a market

derived demand – where the demand for a good or service is dependent upon the use that can be made from it, for example the demand for labour or transport

devaluation – a deliberate decrease in the value of a country's currency relative to that of another country; tends to be used in the context of a fixed exchange rate system

developing economy – any country that has a low income per head relative to the world's developed/high income countries

diminishing marginal utility – as demand for a good or service increases, the additional utility gained from consumption falls

diminishing returns – a situation where the increase in output is less than the additional resources that are used

discretionary fiscal policies – explicit or deliberate changes that are made to a government's own spending or taxation

diseconomies of scale – as the scale of output expands, average costs increase

discount rate – the interest rate that is used when discounting a stream of receipts or benefits to find their present value

dissaving – a situation where households spend more than their income through taking funds from bank accounts or selling assets

division of labour – a situation where workers specialise in a particular task or a part of the production process

double coincidence of wants – in the context of barter where two individuals must have goods or services that are wanted by each other in order for a transaction to take place

dumping – where products are sold or traded in a market at below their cost price

dynamic effects – the wider, non-trade effects arising from the development of economic integration

economic development – the processes through which the quality of life, economically and socially, can be improved

economic efficiency – where an economy is using its resources in an effective way by producing at the lowest possible cost

economic growth – an increase in the productive potential in an economy; it can be shown by an outward shift of the production possibility curve

economic integration – the processes through which a group of economies deliberately seek to form a larger, more powerful economic unit where national boundaries have little relevance

economic problem – infinite wants in relation to finite resources

economic rent – a payment made to a factor of production above what is necessary to keep it in its current use

economic union – the strongest form of integrated economic organisation; takes the form of a customs union, with common macroeconomic policies and may involve a single currency and interest rate. EU12 is a typical example

economies of scale – the benefits gained by a firm through producing on a larger scale; can be shown through falling long-run average costs

effective demand – what consumers are able and willing to buy at a particular period of time

efficiency – getting the maximum possible output from a given set of resources

elasticity – a measure of the responsiveness of the quantity demanded or supplied to a change in one of their determinants

endogenous variable – a variable that comes from the natural workings of the economic system

enterprise – a willingness on the part of an entrepreneur to take a business risk

equi-marginal principle – for a given level of income, a consumer will maximise total utility, where for each product consumed, the marginal utility divided by price is equal

exchange rate – the price of a country's currency with respect to that of another country

exogenous variable – a variable that influences the operations of an economic system from outside; these are invariably unplanned and unexpected

exchange controls – any measure imposed by a government to restrict the flow of currency from an economy

expenditure-dampening policies – fiscal or monetary policies that are designed to reduce domestic demand for imported goods and services

expenditure-switching policies – any policy that is designed to divert expenditure away from imported to domestically produced goods and services

exports – goods and services that are sold abroad

external benefit – a positive effect on third parties arising from the production and consumption decisions of others

external cost – a negative effect on third parties arising from the production and consumption decisions of others

external economies of scale – benefits in terms of falling long-run average costs that apply to firms or an industry as a consequence of factors outside of their direct control, for example benefits due to being concentrated in a particular location

external public debt – public debt owed to creditors overseas

externalities – effects on third parties that arise from the production and consumption decisions of others

factor endowment – the stock of factors of production available in an economy

factor market integration – the processes by which businesses, capital and labour are able to move freely within an integrated economic unit

factor mobility – the extent to which factors of production are able to move freely within an economy or integrated economic unit

factor payments – items such as wages, interest and rent that are the rewards for factors of production

financial account (of the balance of payments) – a record of the flows of investment into and out of an economy

financial economies (of scale) – the benefits, for example lower interest rates, that can be gained by large firms when borrowing money

firm – a generic term to denote any business that hires factors of production and buys and sells goods and services

fiscal balance – the annual difference or gap between government revenue and expenditure

fiscal consolidation – the process used by debtor countries to reduce their level of fiscal deficit

fiscal deficit – a budget situation whereby government expenditure exceeds income from the various forms of taxation

fiscal policy – the use of changes in government expenditure and taxation to manage aggregate demand

fixed capital – the stock of man-made means of production

fixed exchange rate – an exchange rate of a currency that is pre-determined and does not alter

floating exchange rate – an exchange rate of a currency that is determined by the forces of demand and supply in the international currency market

foreign direct investment – capital that flows into a country from elsewhere, usually from multinational corporations

free rider – in the context of public goods, someone who benefits but who does not contribute towards the cost

free trade area – a simple form of integrated economic unit in which members agree to remove trade restrictions between themselves

FTAA – the Free Trade Area of the Americas

functional distribution of income – the way in which national income is divided between the various factor inputs

Giffen goods – an exceptional good for which the quantity demanded falls when its price falls

Gini coefficient – a numerical measure of (say) income equality; it takes a value of between 0 and 1, where 0 represents a completely equal distribution

globalisation – the ways in which virtually all economies of the world have become closely linked with each other through trade, production, technology and finance

government spending – any spending by government at any level; this is one of the components of aggregate demand

Gross Domestic Product – a measure of total output produced in an economy by activities located in that country

Gross National Product – a measure of total output that takes into account the net income of residents from activities carried out abroad as well as in the home country

Herfindahl index – an index of industrial concentration; it is expressed as $H = \Sigma_i s_i^2$, where s_i is the market share of the *i*th firm

Human Development Index – a composite measure of well-being produced by the UN taking into account GDP per head, life expectancy and educational attainment

idle balances – assets temporarily held by households or firms when they believe the returns are too low

immobility of labour – why for social and economic reasons, unemployed workers may not wish to move from where they live in order to get a job

imperfections in the labour market – any obstacle to the free workings of the labour market

imports – goods and services bought from abroad

income effect – that part of the change in demand for a good arising from a change in its price that is attributed to the change in real income

income elasticity of demand – a measure of the responsiveness of demand due to a change in income

increasing returns to scale – a situation where the ratio of output to inputs is rising as inputs are increased

indifference curves – these show the combinations of two goods with which a consumer is equally satisfied

induced investment – investment that is made by a firm in response to changes in output

industry – a generic term that is applied to a collection of firms in a particular form of economic activity

inequality – a measure of the extent to which there is not an even state

infant industries – a new industry that during its early stages is unable to compete with established producers abroad

inferior goods – any good for which demand falls as income rises

inflation – a sustained increase in the general level of prices in an economy

inflationary gap – when there is excess demand in the economy above that which is needed to ensure full employment

information failure – a situation where choices are made on the basis of inaccurate or incomplete information

injections – additions to the circular flow of income, for example investment, government spending and exports

internal economies of scale – benefits to a firm, arising from various sources, leading to a fall in long-run average costs as the scale of output increases

interest – the payment required for borrowing a sum of money in addition to the amount borrowed

international investment position – a measure of the net of receipts and outflows of investment funds

International Monetary Fund – an agency of the United Nations which aims to promote international monetary co-operation and stability

investment – the creation of capital goods or adding to the stock of productive assets in an economy

Keynesians – economists who follow the ideas of John Maynard Keynes; they believe that government intervention in the economy should be used to correct situations where the market mechanism fails

labour – one of the factors of production that is essential for the production of goods and services

land – the factor of production which consists of the natural resources in an economy

leakages – withdrawals from the circular flow of income, for example savings, taxation and imports

lending – the process whereby an institution provides funds for borrowers

life cycle – the lifetime pattern of income and consumption

linear diagram – where the data on an axis are represented in a straight linear form

liquidity preference theory – a Keynesian theory to explain the reasons why people want to hold money

liquidity ratio – the proportion of assets held by a financial institution in liquid form in relation to its total liabilities

liquidity trap – a situation in an economy where real interest rates cannot be reduced any further in order to encourage an upturn in economic activity

loanable funds theory – a theory which states that the rate of interest is determined where the demand for funds for investment and the supply of savings are equated

long run – the time period when a firm is able to alter all of its factor inputs

Lorenz curve – a diagrammatic means of representing inequality

managed float – an exchange rate system whereby a country's monetary authorities try to manage its value through the buying and selling of the currency and through domestic macroeconomic policies

managerial economies – the benefit in terms of falling long-run average costs that can occur when a firm employs specialist managers

marginal cost – the change in total cost when output is increased by one more unit

marginal efficiency of capital – the highest rate of interest at which a capital project can be expected to break even

marginal product – the increase in output that arises from one additional unit of input

marginal propensity to consume – the proportion of an increase in income that is spent on consumption

marginal propensity to import – the proportion of an increase in income that is spent on imports

marginal propensity to save – the proportion of an increase in income that is saved

marginal rate of substitute – the rate at which consumers are willing to substitute one good for another; it is represented by the slope of an indifference curve

marginal revenue – the change in total revenue arising from the sale of one more unit

marginal revenue product – the change in total revenue as a result of employing one more unit of labour

marginal utility – the change in an individual's utility arising from the consumption of one more unit of a good or service

market demand – the total demand for a good or service

market economy – a form of organisation where the allocation decisions of consumers and producers are taken through the price mechanism

market failure – any situation where market forces do not achieve an efficient allocation of resources

marketing economies – the benefits in terms of falling long-run average costs that can occur when large firms are able to bulk buy from suppliers or make savings on their advertising costs

maximisation – any situation where the highest possible value is achieved

maximum – the highest value or point of a function

medium of exchange – money's function in making it possible for transactions to take place

merit goods – products such as health care and education that the government regards as beneficial and that would be underconsumed if left to the individual and market forces

minimum – the lowest value or point of a function

minimum efficient scale – the minimum level of production at which the benefits of all known economies of scale are enjoyed by a firm

mixed economy – the typical form of economic organisation in which resources are allocated through the price mechanism and government involvement or direction

model – used by economists as a simplified means of representing a real-world situation

Monetarists – the school of economists who maintain that control of the money supply is essential for economic stability

money base – money that consists of notes and coins in circulation plus cash that is held in banks or by banks at the central bank

monetary policy – measures that are used by the government or some independent body to control the money supply either directly or through variations in the rate of interest

money supply – the total amount of money in an economy; this includes currency and relevant deposits

monopolistic competition – a market structure in which there are many firms, differentiated products and few barriers to entry and exit

monopoly – a market structure in which there is just one firm, a unique product and high barriers to entry

moral hazard – the effects that being insured has on an individual's behaviour; it could lead to more risky behaviour

moral suasion – in a monetary policy context where the government puts pressure on the central bank to operate in a way that is consistent with its macroeconomic policy

most-favoured-nation-treatment – a WTO principle that no member can give special favours to one member over another

multinational corporation – a firm that operates in more than one country

multiplier – a numerical estimate of the relationship between a change in spending and the final change in expenditure

narrow money – notes and coins in circulation, cash held in banks and balances held by commercial banks at the central bank

national debt – the debt owed by a country's government, to home and overseas creditors

national income – the total income of residents of a country measured at factor cost, allowing for capital consumption

national treatment – an underlying principle of the WTO whereby foreigners and locals should be treated equally

nationalised industry – any activity that is publicly owned and operated

natural monopoly – a monopolistic market where duplication makes no sense; average costs will be lowest where production is by one firm only

negative externality – an activity that produces harmful side effects on third parties, the costs of which are not covered by those producing them

Net Domestic Product – the total value of goods and services produced in an economy, after deducting capital consumption

net exports – the difference between total exports and total imports

Net National Product – the total value of incomes produced by the factors of production owned by residents of a country, after deducting capital consumption

net property income from abroad – the net receipts from property income, including rent, dividends, interest and retained profits received from abroad

new classical economists – the school of economists who believe that markets provide the most efficient allocation of resources

nominal exchange rate – the exchange rate as published in monetary terms

nominal interest rate – the rate of interest in monetary terms

non-discrimination – equal treatment to be applied to all comparable cases

non-excludable – a characteristic of public goods whereby it is impossible to stop all benefiting from consumption

non-linear diagram – a diagram or graph on which one scale is not linear, for example logarithmic

non-price competition – a situation whereby firms compete on the basis of brand, advertising, customer service and so on, rather than by price

non-rival – a characteristic of public goods whereby the benefit of those consuming a good or service is not diminished as more is consumed

normal good – a good where demand increases as income rises

normal profit – a cost of production that is just sufficient to keep a firm in operation in an industry; a long-run characteristic of monopolistic competition and perfect competition

normative economics – concepts and issues of Economics based upon opinions that cannot be tested

notional demand – demand for a good or service that is backed by purchasing power

oligopoly – a market structure with a few large firms and high barriers to entry

open market operations – the buying and selling of securities by the central bank in order to change interest rates and the supply of money

opportunity cost – the cost in terms of the next best alternative forgone

optimum population – the population size that is consistent with the highest level of output per head

ostentatious goods – exceptional goods for which demand increases when their price increases; these are rare and have snob value unlike Giffen goods

parameter – something that is given and cannot be influenced

Pareto efficiency – a situation where it is not possible to alter the existing allocation of resources without making someone else worse off

paternalism – any actions that control what people do, overriding their preferences

perfect competition – a market structure consisting of many firms, identical products and no barriers to entry and exit

permanent income – the amount that someone can consistently spend and maintain at that level in the future

planned economy – a form of economic structure where production and distribution decisions are controlled by a central authority

positive economics – concepts and issues in Economics that originate from empirical investigation

poverty line – the level of income that is just sufficient for a household to survive

precautionary motive – a reason for holding money for unexpected or unforeseen reasons

price agreement – a situation where a firm or others get together to fix a price

price ceiling – a maximum price that is imposed in a market

price discrimination – a feature of monopolistic markets whereby the market is segmented so that different prices are charged to different customers

price elasticity of demand – a numerical measure of the responsiveness of the quantity demanded of a product in relation to a change in its price

price elasticity of supply – a numerical measure of the responsiveness of the quantity supplied of a product in relation to a change in its price

price floor – the lowest price that is imposed in a market

price index – a numerical measure of the prices of goods of a particular type, often over a period of time

price leadership – a market situation where one firm sets the price or alters the price and other firms follow

primary fiscal balance – the fiscal balance excluding interest payments

private costs – costs incurred by those who produce or consume a good or service

privatisation – the sale of publicly owned businesses, assets or services to the private sector

production – the use of resources to make goods and services

production frontier – for two products, the boundary between what can and cannot be produced

production function – this shows the maximum output possible with a given set of inputs

production possibility curve – a representation of the maximum level of output of two types of product that can be produced with a country's existing resources and state of technology

production transformation curve – as production possibility curve

productive efficiency – where a firm produces at the lowest average cost

profit maximisation – assumed to be the usual objective of a firm; it occurs at the level of output where marginal cost equals marginal revenue

profits – the difference between total revenue and total costs of a firm

protectionist policies – any policy that restricts free international trade

public debt – a more up-to-date term for national debt

public goods – goods which are non-rival and non-excludable and that are funded from taxation

Quantity Theory of Money – the theory that the price level in the economy is directly proportional to the money supply; any changes in the money supply have a direct effect on the price level

quota – a physical restriction on the quantity of imports allowed to enter a country; a limit on the supply of a good or service

rate of unemployment – a numerical measure of the number unemployed as a proportion of the labour force

real effective exchange rate – the foreign exchange rate of a currency against that of others taking inflation into account

real exchange rate – the foreign exchange rate of a currency taking inflation into account

real interest rate – the interest rate taking inflation into account

real wage unemployment – voluntary unemployment where workers refuse to work for any wage that is less than the equilibrium real wage

reallocation of resources – any switch in production that takes place from a position of equilibrium

rectangular hyperbola – a mathematical function such as a demand curve that has a unitary value of price elasticity of demand throughout

regulation – rules or procedures that firms are obliged to follow

relative poverty – a situation where households cannot afford what is agreed to be a typical level of consumption

rent – payment made to the owners for the use of land or buildings

rental rate – an alternative to the use of price when applied to factors of production

required rental – the minimum income that allows the buyer of a capital asset to break even over a given period of time

revaluation – a deliberate appreciation in the exchange rate of a currency

risk – recognition that the outcome of any action is not certain

risk-bearing economies – the benefit in terms of falling long-run average costs that can accrue to large firms through being able to spread the likely effects of taking risks

sales maximisation – an alternative objective of firms whereby the aim is to maximise the volume of sales

sales revenue maximisation – an alternative objective of firms where the aim is to maximise sales revenue; this involves producing where marginal revenue is zero

satisficing profits – an alternative objective of firms where the aim is to achieve a level of profits that keeps its owners or shareholders happy

saving – the difference between income and consumption

saving function – the relationship between saving and income

scale of preferences – the rank order of choices made by rational consumers

scarcity – a situation where there are insufficient resources to meet all wants

scatter diagram – the graphical representation of the individual points in a data set

short run – the time period when a firm is unable to alter factor inputs except for one, usually labour

social costs – the total costs to society arising from the production or consumption of a good or service

social welfare – a measure of the total welfare of members of society

socially optimum output – the output that is best for society and when social welfare is maximised

specialisation – the way in which an economy concentrates on producing certain goods and services

speculative motive – a reason for holding money with a view to making expected gains in the future

static effects – in the context of economic integration, these are the effects arising as a consequence of trade creation and trade diversion

stocks – goods that are held by a firm; it is also used as a synonym for shares

store of value – a function of money that reflects its attractiveness when held by its owners

subsidies – a payment made by governments to encourage the production or consumption of goods and services; the effect of subsidies is to reduce market prices

substitutes – goods or services that are seen as realistic alternatives to each other

substitution effect – that part of the effect of a price change on demand that is due to a change in relative prices

supply curve – a curve that shows the relationship between price and the different quantities that producers are willing to supply

supply schedule – data that show the different quantities supplied at various prices

surveillance – one of the functions of the IMF involving taking responsibility for monitoring the economic policies of member countries

sustainable economic growth – growth that is achieved in such a way that it does not endanger a country's ability to grow in the future

tariff – a tax imposed by a government on imports for protectionist reasons

taxes – a compulsory charge that is made by governments on the consumption of goods and services and on factor incomes

technical assistance – advice given by the IMF to provide sound economic policies amongst its members

technical economies – benefits in terms of falling long-run average costs that can arise through the increased use of technology

Tiger economies – a generic term used to describe the rapidly growing economies in Southern Asia

time lag – a delay in the outcome of a particular economic policy

total cost – the total cost of production

total product – the total output of a firm

total revenue – the value of the quantity sold multiplied by price

trade creation – the way in which high-cost domestic production is replaced by more cost efficient imports from within a customs union

trade diversion – the way in which trade is moved from a lower cost source outside a customs union to a higher cost supplier within

trade union – an organisation that represents employees in the collective bargaining process and in other ways relating to their terms of employment

trade weighted exchange rate – the external exchange rate of a currency where the weights are directly proportional to other countries' shares in that economy's trade

transactions motive – the reason why money is held for the day-to-day operation of buying and selling goods and services

transfer earnings – the amount that is earned by a factor of production in its best alternative use

transitory income – any income that is not guaranteed on a regular basis

unemployment – a situation where those who are willing and able to work are unable to obtain a job

unitary elasticity – where the elasticity estimate is equal to 1

unit of account – a characteristic of money which allows the value of an item to be made

utility – a measure of the satisfaction received from the consumption of a good or service

value judgements – where society takes a decision on what is good for say, an individual or the economy as a whole

variable – any measure that can be changed

wages – the money paid to labour in return for its services

wants – anything that an individual or group wishes to consume

weights – values given, say, to goods in a price index to reflect their relative importance in a typical consumer's pattern of expenditure

withdrawals – leakages from the circular flow of income

World Bank – an international organisation that provides various forms of financial help and support

World Trade Organisation – an international organisation that seeks to promote universal free trade

'x' inefficiency – a situation where firms do not produce at the lowest average cost

Index

ability to buy 43
ability to pay 47–8, 111
abnormal profit 72, 90
absolute advantage 233, 235–6
absolute poverty 129–30
accelerator 181–2
active balances 190
active fiscal policies 197
actual input of goods and services 224
actual output of goods and services 224–5
adverse selection 104–5, 137, 138
advertising 87, 136
ageing
  economics of 17–18
  of population 121
aggregate demand 169–70
  aggregate supply and 171–2
aggregate expenditure 175–6
aggregate supply 170–1
  aggregate demand and 171–2
all items price index 6
allocative efficiency 94, 95–7, 135
allocative efficiency output 135
amortisation 206
appreciation in exchange rate 260, 261
Asian financial crisis (1996) 36, 204, 277
asset price 131
Association of South East Asian Nations (ASEAN) 243
asymmetric information 137
automatic stabilisers 198
autonomous investment 181
availability of substitutes 233
average fixed cost 62
average product 60
average propensity to consume 175
average propensity to save 175
average revenue 76
average total cost 62
average variable cost 62

balance of payments 153, 154–7
  definition 250
  disequilibrium in 251–6
  equilibrium in 251
  monetary policy, fiscal policy and 203
  problems 251–3
balance of trade 153
balanced budget 197
balanced budget multiplier 197
bank multiplier 193
Bank of Jamaica 194
bar chart 7, 36
barrier to exit 85
barriers to entry 67, 84, 85–6, 110
barter 186
benefits, welfare 122, 131
black market 112
'boom-bust' cycle 203
brand loyalty 84
brand proliferation 87
broad money 192
budget 196–9
budget constraint 40–1
budget deficit 197
budget line 40–1
budget surplus 197

capital 116, 131
capital account 153, 154
capital consumption 24
capital expenditure 156
capital goods 18, 24–5, 225–6
CARICOM 204, 208, 246–7, 247–8
CARICOM Single Market Economy (CSME) 246–7
cartel 87
causal relationship 45, 66
ceteris paribus 43, 45, 46, 49, 51, 66
change in demand 45, 46
choices 16
circular flow of income 160, 174
classical theory of unemployment 168–9
Code of Fiscal Stability (UK) 198
coefficient 36
collective bargaining 124
collusion between oligopolists 87–8
command (planned) economy 25, 26–8
commercial banks 193–4
common market 243–4

comparative advantage 234, 235–6
competition and markets 107–8
complements 48
concentration ratios 80
constant 36
consumer durables 19
consumer goods 24
consumer loyalty 85, 89
consumer price index 6
consumer spending 169
consumer surplus 45–6
consumers, definition 43
consumption 19, 175–6
consumption function 35, 175
contestable markets 91–2
continuous data 5
continuous relationship 45, 66
contracting out 110
contraction of supply 66
controls 108
co-operation between oligopolists 87–8
cost and revenue curves 35
cost of living index 147
cost opportunity 131
cost(s)
  average fixed 62
  average total 62
  average variable 62
  of depreciation 131
  of economic growth 228
  energy 101
  external 30, 99, 101
  fixed 61
  labour 101
  marginal 62
  private 30, 99, 101
  raw material 101
  shift in supply curve and 67
  in short and long 62–3
  short-run 61–5
  social 30, 99, 101
  total 62
  variable 61–2
cost-push inflation 125
credit creation multiplier 193
credit multiplier 193
credits 250
cross elasticity of demand (XED) 53–4, 56
cross-sectional data 3
cross subsidisation 78
currency substitution 194–5
current account 153–4
  in emerging economies 252–3
current transfers 154
customer loyalty 85, 89
customs union 243, 244

data skills 3–7
debits 250
debt management 212
debt ratio 206
debt service ratio 206
decreasing returns to scale 61
definition of economics 1–3
deflationary fiscal policy 255–6
deflationary gap 179–80
deflationary monetary policy 256
demand, definition 43
demand curve 34–5, 42, 43–5
  attitudes towards products 48
  for capital 131, 132
  exceptions to downward sloping curve 49
  financial ability to pay 47–8
  price, availability and attractiveness of related products 48
  shifts in 46–9
demand for capital 131–2
demand for labour 117–18
demand schedule 44
de-merit goods 103, 104
demography 17–18
dependency ratio 219–20
dependent variable 49
depreciation 24, 131, 159
  in exchange rate 260, 261, 262
deregulation 109–10
derived demand 117
destroyer pricing 86
devaluation 256
developing economies 218
  capital consumption 25
  characteristics 218
  economic growth 224–8
diminishing marginal utility 39
diminishing returns 60
discount rates 192–3
discrete data 3
discretionary fiscal policies 197–8
diseconomies of scale 63
disequilibrium in balance of payments 251–2
  causes 253–4

consequences 254–5
policy measures 255–6
dissaving 175
division of labour 21
Doha Round 268
double coincidence of wants 186
dumping 240
duopoly 86
dynamic effects 245

economic development 216–18
economic efficiency 94
economic growth 23, 152–3, 216
benefits 228
comparison of living standards over time 161–2, 163
comparison of living standards between countries 161–2, 163–5
costs 228
and developing economies 224–8
factors contributing to 225–6
impact of indebtedness on 226
economic integration
costs and benefits of 244–6
meaning of 243–4
economic problems 16–18
economic rent 127–8
economic structure 218–19
economic system 25
economies of scale 63, 86, 107
effective demand 43
efficiency 30–2
elasticity 49
business relevance of 54–6
elasticity of supply (price elasticity of supply) 68–9
emerging economies
current account in 252–3
emigration 122
employment 221
endogenous variables 36
energy costs 101
enterprise (entrepreneurship) 18–19, 116
entry limit pricing 86
environment 137
equilibrium employment 122
equilibrium exchange rate, determination in a free market 260–5
causes of changes 260
equilibrium income
in two-, three- and four-sector economic models 180–1
equilibrium wage 123
equi-marginal principle 39–40
estimates of data 5
European Union 220, 243, 244, 246, 247–8
exchange control 238
exchange rates 150–1, 233
currency flows 259–60
determination in a free market 260–5
determination of 259
effects of changes on the economy 261–3
managed systems 265
regimes 263
excise duties 68
exogenous variables 36
expenditure-dampening policies 239, 255–6
expenditure measure 160
expenditure-switching policies 238, 255
export revenue 232–3
export subsidies 238
exports 231
price of 232
extension of supply 66
external benefit 100
external cost 30, 99, 101
external economy of scale 64
external public debt 206
external trade 221
externalities 30, 99–101, 111
definition 99
negative 99, 101
positive 100, 101
problem created by 100–1
eyeballing 5

factor endowment 19
factor market integration 245
factor mobility 23
factor payments 116
factors of production 18–19, 58, 116
failure of economics 4
fair trade 239
financial account 153, 154
financial economies 64
financial intervention 108–9, 111–12
financial services 137
firm, definition 72, 77
fiscal balance 206, 208
fiscal consolidation 212
fiscal deficit 156, 193
fiscal policy 196
balance of payments and 203

inflation and 201–3
potency of 203–4
unemployment and 200–1
Fisher equation 188
fixed capital 131
fixed costs 61
fixed exchange rate 263
floating exchange rate 263, 264
follow-the-leader agreement 88
forced labour 16
Ford, Henry 21
forecasts 5, 8–9
foreign direct investment (FDI) 272–3
benefits and costs 273–5
four-sector economy 181
franchising 110
free rider issue 106
free trade 267
free trade area 243, 244
Free Trade Area of the Americas (FTAA) 248
Friedman, Milton 157, 188
functional distribution of income 117

General Agreement on Tariffs and Trade (GATT) 238
general price level 147
genetically modified plants 17
geographical immobility of labour 128
Giffen goods 49
Gini coefficient 129
global brands 275–6
global economy 231–2
global sourcing 276–7
globalisation 144, 275–7
effects of 277–8
factors responsible for 277–9
Golden Rule 198
Gorbachev, President 28
government intervention 108–9
impact of 110–12
in wage determination 125
government policy, shift in supply curve and 68
government spending 129, 169, 177
Gross Domestic Product (GDP) 28, 152, 153, 159, 177, 178, 225, 231
at current prices 160
deflator 161
measurement 159–60
gross investment 25
Gross National Product (GNP) 159, 216, 218
'guns and butter' argument 27

health care 137
heavily indebted poor countries (HIPC) 212, 226, 227
Herfindahl index (Herfindahl-Hirschman index) 73
hidden economy 161, 162
hit and run 92
horizontal integration 87
housing 137
human development 223–4
Human Development Index (HDI) 130, 166, 223–4

idle balances 190
immigration 122
immobility of labour 127–8
imperfections in the labour market 124
import penetration ratio 238
imports 231
income 154
income and substitution effects of price change 42
income determination 177–8
income distribution 221
income effect 41, 120, 121
income elasticity of demand (YED) 52–3, 55–6
income groups 218
income increase, effect on consumer choice 42
income inequality measures 128–9
income measure 160
income transfers 110
increasing returns to scale 61
indebtedness, measures of 206
independent variable 49
index numbers 6
indicators of comparative development 218–23
classification according to levels of income 218
classification according to levels of indebtedness 218
indifference curve analysis applied to labour supply 120–8
indifference curves 41–3
indirect taxes 68
induced investment 181
industrial concentration ratio 72–3
industry, revenue 77
inequality 128
infant industry 240
inferior good 42
inflation 145–7, 188
monetary policy, fiscal policy and 201–3
inflationary gap 179–80
informal economy 161

information failure 103, 136–7
injections 178
insurance 137
insurance market 17–8
interest 116
interest rates 148–50
  determination of 189–90
internal economies of scale 63
international investment position 153
International Labour Office (ILO) 151
International Monetary Fund (IMF) 150, 153, 209–10, 268–9
international tourism 233
investment 24, 169, 176–7
  in human capital 225
invisible balance 154
invisible hand 26
isocosts 61
isoquant 59, 61

Jubilee 2000 226–8

key performance indicators (KPIs) 163
Keynes, John Maynard 157
Keynesian 45(diagram 177, 178
Keynesian view 157, 188
kinked demand curve theory 87

labour 18, 116
labour-capital balance, output and 58–9
labour costs 101
labour demand 117–18
labour exploitation 239–40
labour force participation rate 121–2
labour market 117–18
labour shortages 122
labour supply 118–19
  to firm or industry 121
  individual's 119–20
  long-run 121–2
land 18, 116, 132–3
leakages 178
life cycle hypothesis 176
linear data 37
linear relationship 45, 66
liquidity preference 189
liquidity ratio 193
liquidity trap 190, 191
literacy 161–2
living standards 223
  indicators of 65–6
  international comparisons 229
loanable funds theory 189
long run 60–1, 84, 85
  costs in 62–3
long-run aggregate supply (LRAS) 170, 171
long-run supply of labour 121–2
Lorenz curve 128–9

macroeconomic forecasts 9
macroeconomics, definition 1
Malthus, Reverend Thomas 219
managed float 263
managerial economies 64
marginal cost 62
marginal efficiency of capital 182–3
marginal external cost (MEC) 111
marginal product 60
marginal propensity to consume 175
marginal propensity to import 255–6
marginal propensity to save 175
marginal rate of substitution 42
marginal revenue 76
marginal revenue product of capital 131
marginal revenue product of labour 118–20
marginal utility 39, 40
market demand curve 44, 45
market demand schedule 44
market economy 25–6
market failure 30–1, 99
market segmentation 87
market structures 80
market supply curve 65–6
  shifts in 66–8
marketing economies 63–4
Marx, Karl 26
maximum price controls 112
maximum value 35
Measurable Economic Welfare (MEW) 165
medium of exchange 187
MERCOSUR 248
merit goods 30–1, 103, 104, 136
microeconomic forecasts 9
microeconomics, definition 1
migration 127
minimum efficient scale 65
minimum value 35
minimum wage 125, 131
mixed economy 25, 28–30
mobility of labour 127
model, definition 34

Monetarists 157
monetary base 192
monetary policy 196
balance of payments and 203
inflation and 201–3
potency of 203–4
unemployment and 200–1
money, functions and characteristics of 186–7
money (nominal) GDP 160
money hoarding 194–5
money supply 190–2
monopolistic competition 80, 84–5
monopoly 88–9
concentration of power in markets and 107–8
vs perfect competition 89–91
monopsony 125–6
moral hazard 104, 105, 137, 138
moral suasion 193
most-favoured-nation treatment 266
multilateral free trade 233
multinational corporation 272
multiplier 180–1

narrow money 192
national debt 198
national income 159
national income statistics, use of 159
national minimum wage 125
national treatment 267
nationalised industries 109
natural monopoly 64–5, 88, 90
negative externality 99, 101
net domestic assets 194
Net Domestic Product (NDP) 159
Net Economic Welfare (NEW) 165
net exports 169, 177
net international reserves 194
net investment 25
Net National Product (NNP) 159
net property income from abroad 159
new classical economists 157
newly industrialising countries (NICs) 29
nominal exchange rates 150
nominal GDP 160
nominal interest rate 149
nominal terms 147
non-discrimination 266–7
non-excludable good 105
non-linear data 37
non-price competition 84, 87
non-rival good 105
normal goods 42
normal profit 72
normative economics 31–2
normative statements 3
North America Free Trade Agreement (NAFTA) 243
notional demand 43

occupational immobility of labour 128
oligopoly 73, 86–7
open market operations (OMO) 192, 194
opportunity 226
opportunity cost 21–2, 72, 131
optimum output 62
optimum population 220–1
Organisation for Economic Co-operation and Development (OECD) 221
ostentatious goods 49
output measure 160
over-production 101

paradox of thrift 178
parameter 36
Pareto efficiency 30, 97, 98
paternalism 104
perestroika 28
perfect competition 80–3, 98, 107
vs monopoly 89–91
permanent income hypothesis 176
pie chart 7, 36
planned (command) economy 25, 26–8
population growth 219–20
population structure 219–20
positive economics 31–2
positive externalities 100, 101
positive statements 2
poverty 129–31
poverty line 130
precautionary motive 189
predatory pricing 86
price
demand and 43
of exports 232
product, effect on price elasticity of demand 51
price agreement 87
price ceilings 31
price controls 108
price discrimination 88–9
price elasticity of demand (PED) 49–52, 86
downward-sloping linear demand curve and 52

factors influencing 51–2
perfectly elastic 50
perfectly inelastic 50
revenue and 76–7
total expenditure/total revenue and 54–5
unitary elasticity 51
price elasticity of supply (PES) 68–9
price floors 31
price index 147
price inelasticity 221
price leadership 87
price stabilisation 112
price war 68
primary fiscal balance 208
Primary Sector 218
private benefits 99–100
private costs 30, 99, 101
privatisation 4, 28, 109–10, 212
process innovation 87, 90
product, definition 43
product differentiation 84
product innovation 87
product transformation curve 22
production 19
production frontier 22
production function 59–60
production possibility curve 22–5
applications 24–5
command economies 27
shifts in 23–4
production possibility frontier 97
productive efficiency 94, 98
profit maximisation 72, 77–8, 107
profits 72, 116
progressive tax system 111, 129, 130–1
protectionism 237, 238–40
proxies 138
public debt 206
in the Caribbean economies 206–9
causes 209–13
effects on economy 210–11
reducing 211–13
public goods 30, 105–6, 110–11
public sector 28
purchasers (consumers), definition 43

quantities 43
Quantity Theory of Money 35, 188–90
quasi-public goods 105
quotas 237–8

rationing 112
raw material costs 101
real effective exchange rate 151
real exchange rate 150
real GDP 160–1, 163, 198, 203
real interest rate 149–50
real wage unemployment 169
reallocation of resources 23
rectangular hyperbola 53
regulation 108, 111
relative poverty 130
rent 116
rental rate 131, 132–3
required rental 131
resources 16
Retail Prices Index (RPI) 147
revaluation 256
revenue 76–7
revenue deficit 156
risk-bearing economies 64
risk of production 18
rural-urban migration 222

sale revenue maximisation 78
sales maximisation 78
satisfaction 43
satisficing 79, 87
saving 175
saving function 175
scale of preference 19
scarcity 16
scatter diagram 37
Secondary Sector 218
setup costs 85
shadow economy 161
short run 59, 60, 84–5
short-run aggregate supply (SRAS) 170
short-run costs 61–5
shut-down price 82
skills gap 245
slavery 16
Slutsky approach 42–3
Smith, Adam 21, 25–6
social benefits 99–100
social costs 30, 99, 101
social welfare 135
socially optimum output 135
source of data 5
specialisation 20–1
speculative motives 190
standards 111

state production 109
static effects 245
statistical forecasts 8
stocks 131
store of value, money as 187
subsidies 108, 111–12, 129
substitutes 48
  availability of 233
  range and attractiveness, effect on price elasticity of demand 51
substitution effect 41, 120, 121
sunk costs 85
supply curve 65–6
  shifts in 66–8
supply of capital 132
supply of labour 118–19
supply schedule 65
sustainable economic growth 228–9

tariffication 267
tariffs 237, 267
taxes 17, 108, 111
  indirect 68
  Jamaica 108
  level 122
  progressive direct 129, 130–1
  value added 68
technical economies 63
technical efficiency 94
technology 222–3
technology transfer 274
terms of trade 210, 249–2
Tertiary Sector 218
Thatcher, Margaret 28
three-sector economy 180–1
Tiger economies 29
time
  demand and 43
  price elasticity of demand and 52
time-based relationship 45, 66
time lags 203
time series data 3, 6
title of data 5
tool kit 3–7
total cost 62
total output 159
total product 60
total revenue 76
total utility 39
trade 4
trade creation 244
trade diversion 244–5
trade in goods 153
trade in services 154
trade unions 124–5
trade-weighted exchange rates 150–1
transactions motive 189
transfer earnings 127–8
transfers, income 110
transition economies 4
transitory income 176
trickle down effect 216
two-sector economy 180

under-production 101
unemployment 5, 26, 151–2, 221
  monetary policy, fiscal policy and 200–1
unemployment forecasts 9
unemployment rate 151
unit of account 187
unitary elasticity 51
urbanisation 222
Uruguay Round 267
utility 39, 43

value added 160
value added tax 68
value judgement 103–4
variable 36
variable costs 61–2
visibles 153

wage determination
  under free market forces 122–4
  trade unions and government in 124–5
wage differentials 128
wage rate 118
wages 116
wants 16
  unlimited 19–20
weighted average (mean) 5–6
weights 147
willingness to buy 43
withdrawals 178
World Bank 204, 269–70
World Trade Organisation (WTO) 233, 266–8
  agreements 267
  Doha Round 268
writing skills 9–11

x-inefficiency 90, 107, 110

Multiple choice questions

Sample paper, Unit 1

This sample paper covers a range of topics that are included in Unit 1 of the CAPE examinations. It consists of 24 questions.

Each item/question has four suggested answers, A, B, C and D. Read each carefully and then decide which you feel is best or most likely.

1 As an Economics student, you decide to revise for your CAPE examinations rather than play cricket with your friends. What is the opportunity cost of this decision?

A You will get a higher mark in the CAPE examinations.

B Your friends' team loses the cricket match.

C The pleasure you would have got from playing cricket.

D The money you saved on bus fares and drinks by not playing cricket.

2 The diagram below shows the production possibilities of an economy that produces consumer goods and capital goods

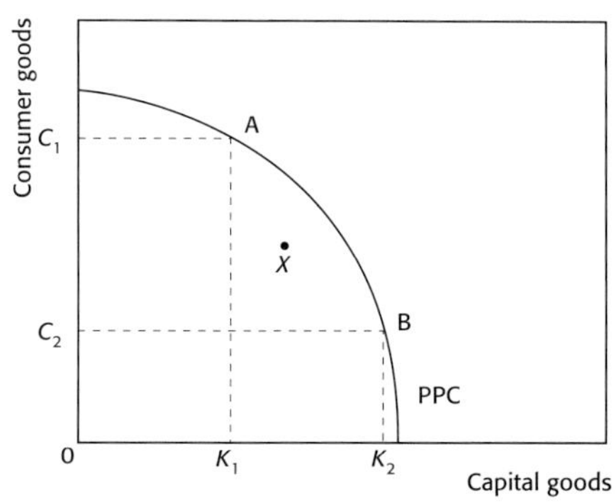

Which of the following is most likely to lead to an improvement in current living standards?

A A movement along the PPC from B to A.

B A movement along the PPC from A to B.

C A movement from X on to the PPC.

D An outward shift of the PPC.

3 Which of these is a positive statement?

A The rate of inflation in Jamaica in 2005 was 9.9 per cent.

B The rate of inflation in Jamaica in 2005 was reasonable.

C The rate of inflation in Jamaica affects the poor more than the rich.

D The rate of inflation in Jamaica could deter international tourists.

4 Which of these events can be classified as an exogenous variable that may have an effect on the well being of the Caribbean tourist industry?

A A rise in the general price level in many Caribbean islands.

B A crash on the US stock market resulting in the immediate depreciation of the dollar.

C British tourists switching demand for holidays in the Caribbean to South East Asia.

D An increase in the size of cruise liners which has meant that access to some Caribbean ports has become more difficult.

5 The diagram below shows the initial supply and demand curves (S and D) for a good.

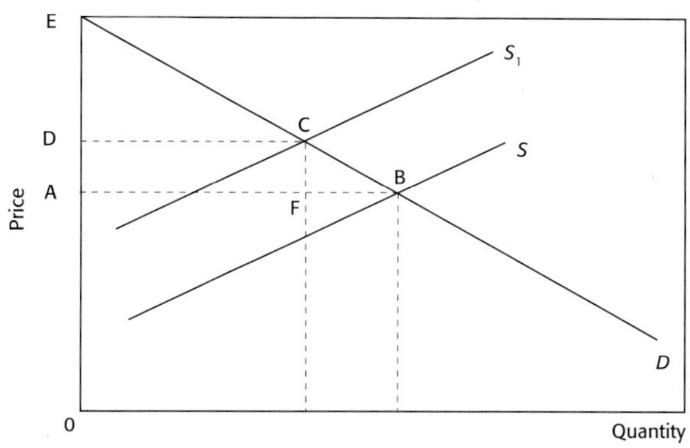

What is the change in consumer surplus when the supply curve shifts from S to S_1?

A DCBA

B DCFA

C EDC

D CBF

6 The diagram below shows two demand curves for lap top computers.

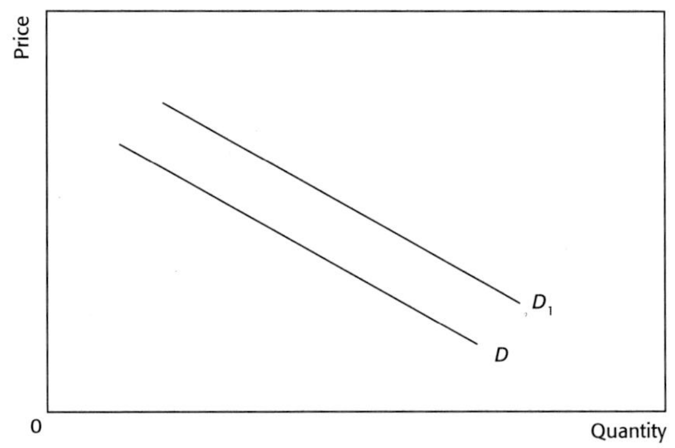

Which of these situations is most likely to have resulted in a shift in the demand curve from D to D_1?

A An increase in demand for personal computers.
B A fall in the price of lap top computers.
C An increase in disposable income.
D A rise in the cost of postage.

7 A Caribbean airline sells 5,000 tickets per month for travel to the UK at an average price to \$600. When it reduces the price to \$540, it sells an average of 6,000 tickets per month. What is the price elasticity of demand?

A –2
B +2
C +0.5
D –0.5

8 The income elasticity of demand for jeans is estimated to be +1.5. Which of the following statements is most correct?

A As income rises, the price of jeans will increase by 50 per cent.
B An increase in income of 10 per cent will see the demand for jeans increase by 5 per cent.
C The consumer will switch demand from other goods to buy more jeans.
D Jeans are a normal good. An increase in income will lead to a greater proportionate increase in demand.

9 According to economic theory, which of these is the usual business objective of a firm?

A To maximise sales revenue.
B Profit maximisation.
C To sell all goods at 10 per cent gross profit.
D To force all opposition out of the market.

10 Which of these market structures has no barriers to entry for new firms that wish to join the market?

A Perfect competition.
B Monopolistic competition.
C Oligopoly.
D Monopoly.

11 A firm has two variable factors of production, labour (L) and capital (K). It uses them at fixed prices, P_L and P_k. AP_L, AP_k and MP_L and MP_k are the average and marginal products of labour and capital.

Which of the following represents the way in which the firm should utilise these factors in order to minimise the costs of producing a given output?

A $\dfrac{MP_L}{MP_k} = \dfrac{P_L}{P_k}$

B $\dfrac{MP_L}{MP_k} = \dfrac{AP_L}{AP_k}$

C $\dfrac{AP_L}{P_L} = \dfrac{AP_k}{P_k}$

D $\dfrac{MP_L}{P_L} = \dfrac{MP_k}{P_k}$

12 If the wage rate is \$8 per hour, an individual worker decides to work for 40 hours per week. When this is increased to \$10 per hour, the individual decides to work for 35 hours per week.

Which of these best explains the fall in hours worked per week?

A The income elasticity of demand for non-working time is negative.
B The income effect is zero.
C The income effect is less than the substitution effect,
D The income effect offsets the substitution effect.

13 A firm can produce up to ten tractors a year with fixed costs of \$20,000. If it builds to its full capacity, the average cost is \$3,000. If it only builds nine tractors, the average cost per tractor is £3,300. What is the marginal cost of building the 10th tractor?
A \$3,300
B \$2,100
C \$3,000
D None of these.

14 Which of these concepts explains why a firm's long-run average cost curve is U-shaped?
A Technology changes as output increases.
B Rising factor prices.
C Productivity is increasing.
D Economies of scale and diseconomies of scale.

15 Merit goods are so called because:
A Consumers deserve them.
B They are provided by governments from tax revenue.
C Their consumption produces negative externalities.
D Consumers do not have proper information on the benefits that can be derived from their consumption.

16 A lighthouse is a typical example of a public good because:
A It is very difficult to collect toll money from passing vessels.
B It is paid for by the government.
C It is there for all vessels to use.
D Without a lighthouse there could be more vessels that have accidents.

17/18 The diagram below shows how the imposition of a green tax seeks to reduce the cost of the negative externalities due to market failure.

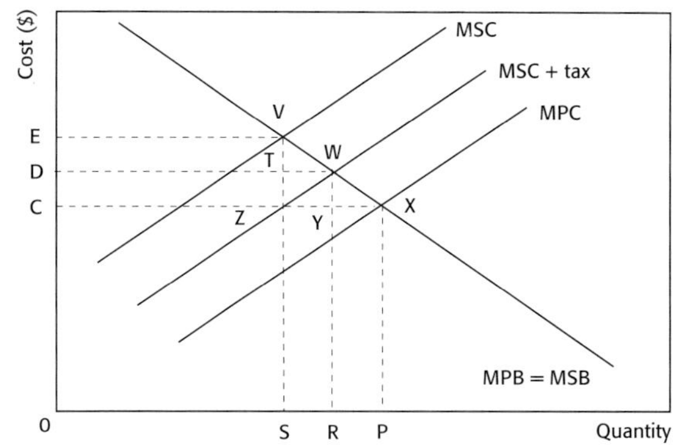

If the market clears at point W:
A This is not an optimal allocation of resources.
B Consumers of the product will complain about the increase in taxation.
C The cost to consumers is lower than at point V.
D There is a fall in quantity consumed compared to point X.

If the market equilibrium is at point X, the deadweight loss triangle is indicated by the area:
A VXZ
B WXY
C TVW
D None of these.

19 The diagram below shows the marginal revenue product (MRP) and supply (*S*) of bauxite workers.

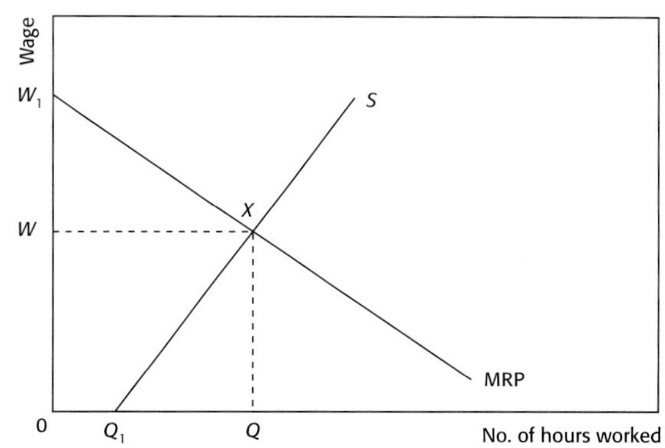

The transfer earnings of bauxite workers is indicated by the area:
A W_1WX
B $WXQ0$
C WXQ_10
D XQ_1Q

20 In theory, in the labour market, trade unions seek to:

A Shift the MRP curve to the right.
B Shift the supply of labour to the right, so increasing employment.
C Ensure that employers pay a wage rate of W_1.
D Increase wages by seeking to restrict the supply of labour.

21 An individual's labour supply curve is backward sloping because:

A Labour supply is inelastic with respect to wages paid.
B The wage rate has no effect on labour supply.
C Labour supply is elastic with respect to wages paid.
D The average working week for most workers has been reduced.

22 Which of these variables is *not* included in the UN's Human Development Index?

A Life expectancy at birth.
B Average daily calorie intake.
C GDP per head.
D Adult literacy rate.

23 Which of these government policies would be unlikely to reduce poverty?

A The introduction of a minimum wage.
B An increase in the income tax threshold.
C A fall in the price of colour televisions.
D An increase in child benefit payments.

24 Social welfare is maximised where:

A The value consumers place on a product is the price that they are prepared to pay.
B Everyone in the population is educated.
C Government spending on social services is at a maximum.
D The production possibility curve shifts outwards.

Sample paper, Unit 2

1 Which of these statements is most consistent with the Keynesian view of the role of government in managing the economy?

A The government should use a deficit budget to increase aggregate demand when there is high unemployment.
B The government should not interfere in the management of the economy even if there is a problem of high unemployment.
C The government should increase the money supply to deal with a problem of high unemployment.
D The government should be more concerned about keeping a low rate of inflation than about reducing a high rate of unemployment.

2/3 The consumption function for an economy with no government sector and no foreign trade is

$C= \$2000 + 0.8Y$

If income increases by \$500, what will be the new level of consumption?

A \$2,500
B \$2,040
C \$2,400
D None of these.

Suppose investment is autonomous and equal to \$3,000. What is the equilibrium level of income?

A \$25,000
B \$7,400
C \$16,000
D Cannot tell.

4 In a closed economy with no government sector, the average propensity to consume is 0.7 and the marginal propensity consume is 0.8. What is the value of the multiper?

A 3.33
B 7
C 8
D 5

5 The government in an economy is undecided as to whether it should increase its own spending on roads by \$50m or reduce direct taxes by \$50m. Why would increasing its own spending have a bigger effect on aggregate demand?
A All of the \$50m spent on roads is added to aggregate demand.
B A reduction in direct taxes takes a long time to have any impact.
C The multiplier does not apply to expenditure on roads.
D Not all of the increase in income will be spent.

6 According to the equation $MV = PT$, what is the cause of inflation in an economy?
A An increase in the cost of imports.
B An increase in the money supply.
C V and T are held constant.
D An increase in aggregate demand.

7 Which of the following would cause the value of the accelerator to increase?
A An increase in the capital–output ratio.
B An increase in income.
C A reduction in the rate of taxation on investment.
D An increase in the value of the multiplier.

8 In 2005, the rate of inflation in an economy was 8 per cent. In 2006 it was 6 per cent. Which of the following deductions is correct?
A The average price level is falling.
B Some prices are increasing, others are falling.
C There has been a 20 per cent reduction in the rate of inflation.
D Between 2005 and 2006 the average price level increased by 6 per cent.

9 Which of these is *not* a fiscal policy measure?
A A fall in the rate of income tax.
B An increase in government spending on education.
C A rise in the base rate of interest.
D A rise in the general service tax rate.

10 One of the functions of money is that it allows prices to be established in a common form, such as in \$BDS and cents. This function of money is known as:
A Medium of exchange.
B Unit of account.
C Store of value.
D Means of deferred payment.

11/12 The diagram below shows how the rate of interest is determined in an economy, where L is the demand for money and MS is the supply of money.

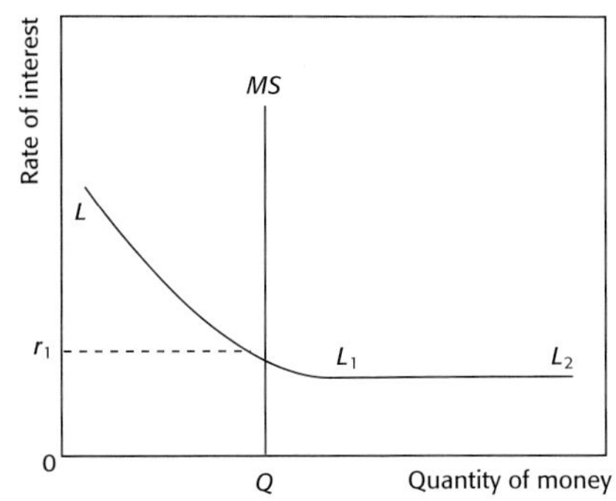

If the supply of money is reduced, which of these statements is correct?
A The rate of interest will rise.
B The rate of interest will fall.
C The rate of interest will remain the same.
D None of these.

The liquidity trap is indicated by:
A An interest rate of r_1.
B The section of the liquidity preference curve between L and L_2.
C The section of the liquidity preference curve between L_1 and L_2.
D The section of the liquidity preference curve between L and L_1.

13 The table below shows the money supply in a Caribbean economy (in 000 $s):

Notes in circulation	276,000
Coins in circulation	12,000
Treasury and Bank cash	60,000
Demand deposits	848,000

What is the value of M1?

A $288,000
B $228,000
C $1,196,000
D $908,000

14 In fiscal policy, an automatic stabiliser is:

A A type of tax that changes automatically with fluctuations in real GDP.
B A type of tax or government expenditure that changes automatically with fluctuations in real GDP.
C A policy measure that automatically occurs once unemployment reaches a certain level.
D A form of tax where the total paid to government remains fixed over time.

15 The table below shows the production possibilities for two countries, India and France, where each uses half of its resources in the production of each product.

	Cloth (Units)	Rice (Units)
India	500	250
France	400	100

Which of these statements is correct?

A France has absolute advantage in the production of cloth and rice.
B India has a comparative advantage in the production of rice.
C India should produce both cloth and rice as it has an absolute advantage in producing both goods.
D France would be better off not trading with India in these two products.

16 The *main* function of an import tariff is:

A To restrict the import of de-merit goods.
B To ensure that consumer welfare is maximised.
C To reduce the supply of imported goods.
D To raise revenue for the government.

17 Which one of these items is *not* included in the current account of the balance of payments?

A Net receipts from international tourism.
B Inward investment from foreign residents.
C The export earnings from banana production.
D Money sent home by Caribbean workers in the UK.

18 The table below shows the average annual price of exports and the average price of imports over a period of two years.

Year	Average price of exports	Average price of imports
1	100	100
2	105	102

Which of the following statements is correct?

A In year 2, the country will have a current account deficit.
B In year 2, the country will have a current account surplus.
C The terms of trade have improved by 2.5 per cent.
D The terms of trade have worsened by 2.5 per cent.

19 The real effective exchange rate is:

A A measure that takes into account differences in inflation and exchange rates between trading countries.
B The exchange rate of a country at a given point in time.
C The exchange rate that is determined by supply and demand in the foreign exchange market.
D The exchange rate of a country once inflation has been taken into account.

20 The debt service ratio for a Caribbean economy fell from 80 per cent to 70 per cent between 2005 and 2006. This means that:

A There has been a fall in the expenditure on imports between 2005 and 2006.
B Some new loans have been taken out in 2005.
C Some loans due for repayment in 2005 have been paid back.
D Some loans due for repayment in 2006 have been paid back.

21 In terms of the forms of economic integration, CARICOM is a typical example of:

A A free trade area.

B A customs union.

C A common market.

D An economic union.

22 Which of these is *not* an example of the dynamic effects of a customs union?

A An opportunity for firms to reorganise in order to benefit from economies of scale.

B Increased competition in all markets.

C A shift in economic potential away from peripheral locations.

D An increase in trade between member states.

23 Study the production possibility curves below.

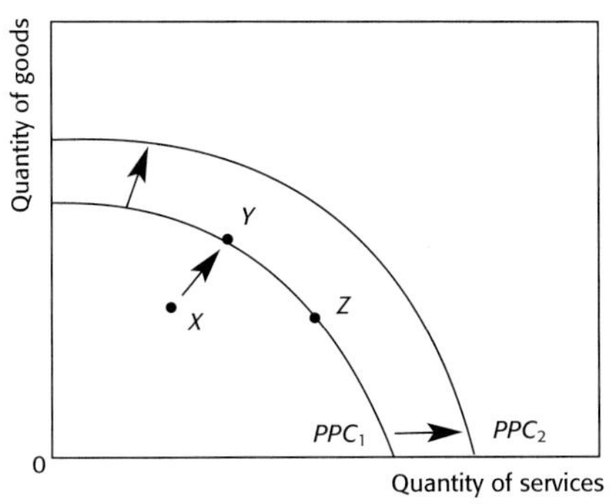

A growth in the potential output of an economy is shown by:

A A shift of the *PPC* from PPC_1 to PPC_2.

B A movement from *X* to *Y*.

C A movement along the *PPC* from *Y* to *Z*.

D A movement along the *PPC* from *Z* to *Y*.

24 Which of these is an example of foreign direct investment in a Caribbean economy?

A Profits made in the Caribbean that are then sent abroad.

B An increase in the number of cruise passengers visiting the economy.

C A Caribbean chilli pepper sauce producer that decides to invest in the UK.

D The construction of a new five star resort by an American leisure company.

Answers – Unit 1

Question	Key	Question	Key
1	C	13	B
2	A	14	D
3	A	15	D
4	B	16	C
5	A	17	A
6	C	18	A
7	B	19	D
8	D	20	D
9	B	21	C
10	A	22	B
11	D	23	C
12	D	24	A

Answers – Unit 2

Question	Key	Question	Key
1	A	13	B
2	C	14	B
3	A	15	B
4	D	16	C
5	A	17	B
6	B	18	C
7	A	19	A
8	D	20	C
9	C	21	C
10	B	22	D
11	A	23	A
12	C	24	D